Wisdom
from
The Greater
Community

VOLUME I

Wisdom
from
The Greater Community

VOLUME I

SECOND EDITION

THE GREATER COMMUNITY
BOOK OF TEACHINGS

Marshall Vian Summers

WISDOM FROM THE GREATER COMMUNITY: *Volume I*

Book design by Alan Bernhard
Argent Associates, Boulder, Colorado

Printed on recycled paper

ISBN: 1-884238-11-4 *Wisdom from the Greater Community: Volume I*
Library of Congress Catalog Card Number: 90-61254

This is the second edition of *Wisdom from the Greater Community: Volume I*

The books of the New Knowledge Library are published by
The Society for The Greater Community Way of Knowledge.
The Society is a religious non-profit organization dedicated to presenting
and teaching The Greater Community Way of Knowledge.

Wisdom from the Greater Community: Volume I along with its companion texts
Steps to Knowledge and *Wisdom from the Greater Community: Volume II*
comprise the first level of study in The Greater Community Way of Knowledge.

PUBLISHER'S CATALOGING IN PUBLICATION

Summers, Marshall.
    Wisdom from the greater community : spiritual preparation for
humanity's emergence into the greater community / Marshall Vian
Summers. — 2nd ed.
    p. cm.
    ISBN (v. 1) : 1-884238-11-4.
    ISBN (v. 2) : 1-884238-12-2.

    1. Society for The Greater Community Way of Knowledge —
Doctrines.   2. Spiritual life — Society for The Greater Community
Way of Knowledge.   I. Society for The Greater Community Way of
Knowledge.   II. Title.

BP605.S58S86 1996   299'.93
                                                        QBI96-20379

To order the books of the New Knowledge Library or to receive information about The Society's
audio recordings, educational programs and contemplative services please write:

The Society for The Greater Community Way of Knowledge
P.O. Box 1724 • Boulder, CO 80306-1724 • (303) 938-8401

Dedicated to the Unseen Ones who carry out

the Creator's will in the world and throughout

the Greater Community

Wisdom
from
The Greater Community

*Y*OU ARE SENT TO THE WORLD FOR A PURPOSE, to contribute your gifts which will emanate from your Knowledge. You have come here for a purpose, to remember your True Home while you are in the world. The great purpose that you carry is with you at this moment, and it will arise in stages as you undergo the preparation that we are providing for you.

Contents

INTRODUCTION

*W*E WELCOME YOU to the Books of Wisdom, *Wisdom from the Greater Community.* Within these pages you will find a new beginning, a great opportunity and a confirmation of your purpose for coming into the world, particularly at this time in the world's destiny and evolution.

Here we present to you a new threshold, a new way, and with this a greater perspective and experience of the magnitude of life and the meaning of the world's emergence into the Greater Community of Worlds. For it is true, as many people have felt, that humanity is at a new beginning. But very few people understand what this new beginning means. They think that the new beginning is simply a continuation of the past and will fulfill the past and continue the past for them. But the new threshold that humanity is facing and approaching now is indeed a new beginning. It is a departure from the past and an entry into a larger arena of life, which we call the Greater Community.

Here humanity will face the reality that it is not alone in the universe or even within its own world. Here humanity will face the real prospect of encountering other forms of intelligent life, for this is the destiny of humanity, and this destiny is upon you now. For this, you will need a greater Knowledge and a greater Wisdom, a Knowledge and Wisdom that human philosophy and human religion alone cannot provide. It is for this reason that the Creator has given you an opportunity now to prepare for the Greater Community and to realize within the larger context of life the meaning and the purpose of your being in the world at this time.

This is not simply another teaching amongst many teachings. It is indeed nothing less than a new testament, for the Creator would not leave humanity alone at the threshold of its emergence into the Greater Community, and that is why The Greater Community Way of Knowledge is being presented. It is being presented in such a way that it will call upon what is most deeply felt and deeply known within you. And it will speak to your deepest needs and your deepest inclinations in words that are simple and unencumbered by religious symbols to as great an extent as is possible.

The Greater Community Way of Knowledge represents a translatable spirituality, a greater spirituality that humanity must learn to embrace if it is to realize its purpose and its destiny in the Greater Community and if it is to find its strength, its cohesion and its integrity as a race. This will enable you to emerge into the Greater Community and to survive within this larger environment. In The Way of Knowledge, you will learn many new things as well as confirm what has already been realized within human history. Here what is most essential in human religion will be emphasized, which is the discovery and the expression of Knowledge, the Greater Mind that the Creator has given to you, your great endowment from the Creator. Here you will learn a new Wisdom, a greater Wisdom, a Wisdom that will enable you to face life, to experience life and to learn to communicate with life in a far greater way than was ever required before.

You may well ask, "Is it possible to learn such things? Is it really necessary? Can *I* learn something like this?" These three questions go together, and the answer to all of them is a resounding "Yes!" But to learn and to live Greater Community Knowledge and Wisdom, you must open your mind as much as you can. You must have a new beginning, and you must find a way to come into the clear where you are not encumbered by your past thoughts or by the conditioning of the world. This is possible now because you have the opportunity to learn a Greater Community Way of Knowledge. Learning The Way of Knowledge will take you beyond the limits and boundaries of human reason, human perception and human understanding. It will liberate you from the constraints and the prejudices of human religions, human values and the limitations of human culture. This does not deny your humanity but instead gives it a greater context and environment and a greater opportunity for expression.

Humanity is endowed with a great spirituality, and this has been kept alive through the centuries by the presence of the Unseen Ones, the Angels of the Creator, and by the revelation, the expression and the contribution of many inspired individuals. Here human religion has played a fundamental role despite its many errors. It has paved the way for a new revelation, a new testament, a new expression of human divinity and a new application and meaning for human wisdom.

It is time now to learn Wisdom from the Greater Community. Real Wisdom must be learned. Knowledge, the Knowing Mind, is already within you. Knowledge only requires that you open yourself to it so that it can express itself and reveal itself to you. Then Knowledge can contribute through you to the world around you. But Wisdom must be learned. Here the application of Knowledge, the meaning of your existence, the development of discernment and discretion, the cultivation of forbearance, compassion, insight and a greater generosity are born of the overflowing nature of your Spirit and the expression of your true spirituality.

fruits of K

Let us now begin to learn a new way and to experience together the new revelation of the Creator. We have come to the world for this purpose. We represent spirituality in the Greater Community. We have selected one individual to be our speaker for this great purpose and mission. Together with him, we are able to introduce to you a Greater Community Way of Knowledge and to express to you in many ways and in many areas of application the meaning and the necessity of learning greater Wisdom, Wisdom from the Greater Community.

"Knock and you shall receive"

Your Knowledge
contains the memory
of your Creator,
of your help
& of your
meaning in the world.

One

THE GREATER RELIGION

TO BEGIN, WE SHALL BE DISCUSSING the Greater Religion, a matter of great importance. Developing Knowledge is a major theme in all of our discussions. Knowledge, relationships and communication permeate all true activity, true development and true progress. They give rise to your spiritual nature and destiny. They call upon your relationship with God, though there are also many practical aspects of life to which they must be continually applied.

Because you have been sent here for a purpose and not only for your own development, your contribution to the world is a primary factor. As you receive, you must give, and this continues within this world and beyond. This procedure is occurring in all worlds, not just this one. Therefore, the Plan of God must account for the needs of many different kinds of beings in many different kinds of environments. How does the Greater Religion relate to you, who are preoccupied with human affairs and this one world? It is directly relevant for three reasons.

First, you are not entirely human. You have not made your major developments only in this world. What you have accumulated in Knowledge accounts not only for your human existence, but for your non-human existence as well. Therefore, to reclaim Knowledge is to reclaim these vital memories. They are not memories of personal traumas or historical events. They are memories of relationships that have been established in truth. Therefore, if you are to reclaim what your Knowledge actually is, then you must be prepared to experience this aspect of yourself, or you will never be able to integrate what you are experiencing into human life. Otherwise, your acquisition, or shall we say reclamation, of Knowledge will be increasingly alienating to you. You will feel increasing estrangement from the world, and this is not our purpose.

Therefore, you must accept your humanity, and you must accept your place in the greater order as well. Only in this way can you fully integrate yourself here, serving this world in its own needs and yet maintaining a greater perspective which is lacking here.

The second reason that the Greater Religion is relevant to you is that your world is emerging into the Greater Community of Worlds. This is the great transition that we have spoken of so often. It is such a great transition that you cannot imagine its consequences or how much it will affect your thinking and your worldly activities.

The third reason is that you need a larger perspective to comprehend the work of God. God is not human. God does not think like a human. God is not made in your image. God has no image. The Source of all life accounts for all life. Think not that God is preoccupied with your life to the exclusion of other life. To begin to approach the Wisdom of God, which is the Knowledge of God, of which you maintain a small but vital part, you must begin to have a larger perspective of life itself.

The evolution of humanity is only one aspect of life itself. You cannot know the whole from an aspect only. Human life does not mirror all life, and yet the reflection of all life is within you. Therefore, religion, which in reality is the experience of the presence of God and your relationship with God, must account for the greater aspects of life.

This is so important for your being human as well, for to be really human, you must have this perspective. You cannot have perspective if being human is all that you are. Being human is very contradictory in many aspects. It is a very self-absorbed and adolescent state. If you are to understand and appreciate the nature of those whom God has sent to help you, then in time you will begin to share their perspective and see what evolution means on a larger scale. Then you will begin to understand your duties and know what growth means here on Earth.

People have so often set ultimate goals for their spiritual growth and have attempted to live by them. Very presumptuous and damaging this is, for failure is inevitable. It is not in the Plan that you should fail by overshooting your true goals in life.

Many of you have felt a desire for union with the Divine, as well as a desire to serve a greater purpose. This is commendable, of course, yet if you wish to serve a greater purpose and experience a greater source, then you must learn what this means. You cannot define the way.

People attempt perfection because they are convinced of error, but they do not know perfection. You cannot know perfection from error. You can only know error. Perfection is not erasing error. It is gaining Wisdom, compassion, ability, capacity and love. Stamping out error does not produce perfection. If you could see evolution on a larger scale, you would most certainly adjust your expectations of yourself.

Upon leaving this life, those few individuals who attained seeming perfection find themselves at a new beginning. Yet they need not be here any longer. Instead of transcending their humanity, they must now encounter the identities of the universe. For this they will need great assistance and exposure.

Their destiny and their way are not your concern. Your concern is your immediate life, your ability to make decisions and to act upon them, your ability to be discerning and your sense of purpose and identity.

People often ask, "Why do I need Teachers?" The answer is very simple. It is because you do not know anything. Yes, you believe many, many things, but your Knowledge is only a small light. You believe that by perfecting your personality or body you will attain great heights, yet we assure you, you will attain great frustration. A perfect personality may have no more Knowledge than an imperfect one. Indeed, your great Teachers in the world have been very notorious—not perfect personalities. That is not the emphasis, though there are adjustments to make in your behavior and thinking, of course.

Perfecting your behavior to meet your standards is not the Path of Knowledge. Knowledge is not ideas. It is experience. It is relationship. It is God. God *is* relationship. It is the attraction between like and like, between the same and the same. That is God in a practical definition.

So, here we have this idea of the Greater Religion. Why is it greater? Greater does not mean better. It is only greater because it accounts for a larger reality. You must understand the evolution of life, not just the evolution of people. You cannot understand this intellectually, for it is far too vast and inclusive, but you can experience it, and you can know what it means in your daily life.

Human beings are not sent here to achieve ultimate reality. That is not your purpose. Your purpose in being here is to complete *being* here. Do you think that you can go from Earth to Heaven and miss all the steps in between? Hopefully, if your progress is true, you will expand your capacity and embrace a larger experience of life, so much larger that being human would be too confining. Why? Because you will be involved in too many relationships.

Your world is about to outgrow its fascination with itself, a necessary stage of maturation. Therefore, a greater experience of religion, or shall we say a religion of many worlds, is appropriate. It is appropriate not only for a greater perspective; it is also appropriate to understand those beings you will be meeting from the Greater Community. They do not think like you necessarily. Not all of them are friendly. You are as strange to them as they are to you. You must see them with Knowledge. This is the perspective.

I said earlier that people need Teachers because they do not know anything. Some people need Teachers but would never allow their presence to be known. For others it would be best if their Teachers were never known. Yet, all have Teachers. You can barely generate enough energy to get through life let alone elevate yourself within it. You must have assistance. Accepting this fact is so important and will give you such a sense of support, grace and appreciation. It also means that you have a purpose that is important and that you do not know everything.

It is true that Knowledge must be gained through experience. An intellectual pursuit it is not. Your intellect was not created to comprehend the universe. It was created to negotiate the particulars of your physical life, in which it has become fairly sophisticated. Yet, it cannot appreciate what is felt and what is known. Therefore, do not use this capacity inappropriately. It has its true application, and a useful one at that. Yet, you must seek a different approach.

Our work, then, is religious in nature because it deals with God. It deals with a greater life. In this world you cannot approach the greatest life; you can only approach a greater life. You must go through the stages of evolution. You cannot skip them all. You cannot.

If this can be comprehended now, then you will be able to recognize what needs to be done, what can be done and what cannot be done. You will see your true involvement and your true requirements, without placing impossible burdens upon your shoulders. This is very important. With impossible burdens you will not even recognize what is essential, and that will produce failure, which will compound your agony. We do not expect perfect behavior. But we cannot help you very effectively if you are insisting absolutely ridiculous accomplishments of yourselves. There are greater beings than you to run the universe.

Therefore, the work to come for you will deal with experiencing God's work within the present religious traditions, both here and abroad. Why is this important? It is not merely fascinating to the mind. It is important because it stimulates contact with your Spiritual Family, both here and abroad. It regenerates ancient memories that are so essential to your experience of continuance, wholeness and inclusion in life.

People are always seeking their Spiritual Family. They seek it in personal relationships. They seek it in political causes and in religious causes. They seek it in peace, and they seek it in war. They do not know what they are seeking, but to be alone in this world is a terrible destiny. Yet, you are not alone. Before you came into this world, you were not alone, and those who were with you then are with you now. To regain this memory is to regain consciousness of life in the visible and life beyond. Then the barriers of illusions begin to fall away. Then you can begin to comprehend Spiritual Presence rather than feel it only. Then your perception becomes refined. If you were not in this world, it would be so much easier to make proper decisions. But you are here. You have taken on the natural inhabitancy of this world in a physical body, but the possibility of true perception still exists.

In preparation of the events to come in the next one hundred and fifty years and in preparation of the religions to come in the next one to three thousand years, the Greater Community practices will be shared for your own development. They are not shared philosophically but given as practices. They are not generated only through intellectual speculation. They are initiatory for you to experience Knowledge, Spiritual Presence and contact. These practices are ancient. Their purpose is to enable you to regain your ancient memories and to regain awareness of your true friends here in this world and your true friends elsewhere as well. From this will spring a much greater sense of purpose, and it is for this reason that these practices are shared.

This is religious experience. Religious experience evolves and necessitates a growing point of view. If you read the history of your religions and known history, as brief as it is, you will see a development. You will begin to see a definite expansion, and thus it continues.

The purpose of this is Knowledge. There is no one to idolize. There are no heroes here. We remain invisible. You cannot worship us. In time you will understand the wisdom of this and why it is so essential in order for us to be effective. Even the great ones in your world who have gone so far and who contributed their Knowledge did not seek to become idols of worship. It is their Knowledge that has been neglected. People are afraid of Knowledge, yet Knowledge is the purpose.

If you yearn for it, seek it. You cannot define it. You cannot predict the outcome. You seek it because it is natural for you to do so. For your Knowledge contains the memory of your Creator, of your help and of your meaning in this world.

*Find
what is true
&
partnership
will find you.*

Two

RELATIONSHIPS & SEXUALITY

I T HAS COME TIME TO SPEAK OF SEXUALITY in the context of relationship and Knowledge. We must speak about relationship and its importance in hindering or in advancing the development of Knowledge. There are many strange beliefs in this world concerning relationships and their relevance to personal growth, to personal healing, to the completion of past incidents, and so forth.

Relationships serve within three primary phases. In the first phase, before Knowledge can emerge, relationships are primarily for the resolution of error. They are to demonstrate illusion and to draw a contrast between illusion and Knowledge, between stimulation and peace of mind. They are completions, you might say, yet the attractions can be very fierce. If a person never enters the second phase in this life, it is possible they may have a long-term relationship, yet it will be flawed and incomplete. It will have inherent difficulties because the individuals involved have not established a common sense of identity. Though they attempt to establish a common bond, their bond is not intrinsic.

In the second phase, which is the emergence of Knowledge in the individual, the unconscious becomes conscious. Then relationships have an entirely different framework and service. Before this, Knowledge was beneath the surface of the mind, exerting influence but in an ill-defined way.

In the third phase, relationships have an entirely different emphasis from the previous two. Now Knowledge has emerged, and the individual is undergoing development in order to serve humanity.

Let us review this now a little bit. In the first stage, which is where the vast majority of people are, relationships are flawed and difficult, yet there are great attempts to make these relationships permanent. These relationships provide a contrast which is essential for self-development. Without this contrast, you would have no way of discerning what is real from what is not. Your errors here are of tremendous value, if you can understand them and comprehend their service.

When Knowledge begins to emerge in the second stage, it seems tremendously disruptive. It provides a relief because it is natural and because it emanates from your own being, yet it seems to draw you away from your former allegiances to a very great extent. It also challenges your former ideas and beliefs, even those ideas concerning personal development and growth. When Knowledge begins to emerge from within you, it does not emerge for growth. Let us make this important point because there are many sad and tragic involvements justified in the name of "growth." This is merely a new form of justification.

Knowledge is not for growth in the usual sense. It is for service and contribution. In this it begins to attract Knowledge in others. It has a resonating effect. Knowledge expands, but you in your true state do not grow. You are merely rediscovered. Growth refers to the body and the personality. It refers to the vehicle for your True Self. The vehicle grows because it changes. Knowledge expands, yet it only does so because it reclaims itself. Therefore, in reality there is no growth. There is only reclamation, which from a personal standpoint looks like tremendous growth. It is as if you are breaking new ground and reclaiming old territory at the same time.

In the second stage, relationships are primarily to serve the emergence of Knowledge. They have far greater relevance to this emergence than to anything else. They are somewhat mysterious because people seem to be sent from nowhere, holding great promise and stimulation for Knowledge. Here the personality is not being so stimulated, for this relationship is not for gratification. It is for true service. It is the beginning of a whole new era of relationship.

In this new era of relationship, if the emergence of Knowledge can take place, you will have relationships of an entirely different nature. They will not be inherently flawed. They will seem to exist already. You do not need to create them. They are established, yet they are new to your experience and so they must find an expression and an acceptance on your part. This is the reclamation of the Spiritual Family within this world, where everyone seems scattered and separate.

Relationships now become something else, but you cannot define them. They seem to defy definition, yet they are so deeply felt and there is such resonance that they cannot be denied. Old friendships fall away now. They do not have this content within them. Old emphases fall away. It is the beginning of something you cannot stop but can only hinder. It is like giving birth. That is the best analogy, perhaps. You cannot stop labor once labor begins. It is a greater force than you can account for within yourself. It is this Greater Power that represents Knowledge.

In the third phase, you are beginning to understand your calling in life and individuals come to find their place with you. There is recognition rather than attraction. There is peace rather than frantic stimulation. There is confirmation in being together. You still have personalities and there are difficulties, conflicts, and so forth because personalities are like that. They have their own inherent discomforts, like your body which has its aches and pains. Just because you have purpose does not mean your body is free of aches and pains. Your personality will have its own aches and pains as well, yet it is no longer a dominant factor. You can be compassionate towards your personality now. It is not ruling you. It is only an occasional nuisance and an occasional pleasure. It finds its rightful place.

As I have said, the vast majority of people are in the first phase. They are in the phase of developing discernment. People in this phase may have tremendous insight, seeming spiritual power, intuitive abilities, and so forth, yet Knowledge has not emerged. They are within an inner cultivation process. It is only through their disappointments and their deeper yearning, which may now emerge, that they will be able to make wise decisions and finally realize that their pursuit of personal fulfillment is fruitless.

Personal fulfillment is not even what you want. You are bereft of happiness because you are separated from Knowledge. You are like a ship without a shore. You cannot make that ship complete for yourself, for it has not found its rightful harbor. You are still alone in the universe. In this stage all you can hope for is to be safe from harm and have adequate pleasurable stimulation to keep you from despair. You will have real joys and real pleasures, but they will not be enough. It is this inherent dissatisfaction with your separated state that will drive you towards union and bring about the emergence of Knowledge. You will lose interest in things sequentially that were stimulating before. Then, when Knowledge begins to emerge, you will have the least possible conflict of interest.

Knowledge will seem a great unknown to you. Even your theories regarding spiritual development will not help you now. You will not know who you are exactly. You are not completely who you were, and you have not become what you are intended to be. During this period you need great assistance. This is when the Inner Teachers begin to emerge, and their emergence has direct relevance for you. This is when you must be selective about whom you spend time with, for each relationship will either help or hinder this emergence. You may think you are being very unloving and selfish, but that is the way it goes.

In the last two phases you still have personal problems, but you also have greater concerns than personal problems. You must still make corrections in your behavior and activities, but you now make adjustments not because it gives you pride, but because it is essential for your well-being. It is no longer a "should." It is a "must." It is a matter of life for you now.

Now let us say what sexuality is for. It serves two functions: First, it serves to regenerate the race, to provide a vehicle of entry for new life here—intelligent life like yourself. Secondly, it is a means of establishing deeper union through the body; it is a physical exercise to experience union. Beyond this, sexuality loses meaning very drastically. When you join your physical electromagnetic system—your body—to another, you are transferring energy to one another. We are not speaking of orgasm. We are speaking of uniting your physical vehicles. This has a very great impact on the body and a very great impact on the emotional self. Your nature does not discriminate at this level. If you have sex with someone, your body and emotions will attempt complete union. Your body and emotions do not discriminate. It is like digesting food.

If you have this engagement with someone you are not in true relationship with, you will damage your physical system and you will disrupt yourself emotionally. You will lose energy and efficacy as a result. This depletion of your physical vehicle and disruption of your emotional nature has serious consequences if it is repeated over and over. This loss of vitality will make you sick. Eventually it will destroy your body's self-maintenance.

This is occurring with the illness that is prevalent now. It is the misalignment of the physical vehicles. It is the destruction, by repeated depletion, of the capability of those vehicles to maintain themselves. This is a very serious matter. You must understand. There is no casual sex; there is no recreational sex. If you attempt this, you will be attempting complete union with no intention whatsoever and will risk your physical well-being. Nature prohibits this. That is why there are so many indigenous illnesses associated with this. It is not wise and it is not natural. It is not good for you, so do not seek this stimulation. Seek true relationship.

You have sexual needs, but they are not sexual in their origin. They represent your yearning for union, which you experience physically, though the cause of this physical sensation is rarely recognized. These impulses, then, are for union. They emanate from your being. You experience them in your body and you feel sexually aroused, so you go out and try to take care of your sexual needs somewhere.

This is a very serious matter. For those of you who are undertaking the reclamation of Knowledge in a conscientious manner, you must attend to this subject very well. There is great hysteria regarding sexual repression and sexual thises and thats. There is great fear that your spiritual life will deprive you of these enjoyments. This is quite ridiculous. Your Knowledge will indicate whether you are to be united sexually with another or not. It is simply given or not.

Because you have such strong views regarding the essential need for sexual involvement, it makes you afraid of your own Knowledge, afraid it will rob and deprive you of your great pleasures in life. I, through my words, cannot reassure you enough that this is not the case. Yet you must discover this for yourself. Your need is for union and for meaningful relationships, relationships for a greater purpose. This is the source of your sexual yearning. This represents the need for reproduction. Reproduction is for a spiritual purpose. If it is misused, it will be damaged. Yet not everyone is intended to have a relationship for this purpose.

There is a serious illness now in your midst. Take heed. This is nature saying "no." This is nature saying, "You cannot do this without harm." Your Knowledge will indicate whom you are to be sexually united with. If you do not trust your Knowledge, then you will have tremendous conflict. Yet, your Knowledge will provide what is needed for your well-being.

In the Greater Community the need for union and reproduction is universal, though the customs regarding sexual engagement vary. Biological processes and the forms of engagement vary, yet the need is universal.

People say, "Well, I cannot wait for true union. I must have sexual fulfillment now. Am I to be celibate until a relationship comes along?" This you pose as a question to me. I anticipate it. Yet, you must ask this of your own Knowledge. Knowledge is not belief. It is not thinking. You must ask this question of yourself. If you understand your true needs, you will see the answer is quite obvious. If you must have sexual gratification without true relationship, you are placing yourself at risk. Even your Teachers cannot save you. You are living dangerously with your body.

In all affairs, people learn by their errors. We do not deprive them of their errors. Yet past a certain point, it is unwise to repeat the same errors over and over again. You are no longer adolescents. You have all made these errors, so you do not need to continue. Life gives you these learning opportunities at an early age. It does not deprive you of exploration, but that is for adolescence. You are adults now. Adolescence in adulthood is destructive.

Sexuality has a new importance now. It is this we must address. People are very compromised in this area. They are unsure of what they want because they do not see the obvious. You are either ready for union or you are not. Is it that clear cut? Yes, it is. If you are not ready for union with another, do not pretend. You will find that your temporary allegiances will be very costly to you. They will leave scars and they will damage you. You will pay a price for them. You must have this early learning in order to learn what is real, yet you cannot persist in this indefinitely. This produces harm.

Sexuality is entirely useless unless it is for reproduction or for union. It is only natural in these realms. If you are not in a position to have either of these two emphases in life, then use this vitality for other constructive purposes. Knowledge will draw tremendous energy from you. That is why it unifies you. You will not have time for things that are not necessary. As a result, you will feel your life is necessary, and you will not have to ponder its worth.

Therefore, if you are not ready for complete relationship, do not play with your body. It is a fragile instrument, tremendously fragile. It is yours to use or abuse. Your emotional state, as well, must find equilibrium now or Knowledge cannot arise, for Knowledge must arise with its own power. If this power is too disruptive to you, naturally it will not occur. Knowledge is something which cultivates itself within you. As it begins to emerge slowly, it will have increasing influence over your thinking and ideas. You will have many signs before you are about to make a mistake, and you will begin to have a broader range of experience.

There are those who are born into this world who, from an early age, recognize that they have intuitive gifts. These people must be especially careful, for their gifts open them to a broader range of experience which they are unlikely to be able to discern properly. For them, the physical body is even more sensitive an instrument. Think of it like this: The more specialized the instrument, the greater the care it requires. Precision instruments require greater maintenance. You cannot bang them around everyday. It is the same for those whose gifts have been evident from an early age.

Many of these people are not from this world. They have immigrated here at this particular time in human history. They have never felt at home here and have always felt displaced. Their awareness of this speaks of an increased sensitivity. For them, personal relationships have wreaked havoc. They are attempting to unite, but they are not with their own kind. Yet, these early sensitivities speak of a greater possibility later. If these individuals can establish a functioning self in this world, they will be in a tremendous position to be of service to the Teachers of God.

You need a witness to your Knowledge in order to accept it. Knowledge always speaks of relationships. These relationships are essential to your well-being. They are strong allegiances, although they may only be

Kate

temporary. It is as if someone had come into your life to help you open, and then they left. Yet even after their departure, you still feel a bond with them. This is relationship at a greater level.

We encourage the development of Knowledge always. This will attract the important people to you. These people will teach you through their demonstration about the difference between reality and error. Many of you have seen enough error. Must you endlessly attempt to experience everything for yourself when people around you are committing every form of self-violation imaginable? You may save yourself great time and difficulty by being observant.

Knowledge speaks of intrinsic relationship, not established relationship. That is why the man or woman of Knowledge is never alone. They have tremendous allies, both here and abroad. Their power comes from their relationship with life. They draw their energy from this. They seem unusual in their abilities because they are not alone and serve as a channel for this greater resource, vitality and direction.

What do you do with all this sexual energy you have? It's swimming around in you; it makes you very angry sometimes. It is Spiritual Presence. People are aroused sexually when they feel Presence. This Presence ignites a yearning for union which raises deep emotions and tremendous sensations physically. This vitality in your body is not to be denied. That is unhealthy. Yet it must be recognized and given constructive expression within your current circumstances.

Recognize this idea, please: The individuals in this world, and in other worlds as well, who have been major contributors to their people were not wasting their vitality in meaningless pursuits. They were drawing upon all their resources for the tasks at hand. They were not casual about anything. Life was too vital for them. It is this vitality you miss. It is this vitality that your Knowledge contains for you. Yet you must seek for it in your current activities.

Part of the attraction of romantic love is that it seems to return vitality to you. Temporarily. It is deeply stimulating to your life force, but it does not give expression or promise to it. The great romantic interludes that you see in your stories and in your pictures are very exciting, but they hold no promise. After you have met this desired one who seems to bring out of you such fascination, enjoyment and self-abandonment, what do you do then? Do you sit around and abandon with each other! There is nothing to do, nowhere to go. Your fascination begins to disappoint. These parodies of relationship must be recognized. True relationship has the intimacy, compassion, and deep pleasure of union because it has promise, direction and purpose.

Therefore, if you seek fulfilling relationships in the world, always seek purpose. It is the foundation. On a personal level, you cannot maintain relationships long term, for your interests will vary. If you are seeking Knowledge, then you will risk these relationships constantly. That is why it is best to seek Knowledge first. Anything you establish as a substitute to this you will risk losing. That is why it can take so very long for those who have made great establishments without Knowledge to turn towards Knowledge for their redemption. They are very fearful of what it may mean. Our comfort for them may not be enough.

People wish to think that they can have everything, you know, but it is not true. You cannot have everything. You can only have ideas of having everything. If you try to have everything, you will be empty-handed and forlorn. Is this negative? No. It is very kind.

Your Knowledge has specific work here. You are placed in time and space, which means you have activities. Self-realization does not leave you dormant. It has a specific application that becomes quite apparent.

You want relationships desperately, but you do not know what to do with them. You are like a person who has an appetite, but does not know how to eat. So you thirst and hunger for the great feast, but when you sit at the table you cannot eat. This is your dilemma.

Many people ask, "How can I find true partnership?" That is not a good question. Find what is true and partnership will find you.

Purpose emanates from your Knowledge. You have had experiences of Knowledge already. It is this that requires cultivation. There is great assistance to help you do this. Then relationship will come to you. That is the way. Learn to eat. Do not seek food. Learn to eat. Or you will sit at the table and realize you cannot fulfill yourself. You will not be satisfied.

Understand this, please: God does not know you personally. That is why you have Teachers, for they can establish personal contact. God only knows what God has created in you. God is in communication with this. God does not know you personally. God does not come from far away to help you out personally. Yet, God serves you personally because of God's Plan.

There are many attempts to personalize God. They are always fruitless and frustrating. "If God is real, why doesn't God come and fix up this world? Why doesn't God come and make my troubles go away? Why doesn't God come and bring peace?"

God has brought peace. God has made trouble go away. Yet no one can see this. God has answered every need, yet no one sees the answer. If God came and made all troubles go away in your physical realm, you would realize you were in Hell already. You are ill-prepared for peace. You could not tolerate peace now. It would show you that you are disassociated from yourself. It would be terrible. It is better that you have a canvas in this life to create anything you want until you find what you really want.

This world is very flexible. Because of the evolution of life, God serves you specifically in every stage you are in. One step ahead of you in your Spiritual Family are your elders who lead and instruct you. They are led and instructed, and so on and so forth. God is the attraction. The Plan is the means. You feel God. God is like a great attraction pulling you. God is pulling everything in.

God has never personally visited this world, for God is not a person. Yet God's Teachers have delivered messages to individuals throughout history. This is difficult to understand, for it can only be known. Can your thoughts accommodate these ideas successfully? My words are approximations only.

In your world there are those who are destined to become speakers for the Greater Reality. You must understand that the Greater Reality is not the Greatest Reality. That is not how life works. God can only communicate through God's Messengers who exist in the next level. Each level serves the level below it. That is how everything progresses.

Therefore, let me now summarize. Sexuality is for reproduction and for union. Sexual energy is only life force experienced in a certain part of the body. Relationships must serve in the current stage of the individuals involved, yet in all stages there can be completion and progress. Serious students of Knowledge must become responsible for their sexual energy and their engagements with others. It becomes evident what must be done if this is their intent.

Sexuality will not be a problem when you are with Knowledge, for you will not be attempting to use your physical vehicle inappropriately. You will experience your energy being drawn where it can be of the greatest service, and your sexuality will be for union. It will not be a problem.

God
Messenger

Elders (Teachers)
spiritual Family
Learner of K (students)

When we speak of
the Greater Community,
we speak of
a larger
perspective
on everything,
including
yourself.

Three

GREATER COMMUNITY

THE GREATER COMMUNITY OF WORLDS is a subject that may be difficult to comprehend intellectually. Yet, if this message stirs a deeper emotion within you, that would be good. When we speak of factual matters that are beyond the sphere of individual concerns, it is most important that you not speculate according to your ideas, for ideas alone cannot account for reality. That is why if you feel stirred in your deeper feelings, it is good.

When we speak about relationships and career in the world, people have a more immediate and direct experience of these things. The experience of the Greater Community of Worlds is not so accessible. It is very interesting, and people are fascinated by it to some degree, but when you go back to your daily personal life, it does not seem very relevant. Yet, it is very relevant to your daily concerns because it is relevant to the direction that your world is traveling.

First, let me say what we mean by the Greater Community. Humanity, unknowingly, is part of a greater association of worlds in this Sector. A Sector is a delineation of space within physical reality—your local universe, you might say. It is not very great in the larger scope of things, yet in contrast to your measurements it is quite large.

We would like to make the information we present very down to earth, if possible. Of course, it isn't really down to earth, yet it is quite relevant to your experience. The reason that it is an important aspect of your daily life is that this world, this planet, is undergoing the transition to emerge into the Greater Community of Worlds. This is its evolutionary stage and its place in history. This may seem very distant from your personal interests, yet I can assure you that it has a direct bearing on all the affairs that are happening now.

To undergo this emergence, your world has had to accelerate technologically and experience a collapse in its tribal cultures and civilizations. When we speak of tribal, we are not speaking of native peoples only. We are speaking of nations that are now being forged into one another, for when a world undergoes the transition into the Greater Community, out of necessity it must unify its own people. This is evolutionary. It occurs in all worlds where intelligent life has been seeded.

Therefore, if you bear witness to the events in your world, you will see that your world is racing to a culminating experience. Everyone feels this, but not many people know what it is about. As in all great turning points, catastrophes, apocalypses and messianic arrivals are predicted. This always occurs at times of transition because people feel they must give some kind of explanation to account for this deeper experience of change.

It is quite essential that you have this viewpoint because it allows you to experience your environment and your relationships from beyond your own personal inventory of feelings and concerns. If you are dominated by your own anxieties and wishes, then you will not be able to see what is happening. You will not be able to perceive life as it is truly functioning and evolving.

Of course, your personal issues must be addressed, and your personal dilemmas must in time find resolution. Yet part of this resolution is realizing that your life is functioning within a greater context. This is as true for you functioning individually in a greater society of people as it is true for your world functioning in a Greater Community of Worlds.

Why is the Greater Community important? It is something everyone knows exists. Your belief system may account for it or not. Your ideas may speak of it or not. It may be a subject of personal interest or not. Yet everyone knows it exists. Everyone knows that this world, in its slight venturings into space, in its rapid technological development, in the collapse of its tribal civilizations, will inevitably emerge into the Greater Community. It is very important to see this because if you fight against the evolutionary forces that are shaping your world, then you will not be in harmony with your own life's purpose.

It has been a central theme in all of our discourses to speak of Higher Purpose in the world, but Higher Purpose cannot be based upon idealism. It cannot be based upon what you think the world should be, for there is no foundation there and you will deceive yourself and others. Your Higher Purpose is based upon the true evolutionary progress that is occurring now. To discover Higher Purpose is to discover your role in serving this constructively. If you think about these things, they will take you beyond your own personal sphere of concerns and wishes. This is healthy. It is important that your world is demanding your attention, yet it must demand your attention in a special way.

Humanity is preoccupied with itself as the adolescent child is preoccupied with himself or herself. Human beings, upon reaching adulthood, mature largely because they begin to account for a greater reality beyond themselves and to respond to the needs of others. This represents the predicament of your world now. It is emerging into a greater reality, yet it is still preoccupied with itself. There are very serious dangers here and very great opportunities.

Many of you have felt strangely moved emotionally in these recent times. You may think it is your own personal development, but that cannot account for everything. You say to yourself, "Something is happening, but I don't know what it is. I can feel it. I know something is about to happen, but I don't know what it is."

The Greater Community is having a tremendous impact here, and it will increase as the years go by. There is much speculation now that your world will undergo tremendous disaster, breakdown, and so forth. We wish to dispel much of this, for this is projection. Yet, it is indeed true that you will undergo a greater change than you have ever known. After all, what is the value of your religion and your sociological emphasis when you see that the universe is not based upon you? This recognition will change things very much. It will also unite your world, for your world will now have a greater problem to contend with.

When we talk about the Greater Community, we are speaking of a tremendous transition in understanding. Here you realize that the God whom you aspire to reach, or perhaps whom you worship or idealize, is not human. In fact, God does not even think like a human because God cannot do that. Here you realize that you are only part of Creation. This becomes much more evident now, requiring a greater vision of the world and a more expansive view of religion and spiritual development.

You see, your religious traditions have been centered upon humanity alone, but you are already part of a Greater Community, and your Ancient Heritage before this life included lives in other worlds as well. That is why many of you have had great difficulty in adjusting to being here. For some of you, your Heritage lies beyond this world and it is strange for you to be here. Why are you here now in a world that seems so odd, so difficult and so alien to you?

It is because people who have this background have a major contribution to make to the world's emergence into the Greater Community. It is their Heritage they must contribute, not only their ideas. Yet until they find this, they will be profoundly alienated, and they will have great difficulty with their own temperament and nature, which in many ways seem incompatible with this world.

Emergence into the Greater Community brings an expansion of love and intrinsic relationship. It also means that your personal lives are seen in a greater context and that your personal problems can be understood from a larger point of view.

There is war in the world now because tribal cultures are breaking down. The world must, out of necessity, become a unified community. Why is this so? It is so because this is evolution. It is completely predictable wherever intelligent life has colonized. When this great turning point comes, it will be a time of tremendous stress and development. This is what many of you feel within yourselves—stress and development. Change is rarely graceful.

The oppositions that exist in this world will be overshadowed by difficulties from abroad. You may say, "We do not need greater difficulties. We have enough difficulties. No more difficulties!" But greater difficulties can solve lesser ones. Many of the preoccupations with your human difficulties will dissolve in the face of a larger challenge. This is good for your people in many ways.

We and members of your Spiritual Family account for life in numerous places. Altogether we bring a larger expanse of understanding, a greater appreciation for life in many forms and an awareness of the difficulties that face true spiritual development everywhere.

The Greater Community is not made up of enlightened beings who are all anxiously waiting to come and enlighten humankind. Your neighbors from abroad share many of your same difficulties. If they were as enlightened as many of you wish they were, they would not be in the physical. Because they exist on the physical plane, they essentially all have the same difficulties that you do. Though their physical, biological, and psychological processes vary greatly, they are not perfect because they are still in the physical. Their technological advances do not necessarily mean that they have advanced in their inner lives, in spiritual matters. Technological development is problematic. It is a different kind of development from spiritual development within a race. Actually, your world is quite evolved spiritually, contrary to what many here think. You are very evolved, very rich.

There are difficulties in the Greater Community as there are difficulties here. They are simply on a greater scale, that is all. There are opposing forces in this Sector that you must realize, for life beyond this world is not that unlike your life here. Conflicts exist, alliances exist, betrayal exists, and the Spiritual Presence works everywhere. So, do not get too involved in the drama of things. It is the Spiritual Presence at work that is the most important.

Your world is undergoing the same problems that you are undergoing individually. It is simply a larger picture of yourself. The Greater Community is simply a larger picture of your world. If you are to function in a Greater Community context, then you must prepare both internally and externally, primarily in your viewpoint and in the foundation of your thinking.

Entering the Greater Community is entering a larger sphere of interaction. If you are idealistic like the young adolescent, you will misperceive the situation and make false assumptions that can only be unlearned through difficulty and error. But if you enter this with an open mind, recognizing how little you know and anxious to learn, then you shall find the counsel you need.

As I have said, your world is preparing technologically, economically and even politically for emergence into the Greater Community. It is as if humanity were unknowingly racing to a certain meeting place. You cannot account for this completely unless you see it within a larger context.

You do not know the importance of this world to the Greater Community. I shall say a few things about this, yet I do not want to arouse idle speculation because that is not helpful. I do, however, wish to arouse your thinking beyond your own personal sphere so that perhaps you can bear witness to something that is actually happening.

This idea of a Greater Community is something that everyone knows, but people do not want to talk about it. It either seems irrelevant to their personal needs, or it is so fantastic that they are afraid others will laugh at them. Yet people do have their deeper feelings.

Why hasn't the Greater Community all landed on the planet and made themselves available? That is a logical question. First, the Greater Community is comprised of many cultures, only a few of which even know you exist. There are only two or three who have ever been here, for your Sector is vast and space travel is very slow. Secondly, your people are too violent, and the presence of an alien force visible to you would endanger them and you as well. It is largely for self-preservation that your neighbors do not reveal themselves here more dramatically. You see, you are like a little village that is about to find itself in the midst of a bigger world. Your little village has never encountered a bigger world, yet you live in one nonetheless.

Before your civilization existed in this world, there was a great deal that took place here. Your recent culture has only been around for a few millennia. This world has never been unified in its native population. People speak of the greater civilizations such as Atlantis and Lemuria existing in early eras, but these were only colonies and quite small actually. Yet, since their time this world has been used as a depository by certain agents of good. Why? Because it is amenable in its climate and environment and because great underground depositories were created long ago, completely unbeknownst to the native peoples.

Many of these depositories were lost because of the changes in the physical climate and the geology of this world. Yet, some of these depositories are quite safely hidden. What is stored there are not only remnants of an ancient colony, but also materials brought here subsequently for storage and safekeeping. Certain of your visitors know this and are very interested in these matters. This world is known to possess certain important information.

It is important that you consider this idea in light of your own Knowledge. You are sitting on a treasure in this world and do not even know it. The treasure you would not find very useful. You would not even know how to use the things that are stored here. However, they have been placed and maintained here for safekeeping. That is part of the reason you will emerge into the Greater Community. Also, you must emerge into the Greater Community for your own survival.

Some of you know this already. No one had to tell you. This world has a certain strategic importance, but you are being scrutinized primarily because this is an emerging world with weaponry, because humanity is aggressive in its nature, and because there are things buried here of great value to others. No one wants to conquer your world. It is far too difficult to do and would be too much to manage. Your neighbors can barely manage themselves. The difference is that they are unified in their own worlds. It is essential if you are to undertake space travel that your planet become one community. That is a requirement. All worlds undergo this. They must be unified to communicate beyond their realm or they cannot do it, and their technology will become destructive.

You must continue to expand as a race. Placed within your Knowledge when you came into this world was certain information that is relevant to your role, should it ever be discovered. That has direct bearing on the events to come because you were placed here in the hope that your Knowledge may be activated and that these gifts may be given at the proper time. Spiritual development in all times and in all places must happen in accordance with the evolution of the world in which individuals are placed, not only for their own individual development but for the well-being of all life living there. Your individual nature and temperament are well-suited to fulfill your function, but if your function is unknown to you, then you will not understand their relevance.

The Greater Community is with you now. All of this emphasis on extraterrestrials is very recent. Of all the illustrations of extraterrestrials, the wild speculation and the fantasy, much of it is useless and nonsense. Yet the seed of it is true. Why is this all happening now? You may say, "What difference does it make to me? I don't care. I have my own problems!" Yet the Greater Community is influencing you emotionally, and it is changing your circumstances.

People are very interested in peace in this world, but there cannot be peace now. Do you know why? It is because of what I speak of. We work for peace always, but we recognize that change is very stressful. It involves decision, commitment and adjustment as well as some sacrifices. This is true of change both on a personal level and on a greater level. Why can't there be peace now? Because your world is attempting to unify itself, and all factions in your world that refuse to do this will wage war. It is very sad that this is true.

Do not demand that everyone settle down in peace. You will be working against the undercurrent in this world. We never advocate conflict, but you must understand that conflict arises in times of great change. With every great advancement in your world, there is tremendous combustion and upheaval. It is not because change requires this. It is simply because people cannot see beyond themselves.

If you look, you will see. But if all you can see are your own thoughts, then that is all you will see. If you are not thinking, you will see what is there. If you are preoccupied with your own thinking, you will see your own thoughts. We want to stimulate people to look without thinking so that they may see what is there and respond to it directly, like your animals do. They do not have the burden of reckless thinking.

The Greater Community must be approached through Knowledge. If you speculate about it intellectually, you will find yourself liking the idea or not, but that says nothing about what you know. Therefore, our primary emphasis is the development of Knowledge so that you may gain access to what is known within you, this precious cargo that you carry unknowingly. Until this happens, your life will not make sense. It will seem aimless and without consistent direction. The only consistency you will have is that you know you are progressing towards something for some reason to serve some greater force.

The more you are with Knowledge, the less the world will affect you because the world cannot touch Knowledge. But Knowledge can touch the world. Knowledge is not swayed by the world. It has one purpose and one direction. As it emerges within the person, the person becomes uniform and focused and then commitment is natural. You couldn't be anything but committed. Commitment is life. To be uncommitted is to be dead. You cannot make commitments. You can make pledges to try to be committed, but your real commitment comes from within you. It commits you. When Knowledge emerges, you will not have any choice about commitment. Your Knowledge is totally committed.

Knowledge is a gift that you have, but it is also your True Being. It has a plan for your life already and once activated, it will begin to exert itself in a much more direct way. You will realize you do not need the burden of decision, for increasingly Knowledge will motivate you, guide you and direct you, gracefully but powerfully. Then you will be able to extend the greatest gift that one can give to another. Your Knowledge will activate their Knowledge, and you will bear witness to this great event. This is true healing, for once this happens, the person's emergence will begin, and they will be entering a Greater Reality while they are still living in the world. It is hard to see that you are already part of something greater that is affecting you very deeply. It is not that you will become part of something. You already are. You are already part of a greater physical reality and a greater spiritual reality.

Why do you need Teachers? Because you cannot cultivate Knowledge on your own. It is far more powerful than you are. It recognizes you as intrinsically part of something already, so separation is already over. It does not act like a separated mind. It is not preoccupied with survival. It does not have defenses. It is the power of the Spiritual Family and the power of God manifested in the physical.

We are here because spiritual teaching at this time must account for the state of the world. You have all been placed in time and space in history. Your Knowledge and your purpose contain a particular application for a particular time. Though spiritual advancement is universal, it is always historically placed. You came here specifically for a purpose to serve in a specific capacity at this time. It behooves you, then, to understand what is happening in the world; otherwise, you will see no relevancy for your sense of purpose. Since purpose speaks of service to a greater reality than your own personal reality, you must see beyond your personal reality, or purpose will be an idea only.

Hear our lesson, please, we will tell you about a race in the Greater Community that was advanced far beyond what you can imagine, yet they did not have Knowledge. They did not become aware of events before they happened. They were not prepared. They were specialists in techno-logical development, yet they fell prey to a Greater Community that they did not understand because they did not have Knowledge. Therefore, they were ignorant of the forces around them. And though they contracted to make devices for other races, they did not understand the intent of the other races, nor did they wish to. They were isolated and ignorant and, as a result, their civilization is no more. This loss was a major loss, even for the Spiritual Families. It was a setback. Yet because truth emanates from beyond time, redemption will occur. But it is a lost opportunity.

If you do not activate Knowledge in your life, your life is a lost opportunity. This you will reflect upon when you leave, as did the seers in this other world. They could not change their world. They could not speak intelligently of Knowledge to their own people. The Unseen Ones con-tacted them, and they were developed while in physical life, yet what the seers spoke of gained very little attention. Their race had created a device of great power. They created it because of their own inventiveness and their own curiosity. Because they lived underground, they wished to learn a means of travel that was not impeded by physical obstacles. It had a very practical benefit, yet they had no idea of the meaning of this to other races. Therefore, they were ignorant of what they were doing. How could the seers of this world dissuade their whole race, who were very excited about these new developments?

It is important that you understand that your world is emerging within itself and beyond itself in the Greater Community and that you are emerging with it. Emergence always has a certain element of risk.

For those of you who have been seeking to find a place to give something you feel you have, the Greater Community will have much bearing on your sense of purpose in the world. You cannot find it in the normal sphere of things. You must think in a bigger way. When we speak of the Greater Community, we speak of a larger perspective on everything, including yourself most assuredly.

Your role is not preordained, but once your purpose is discovered, it will activate your mind and body and guide and direct you to participate with certain people for certain purposes that are greater than even your own development. This is an entirely different way of being in the world. It is what you are striving for primarily.

Therefore, when I speak of the Greater Community, I speak of it as being relevant to your purpose in the world. This world cannot stop where it is going; it must go there. You cannot stop; you must go where you are going. If your destiny is reached through Wisdom, it will be constructive and uplifting and you will progress. Yet, if you interfere with it, fight against it and demand it to be other than it is, you will not be in harmony with your world or with yourself, for your Knowledge is completely joined with the Knowledge that governs this world. That is why we always speak of Knowledge as the most important thing. It is not ideas. It is acting according to your deeper mind. It is a greater instinct.

We do not want to frighten you. We want you to think in a bigger way—not idealistically, not like you want the world to be the way you imagine it should be. You do not even know what this world is for. How can you imagine what it should be for? It will never be Heaven. It will never be home to you completely. You are only visiting here. This is a special place for something special to happen. If you can let down your ideas, then you will begin to know things, just *know* things—that rare experience you have had at times of great distress or great decision. Then this faculty that is your True Mind will begin to be active without confrontation.

Why do people go out and create these terrible situations for themselves? It is because they want to create a situation that forces Knowledge to come to the surface. Knowledge will not arise in a preoccupied mind under normal circumstances. When everything is going your way, you are very stupid. You are half asleep. That is not what brings Knowledge forth.

Yet, if Knowledge is not arising, you will go to extremes to bring it forth. It is like giving birth to something you are carrying and laboring with.

Do you see? The Greater Community will change your ideas about God completely. It will change your ideas about religion completely. You will see that God is not preoccupied with humans. You will see that God is something bigger than what you have ever considered, and you will have to think as a participant in a Greater Reality. This is a great blessing.

Why are nations in this world always threatening each other? They are so similar to one another, yet they accuse each other of the greatest evils. What will resolve the dilemma? They love each other, but they cannot join, so they fight. That is why people fight. They cannot separate. They cannot join. So they fight. That is what is happening between the United States and the Soviet Union. They cannot join, but they cannot separate. They will have to join, let me tell you. They will join because they will realize that they are exactly alike, and they will become increasingly similar in the years to come. Why will they join? Because they will be faced with a Greater Community beyond their borders. This may be the saving grace in this world. Humanity will have to contend with a bigger problem than the differences between nations that are so alike.

There is spiritual advancement happening everywhere. That is why the Teachers of the Spiritual Families serve all worlds. If you ever have the gift of encountering your Teachers who have been assigned to you, you will recognize that not all of them are human. Why is this? Is it not to bring forth your Knowledge which speaks of a Greater Reality and a Greater Community and which takes you beyond your personal sphere to allow you to enter life? We give entering life such great importance.

It is unfortunate if the development of Knowledge is misconstrued to be on a personal level only. Knowledge will make your personal self more harmonious, uniform and consistent but only to have a capacity for something greater. There is a Godseed in all people, but the seed must be germinated and have fertile soil in which to emerge.

Therefore, when I say Greater Community, do not go around thinking about spaceships. That is not the point. I wish for you to think of this in terms of what you experience in life. When you observe others, observe their preoccupation with themselves. They are not available for relationship. They cannot participate in life. Their chief concerns are survival and gratification. That is a very desperate situation to be in—to be in life but cut off.

This you hold in common with your brothers and sisters in the Greater Community: You either have Knowledge or you do not. That is all that matters. Their life is temporary and yours is as well. The seed has been placed within them as well as within you. Grace is available to you so that Knowledge may emerge. You do not need to control the emergence; it is quite natural. But you do need to exert control over your behavior and your tendencies so that it can happen.

It is like a great pregnancy. Your lifestyle and your values must change to accommodate it because like the expectant mother, you will wish to prepare a place for delivery: the proper environment, the proper support and the proper orientation. And you will protect this emergence because it is vital now. There are many people who are experiencing this pregnancy, and it is very difficult on a personal level to account for it. It does not matter that your personal side is so foolish, it does not matter that your body is not perfect, and it does not matter that you are beset by little ideas and fears. These are only minor hindrances compared to what you possess.

It is because you identify completely with your personal side that you are so anxious to make it as perfect as your True Self. But it can never be. It was never meant to be. Therefore, please be kind to yourself. Your vehicle is not your True Self. It is not Knowledge. It is a self-created vehicle for participation.

That is why we wish for people who are experiencing this rapid growth to be very kind, patient and considerate with themselves and others. You will find that your Teachers are very gentle and patient with you. They are not so concerned that you get everything together right away. They are only concerned that you not destroy your opportunity for Knowledge and that you participate fully in your current stage of development. You do not need to constantly aggravate your mind in order to progress in the most direct manner.

Your neighbors in the Greater Community can only be appreciated and understood through Knowledge and intrinsic relationship. Here you won't care what kind of toys they have. You won't care what they look like. You will only care about your experience of being with them. You have friends and you have adversaries in the Greater Community. Your people are very self-preoccupied with human life, human values, human organizations, human gods, human religious paths and human everything! You must become wise and use Knowledge and not be bedazzled by new, grand experiences like in the movies. The man and woman of Knowledge are not preoccupied with what things look like. They are only concerned with the task at hand.

Your Spiritual Family exists in this world and in other worlds. They are not all humankind. You have a human family that raises you in the world, but you have a Spiritual Family that raises you in life. This Family is not all humankind. You are not entirely human. You belong to a Greater Reality. Being a human isn't enough. You are not entirely a human being. When you have this perspective, you will know how to serve people because you will not be trapped in their identity dilemma.

God wishes to make God's Presence manifest in the physical. Yet, God can only do this through the vehicles that exist here. That is the nature of things. God has given this world everything it needs. Now you must use what has been given. God has given this world purpose. God has given this world evolution. God has given this world spiritual assistance of tremendous magnitude. God has planted purpose within you. God has given you life. God has given you Knowledge so that you may fulfill your part in this world at this time.

It
is only as
your deeper nature
emerges
that trust can
finally be
established
within yourself.

Four

TRUST

TRUST IS A VERY FUNDAMENTAL ISSUE and one you are probably familiar with. If you have been progressing, you must be concerned with the development of trust and with what trust must be founded upon. There are two aspects of you that we must talk about, for trust is the empowerment that you give yourself to participate in a Greater Reality while you are still in this world. There is your *personal side*, which you have been developing since you arrived here in this world, and there is your *Impersonal side,* which is something that is intrinsic to you. You have not been developing it; it is intact already.

It is only your Impersonal or deeper nature that can account for Knowledge. If you attempt to develop trust within your personal side, you will have great difficulty. Trust here will seem very complex and confusing, with many adversities and conflicts of interest. The personal side cannot trust because it is alone and afraid. Its foundation is unstable. Its assumptions are weak. Its associations are fragile and uncertain. It has no basis for trust. It is only as your deeper nature emerges that trust can finally be established within yourself, yet you must extend trust to allow this emergence to occur.

People have trouble because they are attempting to use their personal sides to fulfill themselves. They are attempting to fulfill their wishes and their wants and to avoid those things that seem harmful or depriving to them. Very difficult this is, for the personal side does not participate in life and does not understand what is happening.

Therefore, trust becomes very difficult. How can you trust when you are so afraid for yourself? How can you be trusting in a world that is so threatening and that poses so many adversities? How can your trust be genuine and not merely an academic exercise to bolster your sense of immediate security? This is what we must talk about.

It is certainly evident that trust is essential in learning, particularly if you are developing Knowledge. Here you are attempting to receive something that is inexplicable and mysterious. It is a Greater Force within you that accounts for intrinsic relationship and speaks for a Greater Reality. It guides you in directions that you have never gone, and yet it is so natural. What can your personal side do in the face of these things but acquiesce, fight or disassociate? Those are its three possible responses. Yet as Knowledge becomes stronger, your personal side must acquiesce because it is overshadowed.

This is not the stage of development that you are in at this time. You are attempting to establish trust so that you may progress. Your trust must not be based upon this world but upon something greater than the world because there is no foundation for trust here. You cannot base trust upon change. Please understand that. Trust must be based upon something that is constant and established. Then real trust can emerge. It needs a solid foundation that is not threatened by fearful appearances or negative associations.

The difficulty here is that if you live in the personal side, the only reliable source of information for your conclusions is what your senses report to you. Living in the personal side cannot account for a Greater Reality. The personal side hopes that there is a better world somewhere else where you may go when you leave here, but it cannot account for a Greater Reality.

Therefore, people living within this level of mind are very limited and essentially quite frightened. They must base their stability and their strength upon the strength of their ideas alone, and they will develop a rigid structure of thought upon which to base their identity, their direction and their purpose. Ultimately, this structure will fail them.

That is why in preparation for Knowledge you are gently led out of this structure. It is an amazing fact that Knowledge must emerge when the mind is opened and its struggle for identity has failed. Some of you feel as if you are going nowhere, that you are struggling or that your life seems aimless. You cannot generate sufficient enthusiasm. To the personal side, this looks like death and despair. Yet, this is the opportunity that your Teachers have been waiting for for so long. It means that you are now able to respond to something that is beyond your own thoughts, beyond your own wishes and beyond your own plans.

Failure of the personal side to guide and protect the being is the beginning of the emergence of Knowledge. Knowledge begins with failure—failure to organize and direct your life, failure to constitute your relationships based upon your expectations and demands and failure to orchestrate the universe to accommodate your wishes. This failure is a great release from bondage.

People are very adamant that God should come and make the world exactly the way they want it, but God has other plans. God's intention is to free everyone here so that they may return to their natural Home. So, instead of making the world a perfect place for your separation to exist, God has set in motion the forces to break your separation down. Very loving this is. It is not violent at all. God has done this because you have Knowledge and because you cannot make your Impersonal side conform to your personal wishes.

That is why the stronger your Impersonal side becomes, the weaker your personal will is. That is why some of you are running out of interest in this world. If you accept this properly, you will see that it is the emergence of truth within you. Yet, from the personal side's viewpoint, it can indeed be quite frightening. We wish for you to allay your fears and to perceive this in a different way.

God is only interested in re-establishing communication with you. That is all that matters because that is the universe. What can you hope to accomplish here without that? Your span of years is quite brief. Your environment is far more powerful than you are, or seemingly so. There are countless adversities to undermine your progress. There must be something else. This, then, is where your trust must be directed.

Do you see? As long as your primary intent is counter to your Knowledge, you will be in conflict with yourself and with your environment. Your relationships will express this conflict. As much as you want relationship with one another, you will not know what to do with it if you have it. This is a very painful dilemma but not one without resolution.

Gently, gently the Presence of your Spiritual Family wishes to ease your burden of self-determination. You have a greater possibility than your goals can account for. It is this that you may open to quite naturally. Yet if your mind is raging for its wishes, it will perceive this as a complete failure, and it will not abide by this deeper inclination that is so natural to you.

We do not speak of this in terms of passivity, for learning to surrender to Knowledge will require a greater commitment and a greater level of self-determination, self-control and participation with others than you have previously known. This activates all of your natural abilities and gives them a uniform direction.

The distinction between the personal and the Impersonal is so important. When you are in your Impersonal side, you will see an entirely different world than the world you see when you are in your personal viewpoint. Time will stand still. You will be in the present. You are in a different state of mind now. As you experience this, even momentarily, the sense of contrast will give you an inclination of what you must attain to have peace in this world. It will also clarify your values so that you may have a true goal in life—to serve the Greater Reality so that it may emerge within you.

You cannot resolve anything without Knowledge and you will have no foundation for faith, trust or happiness without it. All your pleasures will be temporary, unstable and easily challenged. If you think about this seriously, it becomes quite apparent.

Yet, you are not without hope, for Knowledge is with you. It has its own destiny and its own path. You may pull yourself this way and that, but you cannot convince the deeper aspect of yourself to participate. You see, the resolution to your problems is always quite simple, but your approach to the resolution is quite complex. It is not hard to heal you, but it is difficult for you to want healing. Healing does not happen on your own terms or in your own way because it comes from a greater reality than your personal sphere. It comes from the Greater Reality that you are a part of but cannot govern.

Indeed, you need to govern your thoughts, feelings and activities so that they may be directed according to a deeper experience. You will want this experience of being in the Impersonal increasingly, for here everything settles down and you can begin to see. You will have confidence here because your confidence is based upon something that is sound and established. And you will perceive your personal self like a loving parent who understands the little child screaming and is not offended. Your personal side will eventually integrate itself into Knowledge and find its rightful contribution. Thus, everything will be fulfilled and unified.

You must see that as you live in your personal side, you cannot resolve anything. You will attempt many great resolutions, make new plans, get into new relationships or try to change your scenario, but if your Knowledge is not going in those directions, then you will not have agreement within your own True Being. All of your determination will not sway the true course of your life. Attempting to do this leads to failure which can lead you to the true opening that we are speaking of.

It is Knowledge, then, that requires your trust. Because you live in the personal side, you need to trust the deeper aspect of yourself. You do not consciously live the majority of your life there, yet living there is possible. This is indeed the promise that is given you, but that is not where you are now.

Therefore, the more that you experience Knowledge within yourself, the more that you will naturally have a sense of purpose, direction and identity. With each little increment that you experience this, it makes a permanent mark. You can then return to your personal side, your personal mental framework, but with a little greater perspective and a memory of truth.

Trust, then, is most easily explained in this way: You trust your deeper nature when you are not connected with it. You will see that life is actually conspiring on your own behalf. If you stop attempting to use it for immediate goals, then you will be able to perceive it working on your behalf.

Please realize that the trust you must develop is the trust in Knowledge within you and trust in the Teachers who are here to help you activate that Knowledge and give it meaning. Your development is very much a group process. You cannot fully see and experience this at this moment. That is because you are in your personal side, which does not represent these things.

The question, then, is not, "How can I develop trust?" The question is, "How can I gain access to Knowledge?" Knowledge will provide all of the necessary motivation and justification for true faith, so that when you say to yourself, "I do not need to worry because I know that this situation will work out," you are not simply giving yourself a little pep talk; you are very, very certain. Why? Because you can see it in motion. You are looking without your own thoughts. Your mind is open. It can now perceive the situation as it is truly unfolding.

If you wish for a relationship or are in a relationship, return to Knowledge and you will be able to see what your next step is. Without this, you will vacillate between exhilaration and tremendous fear. Exhilaration and fear. Exhilaration and fear. Wanting and disappointment. Wanting and disappointment.

That is why we say to people who wish to have marriage and true partnership in this life, "Develop Knowledge." Then your relationship will have a foundation, and you can trust this relationship because it has this foundation. This is the wise approach. This is preparing for relationship. This is preparing for purpose in the world.

You see, how can you trust me? I am just a phenomenon. Because you *know* me. That is how you can trust me. It is not because you agree with me or believe in me or any of that sort of thing. I can only be known. You perceive one another, but you do not have a relationship until the relationship becomes known. I am no different. I am simply invisible. But that does not mean that you cannot have as deep a relationship with me as you can with one another, for relationship exists on the level of Knowledge. You cannot point to people and say, "There is a relationship." Relationship is invisible. It is an intrinsic bond between two minds. The two bodies may stand together or rub against each other, but that is not relationship. You cannot see a relationship. You cannot even conceptualize a relationship. It can only be known. You can conceptualize your behavior together, your common interests or the level of stimulation that you hold for one another, but these are all very changeable and can disappear very rapidly. That is not the deeper quality we speak of. We wish for you to appreciate each other, and that is why we offer this insight.

Part of the difficulty in developing trust is your attempt to do impossible things. Therefore, it is necessary for us to counsel you not to do impossible things. They require great energy, even though they seem to stimulate your sense of self-determination. The more difficult the adversity, the greater the prize and the greater the sense of personal reward you anticipate. But in the end, it all becomes impossible and you give up. Then you have the opportunity to know something.

When something is true and you are working at it, even if there is adversity, it is a whole different experience. Everything makes you stronger not weaker. Here cooperation and adversity both activate Knowledge even more powerfully. Instead of becoming weaker, you become stronger. Instead of becoming more disassociated, you become more certain. Why is this? Because you are activating your Impersonal side. It is becoming stronger, and you are trusting it and relying on it increasingly.

It is only by relying upon Knowledge that you can have any com-prehension of what it is and what it can do. That is why when students enter the *Steps to Knowledge* Program, at a certain point we ask them to do something based upon their Knowledge—little things, perhaps, but then great things because this is how Knowledge becomes stronger. This is how trust is truly established. After you have done this successfully, then when you are faced with a new challenge in life, you will be able to recall your former experiences. They will be the demonstration you need that your trust was well founded and that it can indeed do the impossible once again.

Devotion
is
the highest
expression of
love
in the
world.

Five

MARRIAGE

The marriage that we will be talking about is a very, very special kind of relationship. We would like to provide the proper context because the quality of marriage that we would like to address is something that is very rare in the world. It is something you do not see very often, and yet it is something that people strive for knowingly and unknowingly.

We give marriage a very great emphasis because it is the consuming relationship. It is consummate and consuming altogether. True marriage is something that is a source of nourishment for other people as well as for the two people involved. Because we are speaking of marriage in a larger context, we will not only be speaking of marriage between a man and a woman. We will be speaking of marriage as a quality of union that can exist in any relationship, for it is the quality, not the form, that matters. It is the understanding and the experience.

It is appropriate that true marriage be so lofty. It is worth preparing for. It is a natural gift of God to those who are serving their true purpose, for you cannot serve a true purpose alone. You will need true marriage. You will need this kind of assistance.

Because these relationships are so very valuable, great emphasis is placed on preparation. These relationships demonstrate the reality of the Spiritual Family where there can be a bond that is deeper than the personalities involved and stronger than any divergent interests or orientations. This is something that transcends personal realities and has purpose and direction. This is something that is not created by the people involved but is something that they discover together. It is a discovery, and yet it is a discovery with a purpose. It is here to do something.

True union can exist between men and women, between two great friends, or between a parent and a child. It can actually happen between any individuals if they have reached the same point of recognition and if they have an intrinsic bond already.

Obviously, there is a lot of marriage around. Marriage is very common, but how many marriages are an inspiration to you? Not everyone is meant to be in marriage—that is between husband and wife. That is not the appropriate expression of marriage for everybody. However, a relationship based upon Knowledge, recognition and purpose is meant for everyone. When you have experienced that, you will realize that your life is greater than your personality. It will be an experience that will be very confirming for you. Out of this relationship will come devotion, which is the highest expression of love in the world. Devotion is a quality that is very rare. It is not to be confused with obligation or bondage of any kind. It is a free gift that is essential to give.

Many people expect or demand devotion from others but are incapable of giving it themselves, for they wish to bargain with their affection. They wish to make sure that their demands will be met before they are willing to give in. But you see, devotion is not negotiable. You do not bargain for it. It is not giving in. It is something that emerges from the very depth of you, so that you need not create it. It simply arises.

Why is this experience so rare in the world? With so much marriage and so much relationship going on, why is there so little of it that is truly inspiring? Is it because it is a gift that is only given to a few people? Is it because its participants are so pure and so holy and so innocent that it is natural for them? No, it is not for either of these reasons.

Let us give you some ideas now so that you can have a realistic expectation of union for yourself and be able to perceive your current involvements with greater certainty.

First, you will find that this quality of relationship will come to you as you have something important to do in life. People who are actively engaged in life do not have to go searching for relationship. This is a fact. If you have found something truly meaningful to do in this world that it is natural for you to do and that you wish to give yourself to completely, it is a certainty you will not be alone in your giving. It is a certainty that your giving will be shared and will establish a union of great strength. This is because your relationship is pointing outward. You are moving together, and you are not trying to make each other the complete object of your affection, for this is never successful. Devotion is always to something far greater than the personality.

Very few people have this feeling of vitality in their engagement in life and so, to substitute for this, they seek excitement in relationship, some for excitement's sake and some in the name of personal growth. I can assure you there is not enough personal growth in the universe to justify endless involvements. What takes you beyond personal growth is that you become very tired of it, and you now seek refuge, relief and inspiration from some-thing greater. Personal growth is very disappointing because you cannot expand the personal side of you very far. It always has great promise, and it is always very exciting when you are embarking on personal growth, but it quickly begins to get very difficult. Personal growth is natural when you are developing Knowledge, for your mind and body must now accommodate a Greater Power within you. This is the context in which personal growth has value and is governed by necessity and not by preference.

Therefore, relationships for personal growth are by definition very limited. They are limited by your own ambivalence towards growth. They are limited by your objectives, and they are limited because you and the other have somewhat divergent motives. Your personal growth will not yield the completeness of being together that is so very nourishing, for you are trying to use the other to grow and they are trying to use you to grow. Sooner or later you will realize you do not have the same purpose.

This can elapse after a great deal of time because, you see, when you are personally growing, pain seems very justified. Your resistance seems to be a sign you should become more involved, not less. So before you know it, you are now in bondage to participate for fear that you might be a fail-ure of some kind. This is sad, for it can take a great deal of pain to con-vince you that you are on the wrong track.

You do not have much time in this world, my friends. You really do not. Life is short here. Your vitality is limited. It is very important that you seek some very fundamental things and not try to have all of these experiences that seem to be so alluring. There is no evidence that people who are in relationship for personal growth are doing any better than people who are in relationship for other reasons, except perhaps that their engagement is a little more exciting and self-absorbing. But, you see, I want to steer you now to a different emphasis.

Now, I have said that if you are doing something meaningful in the world, people will join you. This is very natural. If your life is given to doing something in the world, people will give their lives to join you. They aren't with you simply because you are entertaining them or because they have wonderful experiences with you. You are an expression of a purpose that they share, so now you have a union that is not based upon likes and dislikes or upon personal goals. It is simply natural to be together, and it would be unnatural to be apart. It is this naturalness that is an indicator that something is going right.

In order to differentiate between recognition and attraction, you must cultivate Knowledge, the ability and the foundation to *know* within your own mind. It is fundamental to everything we teach and advocate.

We are very intent on people having true relationship because that is the greatest expression of Knowledge in this world—meaningful relationship one on one and meaningful relationship in larger arenas as well. What is God, what is the return to God, but the return to relationship? Some people wish to return to God and commit themselves to God, but they cannot be with anybody. And so they are trying to be with everything, but they do not know how to be with any one thing. This leads to idealism of a very unfortunate kind, for people are committed to an idea of God and not to God at all. People are committed to an idea of relationship but cannot participate in relationship.

It is very difficult to create a relationship, is it not? It is always falling apart somewhere. You have to go patch it up. It is always breaking down, and you are always building it up. However, if you are doing something really important in life, you do not have time to constantly be patching up a relationship. Your criteria for a relationship then becomes, does it work or not? It is not whether you are doing a good job or being open or loving. It is not a performance on your part. Your relationship either works or it does not. If it does not, then you lovingly free the person to find his or her right place. Then everything can be rearranged properly.

Now, in all fairness, you have personalities and they create problems. This is true. And you will have to contend with all of the expressions of fearfulness and the desire for separation. But you can confront these things if you have a Greater Power within you. If you do not have this Power, your personality will seem insurmountable. You will be trying to make it comfortable and also be trying to be true to your deeper inclinations. It is very hard to do that.

Marriage is natural for those people who are living a life of Knowledge. We wish to emphasize this. You are here for a purpose. You went to great lengths to be here. You have something to give in being here. You cannot go beyond this world because you have not given what is essential for you to give here. Your giving contains your self-realization, and your Knowledge is your foundation. With this foundation, you will see that life is conspiring on your behalf. Without this foundation, you will feel that you are challenging life and working at variance with life.

It is very important that you understand what relationships are for. Very few people have any idea of this. They are drawn by attraction, they establish a bond, they get all involved emotionally, and then at some later date they find out if they have a relationship or not. This is quite a backwards approach. We wish to advocate a much more direct approach.

Because you are deeply attracted to others does not mean that you should yield yourself to them. If you have been around a little while, you probably have learned that. There are many things that attract people. Until you are aware of your inclinations and until you are aware of the difference between Knowledge and your personal side, between your Spirit and your mind, you will simply be moved around by forces you cannot explain. And those who are more certain than you will certainly dominate you. They are more certain of what they want than you are, and you will feel dominated.

However, if you concentrate on developing Knowledge, you will be able to look and see why you are here and find expression for this—even if it is only a beginning. It does not have to be the ultimate answer. If you find something vital you feel you must do in your life now, then you will find that people will come to participate with you. There is so little vitality in human life that anyone who is experiencing it draws people naturally. People want to come over and find out what is going on. Somebody is alive in their midst! Somebody is not self-preoccupied!

My approach may seem very simple, and it is, but developing Knowledge is quite a challenge. If you seek challenge, I cannot think of a greater one. Without Knowledge, relationship is trial and error only. There are many people who have spent their primal energy on relationships with very little to show for it. They have wasted their lives, and yet they have justified this waste by saying that they have grown personally and that they have learned so very much. But they are right back where they began. They are alone and they are still seeking for a meaningful union.

You have come here for something more important than simply trying to figure out how your mind works. You will not have your personal mind very long, so why devote your life to understanding it? You are not here to do that.

As you begin to develop your spiritual life, your inner life, you realize there are essential qualities in relationship that cannot be neglected. There is a central emphasis that people either have or not. There is no blame here. It is either there for them or it is not. If you are cultivating an inner life and you are attracted to someone who is not, you will begin to see that there is a divergence of purpose that cannot maintain a relationship for very long.

Now, some people have an inner life but never talk about it. Other people have no inner life and that is all they talk about. So, do not think that because people talk intelligently about an inner life that they have one.

If you are developing an inner life, you will seek this in others. Why? Because it is purposeful for you to do this. You will see that a partner for you will either contribute to or hinder this emphasis. If there is hindrance, you will value very different things increasingly, and you will seek different things.

Knowledge always brings people together who have a common intent for union. It also brings some people together who do not share purpose so that they may understand their purpose in contrast. These people cannot join completely, for they cannot function together in the world.

You see, the important thing to consider is the question: Why am I here? This assumes you have come from someplace and that you are going back to someplace. If you can accept that, then you must ask yourself why on earth you are here. And if you are here for something important, then you will naturally want to find out what it is all about. This produces a very essential discrimination in relationship.

There are many people who have been married, who have developed an inner life and who have had to leave their marriage because of it. This is not uncommon. If someone has a destiny in life and they are married, their marriage will produce the environment that will produce the yearning for a Greater Reality and a greater union. If your Spirit is ready to emerge, then fulfillment on the personal side will not be enough. As this emergence continues to be the emphasis, you will feel increasingly restless.

We, of course, wish for everyone to have true marriage. True marriage will come to you if you have found your purpose. People who have purpose can never be alone because their purpose joins them with other people. Nothing can be done alone in this world. Nothing can be done alone in any world or in any dimension. So when you begin to reclaim your Knowledge, which is your true identity, you will begin to reclaim those people who are part of your Knowledge and part of your purpose. They will be specific people, and you will be given very specific things to do with them.

Affections that you have for each other that are not based upon this cannot be maintained. Their initial intensity cannot be maintained continuously. Then what holds people together is convenience, safety and habit. But if they feel a greater yearning, then they cannot stay in this situation. Sooner or later, like breaking out of a shell, they will seek their freedom.

All they are seeking is marriage, and they will feel terrible because they have failed their relationship, or so they think. Their marriage has not consumed them; it has only used a part of them. You see, people are very afraid that marriage will somehow overtake them and destroy their independence. Yet that is exactly what people are truly seeking, to be fully used up somewhere because the more they are used up, the more power they have. The more they are consumed, the more energy they have. The more they are utilized, the greater their Being. Their Being yearns to be used, to be channeled into useful service in the world.

Therefore, if you have this intent to be fully utilized in the world in service to God, it will also satisfy you personally because your personal side does not really want very much. It only wants to be included, to be safe and to have a few basic necessities. Really, you do not need that much, but your Being needs a great deal. It has only one intent and that is to be meaningfully used according to its own design in this life. When we speak of developing Knowledge, we speak of gaining access to your Being and allowing it to express itself and to exert its direction.

Many marriages in the world are purely experiments, that is all. But you see, a marriage that cannot consummate itself requires a lot of energy. In some ways it leaves a scar on you. There is a sense of failure that abides with divorce, even if divorce has become obviously necessary. That is why we do not wish for people to use marriage for experimentation because as it fails, it uses up your vital energy tremendously and it leaves a scar.

Do not look at a person's personality and say, "I will be consummated with this person." Personalities are far too limited to consummate anybody, and they are very wasteful if they are the object of your intent. There are so many experiments in this world to undertake and so many exciting things to pursue, you could quite easily waste your life. There always seem to be new thrills, new inducements, new excitements and new hopes. Yet, as you grow older, your ability to change and your ability to see the truth lessens.

Most relationships that you see are experiments, but they are not necessarily wasteful. You all have to find out the difference between what is meaningful and what is not, and experience is the hardest but most persuasive teacher. When we speak of waste, we are talking about trying to recreate the same thing over and over, thinking that a new exciting person will give you a different result.

Relationships that are for contrast can illustrate the deeper and more important things in life. They do this because they are disappointing. They do this because they do not satisfy you in the way you had thought and so, perhaps, you need something greater. This takes you within yourself and, hopefully, will make you more observant of your environment and your encounters in the world.

We hope that you can receive this in loving kindness because we want people to feel they have meaning in this world, intrinsic meaning, not just something they made up for themselves, not some kind of explanation that they have been using to justify their lives, but something they feel is a guiding force within them. If you are feeling this, then follow it. Do not hold back. There are very few people who have found this, and it will be very sad for you to waste such a rare gift.

Therefore, seek Knowledge. Don't worry about marriage. If you are seeking Knowledge, you will have to have marriage, with someone, in some context, whether you are a householder or celibate. Life won't let you get away without it. You will have to have marriage, for you will thrive on devotion.

I tell you, you will not know God until you are devoted. Devotion is a giving of heart that is spontaneous. It is not something you have to try to do. If it is happening in any realm for you, and it is true and gives you vitality, then please, let this express itself.

Devotion is something you should not judge from the outside. It is like the Kingdom of God in the world. You are either inside or outside the gates. That is all. Things look very different on the outside. From there, the people on the inside look like they are giving things up all the time. It is such a different emphasis. On the inside you keep wanting to give your life all the time because you get it back more powerfully. You do not want to keep anything for yourself because it simply becomes a detriment You want to keep giving because your gift becomes stronger.

Life will conspire to help you value Knowledge. It will also conspire to bring you into contact with people who will teach you what is meaningful and what is not. And if there is opportunity for real devotion, everything will conspire to engage you with this.

When you leave this world, you return to your learning group. There is devotion there. It is not a personal problem. You simply belong. It is evident that you belong. In fact, you will not even think about it because there is no contrast to belonging. Here in the world, there is contrast everywhere to belonging, and so it seems incomprehensible that you could have something like this waiting for you. When you are able to give to this world what you have with your group, then you will no longer need to come here, for the world will no longer be a separate place. It will not be an exception to Knowledge and to true relationship. As each member of your group completes his or her work here, then you will all move on together and you will have a new challenge.

Your Inner Teachers are the advanced members of your group. They need you to progress because if you do not, your group does not progress. You see, do not think of this as obligation. It is simply the way it is. You are not alone; you are part of something. If you do not discover this in this life, then you go Home to your group and you realize, "Ah, I did not do it! I forgot again! How soon can I go back? I want to go back. I know what to do now. It was awful down there, but I have to go back." Why do you have to go back? Because you do. Because that is Knowledge.

This is not you as an individual being a free agent in the universe. There are no free agents in the universe. Why? Because there is no separation in the universe, and without separation the only free agent is everything, and everything works together. Freedom, then, is the ability to be with everything harmoniously. There is nothing else that is free.

Now, when you approach relationship and you are interested in someone and feel drawn, take time with yourself before you get involved sexually and emotionally. Contemplate what is in front of you. Your Knowledge has no answer except "Yes" or "No," or it will give you conditions for participation. That is your Knowledge. If you do not consult it, then you must take your chances. Once you become sexually engaged, you are bonded. It will be very difficult to use Knowledge then, unless, of course, the relationship is completely inappropriate—in which case your Knowledge will kick you out of it.

As you become greater with Knowledge, your Knowledge exerts a greater influence. If you are about to make a mistake, it will certainly let you know. Your reaction to things will become much more intense.

But it is very difficult to use Knowledge when you are emotionally involved because your personal side wants so much. Of course it wants. How can it not want? It is alone; it is seeking desperately. You see, the personal side wants to be alone but not lonely, so it is very difficult for it to maintain a relationship. It wants to be sure the wonderful person is there, but it also wants to be sure it gets its own way. What happens, then, is that you have a conflict of purpose.

Meanwhile, your Knowledge is sleeping within you. It is not involved. It is not in the relationship. You cannot take this person whom you love very much and make your own Being be married. Your own Being knows exactly whom it will be married to, and you cannot tell it to be married to this other person. If you think you can, you have no idea how great your Being is and how tiny your personal side. It is like a little ant telling the mountain to move over. It says, "Move over! I'm coming through."

When your Being recognizes its partner, it will move you along. You will be committed already. You will not even know what is happening to you. It is not like falling in love. It is a different experience. It is not crazy and maddening and frustrating. It is very calm, like you have come home. It is like a little bit of your Spiritual Family is with you now and you begin to have a sense of where you have come from and where you are going. In time, you will remember what you wanted to do here.

So, let us not make marriage the objective. Marriage is the result, not the cause. Let the objective be to cultivate Knowledge, to receive the emissaries from your Spiritual Family who are your Inner Teachers and to begin to look at why you are here. Until you are married to your purpose, marriage with another cannot be consummated.

Purpose is not a definition. It is not enough to go around saying, "This is why I am here." Purpose is an abiding experience of belonging and intent. You are intent upon something. It does not matter so much if you succeed or fail in the world's estimation so long as you can give in this direction. You will give even if you fail all the requirements that the world lays down. That is because your commitment is greater than the world. Your commitment is redemptive to the world. That is why relationships that come together to share this commitment are greater than the personalities involved.

Everyone is seeking their Spiritual Family here. Everyone is seeking this because they miss it. Why would you seek unless you were missing something? It is not only the sense of inclusion you are seeking; it is a sense of specific purpose here as well. Your specific purpose may express itself in a very mundane fashion. You do not all have to be great emancipators for your people. That is quite rare. It is that you have found a place in life to give yourself completely, and you can give yourself without having to negotiate.

People want all kinds of things, or so they say, but all they really want is to belong somewhere. That is the underlying need. If they find where they belong, the central yearning has been answered. Then problems are small, not great. You can own all kinds of things and have all kinds of relationships, but if your central yearning has not been met, you will have a great problem. You will not be satisfied with what you have because it is not consummating you.

In The Greater Community Way of Knowledge, we prepare people for Knowledge—to experience Knowledge and to be activated in Knowledge. Let us give you this idea: The true marriage that we speak of is where two people are activating each other's Knowledge. This is different from two people stimulating each other's personalities. When you are activating each other's Knowledge, which is something that you do not have to try to do, you are more who you are when you are together than when you are not.

So, why try to be so independent and go off and say, "I don't need anybody. I am totally who I am without anybody." And then when you die, you go back to your group and you realize that you made the mistake of trying to be alone again, and you see you are totally not alone.

The Unseen Ones are together, you know. Why are they so bonded? Because their relationship is established in Knowledge. They are wed through their Knowledge. Their minds can melt right into each other, and they have more power as a result.

How are great things done in the world? They are never done by individuals. Greatness always happens because something greater is poured through the individual. It is like a fountain pen: It is not the tip but the vessel that holds all of the ink. In the world you are like the tip touching the paper, but it is because you have a greater vessel to pour through you that you can provide something uncommon, important and lasting here.

When you are acting with Knowledge, you stimulate Knowledge in others. This is the highest service. In fact, you do not even have to be trying to help anybody. Knowledge activates Knowledge. It is spontaneous. Not everyone can accept this, of course, and some people fight you when you try to do this or when you do this without trying, whatever the case may be. Who can be neutral in the face of Knowledge? Who can be unaffected?

For most people, their Knowledge emerges later in life when they have been sufficiently disappointed by the personal side and they have begun to really feel their yearning for God and their yearning for true marriage with others. It is not a want. It is a yearning.

*People
only love
their bodies
when they
serve a
higher purpose.*

Six

HEALTH

W E HAVE BEEN ENDEAVORING to encourage students of Knowledge to develop a high degree of health. Maintaining good health has some very important aspects, particularly for those of you who are developing Knowledge and feel that God has a purpose for you in your life. You see, the development of your health is very essential. We are sad when people neglect this as they undertake spiritual development because it limits their capacity for Knowledge and their effectiveness with other people. It is neglectful because your body is important in serving a higher capacity in this world. It is a fragile instrument that seems to require so much care. Part of the reason for this is that you do not take good care of it, and so it is always failing you and slowing you down.

You see bodies all around, so you take them for granted. Everybody's got a body, and so you think, "Oh, bodies are just bodies. Everybody's got one." And they are a real problem. You've got to feed them and house them and drag them around all day long. They are always demanding and always having aches and pains, having to go to doctors and having to wear clothes and having to stay warm and having to stay dry. You have to give the body all this attention.

And so, when people discover that there is another aspect of themselves that is not the body, they tend to neglect their body because they are tired of taking care of it. It is like a child that never grows up. It is always demanding. It requires a great amount of energy. Besides, it is extremely confining, is it not, to lug this thing around all day? Your True Being would much prefer to fly out the window and go wherever it wants to go—no problem! There will a time for that later, perhaps, but right now you have this delicate instrument to care for.

People develop health for many reasons, you know. Often they develop health because they do not want to be sick, but that is not a sufficient reason to give the attention needed. People want to develop health so that they can look good to other people. That is a very short-range perspective on the value of developing health. Others want to develop health because they see a real benefit. They wish to experience life more deeply, more effectively, and more enjoyably. This, now, is getting to the point, but there is something even beyond this.

You have a responsibility since you have come here, a responsibility that very few people have recalled into their memory. You did not just end up here, surrounded by all these other people who ended up here, not knowing what to do with yourself. No, you have come here for a purpose. You have gone to great lengths to enter the physical body—a painful and difficult journey it is.

If you did not have a body, it would be very difficult for you to communicate with people. It would be very difficult for you to contribute directly to this world that so deeply needs your abilities. It would be very difficult to communicate to your loved ones who are here. You would speak, but they would not hear you, or if they heard you, maybe they would scratch, or turn their head, or feel a strange sensation. But it is unlikely that they would actually hear you speaking to them, for they are too preoccupied with their own thoughts to hear anything beyond their own mind.

So, you have this body. It is meant to be an asset to you. It deserves your careful and conscientious care because it is a gift. You had to wait a long time to come here. You cannot just enter the world at will, you know. You have to wait in line. Very few people remember where they came from, so this all seems a little irrelevant and perhaps controversial.

You are here for a very short time to accomplish a specific task. If you do not accomplish it, you will simply have to go through the process all over again until you can recognize your purpose while you are in the world and complete it. Then you will not need to come back anymore. For those of you who are honest about your experience here, at some point you must come to realize that you really do not want to come back again, particularly if you learn to recognize where you are going and the freedom that it promises for you.

Developing health takes a level of concentration, self-discipline and commitment that anyone would benefit by having. It is not that health is so difficult to maintain. It's that very few people feel they are worth the effort. It is not their bodies that they are evaluating here. It is themselves.

If you have no sense of abiding purpose in your life, then you will feel that your body is just one more nuisance to you. But as you cultivate your awareness of your purpose and as it becomes more real as a guiding force that you feel each day, then you must realize that your physical body is a remarkable achievement.

You know, this world is an ideal little place. Compared to other worlds in the Greater Community, this world is a little gem. Of course, because no one has an understanding of this, most people will spoil their gem.

You see, you have a great opportunity if you are not short-sighted and if you think about your life in a long-term sense. Once you see that you are a visitor in this world and that this is not your home, then perhaps you will begin to realize you have a responsibility to those who have sent you to realize your purpose, to develop the necessary skills and to take good care of your physical vehicle. If you take good care of your physical body, it will serve you well and meet the demands that you place upon it. Indeed, as your purpose is realized, you will discover that your life will become increasingly focused and you will have greater demands upon your energy. They will be regenerative demands; they will be beneficial to you, but you must be physically capable.

Now, you all have Inner Teachers, but if your body is a dull instrument, it will prevent you from responding. Your body needs to be keen. It needs to be an asset. If it is cared for, it is like a window not a wall. You will be able to look through it, and it will not prevent you from receiving more directly the communication that you need to receive from God.

It is true that many people hide within their bodies. From a personal standpoint, this is one of the reasons for having a body. It is a place to hide out so no one can see you. All they can see is your fortress. They cannot even see you. They cannot find you. If they took your fortress and they opened it up, like the surgeons do, they still could not find you. If they took it apart in little teeny squares, they still could not find you. Great hiding place! No one can find you.

But as the body becomes purified, it literally becomes transparent. You are able to see out of it and people are able to see into it. Now it becomes an asset to communication and not an obstacle. It is only when the body becomes empty, clear and clean that the mind will have a greater access to what is calling to it.

If you say, "I want to develop health," and you do this only from a personal standpoint, it is unlikely that you will have enough interest to do it. But if you experience that God wants you to do it and humanity needs you to do it, that would make a very great difference. This is greater than a personal interest in health. Your body now needs to be developed. It needs to be an adequate vehicle and instrument for you to use. Then you will have sufficient purpose, and you can take on the change and the initial discomforts that are required, whatever they may be.

It would be a shame if your body failed you, leaving your purpose undone. Bodies are very fallible and breakable, you know. People attribute magical powers to bodies, but they are really not very magical. They are simply machines. They are beautiful mechanisms, and if they break beyond a certain point, you will not be able to repair them. So, do not use your body with negligence, thinking, "Well, if I wear it out or if it falls apart, God will come along and fix it up for me." This vehicle of communication is a gift that others can recognize.

In your own Knowledge, you know you have to do certain things. We are not speaking of extremes. We are saying that you know your body needs to be healthy. It is part of your Knowledge that knows that this is true, and any reason you give to excuse yourself will not prevail against Knowledge itself.

As we said, if your body is neglected and does not function properly, then it will be an obstruction and a problem to you. It will slow you down and interfere. It will dull your mind. It will not be what it is intended to be.

As your body becomes more efficient in its functioning, you will be able to devote yourself to developing your deeper abilities. The body now is no longer a constant adversary. It is simply a useful instrument. It does not matter if it is beautiful or not. That is not the point. What matters is that it functions properly so that you can be in it comfortably and use it for a good purpose.

It takes some discipline, commitment and consistent self-application to develop your physical vehicle. It takes the same intent to develop your mental abilities.

You see, progress in this world is actually being furthered by a very small percentage of the population who are doing all the work for every-one else. Maybe twenty percent of your population is doing all the work. They are really breaking new ground. Everyone else is working, but they are simply dragging along.

I give this perspective not to condemn you at all, but in relation to your neighbors in the Greater Community, your people are extremely lazy and ineffective. This is partly due to the fact that your environment is so easy and requires so little. This is quite rare in the Greater Community where, in order to survive and maintain their development, races have had to cultivate themselves. It is not a matter of "Do I really want to or not?" It is simply necessary. Here it is not necessary because everything is so easy.

People often ask me for very great things. They wish for me to explain their purpose, their future or the outcome of their involvements. And you know, sometimes I cannot answer because they are not able to carry out what I might tell them because they do not have enough energy or vitality. They cannot even fulfill their own objectives because they do not have vitality.

You see, as you develop Knowledge and your mind becomes more refined, it becomes more focused and has greater concentration. Your physical body is then able to exercise greater energy, and it is able to accomplish more.

Therefore, you must be able to conserve your efforts. Your body must be able to act upon the incentive of the mind. You see, that is why people who are really going to do something important in this world are very single-minded. They are not constantly being swept away by all the pleasurable inducements around them. If they partake of these inducements, it is only to a limited degree because they need their resources. They cannot squander their time or energy on things not directly relevant to their central area of concentration. They must be physically and mentally able and to the degree to which they are, they are demonstrating health, for their minds and bodies are now able to serve their intention.

That is why we wish to recommend a very moderate program of development of physical health because this will enable your body to express more profound things. It will allow your mind to become more direct, more acute, more sensitive, more aware, more able to respond and so forth. Your mind will then become a sensitive instrument. Then, when there is something important happening, you will be able to respond. Your body, then, will not be a great weight upon you, a great burden.

This body is always an object of your concern: "I have to change it. I have to do this or that to it." What a waste of your time to always be working on a body. By the time you finally get it together, if you ever do, it will be time to give it up!

You are not here to work on a body. You are simply asked not to damage it so that you can accomplish something of importance here. Then when you leave this world, you will know you have accomplished your purpose successfully. Not only will you be successful as a result, but the others who are depending upon you and who need you to make your contribution here will be successful as well.

The fundamental understanding is the realization that you are already part of something that is established. The world does not demonstrate this, so you must know it within yourself. Knowing this, you realize you have a responsibility to a community that exists already. This responsibility is what will encourage and empower you to do great things in the world.

People do not do great things for personal interests. Personal interests are not strong enough to lead to great acts and important contributions or to lead people beyond ordinary things to the important things that can elevate your whole race.

People are very depressed because they do not have any vitality. They have no sense of purpose, no sense of being. They blame their bodies because their bodies are always hurting them, and they blame their environment because their environment is always obstructing them. But the problem is that they do not experience their own vitality. They are not experiencing life. They are bogged down within themselves and are not with life.

Being with life is so essential. It is why you have come here. Because when you are with life, you will know what to do in order to serve it and you will be able to receive its tremendous gifts as well. It is valuing something that is not temporary, and it is valuing the temporary for serving something that is not temporary. Your body is something temporary that serves something eternal. That is when you realize your responsibility to maintain it, to care for it and to use it properly.

It is difficult, I understand, to do this in your current society because your environment is always encouraging you to hurt your physical body, to misuse it and neglect it, as if doing so leads to greater enjoyment. Only your suffering must persuade you to the contrary. Abuse does not lead to enjoyment and does not increase your vitality.

Your vitality will make every day essential to you regardless of what is going on around you or how you feel. Whether you have a good day or a bad day, today is still very meaningful. Today is another opportunity to develop yourself and to contribute to your world. It is this sense of vitality that overrides all of the small objections that affect most people so much. You are not held back by little things when you are involved in something great.

One of the reasons war is created in this world is because it is far more exciting than peaceful living here. You notice when peaceful times exist, society starts to become degenerated and there is a big war. Everyone then gets a tremendous sense of temporary purpose and vitality. War is over with terrible destruction, people enjoy peace for a few years, and then there is a new war.

Everyone talks about peace on the planet, but you know, there are very few people who could stand it. There are very few people who could live in a world of peace. They are ill prepared. You have left a world of peace to come into this world. Peace is possible here, but you must prepare yourself for it. You cannot be living in conflict and hope to have a world of peace. The bullets will still fly and nations will still assault one another.

No one can tolerate peace for long because if your environment is peaceful, your anger begins to come forth. If your environment is not peaceful, you do not realize your own anger. If I took you and put you in a room with no stimulation at all, a very peaceful room with no aggravation, your own anger would come forth. You would realize that you are at war already. You are struggling against your own Knowledge. You are fighting with yourself. That is why there is not peace in the world. There is only peace to the extent that people can stand it. So, you will not have peace in the next decade. Why? Because people cannot stand it. If the world were without conflict, it would be like the little room with very little stimulation.

To the mind that is cultivated, the room without stimulation is a wonderful place. To the mind that is in conflict, the room without stimulation is a terrible place. To the mind that has been refined, the silence of the wilderness is a wonderful experience to be cherished. To the mind in conflict, it is an aggravation.

You have two things to accomplish, which are quite essential to your being here. You cannot neglect them, regardless of your beliefs or point of view. You must develop yourself, your inherent abilities, and you must contribute something vital to the world. Your own Being knows this, even if your thoughts do not. Your own Being will be aggravated until it can accomplish these two things, which together comprise your purpose.

We have spoken of the physical body, but that is only one aspect of health because if your mind is at war, it will not want a healthy body. Why? Because the body will be like the silent room and will be an aggravation. The silent room is very boring to the mind in conflict. It cannot stand it. Yet as you begin to value inner peace more and more, you will seek for quiet. You will want your body to be quiet. You will not want it constantly complaining. You will want the quiet room. You will want a peaceful world. Why? Because in the quietness you experience God, and all that is meaningful returns to you.

So, use the body as a room. It is either loud and clashing or it is quiet and empty. A quiet and empty room is a wonderful gift to the mind that appreciates it, a wonderful sanctuary. It functions in its capacity without complaint. Then, when it is time for you to leave this world, you will thank your body for being a gracious temporary dwelling.

To spend your life struggling with your body is really very wasteful. You will reflect upon this once you leave. I will give you this analogy: It is as if you wake up in the morning and you cannot decide what to put on. You spend the whole day going through your wardrobe and then it is nighttime, but you did not even go out at all and the day is gone. Put something on and go out!

People only love their bodies when they serve a higher purpose. To love your body for any other reason is simply to use it for selfish reasons, which will breed resentment. Your body must enable you to extend your sense of relationship in life. If it does not do this, it is a prison. It is holding you back and shutting you in. And the mind still feels trapped. It has this tremendous obligation now to make everyone like the body.

You see, we do not want the body to be a problem. We want it to be an asset. You know this already. You know that your body needs to function properly, and you know what you need to do. It is not for vanity's sake that you do this. It is simply that part of your vehicle in this world, which is your body, is slowing you down. Even the cripple can use the body effectively. Even the blind man can use the body effectively. That is not such a great liability. It is the use of the body that matters.

What this means in actuality is you must be very conscientious about what you eat. You must be conscientious about sexual engagements. You must be very conscientious about where you take your body and how you expose it to the environment. It will take less energy to maintain health than it does to damage your body. If your lifestyle is based upon neglect, then it is hard for you to realize how much energy you are putting into your neglect.

In the development of Knowledge, the mind is discovering its True Source and its True Self. As this proceeds, you become increasingly sensitive, even in your physical body, and you naturally steer yourself away from environments that are disruptive or that hinder your abilities. Likewise, you will become increasingly intolerant of foods that are counter-productive to your well-being.

You do not need to have very interesting beliefs about this. It is a natural process of change. You are now becoming pragmatic about your body. You simply want it to work properly, and that becomes the criteria for any changes you might make in your habits. You have to do this with very little agreement from your world because your world does not value these things.

You live in a society that is very tolerant, regardless of your complaints. Compared to the Greater Community, it is extremely lenient. This has its assets and its liabilities. Its assets are that your society fosters a freedom of expression and exploration that has produced great things. Its liability, however, is that its population is weak, self-indulgent and incapable of responding to change very effectively.

Any circumstance has possibilities and obstacles, so this is the environment we must work within. It is not an environment that fosters dedication particularly. It is an environment that gives freedom of discovery, though it does not foster the ability necessary to make your discovery effective.

The mental equivalent of developing health is that your mind becomes focused on its primary purpose. All of its conflicts with itself, its wants and its interests now begin to fall away because its predominant emphasis is taking over. You have something very important to do and other things don't matter so much.

What happens to you physically here is that you simply want your body to serve you. You do not want to serve it. It becomes a servant and not a master to you. Those of you who have not acquired a functioning level of health are servants to your body. It is governing and limiting you unnecessarily.

You see, health is natural. You do not need to be spectacular physically and run over mountains and swim across great distances. That is for acrobats and exhibitionists. You only need to be able to adequately complete each day without any obstruction from your physical body and to be able to live your span of life here in this world in health, longevity, and accomplishment.

It is a remarkable aspect of human evolution that grave circumstances are created to promote advancement. This is, in fact, a common feature of the physical universe. Has it not been curious to you that as your life becomes easier, you lose vitality? This is worth considering because if you honestly look at this without preference and without trying to justify things that you might want, it allows you to look and ask, "What is really important here? If I become well off and have comforts, will that produce greater vitality for me? I cannot have conflict all the time because that wears me down and that does not produce greater vitality." Vitality is health. That is what I am speaking of.

People want to have greater security in the world. Does that produce greater vitality? People want to fill their "want" list to make sure they get all the things that they are demanding from life. They are demanding a perfect relationship, a beautiful body and good employment. They are demanding that God show up whenever they want. Does that produce vitality? If you become a very wealthy person and your children grow up in wealth, does that produce vitality for them?

These are important questions because they allow you to look at life more objectively. "What produces the greatest vitality? Do I need to have war in order to give myself a temporary sense of purpose and determination? Do I have to let my physical health become so denigrated that I finally have conviction regarding its improvement? Do I have to let my relationships become so intolerable before I am willing to be responsible for what I know?"

Vitality is the issue. When I speak of health, I speak of vitality. You can have a beautiful body, run over mountains and have no vitality at all but be a dead person in a very handsome body. Or you can be an unspectacular looking person and be absolutely radiant. Why radiant? Because you are experiencing life. And you are radiant no matter what is going on because everything counts: the good things which are rewards and the bad things which are opportunities. If you make your life too easy, you will not apply yourself and will become depressed. So why make life so easy? Why not make life more vital? Easy is not better. The only value in ease is that it gives you the freedom to involve yourself in something that produces greater vitality.

We are at work all the time. We do not take days off and go out on holiday. You would be in trouble if we did! There is no separation between work and play because the work creates vitality. People consider work to be something that robs them of vitality and so they go rest, which does not give them much vitality either. They do not know what vitality is.

You do not have to have magical or mystical experiences or go to great heights or have beautiful visions or see angels dancing about to have vitality. That is not vitality. Vitality is tapping your own Knowledge and allowing it to express itself through you. It is tapping the Divine vibrant force within you and allowing it to express itself into life through your physical vehicle.

Let us now take a moment of quiet together. Let us for a moment allow our bodies to be the quiet room, the room without stimulation, in order that we may feel the content of life, the Presence of life that is God. Let this body that conceals you be your sanctuary of prayer, a holy place.

*Your freedom is
to discover
Knowledge.
That is why
you have come
into
this world.*

Seven

FREEDOM

WE WOULD LIKE TO SPEAK ABOUT FREEDOM, a very important subject and one that is given a great deal of attention in this society in particular. But we must speak about freedom now in a larger context and give some ideas that will be very thought provoking to you. Perhaps they will challenge some deeply held ideas and confirm some deeper inclinations as well.

There is a great deal of hysteria about freedom, personal freedom, especially in this country. Freedom is taken to very great lengths here. Indeed, freedom is a very important aspect of your pursuit in life. It is very confusing, though, because it has some adversities—some obvious and others perhaps that are never accounted for.

Those who have attained Wisdom in this world, and in other worlds as well, who have discovered the gift of Knowledge and cultivated it with their full intention, have come to certain basic realizations that are common everywhere, regardless of culture, environment, religion, language, and so forth. One of the things they have discovered uniformly is that the greater the Knowledge, the greater the power and the less the personal freedom. I shall repeat that: the greater the Knowledge, the greater the power and the less the personal freedom.

Of course, people here want both. They want greater power. They want to cultivate their Knowledge so that they can have more certainty and direction in life. And they want more personal freedom. Yet the Wise have discovered that when the true steps to the reclamation of Knowledge are underway, the desire for greater personal freedom is somehow affected or obstructed.

Another thing that the Wise have discovered is that freedom and purpose can be mutually exclusive, given people's normal definitions. Again, people want purpose because it offers direction, promise of a meaningful future and meaningful current engagements. They want greater personal freedom as well. Yet, when the opportunity to undertake the discovery of purpose is given to them in a recognizable form, they are afraid of what they might have to give up to pursue it. So, the issue of freedom becomes an issue of contention.

Freedom is often considered the ability to act and participate in whatever way you want without obstruction or hindrance from others. Of course, Inner Teachers are considered very threatening here because it always seems they are going to tell you all the things you cannot have. As much as you would like the contact because it is meaningful, there is a fear of loss of freedom; there is a fear that somehow you will be told what to do and not be able to make all the decisions yourself.

People don't really want to make many meaningful decisions, but they will not let anyone else make them, so the whole thing becomes very confused. Teachers are asked to provide everything of value and ask nothing in return. People want instant gratification, instant purpose, instant Knowledge and yet want to yield nothing.

So, let us explore this a little bit because there is really no contradiction between purpose and freedom if you perceive things correctly. What is freedom but the ability to reclaim your Knowledge, which is your destiny and your heritage? That is all that freedom is for.

Without Knowledge you are in bondage to your own thoughts, and you are in bondage to the forces in this world. Your personal freedom is useless and painful here. What has it given you? Trial and error is a very poor learning device. It is very slow and difficult and is necessary only to a point.

Your freedom now is the freedom to pursue Knowledge, which offers the only freedom there is because it recalls to you your Spiritual Family. It recalls to you your commitment for coming into the world. It recalls to you your destiny, and you begin to see your life as continuous, not just conceptually but really continuous. All of a sudden the world that was so difficult and intimidating does not have quite so much weight. It is not quite so terrifying now.

Here you realize that you are only free to participate in life. What is individual freedom if it does not lead to full participation in what life really is? In this country people are very covetous of their personal freedom, and yet what has it given them but greater isolation and frustration? They have lost the unity of the ancient tribal cultures where purpose was given to you, provided out of necessity. Now, no one cares who you are or what you do and you are free, to a point.

Yet, your remarkable society is so important because it gives you the greatest opportunity to discover your Knowledge and express it with a minimum of hindrance. It is an unprecedented achievement that you have this great freedom, but how many people can use it properly and receive its great benefit?

Your only real freedom is the freedom to live your purpose. Freedom without purpose is chaos. It is living aimlessly without direction, with only your fears for survival, your wants and your desires to motivate you. It is a very desperate situation. And so, people seek bondage. How many people here have sought bondage in personal relationships? "I would rather be in a relationship that is painful without promise than to be free once again, for my freedom is a more terrible burden."

Personal freedom, if it is coveted too much, keeps people from being able to give themselves. In fact, it is thought that if you give yourself to something, you are losing something of tremendous value. "Do not give yourself to anything completely! Don't let anything use you up! Save yourself!" And yet, the only people who achieve harmony and empowerment are those who give themselves completely, with nothing behind them to save for themselves. But personal freedom says, "No. Do not be conned. Do not give yourself away. Do not give up your personal empowerment. You must be in charge of everything in your life." This becomes the reason not to be in relationship completely. So, in marriage you try to be together, but not completely. You try to give, but only to a point. You want to protect your private incentives, and yet they are painful to you because you cannot seem to engage completely with the other person.

You see, your freedom is to discover Knowledge. That is why you have come into this world. You have come from an easier place to a more difficult place to achieve something. If you were sent to a place that was in a great deal of trouble, you would not go there for a vacation. You would go there to work. If a forest fire were raging north of the city, you would not go there with a camper and swimsuit. You would go there with a shovel to get something done. And if you went there and you didn't know what to do, you would feel a great loss. "I'm here. I made it. But I don't know what to do!" There is no amount of comfort you can give to yourself to appease that need to contribute.

Knowledge resolves the issue of freedom naturally because it engages you completely in life and gives you the freedom to do this. It is the freedom of complete relinquishment to life that is real freedom, for life is the only thing that is free. You alone cannot be free, for you will spend your life fighting off relationships and yearning for them all at the same time. You will brush them away and pull them in and push them away, and you will go from person to person desperately.

Personal relationships are very coveted because it is believed that they will give greater personal freedom. "I will be happy if I have someone to share my personal freedom with." But it is very difficult to share personal freedom because the other person always wants to take some of it away, and you have to make compromises to be in relationship. If you are married, you cannot be free to go out and be in relationship with anyone you want. That freedom is sacrificed. And yet, if you are not married, you may want to be in union with someone meaningfully.

So, when the Wise say, "The greater the power, the less the freedom," that is one aspect of this insight. The other aspect is that as you engage with Knowledge, even as you approach it, you will lose interest in most things that are not related to it. You will not want to run around so much. You will be drawn increasingly inward, as if a great attraction were pulling you to the very center of yourself. Now you will not want so much stimulation. In fact, you will begin to value quiet and peacefulness more and more and value noise and aggravation less and less. You will be less concerned with your former ambitions and more concerned with things of more central importance to you. To your friends you will seem less free. "Let's go out dancing!" And you say, "I can't. It just doesn't feel right." And they look at you and they say, "What's wrong with you? You used to go dancing all the time and now you're a dud! You're no fun anymore!" This is natural. People in life who are meaningfully engaged are not bogged down in their own personal problems. They do not have time. They are needed too much. Therefore, the Wise say, "The greater the power, the less the freedom."

You will neither want to nor be able to pursue everything at will or on impulse. You will live a much more uniform and, in some ways, isolated life. Your discernment in relationship will grow tremendously because the criteria for a relationship will be whether it encourages Knowledge or not. Other attractions begin to be recognized as very temporary and dangerous if pursued wholeheartedly. This, too, is natural.

The man or woman of Knowledge never has to be concerned about having a relationship because people will want to be with them all the time. Their problem is discernment because a person of Knowledge is going somewhere, surrounded by people who are standing and waiting. Anyone who is truly moving will draw others. That is why the very Wise are often secluded in life because if they go out in public, everyone makes a big fuss—not because they are particularly brilliant or beautiful, but simply because their life is totally involved, and it is that involvement that brings such a strong reaction.

Therefore, in the pursuit of Knowledge you will value freedom in order to pursue Knowledge. Here you will thank your parents, you will thank your society and you will thank your painful experiences of the past for bringing you to value this freedom and for showing you that other freedoms lead nowhere. They are empty.

At some point, perhaps, you will welcome your Inner Teachers because you need their assistance, and you are not concerned about what you will lose. You are concerned about what you must receive. People who are terrified of losing are afraid to receive. The cost is always too great for them. If you are to be fully engaged in life individually and as a society, it will cost everything you have. You will end your life completely used up like a great vessel that has been emptied. It is that complete utilization that will fulfill you in this world and will make it unnecessary for you to return. You have given everything you have brought with you. You are completely used up. You are not ravaged or exhausted. You are satisfied.

So, do not be concerned about the cost. The cost is everything that you see for everything that you cannot see, and what you see is such a small portion of life and what you cannot see is so great. You cannot see where you have come from or where you are going. You cannot see your Teachers. You cannot see, except in rare circumstances, your Spiritual Family. You have descended into the visible world to get something done and to learn to discern what is of value and what is not, what has permanent meaning and what is a temporary stimulation only.

When you value the permanent, then you can enjoy the temporary because it is no longer a restraint or a curse. It is a temporary pleasure. You eat the cookie and you say, "Good cookie." You do not look at the cookie and say, "You are my master. I cannot not eat you." You do not look at the body and say, "You are my prison. I have to care for you night and day. You never grow up. You are like a child forever, and you will hurt me every day of my life." You look at the body and say, "You are my vehicle and I will use you to the fullest. I will wear you out through full utilization and I will not abuse you, for you are my gift. You are my microphone, and through you I can touch another in the way that is most meaningful here."

So, when the Wise say, "The greater the power, the less the freedom," they also mean that the more power you have, the more responsibility is placed upon your shoulders and the greater the risk. That is why the Wise are not running about going to every new movie and seeking every new sensation. They have too much responsibility. Those of you who are parents realize the responsibility and the cost, and yet your children give you something you never would have gotten otherwise.

There will be plenty of time to rest when you leave this world. Then you go on vacation, all dirty from fighting the forest fires and so glad to have a rest. People do not know this because Knowledge has not arisen sufficiently to offset their grave fears. Indeed, as Knowledge becomes potent within you, you will be anxious to leave this world. You will be anxious to complete your task. You will be grateful for every opportunity to do so, and you will leave gratefully, saying "Thank you very much!"

Why is it important to hear someone like me? Because I represent your life beyond the world. If you recall that, even incrementally, it will dissolve your fear because you will know that you are not isolated and alone in this world. You will know that your stay here is temporary and that not quite as much is expected of you as you had thought. You do not have to be God in your universe. You do not have a universe. You are in the universe. You do not have to quest for personal power because you have real power.

What is personal power? It is power over something that is tempo-rary. You spend your whole life having personal power, and then you give up the personal. Everything you have strived for then falls away. You leave the world empty-handed and you say, "What happened to my personal power?" Well, it was left back there with your personal side. It got dis-carded with your garments. When the King and the Queen leave the world, their crowns and jewels and sepulchers are left behind. When you leave the world, your achievements are left behind except for one thing—your Knowledge. That is life within you, and that will be life within you when you leave this world as it is now.

When people become students involved in The Way of Knowledge, there are many issues which arise regarding freedom. There is a great deal of concern over who is in charge. "Am I in charge or am I simply follow-ing orders? Do I have any say about what happens to me? Am I being manipulated or used?"

These are very serious questions, though Knowledge solves them instantly. To give up your personal freedom is to reclaim God and all your real power. Your personal freedom is driving you crazy.

What do we have to offer you? We offer a reminder and assistance to reclaim your Knowledge. That is empowerment for you, but it is an empowerment that changes you a little bit, you see, because before you were only partially yourself. Now you are becoming completely yourself, and it is strange how you feel differently about everything. You feel more like yourself in those wonderful moments when there is no future or past and you are not concerned for yourself. You are concerned for the world, and you are perceiving the world and not yourself.

Personal freedom is valuable only in that it gives you this opportunity to find Knowledge. It is an exchange, you see. It is giving up a certain amount of the domination you maintain over your life in order to receive a greater Wisdom. The child must give up childhood to enter adolescence. It is relinquishment and receiving all at once. If you do not give up childishness in childhood, you will keep it and not receive the next gift. Receiving Knowledge is even more natural than this.

We value freedom very highly because freedom is what Knowledge is. It is not the freedom to get things. You know, everyone has his or her list. People are going through life, and they are determined to get a relationship, a job, a car and all the other stuff. And, of course, if they get them, it is hard to keep them because the relationships are always falling apart and need all kinds of work. Cars get old and you must get a new one. These things are not bad, but they come naturally when you are pursuing something far more essential to yourself and to everyone.

There is not a person in the world who does not have Knowledge. The differences, then, are the differences in the level of development, attunement and realization. The only common ingredient to everyone is Knowledge. At that level, there is no disagreement. So, if you want to be in total agreement with life, then your personal side must be transparent enough so that it does not obstruct your attention. Then you can begin to perceive life moving through yourself and others. You can see the movement of things. You can recognize those who are wise and look upon those who are ignorant with compassion. There is no blame now. There is patience. There is patience of such magnitude!

Imagine for a moment that you were your own Teacher and you were high above yourself personally, watching this person go through life. Imagine the patience you must have. All these little things you plant here and there, and maybe the person will come over here and see this. They miss ninety percent of what you plant and of the ten percent they don't miss, usually they misinterpret the whole thing anyway! So, you are always plotting to bring them to themselves, and they are always plotting to get farther away. It takes great patience, but the result is worth the effort.

The only thing that matters in this world is Knowledge. Knowledge is not ideas or philosophy. It is profound experience. It is universal and timeless, and it is valid for all dimensions. But it is scary. You have to give up the freedom you are used to, which is the privilege to be chaotic, for the freedom to be uniform and to have direction. When you have direction, your choices are limited. Indeed, as Knowledge becomes stronger, after awhile there is no choice. That is freedom. Freedom is a state of no-choice. Now you are dealing with what is unequivocal and absolutely vital; you are not dealing with casual choices. Life is vital every moment. If you are entertaining choices, you can be certain you have not arrived at Knowledge in that situation.

The compelling force of Knowledge is so strong that it overrides anything that the world can set in its way. This level of commitment is the greatest demonstration of God. It is powerful, unending and compassionate. It has vitality. It is driven from something beyond this world. It is an uncommon, relentless force. It does not care about costs and obstacles; it cares about practical functioning. People with Knowledge will be uncommon and potent. They will not be alone, unless by choice.

So, the Wise say choice is something to be escaped, and yet choice is so valued in this world. "I must have choice in everything. The government cannot tell me what to do. My wife cannot tell me. My friend cannot tell me. My body cannot tell me. The weather cannot tell me. I must be at choice. It is *my* choice!" Like a little child. "Mine!" It does not matter if it is good for you or not. It matters if it is "mine!"

But you see, as Knowledge emerges, everything begins to fall into place. There are not so many choices. You feel a very strong attraction to another person, the kind that sort of sweeps you away, and instead of saying, "Oh, how wonderful! Attraction!" and being swept away and then finding out later if there is any relationship there, you stop and you see if this is Knowledge or not. You are able to check yourself. This keeps you returning to what is vital to your own fulfillment and to your own contribution to others.

Then you ask, "Where do I give myself totally?" You look about and there is not much that is very inspiring to give yourself to, so you must give yourself to your preparation. You must see what the world is asking of you because now you see your life is not this desperate attempt to acquire things in a brief period of time. It is a place where you come to contribute and to receive.

Why is the world such a tough place? There is a great deal of emphasis now to make the world a place that is not tough at all. But do you see the contradiction in this? There is a contradiction. The question is not whether life is difficult or easy. The question is whether it is vital. There are people who have very easy lives and they are dead inside. Their vitality escaped them long ago. All they can hope for now is a buffering against their death and some kind of continued pleasurable stimulation.

Sometimes when life is difficult, your vitality shows through. If you make life too easy, you will be asleep—comfortable and at ease. Nothing asked, nothing vital. You will work your whole life, earn lots of money and your children will grow up with nothing vital at all. This is so evident. You can see it all about you.

Life is not passive. It is a vital and powerful force, a serious and complete engagement, not a casual engagement. There is nothing casual about life. Whether it is quiet or active, it is extremely involved.

Things happen out of necessity, not out of want. The clouds do not come by because they want to. They are pulled here. They have to come and they come. They do not rain because it is fun. They rain because they must rain. You come to the world to give because you must give. That is your nature. If you do not give, you will be unhappy and blame everybody for it, even yourself, but you will not be happy.

You must prepare yourself to give. Knowledge is a responsibility. You must be a person capable of bearing it. You cannot be like a child and assume the responsibility. You must prepare. Life will do this for you, and you must do it on your own accord. If you wish to uncover the mystery of your existence here, then you must give it great attention. Perhaps you will not be quite as personally free if you do that, but it is okay because this is more important.

I will tell you a little story now about the history of another world. In this world, the wisest have very little personal freedom. In fact, they don't run around at all. They don't take vacations. They don't need to. The ones who have the least insight have the greatest freedom. They can do all kinds of things within certain guidelines. They do not need to discriminate between what they think and what they say. Yet, those who are wise must discriminate every second, but they have the power and the incentive to do this because every second is complete for them. They have attained a state in which they can do very little except what is absolutely essential to them. And this they do with extraordinary ability. In fact, it is so extraordinary in contrast to your world and your society that your people would seem incredibly lazy and idle in comparison. But you are not this race, and they have a different nature from you. Yet, Knowledge is the same in all worlds. It is the common factor in all intelligent life.

It is not so different in other worlds. Just because they have new machinery does not mean that the nature of things is that different. Why is this important for you to know? Because what is out there is your future as a race. You are looking at your future. It is this you are racing towards in your technology. It is this that you are preparing for emotionally. It is this that is changing every aspect of your life. It is this that is destroying tribal societies at a rapid rate. It is this that is forcing your world to become unified.

The difference between the Wise and the unwise will still be the same. Though you may have much more information than your ancestors and though you may have wonderful gadgets and wonderful machinery, you will still be faced with your Knowledge, either discovered or undiscovered. Believe me, there are not many Wise in the physical universe, regardless of culture. Do you know why that is? It is because the Wise must hide. They must hide because their gifts are meant for certain individuals only, and they must hide to maintain their freedom to give.

Your Knowledge at this period in time has a specific task to accomplish because when you enter the world from your Spiritual Family, you enter in a period of history, and your contribution is geared to that period in history. How could it be otherwise? When you have a task to do, it must be relevant to the times in which you arrive. You cannot go to the forest fire with a stone ax. You must go with a fire engine because a fire engine is what is needed.

People in this society have great freedom and great luxury, but there is very little duty, and people are very lonely for it. It is not natural to be so separated. People hate duty here. They think it is a tremendous loss of freedom, but duty in its real essence represents meaningful engagement, not obligation. Where else would I be but here? I could go anyplace and I would still have to be here, so choice is rather meaningless for me. The endless choosing, the endless debate—I am free from that now. That is freedom. The endless deliberation, "What do I want?" The endless deliberation. I do not have to concern myself with that, you see, because Knowledge has overtaken me.

Freedom is the great reason people will not accept God, and yet God gives you freedom and power of such magnitude that you could not give it to yourself meaningfully. God gives you responsibility so that you may reclaim your power and value yourself. You cannot come closer to God unless you have this value. You cannot be a little crumb and go to God! God does not know you as a little crumb. God knows you as a magnificent creation. You cannot go to God all self-inflated with a big name tag saying, "I am a magnificent creation!" and be a little crumb inside, either. You must go to God as God made you, not as you made yourself.

This is why God pulls you from beneath your awareness—the great vacuum pulling everything back to God! That is why there are Spiritual Families. That is why there are teachers and students at all levels. I have Teachers, too, you know. They pull me. I pull you. You pull someone else. That is the great tug. That is how everything is being drawn back to your Homeland. And to the extent that Knowledge has been activated in you, you will naturally contribute it. How could you do otherwise?

*This preparation
will engage you
meaningfully
in every moment
while preparing you
for the future.*

Eight

PREPARING FOR THE FUTURE

THE FUTURE IS VERY TANTALIZING, you know. People want to know a great deal about it, but at the same time they do not want to know about it, either. They want to make sure that everything they have will be guaranteed to them and that more will be given in a future that is to their liking, as if you can secure a guarantee.

Your future draws you away from the present. If the present seems secure, there is no guarantee the future will be, so you must secure the future to assure the present. This, of course, leads to tremendous unhappiness since the present is never secure because the future is never secure. You hope that someone like me can provide a guarantee of the future so that you can have more peace of mind in the moment. But, of course, I will not provide you that guarantee. What I will provide, however, is an invitation to learn to be able to provide for the future and to respond to the present. This is true preparation. *steps to Knowledge*

Having certainty about future events is always illusory because you cannot have complete certainty about the future. Even if your Knowledge indicates a future event, it will not be exactly like that when the event occurs. Any precognitive experience you might have of the future will only be a part of what will actually occur.

The future is being created right now. It is being formed. How can you prepare for something that does not exist? How can you secure that which is not yet manifest? Life is always preparing for the future. You cannot take the other position and say, "There is no future. I shall live completely in the moment, without concern." This seems like a tremendous relief from the terrible anxiety that hangs over you. If the moment is absolutely adequate and there is no future to be concerned with, true happiness does seem to be possible.

This is very tantalizing, but it is not complete for some very important reasons. The present is the preparation for the future and you, whether you accept the responsibility for this preparation or not, are in preparation for the future as well. This time will lead to the next time and will prepare it. So, it is a matter of whether you want to be responsible for preparing for the future or not. If you are irresponsible, the future will terrify you because it will overwhelm you, shock you and deprive you, and you will not be prepared for it.

If you are without preference of any kind and have no desire whatsoever, it is theoretically possible that you could enjoy the moment regardless of what happens. But, of course, this is not the case with human beings because the process of life is a preparation. Your being in this world is for preparation. You are not here simply to be here for the moment only. You are here for a purpose, and your purpose is preparation.

So, you cannot escape the future, but you need not dwell upon it fearfully either. The only way you can live in the moment successfully is to live in Knowledge, for Knowledge is completely in the moment and is completely preparing for the future all at the same time. It accounts for the past, the present and the future. It lives only in the present, yet it paves the way for the future and guides you forward.

You cannot prepare for the future by securing it or making it predictable. It will never be predictable and if you attempt to make it so, your life will become very dull and empty. Your need for comfort and your desire for reprieve against your own fear cannot be accomplished by eliminating all possible change from your life.

Your greatest concern is that you will not accomplish what you came here to do. If you truly examined your mind and undertook the reclamation of Knowledge, you would realize that this is your greatest concern. There is nothing the world could do to you that would be a greater concern because you are only here for a little bit of time, and whatever the world could do to you would only be for brief moments in your great span of life. But not fulfilling your destiny here leads to disappointment and requires your return. This is more uncomfortable in the long term.

Once Knowledge has been recognized within your own life, you will see that your drive and your desire to fulfill it are stronger than anything else. Eventually, this will overcome your need for safety and security, your need to have a predictable future and your need to have all the things that you feel are absolutely vital for your happiness. There will only be this desire to express and complete your purpose. That is when your life will be uniform and when you will have true power. Then the future cannot threaten you because you will express and complete your purpose regardless of what happens. Each new situation simply gives a new opportunity to fulfill your purpose. It is not seen as a possible loss. It is seen as a possible opportunity. If times get worse, that does not diminish your opportunity. If times get better, that does not diminish your opportunity. Doors may close. Others may open. You are intent on doing something, and you will use whatever your circumstances may be to accomplish that.

If your purpose has not been discovered, then survival is your main concern, and out of fearfulness you will attempt to secure a future that is predictable and prepare yourself for it. This will destroy your experience of the present and lead you into some very erratic and compulsive behavior. It will make you profoundly unhappy with very little relief, for here the future will always elude you and disappoint you in certain ways.

So, I will not guarantee your future. I cannot. How can I? If I tell you anything about your future, it is but one facet of your future, and it is possible it may not occur given your own decisions in the interim. So, what is the value of making predictions? Occasionally, predictions are very important to incite responsibility and constructive action in people. If there is something important or difficult that is about to happen and people need to know about it, a prediction is quite essential, but this is fairly rare.

Your role here is not simply to prepare for disaster or to find a safer, more secure hiding place so that the storms of this world will not overtake you. You have not come all the way here to hide out. You do not want to hide out. You will even destroy your own security if it becomes too overbearing. Why do people destroy all that they have created that makes them so secure? Because it is imprisoning them, and they cannot stand it anymore. They would rather start all over again. So, if your own stability begins to eliminate your possibility for progress, you will destroy it. You will destroy your financial state, your health, your relationships—whatever seems to be infringing upon you.

This is not for freedom's sake, for freedom without purpose is quite meaningless. What is the value of freedom if there is no purpose? It is only license to be chaotic. But the true meaning of freedom is so that true purpose may continue to be discovered and expressed. To have this freedom, you must learn to live in Knowledge and to use Knowledge. If you do not use Knowledge, you will only have your thoughts to guide you, and they are remarkably chaotic. They are so temporary, sporadic and conflicted that they make a very poor guide for you.

Therefore, you must learn how to prepare for the future since you are preparing anyway, like it or not. That is the great thing about life. It is the way it is. Your perspective only enables you to become engaged more effectively. It does not change your true circumstances.

This gets very confusing for advancing students of Knowledge because they thought they were here to make the world a perfect place or at least a better place, but now they are not so sure. If you follow Knowledge, it does not always seem to lead in this direction. It does not always meet your criteria for improvement for yourself or for others. You find out that much of your desire for self-improvement is simply to have a better appearance, to look better to yourself and to others. "Look at me. I am doing well."

When you follow Knowledge, it does not have this emphasis, yet it breathes life into you increasingly until you are filled with life. Then you are no longer a person estranged by ideas. You are now a person who is filled with life. Your ideas are secondary. You will have them because you have a mind that thinks, but it is the Spiritual Presence around you and with you that will influence people.

So, how do you prepare for this future? It is quite obvious that you are living in a time of unprecedented change. You yourself are undergoing unprecedented change, which is quite related to the times in which you live. You prepare for the future by being able to respond to it. Knowledge will indicate what things you must develop and how you must prepare for your own specific role. Some of you will need to go into the future with no money at all. Others will need to go into the future with a great deal. Given a human value system, this seems very inconsistent, yet it is related to what you are meant to do. Some people will never undertake their purpose if their hands are full of money. Others will never undertake their purpose if their hands are empty. Who can say? Who can determine what will give each person the best opportunity?

If you give people lots of money, you know, they fall apart. If you take money away from people, they fall apart. There is no social ethic or moral philosophy that can account for the evolution of life. Life is not about these things, yet it can be profoundly experienced. In fact, it is the only thing that can be profoundly experienced. Can you profoundly experience an idea? If you experience an idea profoundly, there is no more idea. You have evaporated it because ideas are not experience, though they may lead to experience.

Your preparation is to be able to respond to the future and to what the preparation is at this moment. You have been given the blueprint for your own development. It is within you. You cannot cultivate it alone because a major part of your advancement is realizing you are not alone and that you are part of a Greater Community.

You cannot say, "Give me the blueprint and I will carry it out," because, you see, you only have part of the blueprint. Your Teachers have part of the blueprint. People in your life have part of the blueprint. People you have not even met yet have part of the blueprint. Therefore, do not be idealistic and say, "Tell me the plan and I will go forward. Tell me who I will be and I will prepare now."

If I told people what they would be, from their current standpoint it would look either impossible or personally not preferred. Sometimes I tell people what they want to be so they can realize that it is not what they want to be. Sometimes I tell people what they want to be so that they will finally support themselves and take responsibility for what they know and move forward aggressively.

Therefore, how are you to be able to respond? Being response-able is a very good concept. If you are fixed in your viewpoint about who you are, what life must be, how everything must happen, who God is and what God is doing here, then obviously you can only respond to your fixed position, and you will insist that the world support your fixed position, which, of course, it does not.

You are not working with life then. You are trying to direct life to fortify your own identity. Your real identity is quite safe. It is established by God and does not need you to invent it, uphold it and make the world agree it is true. Yet, the identity that God created is hidden and must be discovered. As it is discovered, it will dissolve all other identities within you. Your identity will be experienced by carrying out your purpose because identity is life in action. It is experiencing yourself living a life that is vital, essential and real. It is observing the results of your actions and the relationships that are developed as a result, for who God created in you is not an individual; it is part of a greater fabric.

So, you can look at yourself alone and say, "Who am I? I must be something very mysterious because I know I am not merely a body. I am not merely my ideas. I am not merely my name and history. I know I continue after death. I know I have been somewhere before coming here." These ideas, of course, are obvious to anyone who is open to them. But who is this individual? You see, your purpose reveals your self in its relationship to others. You did not come here just to grow up. You came here to get something done. This world is in a lot of trouble. It is created that way so that people who need to get something done can do it!

Why doesn't the world become a perfect place when people are so intelligent and so loving in their true nature? Why isn't the world the way it is supposed to be? Because it is an environment where people who have not accepted the responsibility for service can have an opportunity to do so. If there were no improvements to be made here, you would be quite lost because your stage in life is to contribute. If you think your life is just for your own growth, you will become self-absorbed and miss the whole point. We wish to take you out of being self-absorbed so that you can be engaged with life. That will produce all the growth you can handle and will rekindle relationship, a sense of belonging and a sense of place that are so fundamental.

People say, "I want relationship and I want career and I want the promise of longevity and I want all these things as soon as possible." Well, there are people who have all these things, you know, and they are not doing much better than you are. That is evident. People who are not in relationship do not want to hang out with people who are because they do not want to see that what they want is probably not sufficient to their need. They want to be a have-not and envy those who have. And so, they go to movies and watch people in relationship falling in love, but they do not want to go into households with lots of kids and see what marriage is really like.

Relationship is very important, of course, but even it is not the primary thing. If you go into the future wanting relationship so desperately— "Just give me a relationship. That's all I want!"—you are at great risk of disappointment. You are not coming from Knowledge now.

When you are with Knowledge, you will understand the future because the future is to bring forth your Knowledge. Times may get worse. That is okay. It brings forth Knowledge. Times may get better. That is okay. It brings forth Knowledge.

You work diligently to improve the quality of life here, but it is more mysterious than simply making everything look better, making all people look better and making all pain seem to go away. People did not come here to be painless. That is like going to the ocean and refusing to get wet. If you wish to get involved, you must accept some degree of discomfort. There are painful circumstances here. You will have little aches and pains even if you live an immaculate life. Yet when you are living with Knowledge, these irritations are not sufficient to overcome your awareness. They are simply seen as indigenous to this environment, not big pains but little pains. You have already given up the big pains to enter the life of Knowledge, for what is a big pain but living without Knowledge?

Therefore, do not go into the future with your list of demands because you will be very frightened that you may be disappointed, and that fear will haunt you. And as you get older and you see that certain things have not been fulfilled, you will be extremely anxious for yourself and ill prepared to deal with what the future holds. The future holds promise, but if you have your demand list, you will not see the promise.

How do you prepare to be able to respond? By developing Knowledge in the moment now. There is so much for you to do with Knowledge right now! It does not mean that you know who you are or what you will be twenty years from now or that the future is secure or that your identity is fully established or that you will have all the things that you have ever wanted.

What it does mean is that your life is being revitalized. Knowledge is breathing life back into you. You have become forlorn, and as life is breathed back into you, you do not have to worry about direction because you are moving now. You are not standing at the sidelines asking, "Who am I? What am I? Why am I here? Where am I going?" You are just going and now that you are going, you realize you have a sense of direction. You cannot experience direction if you are standing still. When you are moving, you are moving in a certain direction. That is how direction is discerned.

When you begin preparing in *Steps to Knowledge*, we want to get you moving. We do not want you sitting around, looking at your ideas and saying, "Where is the truth now?" We want to get you moving because when you have traveled a little bit, then you will be able to discern your direction. "I was back there. Now I am here. This is my direction." You must be moving to experience purpose. You cannot be stagnant.

Therefore, I don't say, "Don't worry about the future." If you are not with Knowledge, all you can do with the future is worry about it! I don't say, "Escape into the moment. There is no future," because this is merely irresponsible. I say, "Develop Knowledge now. Use it effectively now and realize you are here for a purpose, even if it is ill defined."

You see, you will not have a full understanding of your purpose until your life is over. Then you will look back and say, "This is what actually happened." You may have a very consistent and substantiated idea of purpose, but it will not be complete until you are at the end of your journey here looking back and saying, "Yes, now I understand my purpose." Why do you understand it then? Because it has brought you to the juncture between this life and your Spiritual Family that awaits you beyond this life. You cannot have a full sense of purpose while you are in the world because this is only half the picture. The other half is on the other side of the veil.

Therefore, do not spend your life seeking for definitions. To understand half the story of your purpose is to be a person of remarkable Wisdom. To accept the limits of awareness here enables you to have

Knowledge in the world. Now you are in a position to contribute because your demands are not so great. You are not saying to life, "Give me a complete definition of who I am. Give me complete satisfaction. Give me complete fulfillment. Give me. Give me. Give me!" You are not standing at the side of the road complaining. You are actually moving now and you can contribute. This is how you realize your gifts. That is why we want to get everyone moving in a meaningful way. With movement comes vitality and a sense of direction.

There is a great deal of emphasis now on revitalizing the past, understanding everything that happened in childhood and going back into past incarnations and experiencing yourself as a King of England. (There are so many people who have experienced themselves as the King of England that it is remarkable!)

There are times when your past lives must be re-experienced, but you do not need to seek them out. They simply arise. There is a wave of emotion and then it is gone. It is the emotion that needs to be released. It does not matter what you did before. It is over. Likewise, only in rare cases do people need to resurrect their early years so that they can release their emotion so that they may come back into present time.

All you have at any moment in this life is your Knowledge, discovered or undiscovered, used or unused. Therefore, you must look to the moment no matter what your difficulties or obstructions. Take stock of what you are doing that is essential, vital and real and what is not, where you are using Knowledge and where you are not. This kind of life inventory is essential because you have finally arrived at a beginning place. Before this, you were merely trying to convince yourself that you were better off or worse off than you were before. Now there is no need to convince yourself because you are looking.

This is preparation for the future because the future will confront you with things, and you must be available. If you are self-absorbed, how can you be available when events occur?

"What if there is another earthquake?" Many people want to know. "When is it going to happen?" Well, what difference does it make? The only important thing is how will you be prepared for it. You could say, "Well, an earthquake is coming to this town. I am going to move to the next town." So, you pack up everything, move to the next town and get killed in an automobile accident as soon as you enter the new town! No earthquakes there, but you get wiped out. So much for safety.

It is pointless to try to be safe. It is hopeless. Life will get you sooner or later. Being safe as a main emphasis makes you far more vulnerable because you are far less able to deal with change and circumstances. You do not meet them; you avoid them, and so they overtake you. If you are running from life, it will seem to overtake you. If you are running to life, it will embrace you. Then you will be vital in your time in history, and you will leave this world with your accomplishments made.

It is this ability to prepare that is your genius because this will engage you meaningfully in every moment while preparing you for the future. Therefore, do not worry about future events. Be current with yourself now and do whatever your Knowledge indicates. That is preparation. It is living in the moment in a vital way and preparing for the future in a meaningful way. Then there is a present and a future all together. You have a sense of destiny which indicates a future. You have a sense of purpose which indicates a future. Do not be without a future, or you will simply be lying to yourself. You will have one, like it or not. The future is coming!

As for relationship, you cannot guarantee yourself partnership, but if your life is meaningful and vital and you are really engaged, how can there not be relationship in your life? When you are vital in life, you will attract people by your vitality and your direction. When you are moving, people see you and respond to you. You have to respond to someone who is moving because they have power. When you cease moving, you cease having power and you become like an invisible person.

This requires great faith, of course. You cannot experience Knowledge at every moment. It will be intermittent, but even in an intermittent phase it will be substantial. Here you must have faith and abide by it. If Knowledge last indicated that you must do something, then continue to do it until Knowledge indicates otherwise. You do not have to go back every five minutes and say, "Well, let us re-evaluate the situation. Am I still supposed to be doing this?" When you do that, you start to stop. Living with Knowledge will take you from juncture to juncture, bringing forth all your best abilities and minimizing all your difficult or negative acquisitions. It is Knowledge that we always advocate. It is mysterious and profound, yet it is absolutely essential.

We have spoken before of events to come, the nature of the time and era that you live in and the kind of preparation that is required. You live at a time when the world is being forced to unify itself, not because this is its moral prerogative but because you are emerging into the Greater Community of Worlds. You are venturing into space, and your neighbors from beyond are venturing into your realm increasingly. This is the larger picture.

Your Knowledge will account for this, but your personal wishes may not. If you are still having your demands that life give you all these specific things, how can you attend to these greater forces? How can you see the movement of things within a larger context? You only see them in terms of whether they give you a greater promise or a greater liability in fulfilling your wishes.

That is why it is so easy to misinterpret current events because you see them from such a limited perspective. You are very afraid that changes in your economy or your politics may limit your freedoms and your acquisitions. Yet these forces will continue. If you are to successfully move with them and serve them, you cannot be fighting against them. You cannot be fighting those things you are meant to serve.

You see, knowing that the world is emerging into the Greater Community gives you such a greater perspective on events that it allows you to be compassionate with people. It gives you a perspective that is very essential. We say these things because it helps people prepare for the future. Now they can begin to escape their own personal viewpoint that confines their perspective and begin to see things in a larger way.

When it is essential for you to have new information that is crucial to your future, this will come to you through Knowledge. You will end up in places not exactly knowing why. Perhaps you have reasons, but that is not important. What is important is there is something there for you. And tomorrow, if there is something you need that will help prepare you, you will go there. The more that you can respond to this natural inner guidance, the more your life will be vital and meaningful. And you will be very excited—not because everything is wonderful, but because you know you are here to serve a purpose.

God
does not have to
figure out
your dilemma.
God
just attracts you
&
your dilemma
falls apart.

Nine

SPIRITUAL TRUTHS

NOW WE WOULD LIKE TO SPEAK ABOUT Spiritual Truths. There is much presumption and misunderstanding about very basic things, which makes the direct approach to Knowledge seem more complicated than it needs to be. We talk about the development of Knowledge, relationships and world events in a very direct manner, but people are still very confused because they have assumed that spiritual life, spiritual teachers, spiritual teaching and spiritual ideas must have a certain conformity. Therefore, it is appropriate to talk about Spiritual Truths.

First, it is very important that you realize that there is no absolute truth in physical life. This is very important to understand because absolute truth is reserved for an absolute state of being and physical life, obviously, is not that. So, instead we have relative truth, relative to this state of being.

God is functioning here in a relative reality. It is relative here because it is changing. An absolute reality is an unchanging reality. It is a steady state and completely at peace because it is not going anywhere. You are not in that reality, nor do you even seek it for the most part here because that is not your need. You are not ready for absolute reality. It is not your step in life. You must first accomplish your task here in this relative reality.

When people start to think that God has an absolute truth for their relative reality, this begins a form of tyranny that is very dangerous and difficult to overcome. Religious tyranny, political tyranny and personal tyranny are evident within people and within societies at large. Attempting to apply an absolute truth to a relative situation produces bondage and slavery and is completely counter productive. Its initial intent may have been well-meaning, but soon it produces violence and attack.

The challenge for each and every one of you is to accept that you are in a stage of development and to try to not rest your sense of identity upon absolutes. You must be open and yet very firm about what you know already. This firmness and openness is the achievement. What has been discovered thus far that you *know* to be irrevocably true? This you must hold to with great reverence. Yet, it is more a Spiritual Presence than an idea, a deep sense of relationship and direction in life rather than a series of beliefs or postulates.

You cannot approach an absolute God in a relative reality. It does not work because that is not where you are. It is one in ten million people who are prepared for an absolute encounter. This is not the need of humanity. God is not reserved for the one in ten million. God's Plan includes all and guarantees fulfillment and advancement in this reality that you live in.

The next stage of life beyond the physical realm will be a relative reality as well, but it will be absolute to your needs because relative truth is absolute to your needs. So, do not think it is not meaningful or effective. It is tremendously effective. It is more powerful than anything you can see or imagine and it is moving. It is going somewhere.

What is purpose in life? It is not a definition. It is not adherence to a belief. It is moving with life. It is movement. That's what makes it relative. It is going from here to there. It is going somewhere. Absolutes are not going anywhere. They have already arrived. There is no further movement. You are not at a place of absolute reality yet. Therefore, your attempt for absolute truth will be self-deceiving and will keep you from the true accomplishment that you could be making now.

Religious tyranny will become very evident in the world in the years to come. This is the result of people holding to an absolute idea in a relative reality. It will breed violence and hatred—everything that is counter productive.

Therefore, if you are serious about developing Knowledge and reaping true satisfaction in this life, you must be very firm but very open. You must adhere to what is known now but not believe that it is the end point. You are in movement from one place to another, so do not become settled on the way things seem to be.

Your future will largely be determined by your ability to respond to events externally and to your own Knowledge internally. You cannot do this if you are basing your life on an absolute idea because the moment you do that you stop. You are not going anywhere now. You are standing by the side of the road holding your sign for the world to see and life will be passing you by, most assuredly, for it is going somewhere. Its destiny is beyond this world because that is where you are going.

You did not come to this world to stay here very long, so you are obviously always returning. From the moment of birth you are returning Homeward. You have come here for two reasons, and these reasons are contradictory: You have come here to hide from God because this is the place where God does not seem to exist, and you have come here to serve God. These reasons are only contradictory because they represent the two aspects of your mind—the part of you that believes you have left God and the part of you that has never left God. The part of you that has never left God can only serve God, for you were created to serve God. It is your joy and ecstasy to serve God, hardly a form of bondage. A true delight, indeed!

But that is your Knowledge; it is not your personal reality. Your personal reality is about hiding from God, and so the world becomes a place where you learn to fill up every moment of time with sensation and stimulation so you do not have to think about God. It is only when this stimulation begins to fail and disappoint you consistently that you turn your attention to Knowledge because after awhile God is really the only thing that is left. It does not matter if God is irrational or if nobody else thinks about God; you will now think about God because there is nothing else to do. You have exhausted all of your substitutes, and so you start to think about God.

You may not necessarily think about God as God, but you will start to think about the qualities that are of God—the desire to serve humanity, the desire for peace over stimulation, the desire for equanimity over excitement, the desire for wholeness and honesty, the desire for movement and progress. This is thinking about God, too.

These are not things you think about if your primary aim is to hide. When you are hiding, you want to forget you are hiding because hiding is fearful and not really fun. You do not want to be fearful all the time, so you try to make hiding fun. But it is not fun, for you are alone and estranged in a very harsh reality that you hope will be kind to you. You hope there is a God, but you hope that you will not meet God today because meeting God today would be too much. But you hope that God is there when you need God. It is like being a child who does not want to be around his or her parents but hopes the parents are there in case trouble arises.

It is fun to run away from home until things get dark and you become hungry. Then you want to go home because all of the motivation to run away has left you now. You seek shelter and comfort and security. But when you come into the world and you become tired and hungry, you cannot go home because you are here. But God has come too! God tags along everywhere. So, you run away and God tags along. You cannot shake God loose. Fortunately, this is true.

You cannot only believe in God and hold, "This is God's word from this book" or "This is the way God's reality must be in order for God to be meaningful and good." It is not enough to simply try to resolve the seeming contradictions about God. God does not need to resolve these contradictions, for God is just God.

Your world is contradictory because it is a hiding place, a place where people go who do not want to know anything. Yet your purpose in being here is to remember what you know and to support others in remembering what they know. When you are hiding, you think someone is going to punish you. You have been bad. It is like running away from home as a little child. You run away and you are afraid to go home because your parents will punish you.

Now you have run away a long way, and it's very scary to go home. As much as you want to, it is very scary. "Oh, I cannot go home!" This is the root of all of your fear. It is beneath your psychology and so fundamental that to address it directly would separate the many layers of delusion that confront you everyday.

When people begin an earnest development of Knowledge, they begin to encounter their root fear of God. For some reason, they have trouble doing this or that exercise, even though the exercises are easy. Or they are forgetful. Or if they feel the Presence, they do not want to feel it for more than a few minutes. It is too much. There is nothing wrong with this. It is simply a time-consuming process to become reacquainted with Home. The more you are reacquainted with Home, the less significance your hiding place has for you, and the more you realize you are here to contribute something, not to get something.

There is very little the world can do for you, but there is a great deal you can do for the world. The only way you can embrace this Spiritual Truth is to have a profound sense of your origin and your destiny, and this cannot merely be appreciated philosophically or theologically. It must be born of profound experience within yourself.

So, the first Spiritual Truth is that there is no absolute truth here. Do not make an absolute truth or you will put yourself in bondage and if you teach it, you will put others in bondage as well.

The next Spiritual Truth is that God has already established a Plan and you cannot change it. So, there is a Plan in motion already. Not only can you not change it, you cannot even understand it. For you to understand God's Plan, you would have to have God's mind, which at this moment you do not have. It is like little children trying to understand why their parents go away every day to work. You do not understand. You have not achieved that level of participation. A relative reality cannot appreciate an absolute reality, even though the relative reality is moving towards the absolute. You are moving towards the absolute.

People often like to say, "Well, I will be growing and developing forever." But the more you grow and develop truthfully and not merely in fantasy, the more you will see how difficult and taxing it is, and towards the end of growing and developing, you become very tired of it. You just want to go Home now. The great adventure is over. But this is not a resignation; it is the re-emergence of your true reality within yourself. So, halfway through the journey, you are halfway Home already, and the more you are Home already, the more you want to pull the rest of yourself in with you. And the more you are Home already, the more you will want to pull everyone with you. This is a natural attraction. It is not philosophy or a holy idea. Every little increment of Knowledge that you reclaim, you will naturally want to extend to others. That is all that can be done with it.

The contradiction of living in this world is that it is a hiding place. People are afraid to give and afraid to receive because when you start giving and receiving, the whole idea of hiding begins to dissolve, and you realize that God has caught up with you already.

To your True Mind this is the great reunion. To your personal side, it looks like death and vanquishment. The personal side of your mind is something that you have acquired in being here. It does not know of God. You have to teach it about God like a little child, to assure it that it will be okay. Do not fight it or punish it like a bad child. Do not abuse it for being stupid. It is afraid for its own survival.

Therefore, God has created a Plan already. You are either with it or you are not. It is possible not to be with it. You cannot actually be outside of it, but you can be idle within it, not participating. It is like a big dance. Many people come, but only a few people dance. Everyone else is standing around not knowing what to do. A very unhappy situation.

Your ideas about God's Plan will always fall short of the reality because the reality is too great and too inclusive. It includes everyone. God is very smart. God takes everything that you have made and every reality that you have imagined and sets it all into motion with a great attraction to return Homeward.

Within your own Knowledge you have this attraction. It is the great attraction from the Creator to the Created. If you are moving with it, you will demonstrate extraordinary power and grace in this world, not because you are a special person, but simply because your Knowledge has had the opportunity to shine through. You will still have a personal side and a personal life, but there will be grace with you because grace is being released. Your treasure now is beginning to show.

Let us go on to another Spiritual Truth. Let us give the truth about relationships. There are two kinds of relationships that are available to you with one another. They reflect the two aspects of mind that you possess. There are relationships for unlearning, and there are relationships for true accomplishment.

Relationships for unlearning are where you come together to commit errors with each other and learn from them. They naturally violate your Knowledge because that is the error. You seek them out because they stimulate you. Your purpose in them is usually to make your hiding more pleasurable and to give you a sense of purpose, direction, involvement and relationship that is naturally lacking in a state of hiding because hiding is very lonely. And so these relationships, which are the predominant relationships in this world, are for unlearning and undoing. They are disappointing, but they are very, very illuminating because they teach you Wisdom and they teach you to value what you know.

The other kind of relationship is for people who know they are going somewhere and who join together to go somewhere together. They are joined because they feel the Presence and because their lives are truly compatible. These relationships are rare, but they are available to everyone. They are for real learning and not for unlearning. Unlearning eliminates things. Real learning adds things. These relationships are for adding, but not just things of this world. They are for cultivating Knowledge and for bringing forth things that have a permanent result. They are not just between a man and a woman and are not exclusive to husband and wife. Their highest expression is devotion, for devotion emanates from Knowledge if it is true. Devotion is not based on personal preference or attachment. It is something that emanates naturally. You do not have to try to be devoted. You either are or you are not. It is okay.

Since God is calling you to go somewhere that you are going anyway, the more you feel you are going somewhere, the more you have real criteria for relationship because relationship is for participation.

Everyone must go through unlearning in relationship, but if this unlearning continues far into adulthood, it limits your opportunity to experience true bonding.

You will give up so little to gain so much. You do not have to be celibate and live in a monastery, but you will need to relinquish many of your ideas because they are inappropriate for true association. There is a certain sadness in giving up ideas, but ideas are so limited and minimal compared to life itself.

This leads me to the next Spiritual Truth. There are only three things in life in this world—There are thoughts, there are images and there is Presence. Thoughts, images and Presence. That is it!

As you learn to observe yourself, you will start to see that you are experiencing mostly your thoughts, and you are valuing mostly your images. Self-observation makes this most evident because you see that what you are reacting to is something that is not even there. The more you learn to experience and follow Knowledge in life, the more you value the experience of Presence because Presence teaches you what is actually there. Your thoughts about it and your images of it are secondary.

For instance, you meet someone you are very attracted to and you decide, "Oh! I have not felt this way in so long. I am going to be with this person. It feels so wonderful!" You have thoughts and you have images, and they are wonderful thoughts and images. You are with this person, and they excite your thoughts and images. Then at some point later on you find out who the other person is, and it's disappointing. They are not quite as glamorous as your thoughts and images. You were in love with your thoughts and images and discovered the person later.

But when you are with Knowledge, you discover the person first. Whatever thoughts and images are acquired are based upon experience of the person—their Presence, their Being and their Mind. Your relationship is based upon whether you are going to the same place and if you can go together. This is Wisdom in relationship. You cannot fall in love with someone and hope to go to the same place together. If you are going in opposite directions, then so be it. You may still love them intensely because you love their Presence, but you must set them free to participate in life. You'll see them later. Remember, this is only a temporary visit here. Back on the other side of things you can reminisce.

So, what you experience in this world are thoughts, images and Presence. There is nothing wrong with thoughts and images except that they dominate people's experience. You will have thoughts because you have a mind, and you will have images because you have senses, so you cannot eliminate these and be here. But if they predominate, then you will not feel the Presence of anything. You will not feel your own Presence, the Presence of another, the Presence of life or the movement of life. You will not be present for anything. You will be completely absorbed in your own internal process. Therefore, the objective of your true Teachers is to take you out of this self-absorption and to re-engage you meaningfully in life. There is nothing but expectation and disappointment in being involved with your thoughts all the time.

Life is going somewhere. Do not let it go without you. That is my point here. Presence will always move you because it is going somewhere. It is not fantastic images; it is experiencing the Presence of another. It is experiencing someone else's reality directly, not only intellectually. Then you can look and see if the person who attracts you so strongly is going where you are going because you have a sense of going somewhere.

Most people do not have a sense of going anywhere, and they hope that their romance will provide some direction. And so there are two people not going anywhere waiting for the other to lead the way, hoping circumstances will require them to go somewhere. "Well, if we have many children, that will require us to do something." That is valid. But for you who have shown interest in Knowledge, it will not be enough to let your circumstances completely dictate your movement in life.

Let us go on to the next Spiritual Truth. You are not alone in your efforts to cultivate Knowledge. Members of your Spiritual Family who are inherently related to you are assisting you, both from beyond your visible range and within the world itself. Therefore, do not think you have to rely on your own efforts alone to achieve greatness, which is actually just naturalness.

So, you have Teachers and you have assistance. If you want to be alone with your thoughts, you are free to do so because you can do that in a hiding place. Your mind is your only hiding place. Even this physical world, as difficult as it is, is not really a hiding place. So, the only place you can hide is in your thoughts. If your thoughts begin to open up and clear away a little bit, you will see that there are many people looking at you, very lovingly. This is your Spiritual Family. This is direct experience of relationship. This is life.

The only place you can hide is in your thoughts. You can think from the moment you awake to the moment you sleep and never be outside your thoughts. So, it looks like you are completely alone in your thoughts. It is only when something dramatic happens to you and snaps you out of your thoughts a little bit that you have a moment to experience yourself in life.

Your Teachers are with you, though they may never become known to you in this life. Only if you have been given a calling and have responded to it will their Presence become stronger because you will need to know that their assistance is with you in a very demonstrative way.

Many people will not accept help, and so they must be given gifts without knowing where the gifts come from. Their efforts, if they are truly motivated, will bring them into true relationship anyway. They will realize that what they have done was the product of relationship and not the product of an individual, for individuals do not accomplish anything.

There is no individual creativity in the universe. Creativity is a natural by-product of relationship, whether it is relationship you see or don't see. "Creative individual" is a contradiction in terminology. There are only creative relationships. Somewhere, someone has connected to something else that is real, inherent and genuine, and this produces a remarkable contribution. This is creativity, and it is very exciting because the individuals involved realize they are part of something greater that is working through them.

True marriage is creative. True friendship is creative. True religion is creative. True work in the world is creative. Why? Because each joins you with something that yields something greater than what you alone could produce.

Now, as I have said, the fundamental fear in all people is a fear of God, a fear that God will catch up with them and beat them up! So, subliminally, God is like the devil who will punish you and persecute you for being so stupid and such a lamehead. Or, there is the belief that when God shows up, you will have to give up everything in the world that is fun and happy that you enjoy. This represents another form of persecution because God will take it all away and make some kind of unhappy cleric out of you. This is very ridiculous, of course, but it is at the core of most people's thinking. That is why people accept absolute ideas, but not God.

God's service is everywhere. It moves through so many channels. Why does it do this? Because it is a natural force of attraction. It is like gravity. It finds its way through everything. It will rearrange physical reality to accommodate it, not because it is meddling, but simply because it is a natural force that attracts.

What are Spiritual Families but groups of individuals who have joined together out of this attraction and who, in a higher state of reality, will join with other great groups, like rivers joining together on their way to the sea. It is a greater and greater association based upon natural attraction, which at higher levels becomes increasingly powerful.

Here you increasingly become the contributing force that you truly are because there is nothing else to do. You are being reclaimed slowly, but while you are being reclaimed you are also contributing to everyone and everything, and this redeems your own value to yourself. You cannot return to God if you are a stupid idiot. You would be too ashamed. You would not have capacity for the relationship. So, in all stages of your reclamation, you contribute gifts of value and this redeems your value. You must return to God as part of Creation, not as a miserable person. God does not know about miserable persons. God did not create miserable persons, but God will attract the miserable person nonetheless because God is everywhere, and the attraction to God is everywhere. It cannot be escaped forever.

The next Spiritual Truth is that the curriculum that is given on an individual level is quite specific. Many people need a very regimented life with tremendous self-discipline and structure in order to achieve anything, to gather their resources internally and to organize their thinking and affairs. Other people need to give up all regimentation and confront space, nothingness and openness directly.

Everyone is in a hiding place, but God has the key. Different keys fit different locks. How can God know what to do for each person? God does not have to figure out your dilemma. God just attracts you and your dilemma falls apart. That is the genius. That is how life works. It does not need to figure out all of the complexities of your problem and all the issues of your life.

Your Teachers do not stay up nights thinking about how they are going to rescue you from the next error you are about to commit. They are simply with the attraction. They amplify the attraction and they express the attraction. That will undo all of your errors. God is pulling you Home. Even the overwhelming threat of this world and all of its attractions, fears and inducements that seem to dominate every moment of your life are nothing compared to the pull of God.

*True service
accomplishes
two goals:
It meets
the world's present
needs
&
it prepares
you & the world
for the future.*

Ten

SERVICE IN THE WORLD

OW WE WILL TALK ABOUT SERVICE IN THE
WORLD, a very big subject. We are here for a specific purpose
in our service to the world. Like other Teachers at our level, we
are here to seek out certain individuals who are inherently connected to
us so that their own Knowledge and the memory of their true origin may
be rekindled in this life. As this is brought about, they will be able to activate Knowledge in others and thus part the veil between this world and
life beyond this world. We have a specific purpose to reach specific people,
and yet our very nature and presence allow us to demonstrate a Greater
Reality and context for relationship that is relevant to everyone.

We are here to impart Knowledge in those individuals whom we are
called to serve specifically. It is not so much that we give Knowledge, but
that we activate it within them. You see, only through purposeful relationship can Knowledge be activated. Each of you carries a treasure of
Knowledge internally, but you cannot activate it yourself. You do not even
know where it is. You live at the surface of your Being and cannot penetrate to the core without great assistance, from others amongst yourselves
and from greater powers beyond.

This is because Knowledge is in a different part of your mind. It is in
the part of your mind that is not attempting to be an individual. It is
rooted in the soil of all intelligence. Though above this soil you stand individually as a unique expression, your very foundation is based upon a

commonality that is so fundamental it is difficult to appreciate in this world. Though your roots are very specific, they share a common soil.

Therefore, your Knowledge must be activated through a meaningful relationship. That is how it works because at the deeper level of your mind, everything is relationship. Everyone in this world is seeking intently to discover relationship. All of you are seeking relationship because relationship is the only thing that matters. Anything else that you wish to acquire is still relationship. Break it down into its fundamental parts, and it is all relationship. Relationship is everything.

Unfortunately, living in their personal minds, people believe very intently that the only opportunity to experience profound relationship is in romance or in family. We wish to broaden the context of relationship because many of you will not have partnership in this life in that way. Your partnership will be in a different form. Unless you can entertain this possibility, you will strive for the impossible and spend your life attempting to accomplish something that is not intended for you.

If you seek for small things, small things will be your reward. If you seek for temporary experiences and excitement, you will have temporary relationships. If you seek momentary experiences, you will have momentary involvements. Do not be surprised if this does not satisfy your deeper nature and inclination.

If you seek Knowledge, you will be disappointed in many relationships because they cannot provide the context within which Knowledge can emerge. It is only when you join with another who shares this intent, whose nature is akin to your own and whose origins before this life are associated with yours quite specifically that this can be fully brought about. You are actually meant to be together. You are not together because you attract each other or because you fulfill each other's expectations or because you are thrilling or because you present a very pleasurable and exciting appearance. You are together because you must be. You are drawn by something deeper.

Many people ask, "When will I meet my soulmate, my true partner?" How can I respond except by leading you into this deeper inclination for Knowledge. That is the only foundation for true relationship. This relationship will not die with the body. It will not age with your personality. It will be as youthful and vital in your old age as it is now. It is not based upon your experience in the world. It is based upon your experience before coming into the world, which is directly related to what you will encounter when you leave here.

Why is this relevant to service in the world? Because your ability to discover and to carry out your true function in the world will be dependent upon your ability to participate with others, to experience affinity with others and to share a higher goal than you individually would seek for yourself.

There are many fine things to do in the world. Indeed, this world has great needs and anything that you can give to serve its needs will benefit you very directly. But your greatest gift is to give your Knowledge. There is no greater gift than this. Knowledge is not ideas; it is not information. It is the regenerating force of life within you, but you cannot activate it yourself, try as you may. You can meditate for a lifetime. You can practice austerities. You can deprive yourself of pleasures, but you will merely aggravate and ruin your personal mind. It is something from beyond your own sphere that must reach you because that represents the greater part of you.

People think it is quite phenomenal that Teachers such as ourselves come on the scene. Some people regard our presence as intrusive. Others accept it with a sigh of relief. But it is Teachers such as ourselves, indeed all members of your Spiritual Family, who have made all of your progress possible. Because you live within the context of individuality, it is very difficult for you to account for a larger context in which individuality plays such a very small part. This is an entirely different view of the universe and of relationship. You have had to learn your individuality very painfully. It has been taught to you from the day you were born. But viewing life within the context of true relationship is much more natural.

As I have said, there are many fine things to do in this world, and you will feel compelled to give certain things to certain people, but your gifts cannot even approximate your Knowledge. Why is this? Because if Knowledge can be activated in you, it will affect everyone with whom you come in contact. Indeed, it will affect people who are not even in your physical proximity. When you are activated, others are activated as a result. This is the spark to awaken, and with it come the specific tasks for you to do in life.

Prior to this, Knowledge will organize your thinking and behavior and make you one person. You will not be a fragmented person. You will be one person with one frame of reference and one goal, and this will make you very powerful. If you are not fragmented, if your thoughts and actions are uniform, you will be extremely magnified without trying to be.

People will love you or hate you, be drawn to you or go away from you inexplicably. Some will go away from you without reason. Why will people respond so strongly to you? Because you are uniform and they are fragmented. You represent their higher calling which they may not be able to respond to, and so their own conflicts of interest arise around you. Notice your own discomfort when you are in the presence of someone who is very committed to something in life and you are not committed to anything. Feel your discomfort when you are with someone who is not interested in personal dilemmas at all, and yet they are very loving and compassionate. It is a relief and a discomfort all at once.

How can you give Knowledge? Well, you cannot. It gives itself. Then, everywhere you go people will respond to you, even if you are not trying to give people anything. There is something in you now that is giving you to people. It is not you giving it. It is giving you.

Your life is very distressed because you are attempting to fulfill yourself. You want to be sure that you have the relationships you want. You want to be sure that you have fulfilling experiences. You want to be sure that you will not have pain or distress or disaster. You want to be sure that the world is safe, that your ideas are accepted, that you are loved and appreciated and that you have financial security.

Consider the effort it takes to guarantee that you will have all these things. Consider how limited your success will be because you cannot control everything around you. Indeed, controlling your own mind is an enormous task in and of itself. But now you must control the minds of others. You must control the forces of life. This is a terrible burden. If you spend your time yearning, wanting, planning and scheming for that perfect person, but they are not scheduled to arrive for five years, what will you do for the next five years but aggravate yourself enormously?

Because people have difficulty waiting for anything, they will attempt to fulfill themselves with whatever is available now. You as a race are not well trained to wait for anything, particularly in this nation where instant success is the motto. But when you begin to tire of this constant attempt to fulfill your life, you will begin to open. This is part of the preparation for Knowledge, for without your constant attempt to manage and control your destiny, something else begins to emerge within you. It is very difficult to trust this at first because your basic assumption is that you are alone in the universe and there is nothing to help you. But Knowledge will begin to arise when it has this opportunity, and it will arise fully if you cultivate it, nurture it and give it increasing priority in your life. It is mysterious, inexplicable and powerful.

How can you give to the world? How can you be sure that what you want the world to be is what it is supposed to be? How can you be certain of all the effects of your actions? How can you be certain of what helping people really means? Your Knowledge knows, but you are uncertain.

If you read about the lives of very great people, you will realize that their methods of helping people were quite unorthodox, and often they did not appear to be helping anyone at all. Yet their lives were completely given to contribution. Your life is given to fulfillment. That is why you suffer. Their lives were given to contribution. My life is given to contribution. I contribute everywhere in every opportunity. That is my need. Your life is for fulfillment, so you even give for fulfillment. But giving for fulfillment is not very fulfilling.

So, what does service in the world mean? You should give what is meaningful to you whenever you can at every opportunity you see. Yet there is a greater gift inherent within you that will give in and of itself, for all it can do is contribute. All you can do now is recognize its appearance whenever it emerges, whenever you feel it. It is like a warm glow inside of yourself. On occasion it will give specific directions to you. It will save you from disaster and guide you into the proper relationships. It will teach you to discern what is helpful and what is not, what is encouraging and what is discouraging, what strengthens you and what weakens you.

As this greater gift becomes more predominant within you, it literally takes you over. It is as if your Being now takes over your mind, and the mind now has something truly to serve. This can be a scary experience. You may ask, "What is this great power emerging in me?" This power is growing stronger and you think that you are losing your mind and you are unsafe. But I assure you that unless you attempt to use this power inappropriately, it will draw to you all the people who are most needed in your life, and it will bring into your awareness the Greater Power that exists from beyond this world.

Now, let us look at a little different aspect of service in the world. True service in the world accomplishes two goals: It meets the world's needs in the present time, and it prepares you and the world for the future. Your Teachers represent the future because they are what will be awaiting you when you leave this world. Your life is, in part, preparation for the next step beyond. Your contribution to the world now will guarantee your success in the future, for you have only come here to contribute.

What can the world give to fulfill you? You are not here long enough. Your visit is so brief that whatever it could provide you would be gone in such short notice. This world offers pleasures and stimulants and valuable friendships, but most important is that the world offers you the opportunity to experience and to contribute what exists beyond the world in your Ancient Home. That is the world's greatest contribution. That is your greatest contribution.

If you feed a hungry man today, he will be hungry tomorrow. But if your Knowledge activates his Knowledge, his life will never be the same. It may be a thought, a word or a touch, and his life will be changed. You will not know who changed it, and he will not know who changed it. He will perhaps think it was you because it happened in your proximity. If you build a bridge today, it will be gone in a hundred years. It will serve a temporary service. If you give Knowledge today, it will change a life forever. If you change one life forever, your work in this world is complete because your Knowledge has become so strong that it has activated another's Knowledge, and it has ended separation to the extent that you no longer need to be in this world.

Therefore, there are two aspects to service in the world. There is contributing to the world in its immediate needs, which means feeding people and building bridges. And there is preparation for the next step, which means cultivating Knowledge so that it may serve other people. Our Teaching is for the activation of Knowledge. This is our mission.

If you have this experience of Knowledge, you will be what the world needs. Do you see? The world has not changed, really. Though your lifestyle is different, your needs have not changed. Though you are not as hungry as your ancestors and your life is not as brutal, living in the personal side of your mind is as aggravating as ever. In fact, it is more complex now than it used to be. Before, survival was the issue, but now you are faced not only with survival but with fulfillment—an impossible task. How on earth can you fulfill yourself when you do not know who you are, where you are going, where you have been, or what anything is for? Can you be god and fulfill yourself?

Every personal relationship you have will disappear. Every acquisition you have will be given away. Only something that has a deeper nature within you will last. If you develop true association with any person in this life, it will be carried forward. This is part of your success. What is success in life but the establishment of true relationships? This represents all your accomplishments so far. What you have really brought with you to this life are all the relationships where true recognition has occurred. That is your Ancient Heritage. That is your Spiritual Family.

People want to believe that everyone is equal in his or her capacity and possibilities, but this is not the case. People have come into this world with different capacities and specific work to do. Occasionally, an individual will come who is a leader, and there will be many people whose function it is to serve that leader. They are as important as the leader, but their function is to serve the leader.

If you try to be a leader when your function is to serve a leader, your life will be very frustrated and confused, and you will be jealous and resentful. I can assure you that if you experience jealousy, it is because you are attempting a function that is not yours because jealousy is the opposite of confirmation. It will give you such great peace to recognize your place. All places in this world are temporary. Grandeur is not of the world, so do not worry about a grand position in life.

Any of you who wish to be very noteworthy in your spiritual success must accept that people will abuse you very greatly. So, be prepared to experience tremendous abuse if you want to be popular. That is why the Wise are hidden and you cannot find them. When you are ready, they come and find you. They take you to their hiding place where they can prepare you, and they do not show themselves in public. The most powerful teachers you will rarely ever see. Why? Because their power would instigate such confusion and such a potent response, and they do not want this.

Many people hope that Jesus will return and walk this earth. If he did that, he would produce World War III more rapidly than anything I could think of! Not only would his life be forfeited in short order, but he would generate conflict of a greater nature than you can imagine because the believers and the non-believers would go to war. His purpose is not war and he is not stupid. He made his brief announcement. That is good enough. It set the process in motion for the next stage.

What is service in the world, then? You must prepare. You cannot feed people without preparation. You cannot build bridges without preparation. And you cannot activate Knowledge in others without preparation.

There are two aspects of preparation. The first is to give by meeting people's specific worldly needs and the second is to develop Knowledge and to find a meaningful role in participating with others.

But, you see, the problem for people here is that these criteria have nothing to do with fulfillment. You cannot use these things for fulfillment. How can you use Knowledge for fulfillment? That is ridiculous. Knowledge will use you for fulfillment. No one can see this because everyone is too involved in fulfillment. Because fulfillment is always being threatened by everything, hope and fear become the preoccupying factors of your life—hope that you will have more tomorrow and fear of losing what you have today. The only way that you can participate in hope and fear is to be completely absorbed in your own thinking, which is what separation means. God wishes to take you out of your own thinking because your own thinking isolates you. Even if you are with others who share your thinking, you are isolated from them as well. No one has touched you yet.

Because whatever success you acquire in the quest for fulfillment can be lost tomorrow, there is no peace of mind possible. It is really very sad, but this is the predicament of the world. Some people wish to create Heaven on earth and have no more war, but they also advocate tremendous personal growth for everyone. Well, if you advocate tremendous personal growth, you will advocate change, and change brings conflict, and conflict breeds war. So, if you want peace in the world, it must be a world of no change. People do not change gracefully, not at this stage at any rate. They change with great emotion and stress. In kindergarten the kids fight, and the teacher needs to keep them from fighting so that they can progress with a minimum of discord. This world is like kindergarten, and the participants are combative.

There is great joy in this world for those who are not attempting to use the world to fulfill themselves. There is great peace of mind in knowing you are here for a purpose. There is a great confirmation of your deepest feelings to know that your Teachers are with you. Your greatest fear is that the madness that you have created for yourself is, in fact, reality. Yet, finding out that it is not, if you can really experience this, is such a joy!

So, proceed, then, with an open mind. You do not know the cosmology of the universe. You do not know how God acts or creates. You do not even know how your mind thinks or how your hand moves or why you feel certain things you feel or why you have hundreds of thoughts every hour. This life is wonderfully mysterious, yet if you are hell-bent upon fulfilling yourself, you miss all that. You are trying to get the things you want from everyone you come in contact with. You are like a person on a shopping spree, unmindful of anything else but getting the best deal. Life is this wonderful mystery, and you are on a shopping spree—absolutely crazed!

You have come here for a purpose. Your purpose is to discover your Knowledge and to allow it to emerge. That is everyone's greater purpose, beyond survival and fulfillment. From your purpose will come a specific role and calling in life that will engage you with everyone in a meaningful way. This is your purpose, but very few can even approach it.

Your fulfillment must fail you to some degree for you to value something greater. You see, people want to meditate and have spiritual experiences for their fulfillment, too. No one wants to be without God, really, so God is included as a minor aspect. Not as important as romance, of course, but everyone should have a little God here too, yes?

What I am speaking of you must feel. You cannot think it. Thinking will help, but it cannot approximate the experience. You will all be leaving this world so soon. What is there to gain from being here? What is a few years? Then you leave the world, and you go back to your Spiritual Family. You look at what you have done and have not done, and you say, "My, it is all so clear to me now. Of course! It is so obvious what I had to do."

Being in this world is like someone coming along, hitting you on the head with a bat and knocking you out. A few days later you come back and you say, "My God! Where have I been?" But the point is, you must come back while you are still here. That is the difference. You must snap out if it while you are still here, not when you leave. You have been hit over the head with a bat. That is why you forgot everything, but you must remember while you are here. Everyone snaps out of it to some degree when they leave. You must snap out of it here.

The only way Heaven can be brought to earth is through your memory. Heaven is already here, but no one can see it because it is not moving. It is so still, and you are only looking for things that are moving because only things that are moving are fulfilling.

Your Spiritual Family is here. They are not moving and you cannot see them. They are watching you sleep. Your Teacher, the head of your small group, is sending communication to you because your Teacher is the only one who can bridge the gap between your state here and your true life beyond. Your Teacher will activate your Knowledge and bring you into contact with others who will activate your Knowledge because your relationships need to be re-established in both directions—both vertically to your Teacher and horizontally to one another.

You must get out of the frame of reference that everything is for you personally. It is exactly the opposite. You are for everything. That is what makes you so wonderful. It is not that you cannot want things for yourself. That is okay, but your whole frame of reference will need to shift from fulfillment to contribution because contribution gives more. If you use contribution for fulfillment, you will feel like you are giving and not receiving. But if you give for contribution's sake, you will receive more than you give. That is the difference.

Now, I have already told you what your purpose is, so please do not ask what your purpose is. But its meaning is something you must penetrate, and to do this you must really look at some very serious questions about why you are here. Do not be satisfied with definitions. Definitions do not give you life. Think of the moments in your life when you felt an intrinsic relationship with life itself, and you felt a Greater Presence was with you. Think of the moments when you felt complete affinity with another. Think of the moments when you felt your life had meaning and purpose, however undefined, and that you were not just here to struggle to get all the things you want and then die with your hands full. Think of those times. They are very important. They are moments and glimpses.

You cannot have a consistent experience of Knowledge because you do not have the capacity yet. That will come later. Now you need moments, and the moments need to be frequent enough so that when they are over and you return to your personal mind that is seeking fulfillment, you will remember that there is something else that is more important, that you are not alone and that your life has meaning.

The only fulfillment here is Knowledge because only Knowledge connects your life here with your life beyond. It brings your life from beyond here, and that is fulfilling because now life has been brought into the world. Now the world is no longer just a terrible, desperate experience. It is life itself.

You will then have a different vision of contribution and of service in the world. You will not attempt to make the world look good, as is the intention of most helping. Most people want to give in order to look good and they want the result to look good. But you will have a new vision of what is possible and what is needed. So when you feed someone, you give something greater than food. And when you build a bridge, everyone who crosses it feels your presence. The great saints in this world, for the most part, did not feed people and build bridges. They gave a greater food. They built a greater bridge.

Think not that my discourse is not relevant to every interest that you have. It is, most certainly. Do not be obsessed with romantic relationships. They are far too limited to fulfill you. It is unfortunate in this world that there is so little context for true involvement with one another that romance is the only consideration.

You must be married to something in life, but your marriage must come from within you. It must marry you, not you marry it. People marry. They say, "Well, I will marry you if you meet all of these demands," which, of course, the other person can't. So there is breakdown, and there is change and that is all there is.

A marriage from a Greater Source will marry you. It will say, "Marry this person." It will marry you. God marries you. That is marriage. God can marry you to a person of the opposite sex. God can marry you to a great friendship. God can marry you to religion. God can marry you to a community. God can marry you to a cause in the world. God can marry you to someone who is very sick. This is a marriage that is greater than any that your romantic ideas can conjure up. This is a relationship that is devoted beyond personal interests. What difference does fulfillment make now? You are being fed by your own devotion. You are with life now. You are not shopping anymore. You have stopped to buy. You are purchasing life now. You are not simply a spectator of a process that is beyond your reach. God wants to marry you in this world so that you may feel the greatness of relationship.

Therefore, seek in your requests to be married. "Marry me to something that is real and genuine that will give me great happiness." You are asking life, then, to give you what you possess. Then, when you leave this world, you will leave with a feeling that you have established something important here, something that you will take with you. Then, when you return to your Spiritual Family, you will not return empty handed. That is what breaks open the mysterious veil that separates this world from life itself.

*When you think
of becoming
more powerful,
think of having
great
responsibilities.*

Eleven

POWER & RESPONSIBILITY

ANY PEOPLE'S INTEREST in personal development, in spiritual growth and in cultivating their abilities is associated with the issue of power. It is very essential that you realize that power and responsibility are intrinsically tied together. You cannot separate them.

So, let us look at power. Power is the ability to take care of people. That is my definition of power for now. There are other very good definitions, of course. Many of you will think, "Power is the ability to overcome obstacles, or handicaps or hindrances. Power is the ability to get things done in the world. Power is the ability to maintain a state of equanimity." This is all true, but I will talk about power in the context of providership, the ability to take care of others without loss but with gain. That is my definition of power. It is not the only definition, but it is relevant to my discourse.

Responsibility is the ability to respond to your truest inclinations as well as to the needs of others. Therefore, responsibility is associated with providership as well. As you provide more for others, you must call upon your own strength. You cannot be obsessed with your needs, wants and difficulties because you have placed yourself in a situation that requires you to rise to a greater occasion and ability.

Now, you cannot just take care of people like that. You must prepare. Here you do not become strong and then take care of people. You do not become powerful and then have responsibility. It does not work like that.

There is a great preoccupation in your society with personal freedom, the ability to determine and carry out your own destiny. This is a very rare freedom you have, rare in your own world and rare in the context of the Greater Community of Worlds, where personal freedom is extremely rare. There is an obsession here with personal freedom. People wish to reclaim power, ability, relationship and resourcefulness, but they want it without any infringement upon their freedom at all. It cannot be that way. There is a direct relationship between power and freedom.

The more powerful you are, the less personal freedom you have, yet the greater the internal freedom you have. Here, you do not have the freedom to go wherever you want and do whatever you like at any time because you are carrying responsibility. You are answerable to other people through taking care of them and through providing service. You cannot just do whatever you want at any hour of the day. With greater power and ability, you have a greater sense that your life has destiny, purpose and direction, and this is the greater context for freedom.

Personal freedom becomes very obsessive because it demands things from life that you yourself cannot provide. People say, "I want to have complete peace, complete power and complete ability. I want to be able to do what anyone can do, but I do not want anything to hold me back, restrict me, restrain me, or bind me. I want to feel good about myself at every moment. I do not want to be in nasty situations. I do not want to be confronted with ugly things. I want the world to be an absolutely wonderful place so that I can have personal freedom and not hurt anybody."

How can there be peace unless you have regained your power? Peace is not a state where the world does not infringe upon you. Peace is a state of inner discovery where you have realized that you are part of life, that there are intrinsic relationships and that your Spiritual Teachers are real and exist within you. You realize that you have assistance from without and from within—a greater resource than you could provide for yourself. This is what enables you to take on great tasks and carry burdens. This life is so short here. You are not here a very long time, but you can do major things here, important things.

In this society, you have both an opportunity and a handicap. Your great opportunity is the freedom to seek Knowledge and to express your inner life openly. This freedom is unprecedented, I assure you. Your handicap is that you have very few models for true power or ability and very few models for successful relationship. Your society seems self-indulgent and very chaotic. You are free to shop, but the selection is very great, and you have very little reference on how to make the best choice.

You are free now to have relationships with very little limitation. Men and women are extremely available to each other as never before. They are not held apart by social castes or economic lines. You have tremendous wealth available to you. Your life is easy and your fundamental needs are being met, for the most part. You have houses to sleep in, clothes to wear and food to eat.

So, with your freedom you seek to regain your power. Yet, if you try to do this without assuming the burden of responsibility, then your search will be fruitless. You will be demanding from others that they accept you and give you the freedom and license that you yourself cannot provide. This attempt is very disappointing. It is focused on taking and not on giving.

Many people have often asked, "What can I do now to have greater ability?" On occasion they were given specific indications. Often these were not met with favorably because it meant restricting their personal freedom. They were told, "Go assume this role." "Get married. Have children." Begin a business enterprise." But people then thought, "Oh, I don't want to do that. It is too hard. It is too much. I would have to give up my play, my little happinesses."

You see, people rarely grow and develop on their own initiative. People usually grow because they must, not because they want to. There is complacency that is inherent in intelligent life, and your environment is so easy that complacency is built in. If you lived in a more demanding environment where your choices were limited, then you would value your decisions far more because they would have much more serious consequences.

Responsibility is difficult, but it is also very rewarding if it is placed in the proper perspective and given in the right area. You must choose wisely what burden you will carry, whom you will take care of and for what reason. You will be happier if you can provide for others beyond your own choice. For example, if you have children, well, some days you want to be a parent and some days you do not, but you are a parent every day. If you own a business enterprise, you carry that business on days when you like having a business and on days when you do not. Here your rewards are greater and more long term than the freedom to go and have a day off whenever the impulse strikes you.

Therefore, in whatever employment you are engaged, concentrate on contributing to people. Do not concentrate on being liked and accepted. Do not concentrate on having the license to express yourself without other people's disagreement. Do not seek for freedom. Seek for contribution. You are free to contribute in your society to a very great degree. This freedom is worthwhile. When you leave this world, you will not have to feed and house yourself. You will not have to take care of a physical body. You will not have all these trials and difficulties.

It is a characteristic of all men and women who have regained Knowledge that they can take care of other people effectively, without a loss of vitality. This does not mean that it is easy. This does not mean that it is always a pleasure, and it does not mean that they do it gracefully, necessarily. But they are capable of doing it.

There are two aspects of mind in every individual, and I would like to address them so that you can have a proper perspective on these things. I will use the terminology personal side and Impersonal side.

Your personal side, which is your personality, is the aspect of mind that you have acquired and developed in your own brief life here. Your Impersonal side is the aspect of mind that you have brought with you. It is intrinsic to you. It is actually your reality beyond this world as it exists in this moment, which we also call Knowledge.

Now, within the personal side there are many points of view, but they are all personal. There is a fundamental difference between a viewpoint from your personal side and a viewpoint from your Impersonal side. From your personal side, your life looks one way. From the Impersonal, it looks an entirely different way.

The personal side is fundamentally concerned with survival. Once it has made sure it has enough food for the body, enough clothing and shelter, it goes about seeking approval, for that is its desperate need, which is also based on survival. It is very needy. It has great anxiety about life because it is temporary, and it faces annihilation or infringement from so many different sources that it cannot account for them all. Therefore, it is fundamentally fearful and unhappy. To allay its unhappiness, it seeks for stimulation and escape. It does not want to know, for Knowledge is fearful to it. Knowledge represents pain and loss and a threat to its survival. The personal side is not evil; it is only helpless. It cannot function on its own because it is like a child.

Your Impersonal side is fundamentally concerned with contribution, for that is why you have chosen to come into this world. You did not come here only for your own development. You came here with resources from your Spiritual Family beyond this world to contribute specific things in this time and place. Therefore, the Impersonal side is fundamentally concerned with contribution. Survival is not an issue with it except inso-far that it wants to maintain the mind and the body in a healthy state. It wants to keep you out of danger and to make sure that you go to the right places and find the right people. Its perspective on life is extremely different from the personal side. Its priorities are different, its frame of ref-erence is different and its concept of relationship is different. Its under-standing about success, survival and well-being is different. It is a different perception altogether.

Our work is to provide a shift into the Impersonal, for until that hap-pens and becomes a foundation for perception and decision making, your life will still seem reckless and inconsistent. You will go from happiness to sadness, back and forth, back and forth. You will have brief moments of insight and long periods of emptiness and frustration.

I want to reiterate that perception from these two states of mind is extremely different. From your Impersonal side, once you gain a foundation there, you will look at life as if you were a visitor from your Spiritual Family, whom you were sent here to serve. You will not be intimidated by the world because you will know it is a transient, temporary state and it cannot touch you. It can only hinder your ability to contribute. Your Inner Teachers are related to your Impersonal side. That is why contacting them is very valuable because they have the ability to initiate you into Knowledge.

But, of course, people live in their personal sides. You were born in a state of amnesia, and you have grown up developing your personal mind so that it can communicate and survive in this world. Communication and survival were necessary steps which you could not bypass in order to function here. You must have a personal mind because it provides access to other beings here. It enables you to survive here in a physical state, but its duties and responsibilities are so limited when compared to your Knowledge that you cannot give these two aspects of mind equal footing.

Let us say that your personal mind is about ten percent of you and it is the ten percent that you live in. Taking you beyond your personal mind gives you a vision of life and a direct experience of your purpose. In time, as you gain further and further access to this, you will have the foundation for true accomplishment.

Now, when people talk about intuition, they are feeling the effects of the Impersonal on the personal, but they are still in the personal. They are still concerned with getting things they want so that they can survive. This also includes happiness because if you do not get enough happiness, you will lose interest in survival and destroy yourself anyway. This is why people do all manner of harmful things to themselves physically and mentally. They don't care anymore.

The personal side is all about fear and survival. It knows that it cannot overcome the forces of nature and that its fight to survive will in time be overwhelmed, and so it seeks comfort and escape. It wants to make sure that it has everything that it feels will give it some sense of identity, purpose and direction. It wants this because, without your Being, it is lost. It is like a little child in a big world with no guardian. Your Impersonal side is the guardian of your personal side. Your Being is the guardian of your mind.

To be initiated into Knowledge is to shift your frame of reference from your mind to your Being. It is fundamentally a shift in perception, for as long as you are in your personal mind, everything looks one way. Yet, as you gain access to Knowledge and are able to experience it with greater frequency, you will notice this dramatic shift. Here, you will not attempt to work out your personal problems while you are in your personal mind. You will only attempt to implement certain practices or procedures that will help you maintain what you know while you are in a state of unknowing.

It is very damaging to believe that your personal mind is evil or terrible when it is really pathetic. This is like punishing a child for being a child, for not being an adult. Can you create a mind in a few years that can match the magnitude of your true identity? Can you mock God like that? Can you create an awareness or a belief system that can in any way match the power of Knowledge? Of course not.

Your personal mind needs your Impersonal mind to be safe. As your Impersonal emerges, you will feel increasingly safe and secure, yet there will be resistance at the beginning because of this survival issue. As you learn to receive instruction from your Teachers, you begin to relinquish some control over things. The obsession with personal freedom, which is the personal side's obsession with survival and fulfillment, begins to be transferred to a Greater Power within you. You are now accepting relationship into your life.

You live in this great country, and yet you live little lives obsessed with ridiculous things. When you are scared, you go seek relationship, and it gives you temporary relief. You do not know what to do with your freedom. God is not interfering. You can do anything here, but very few people know what to do with their freedom. It is very sad because you have everything and you are still empty. Your true desire inside has not been quenched.

What begins to restore you, then, is responsibility. Your Knowledge will always direct you to begin to serve people, to care for them, to act in a responsible manner and to be effective in communication. It will help you discern whom to take care of and whom not to take care of. Human beings must serve. You were made for this. In fact, all beings were made to serve. If you are a taker in life, you will be very unhappy. Life here cannot give you enough to satisfy you. It is always taking things away, so it is extremely sad.

Knowledge is with you. It is a tremendous Presence. It is so powerful that it is frightening to encounter at first. You can only gain access to it in small degrees because you do not yet have the capacity to accept such magnitude of mind. That is why when people have an experience of Knowledge, they run away and go hide. They go back into romance or intoxication or some kind of debilitating activity where they can hide because Knowledge is so great. *Hospitable experiences*

Because your life is part of a Greater Plan, you have an intrinsic role to assume. This always engages you in relationship with others in a very profound way. Now you are not in relationship for personal freedom or personal fulfillment. You are now in relationship, perhaps, for reasons you cannot even describe, but you must be together. As you are together, your life begins to feel more at ease, and there is greater self-acceptance. You see that your nature is geared towards a certain role that is best for you.

God knows that if you found your rightful place, much of your current turmoil would disappear. You'd be happy just to do your part. Yet, because your part is in contrast to so many of your former goals and ambitions and because your personal side fears that your part may not be real or true, it is not sought after.

You see, there are turning points in life. Let us say that life has three periods: a period of denial, a period of discovery and a period of accomplishment.

In the first period, your life is really about escaping Knowledge. It is preoccupied with excitement, sensation and stimulation so that your mind won't know anything.

The second period is the stage of discovery. It is born of the fact that the first stage is so terribly disappointing. Now you realize that there are important things you must learn and discern in order not to repeat old mistakes. You have a greater sense now that you could be far more happy, far more involved and a greater asset than you had considered possible before. So, you begin to discern what is right and good and what is wrong or bad for you.

This, in time, leads to the discovery that you do have a purpose and that you must engage yourself in a certain way in life to discover this purpose and live it, for it is in living this purpose that it is discovered. I cannot give you a definition and say, "You are this," and you say, "Oh, I'm happy. I know that I am this." You must live it. It must grow for you. It is so great that you cannot simply accept it and have it happen.

Your Teachers do not want to bring the realization of purpose about prematurely. It cannot be brought about until you are ready, willing and able to carry its responsibilities. Discovering Knowledge means that you will be asked to do things in life that perhaps are not based upon former goals. But if you do them, you will respect yourself and feel at home within yourself because they will be so right for you.

The greatest struggle for freedom is always to escape the personal side to find Knowledge. But if you are afraid of your Impersonal side, which everyone is, and have not ventured there effectively, then you will attempt to make other people love and accept you, either by force or persuasion, and make sure that no one infringes on you in any way. "No one can tell me what to do!" You see, that is the problem with Spiritual Teachers. They tell you what to do and you need their advice greatly, but they also teach you how to make decisions.

If you cannot be infringed upon by anyone, then there will be great conflict regarding authority. "I must determine what I do in life. No one can tell me anything." That produces a very difficult teaching situation, for the student now is demanding great things but will not receive advice or direction from anyone. So, the Teachers cannot arise. They must be in the background, sending their thoughts into the student's mind. The student will think it is his or her thoughts: "Ah, I had a marvelous idea today!" and the student will be restored.

As students learn to follow, they begin to have a sense that their direction is not coming from them alone, that there really is a very great Presence with them. It is not just their Presence, for what is Presence but relationship? You as an individual have no Presence. You cannot have Presence and be separate from life. You have Presence because you are intrinsically joined with life, and that's what produces Presence.

There are no powerful individuals. What can a powerful individual be? Powerful individuals are expressions of something greater than individuality, and that is what makes them powerful. That is why we say there are no great individuals, but there are great relationships.

Because of humanity's social and political needs, you will become increasingly reliant upon one another in the years to come. The emphasis on personal freedom will be restricted by your circumstances. You see, people want the world to be like a Garden of Eden so that they can have total freedom to explore and express, but the reality is that they have created something very different which requires them to be in relationship with one another and learn to cooperate and take care of people. If you lived in a Garden of Eden, you would be very unhappy because it would not be requiring anything of you. You would be in a very beautiful isolation.

What you will create are the conditions that will make relationship necessary because most people grow out of necessity and not out of preference. Real growth requires challenge, change and adjustment. It requires that you relinquish a little bit of personal freedom and yet it makes internal freedom possible.

How can you know your abilities unless you take care of people? How can you achieve anything without carrying a burden of responsibility? How can true friendship or true marriage ever be established unless you risk your own personal interests for someone else? That is why having children is beneficial to many people. Then life is more about providing for others. There is a certain peace in this, even though it is not easy. Here you do not have time to be constantly questioning, "Who am I? How am I doing today? What is my mental state? What is my physical state?" You have to take care of people.

When you graduate from this world, for those of you who evolve beyond this world's learning, you will have to take care of people. That will be your task. Just like us. In specific ways, you will have to take care of people. When you are beyond this life, you will find that caring for those who are still here is very challenging because they are ambivalent regarding your existence. They are ambivalent regarding their relationship with you, if they are aware of it at all, and they have very conflicting views about everything. So, if you wish to contact them or give them something helpful, you are met with very limited results, not because they are bad but because they are part of a world that is without Knowledge.

Listen. I am not belittling you at all. I am speaking of the greatness that is hidden within you. This greatness comes with a price, but the price is so small and the reward is so great that it is really without a price when you think about it.

We ask that students of Knowledge consider their relationships seriously because relationships are very important. We have asked them to consider their lives as having purpose and everything they do as being related to this purpose in some way.

You must be engaged with people in a special way to activate Knowledge in each other. These relationships based on Knowledge are not merely therapeutic. They do not merely put the personal side at ease. They are really for something greater.

Your challenge now is to learn to contribute to the right people for the right purpose without putting yourself at risk unnecessarily. This calls for Wisdom, a whole other aspect of learning. Yet, learning Wisdom goes along with the discovery of Knowledge.

Let us give you this important idea that may perhaps be contrary to many of your ambitions. This idea is worth thinking about a great deal: The more powerful you are, the more hidden you must be. The greater your capacity for Knowledge, the less you will want to show it to others. Those who have Knowledge do not display it except in certain circumstances and with certain individuals. Why is this so? Because otherwise it generates conflict, fear and hostility towards the giver. It gives rise to the most deeply held conflicts of mind in the recipient. It can activate change before a person is ready for change and can stimulate a power in the recipient for which they may not have the capacity. Therefore, the more power you have, the more hidden you must be. For those of you who have thought about transforming the world or making a big show by demonstrating some great virtue, you must think very carefully now.

If Jesus Christ came tomorrow, he would begin the next world war. I assure you this would be the case—the believers against the non-believers. It would be terrible. Whenever any great soul has become public, there has been much conflict and discord. It has set in motion great forces of change. It has activated many people. Yet, when you are activated by Knowledge and you cannot accept it, you will fight the giver. Has Jesus Christ brought peace to the world? He has brought the activation of Knowledge. Many wars followed his presence here. He knew this would happen, of course. Thus, even he had a conflict with giving.

You do not give children power. You raise them so that they may become powerful. Yet, at certain junctures in history, individuals of Knowledge must become open and display their ability, which is not their individual ability. This is what keeps your evolution going. These displays are very rare. Do not think that if you cultivate Knowledge, you will be asked to display it very often, though you will be asked to use it constantly. If you give it indiscriminately, you will be very disappointed because you will find that most people are not interested and if you press them, they will become belligerent. It is very hard, then, not to be critical of others or demean your own gift.

Knowledge is a state of direct realization and it is extremely powerful.

It is not meant for everybody at this moment. Yet if it is passed on and given to the individuals who are prepared for it, then this world will accelerate its evolution, and the results of this giving will have impact on all levels of human endeavor.

You see, God does not want to activate Knowledge in each individual completely at this moment. It is not God's Plan to do this because it does not work. There are certain individuals who need to be activated to a certain degree, and as they accept this and accept their function that arises from it, then they give certain specific gifts to others. Those people then pass on their abilities, and so forth. So, it grows extensively. If one person gives the gift of Knowledge to another, the other will then feel motivated to give to others, and those who receive will give, and so forth. Therefore, the initial gift will grow tremendously and have a resonating effect. That is how God brings about fundamental change with a minimum of disruption. That is how a greater ability of mind is brought into play without producing terror or conflict. The Wise know this to be so. That is why they say, "The greater your power, the more hidden you are."

If you wish to be popular and have great accolades for yourself, then do not share Knowledge directly. Keep the pearl within your heart and give the ideas that emanate from Knowledge because ideas are something the world can engage with. You cannot activate another's Knowledge. You cannot teach Knowledge. It cannot be taught; it can only be passed on by a process that is very mysterious. You can only bear witness to it.

Knowledge activates Knowledge. You cannot say, "I am going to activate your Knowledge. I am going to get you in touch with your Knowledge." That is not successful. You do not know how willing, ready or capable the other person is.

People know many things that they do not accept. You know things about your life that you have not accepted. You know what to eat and what not to eat, but you do not follow this. You know which relationships are wasting your life, but you will not disengage. Why? Because you are not ready. You do not have the capacity for this change, and you may not be able to accept what it will bring to you as a result. That is okay, but if you try to teach people Knowledge, you will try to change them, ignorant of their level of preparedness.

Knowledge activates Knowledge. Therefore, your first responsibility is to become a student and a recipient of Knowledge. Then Knowledge does the work itself. Ideas are very important because they prepare people to discover Knowledge, but ideas are not Knowledge. All that they can do is prepare a mental framework where Knowledge can arise most easily.

It is the work of your true Teachers that activates Knowledge in you because they are a force for Knowledge. It is not their personalities that are important. It is their power in activating Knowledge.

Therefore, when you think of becoming more powerful, think of having great responsibilities. If you want power without responsibility, you will end up fighting people and blaming them for your difficulties. If you want more power, you will have less personal freedom and will have to be more discriminating in relationships. Even though some may feel that they are very advanced, there is no one in this world who is advanced. No one in this world is beyond temptation or fear, so do not think that you can overcome the world.

People will either strengthen you or weaken you. There are no neutral forces in life. At your current stage of development, people will either strengthen you or weaken you. Even if they are not harmful and are very loving people, if they are not directly involved in the enhancement of your Knowledge, they are weakening you to a subtle but very real extent. Your time is precious. People say, "I want to have relationship with anybody I want. Why am I so limited? I try to go be with someone and my internal state says No!"

There is an infringement upon your freedom when you are assuming greater responsibilities. If you become married, you cannot have sex with anyone you want. If you have children, you cannot go out and play at will. If you have a business enterprise, you will have great burdens and concerns. Attempt anything important and there will be an infringement on your personal freedom. This is okay because it offers you something better.

*Love arises when
you honor
your nature
because
that is the
fundamental act of
self-acceptance.*

Twelve

LOVE

*L*OVE IS A SUBJECT WE HAVE NOT SPOKEN OF directly before for a very specific reason. The reason is that love requires some preparation to comprehend its power and magnitude. The problem with love is that people try to love. They try to be loving. They even try to be loved. It does not work very well to do this because to be loving is not the first step.

Many people talk about love saying, "Well, if you are loving, then this will happen, and your life will become more joyful, and people will respond to you more positively. If you are more loving, you will have a greater degree of friendship and companionship. If you are more loving, you will experience God more directly."

The problem with this approach is that people cannot try to be loving. They try to be loving on top of their current experience, which often is not very loving. You cannot place a sentiment on top of your experience and hope that your sentiment will be successful. Love is an expression of your own Knowledge. It is an expression of your True Mind.

So, then, let us not try to be loving so that we can be more honest with each other. Honesty requires that you begin where you really are. You cannot begin from where you want to be. You cannot be where you want to be. You can only be where you are. If your current state at this moment is not a state of profound love, then you must express that state and find constructive ways of doing that.

This in itself is a great step forward. It requires you to become self-observant and to disassociate yourself from your experience enough so that you can look at it objectively. This involves a certain degree of self-acceptance. You must accept your current state. You cannot be waging war against it, even in the attempt to become more loving. That is fruitless and will lead to a greater sense of personal failure, which you do not need.

I tell you, love will come naturally in its own way. You do not need to create it. It will emanate from you when the conditions are right, and other people will respond to it. You will not be trying to be loving or kind or nice or lovable.

The problem with trying to be loving is that you lose respect for yourself because trying to be loving is a form of self-denial. It is saying, "My current state is repugnant. I will not honor it, and I will attempt to be in a more desirable state." Well, a more desirable state may indeed be worthwhile, but you cannot attain it through self-repudiation.

So, let us talk about love in terms of preparation, the kind of preparation that allows love to emerge naturally. When love emerges naturally, there is no dishonesty. There is no self-denial. Love is happening. Your challenge now is merely to accept it and to allow it to emanate. You will be as much a recipient of it as those with whom you are engaged.

Let us make a few important points regarding this. First of all, you do not create love. You cannot manipulate love. In fact, you cannot do anything with love, but it can do something with you. You cannot drum it up. You cannot add it on. You cannot strive for it. It is elusive, if you do. If you are open and cultivating yourself correctly, it will be a natural emanation. It is both a result and a cause in and of itself. Like Knowledge, it is a force that is latent within you. As you focus upon it and allow it to express itself, and as you become a substantial person who has a capacity for Knowledge, love will emanate naturally.

Let us say that love is not an emotion. It is not always kind. It does not maintain one appearance only. Ideas of being loving and lovable conjure up certain forms of behavior and mannerisms and certain forms of etiquette and social obligation. But this is only acting at love. Love is very powerful. It does not need your creations. It only needs for you to become an empty vessel through which it can express itself.

So, love may make many appearances. If you think about this, you will realize that there have been times in your life that were extremely difficult and very challenging, times that you rejected and could not stand. Yet, their result was a greater experience of love and relationship. Those "great romances" that failed you, did they not save you from a worse calamity? And in retrospect, could you not look back and say, "My God! I almost married that person! I am so glad it did not go that way!" But at the time was it not terribly painful? That was love in action, too, but it did not look loving at the time.

It is only when you look at your life from a greater perspective that you see and sense that your life is being gently guided along. And when it is not gently guided, it means that you have gone too far away, and you need a stronger assistance. Therefore, you get a little push now. It is not so gentle, but you need this because you have disassociated yourself from your own Knowledge substantially, and you need a strong correction from life.

Love is mysterious. It is not always happy; it is not always kind, but it always carries you forward toward the source of love itself.

God's purpose in life is to unburden you. That is God's first purpose. God cannot give you anything until you are unburdened. You cannot carry a gift from God if your hands are full of your own necessities. People at the beginning ask God, "Help me get what I want. I want this and I want that, and I want you to make sure I get it. If you are real, you will do this for me." Here you are not quite sure if the things you want are not merely burdens for you. If you keep demanding from life that you have these things without result, well, maybe it is not in your best interests or maybe it is not time for such things.

God's first purpose is to unburden you, and the unburdening is an act of love. In fact, you will do most of the work. Do you know why? Because trying to fulfill yourself is so terribly disappointing. Only God can fulfill you and only you can fulfill God.

God knows this, so God is not counting on anything else. You are trying to correct your life, rearrange your life, re-establish your life, and fulfill yourself through your relationships, your career and so forth. But it is never enough. Even if you have money, a beautiful partner and wonderful times, your longing will be even stronger than ever because it can only be satisfied by having a greater purpose in life.

Therefore, God's first emphasis is to unburden you. God does not want to deprive you of anything that is truly beneficial for your happiness. This you must learn through experience because my reassurance will not be enough. Until you are unburdened, you will be asking God to increase your burden and not lessen it.

As you seek for greater purpose, often as the result of personal failure, then something else can be given to you because you are laying down your shields. That is love. If you are terribly burdened, how can you be loving? You are attempting to control life to assure that your survival and happiness will be guaranteed. You are trying to determine that people will respond to you in a predictable manner. You are often trying to get results that are in conflict with one another. It is extremely difficult, and it need not be so.

The most loving kindness given to one who is burdened is to share their burden, but they must give away their burden for it to be shared. If you say, "Jesus will carry my burden for me," you must give it to Jesus, and what he does with it you cannot control. Who knows? He might give it away to someone else. He cannot carry everyone's burden, but it is not your burden anymore.

When you are unburdened to some degree, God can give you a new responsibility and that is the meaning of higher purpose: a greater responsibility. By responsibility, I mean your ability to respond to God in your life truthfully, honestly and effectively, without deception or distortion. That is your responsibility. Responsibility *is* higher purpose. Now you are the recipient and the giver of something greater. It is a power and a force. It is your Knowledge, and we shall also call it your love. Then you will want to unburden others because that is the natural extension of what you have received.

God always gives to givers because they naturally amplify the gift. God also gives to takers, but they do not experience the gift. What God gives to takers is an opportunity to give. What takers need to experience is the need to give because that is what will redeem them. When they become givers, naturally, then the whole process of giving and receiving can truly begin.

Your giving must be determined by a Greater Force within you. People have very strong ideas on what should be given, how it should be given, what the result must look like, who should receive it, how they should receive it, what they should do with it, and so forth. It is very hard to give with all these requirements!

Therefore, let us separate love from sentimentality. Let us separate love from trying to make happy appearances. If you go around smiling at everyone, you will be disgusting, and you will not understand why people do not want to be around you. But if something is happening in your life that is great and inexplicable and you are as much in amazement about it as anyone else, then you will influence and affect everyone you come in contact with. It will not be born of your ambition or personal needs. It is something that is happening in your life.

When students develop in Knowledge, either in this preparation or in another, they have an opportunity to experience relationship in a very direct manner. They can become an intermediary. An intermediary is one who translates Knowledge from one level to another and demonstrates that you can be an intermediary between God and the world. As a matter of fact, God needs Teachers such as myself to be intermediaries because that is the only way that God can contact the personal side of your mind. God has no personal side, and so God does not relate to the personal side of human beings.

Making God a person is pathetic because an omnipotent Presence cannot be a personality. They are mutually exclusive. God is a Presence and a Force, the true attraction in all of life. God speaks to you through your Teachers because they are the intermediaries at this level of existence. Indeed, God speaks to me through intermediaries. Do you know why this is so? Do you know why you cannot just go to God directly? Many people ask that, you know. "Well, why can't I just go to God directly?"

It is because God wants to join you with others. God's Plan is a Plan of rejoining of relationships in their true function and capacity. God's purpose here is to unburden you and to prepare you for true relationship because you will not be able to do anything in life without true relationship. You will not be able to be a bringer of grace without relationship because grace is a product of relationship.

So, what do you do now to have more love in your life? What do you do now to experience the rewards of being loving and lovable without becoming dishonest or self-degrading? I will tell you a little secret. If you want to experience love with people, it is very simple. People don't think of this because they are associating love with behavior and not necessarily with experience. When you are with another, be present to that person. Being present means that you are more with them than with your own thoughts. You are not preoccupied with your thoughts. You are not preoccupied with them, either. You are just being present. It is a state of being an observer without preference. It is amazing what this can yield, but it takes mental preparation.

The problem in relationships is that people are completely consumed with their own thoughts. In fact, they are so consumed with their own thoughts that they aren't even relating to one another. They are relating to their thoughts about one another. Indeed, people can be together for long periods of time and not experience each other at all. They are attempting to use the relationship to validate their thoughts about each other and their expectations, needs, and so forth. But if you are present with another, which means that you are observant without preference and without conclusion, then you will have an opportunity to experience something very great.

I am not talking about relationship yet. I am talking about recognition, which is the beginning of relationship. It is the beginning of a true experience of love. I am also not talking about empathizing with people. That is relating to another person's experience, which is actually more about you than it is about them. It confirms that you are not alone. It relieves the burden and anxiety of separation momentarily, which gives you an experience of relief and happiness briefly. This is worthwhile, but I am speaking of something far more powerful.

Do not try to be loving. Do not try to look good. Do not try to look anything. You do not matter. Be only all eyes and ears and feeling. Do not use the encounter to try to prove something. The results of doing this are very immediate.

The attractions that individuals feel for each other are not always this recognition that I speak of, which is not passionate and does not make you feel like a crazy person who has taken a strong drug and has gone into some kind of great tornado of passions. It is a deep feeling and it is calm. It is recognition, not stimulation. It is not like taking a great romantic journey. It is a calm settling down within yourself, for your True Self has just been honored and discovered through this encounter. Do not think, however, that because you have had an experience of recognition that relationship is instantaneous or guaranteed. Relationship is based upon what you can do together in life.

The major factor for true relationship is greater compatibility. Greater means that it is larger than the idea of compatibility that is generally assumed. It means that you are compatible in your natures. It does not necessarily mean that you are compatible in your judgments, evaluations and preferences, for these are things on the surface of your mind. Greater compatibility means that the deeper you go together, the greater the resonance between you. It means that you are not opposed to each other's spiritual calling. In fact, you complement each other's spiritual calling. This is always greater than your understanding. With greater compatibility, your natures resonate with each other. Being together produces a better result than you could produce alone. Now, you are both able and prepared to acknowledge the spiritual life that is destined for you.

So, we have recognition and we have greater compatibility. Greater compatibility must be discovered through action, time and challenge. Indeed, as you face challenge together, your compatibility grows deeper and deeper. It is not exhausted or eliminated, but it must be supported. This provides the foundation for love to emerge.

Relationships of this kind are not common. Do not think you can have them with many people. You can experience recognition with many people, but greater compatibility in physical life is something that is more specific. It has to do with your calling in life, which leads you in specific ways to meet specific people for specific purposes. Your calling is mysterious, yet there is nothing in life that is more powerful, more engaging and more relevant to all of your needs.

Now this brings us to the problem of self-love. Love arises when you honor your nature because that is the fundamental act of self-acceptance. Very few people do this, you know. People want to be something else.

They carry this burden of insisting that they be something else. Life is not very accommodating here because it does not give you something else.

If people find their rightful place with others, most of their problems will go away. Why? Because they can settle down now and participate. They are not constantly questioning who they are, why they are here, what they must do to be happy, what they must do to avoid pain or what they must do to find peace. They can now simply participate.

Many of you would like to be like a Buddha or a Jesus or a Mother Teresa because these individuals represent everything that I am talking about. Individuals such as these are not trying anything. Life is moving them. They are unburdened so they can follow life. It is not that they have few possessions. That is not the issue. It is that they have very little insistence upon life; yet they are fully able and desiring to participate.

So, if I say, "Be present with others whom you meet," you will have a result, and the result will be an experience of recognition if you are very serious in your intent. But then a problem arises. The problem is that love can be very difficult to accept. In your relationships, you will seek out those who have as great a capacity for love as you do. A relationship requires a capacity for love, which is the capacity to experience relationship and the ability and desire to participate. The experience of love melts you away. Your personal side, that tiny part of your mind in which you live, melts into your Impersonal Self, or True Self, because it is overtaken. That is surrender.

If you are determined that your well-being, happiness, fulfillment and longevity are entirely dependent upon your attempt to fulfill yourself, then this surrender will be very terrifying for you. But when you are tired, forlorn and have had enough and know that the next attempt will be as futile as the last, then you will accept this great gift from God which is called love.

Love is when God overtakes you. You have stopped running. At that time you do not care about personal fulfillment. You only want help and you only want to know. "What is it? I give up!" Then something very powerful happens. Love starts to overtake you, and you start to have an influence on other people.

The only way that you can heal another, the only way, is that your Knowledge is powerful enough to activate Knowledge in another. This is something that is entirely beyond your conscious control. It will be as amazing to you as it is to anyone else, but very natural.

We find it unfortunate that people think that self-improvement is about making life a better movie for themselves. We know that sounds hopeful, but that is not what will give you freedom, for freedom is escape from your personal side. Your personal side here is not destroyed or abandoned. It is only that your foundation has shifted. Then your life is no longer about survival. It is about contribution, and it happens naturally.

We want to unburden people. We want them to sit back in themselves and not try to dismantle themselves by saying, "Well, if I did not have these fears or these barriers, I would be perfect, radiant and happy all day long." That is a very common assumption. "Well, if I had no resistance, I would be absolutely magnificent." That is not the Path of Knowledge. That is the path of personal fulfillment. It is the path of trying to be God, trying to fulfill yourself and trying to make your world a Heaven on earth. What happens is that you do not understand what God is doing here.

God wills for you to join with your Spiritual Family so that you may learn the law and the reality of joining because this is the foundation for true love. For this you need your Teachers, though many of you will not experience them directly. They are watching over you.

Why are Inner Teachers important? Because they bring to you the memory of your life beyond this world and with it the realization of your purpose in being here. You cannot truly find your purpose without this greater sense of destiny and origin. Your purpose in the world is totally relevant to where you have come from and where you are going because you are a visitor. You have come from someplace and you have not come empty-handed, but your gift is hidden deep within you. It is hidden in your Knowledge.

You may attempt to do anything you like in this world, and you will not ruin your gift. The only failure possible is that you will not find your gift, or you may find it but not be able to contribute it. It is to guarantee as much as possible against this failure that we and other Teachers like us have provided trainings at various levels for various individuals in special stages of development.

This is God working in the world. God does not come because God is everywhere, so how can God leave somewhere else and come here? Coming here and going there is meaningless to God. God's Will is a force of attraction that organizes all individuals that are separated at all levels of existence. This force organizes everyone into perfect complements of each other and this is what brings everything back to God.

Your Teachers need you because you are emissaries in the world. You have not come here merely for therapeutic reasons. This world is not a mental hospital. I know people are very excited about working out past mistakes in all lifetimes, but that is not what God asks you to do. How can you work out anything in the past? It is over. You are still carrying it around like a great bundle. Your journeys into the physical do not account for your Greater Reality.

So, you need your Inner Teachers and they need you. It does not matter for all of you that you have conscious contact, though for some of you it is quite significant. It is always worth your concern and focus, however, because it is the reclamation of true relationship. Fully comprehending the Presence of your Teachers in this life is to have an experience of relationship directly. This will prepare you to be in meaningful relationships with other people with far greater ability and resourcefulness.

You know, when people first have any idea of Inner Teachers, they project all of their ideas upon them. "Let us make Teachers look like this or like that. Let us have them act very angelic or very powerful and very commanding." Some people want Teachers to just be like little helpers to kind of help them along. There are some people who have received ideas from their Teachers and have even heard their voices, but they have no idea who they are. It is only when you and your Teachers actually do something together that your relationship becomes comprehensible.

This is the foundation for love. Love will arise naturally when you are present for people and when you have come to terms with your true inclinations in life. Then love begins to permeate your life and activities. It is something that abides with you, not something that you stir up. You continue to be foolish and put on a little show perhaps, but this Presence is abiding with you increasingly, and it goes with you. This is the purpose of our work, to provide an environment and a curriculum that makes this truly possible in a short period of time.

When people respond to someone who is advanced, they are not responding to the person. They are responding to the Presence that is with the person. Often advanced individuals say, "No, it is not me. Do not look at me. I am not doing it. It is with me." There is a lot of emptiness in their lives for this grace to fill.

We are very blessed to receive the Presence of one another, to be able to touch life with life, to be able to touch this worldly life with life beyond the world. I am nourished through this contact. I am heard and I hear you. I give thanks for this opportunity. Nasi Novare Coram.

Think of
Spiritual Community
like a marriage
because
marriage thrives on
recognition,
true participation
&
devotion.

Thirteen

SPIRITUAL COMMUNITY

WE WOULD LIKE TO SPEAK ABOUT Spiritual Community and expand on this idea so you may understand the nature and purpose of relationships far more deeply.

Community is an essential foundation for true personal development and a perfect environment for complete contribution. It is something that has a lot of speculation surrounding it, a lot of judgment and ideas. The world serves as a very poor example of true community. There are very few good examples to draw from, so it is hard to have a healthy idea of this without many inadequate associations.

We treat true community like marriage because it is marriage. When you become married, it is not merely a personal association where you say, "I will get along with you if you get along with me because I have a great attraction for you, and we have many things in common." It is far greater than that.

If marriage is based merely on personal attraction, it will run dry. It must yield something greater and produce community—either children or a circle of people, a family. That is what marriage is for; it is for community. That is when marriage has a greater context in which to grow and where you find escape from personal dilemmas that can otherwise dominate you.

So, let us, then, think of Spiritual Community like a marriage because marriage thrives on recognition, true participation and devotion. It needs a foundation. Community as a marriage that is extended beyond two people requires the same things. You must have the proper incentive for participation, an understanding of participation and a preparedness for participation.

Obviously, there is a great deal of marriage going on around here without much success, so this is very relevant. When I speak of community, think also of marriage because you must marry something in life. You cannot go through life just being a spectator with a grand viewpoint and a more spiritual outlook about everything that is going on. You are still isolated. Until that isolation has been breached, your predicament has not been solved.

Now, there is a great deal to join in life—political movements and social movements and social clubs and fan clubs and all kinds of clubs, but this is not the community that I speak of. Community is an environment where you can contribute yourself completely and find escape from your own mind. What is freedom for any of you but freedom from your own mind? What separates you from God but your own mind? That is your oppressor; it must be your servant. But you need people to help you do this. You need forces that you can recognize and forces that are unseen as well because your life here is preparation for life beyond, so the forces from beyond are a factor.

This life is a transition to another life. To come into this world, you are born into a life from a life. You go through this life and enter into another life. People think of lifetimes only in terms of visitation rights to this planet, but you go from life to life, context to context. Why is the future relevant here? Why are these spiritual things so important? This life is preparation, like childhood is preparation for adulthood. Adulthood is preparation for your Spiritual Family, who will be waiting for you when you arrive and pass through the thin membrane that separates these two realms of existence.

Now, everyone wants community because human beings were not fashioned to be separate. It is a very grand idea that people can be completely self-sufficient, a great ideal for people. "I don't need anybody." It is a sign of weakness to need anyone, yes? So, personal fulfillment is the great pursuit: to be a little god in the world.

That is not what people want. It is neither their will nor their Knowledge to be so. You will need to be self-sufficient to comprehend and to follow your own Knowledge. I assure you that this will produce all the personal growth you could ever want because your personal side will need to grow to keep up with you. However, it will not be the dominating factor any longer.

You are here in this world, alone. You are seeking for your Spiritual Family. Why? Because that is what you have come from, and that is what you will return to. So, you seek it here as well because this is natural. And you run into a very difficult learning situation in this world because individuality and community have such strange associations. You seek for communion with others, and yet you seek with the incentive of using the other person so that you can be more of an individual. That is contradictory because the more you join with others, the less individual you are and the more you are a function of that relationship.

So, you must be very discerning of where you join and whom you join, but the inclination is still there. You cannot join with life if you are living in your thoughts, and it takes others to bring you out of your thoughts. You came here to find certain individuals who will bring your Knowledge forth. You did this so that you may discover and discern your true contribution in life and develop sufficiently so that you will be able to recognize it and yield it to the world. This is the beginning of community.

True community begins because an individual is experiencing Spiritual Presence to a very great degree. They are being called by something; something inside of them is calling them. If they can open themselves to this and follow its direction, then other people will be drawn to them, and they will be the seed for community. This is community in the truest sense. It is the product of one person responding to God. Now, the person responding does not have to be pure or lofty or exemplary. There have been very great scoundrels who have responded—notorious, controversial beings—though they needed to be purified in time. You do not need to be a perfect person.

This is what generates community. It is entirely natural. It is when people try to make community that they run into problems. "Let's make a community!" The world is full of this. "We will all join together to bring about this result in life." That does not produce community of the kind I am speaking of. Community is a natural process of attraction because one individual will draw and gather other individuals around him or her. It will be absolutely vital for their development and expression.

One of the most important things that individuals who are feeling this great Presence must learn is to follow that Presence. Their ability to follow will determine their ability to lead. If they try to use that Presence to fulfill their own ambitions, then there will be trouble and the Presence will leave them. If they think that the people are following *them*, there will be great difficulty. It is not the person you follow; it is the Presence with that person, the Presence that he or she is following. That is the true Presence. It is inexplicable. You can always argue that it is not there because it cannot be seen, and yet it will generate the greatest devotion a human being is capable of—the greatest empowerment and the greatest direction. What is it? It is like vapor. No one can catch it and study it.

Therefore, community is a natural creation. It is not created by ambition or philosophy because these do not generate devotion. Communities created by ambition or philosophy can only be held together by submission, and they require adversaries. In other words, "We will organize society because we have a common enemy." We see much of this in the world. That is participation through submission. That is not what yields Knowledge. Your Knowledge cannot emerge within you alone. It must emerge in the context of relationship. It is absolutely hopeless for you alone to find out why you are here. You may have some wonderful definitions, but you are still a slave to your mind.

When you open beyond your own thoughts, you will comprehend the Presence that calls you and attracts you. You will find it is more powerful than anything you can see or discern in this life. A man or woman of Knowledge is more powerful than the world, for what can the world claim from them? Yes, it can take their possessions from them and kill their body, but it cannot deprive them of their Heritage. These people will naturally create community and join in community because to them a separate life is incomprehensible.

Therefore, we say cultivate Knowledge and Knowledge will bring to you all the relationships you truly need. Those you do not truly need will find no purpose here, and so your life will not be hindered and held back by inappropriate engagements. Now, it is quite possible to be inappropriately engaged, yes? It is very tempting to make all engagements justifiable, but you do so at the cost of Knowledge. You do not need to make something right to keep from making it wrong. It does not have to be good to not be bad.

When you are truly engaged with those individuals whom you have sought, something very important will happen inside of you. You will feel energized, and you will feel more at home than you have ever felt before. It is an indescribable feeling of coming home in the world.

The reason that certain individuals are the seed of community is that they are experiencing community within themselves. Their body is no longer a hiding place for one being. It is a meeting ground now. Something is happening. The body is not a sanctuary for one; it is a temple for many. We call this community Spiritual Family. We use the word "family" because family is the closest approximation that you have in this life to intrinsic relationship.

Now, true community in the world must be very small, or it cannot be a Community of Knowledge. The world must join in community, but it will not be a Community of Knowledge because Knowledge is not preferred here. The results of Knowledge, however, are greatly needed because the results of Knowledge care for people.

The average person here is not interested in Knowledge because the race has not evolved that far. So, it is not wise to go out and try to change people because you will hurt them if you do. If you take a society of people and try to make life better for them, you will end up killing half of them. This is not a negative thought. It is real.

You see, God does not expect everyone to get it together now. Everything is moving along. Yet, *you* can feel the fire of contribution. Something must be done; you must be the person to do it, and you must gather others to help you. This fire of contribution is in no way contradictory to accepting the world exactly the way it is. It is only contradictory in terms of ambitions. The man and woman of Knowledge will go about their work regardless of circumstances, and if the world in general is no better at the end of their life, what does it matter? They gave all. They do not take people and condemn them for not getting better.

So, community must be very small because it is extremely intimate, but it will be life giving to the community at large, which is society. It is these little embers that keep the fire going. What has kept Knowledge alive in the world? What has enabled humanity to progress as a race but small enclaves of individuals, hidden, working away. Occasionally, an individual will come forth who will make a public display or demonstration. This is what has kept the embers burning.

Think not that God is going to ask you to go out and make the world better. It is not like that. Something inside of you will overtake you. Something greater than your mind will overtake you and lead you to certain people. It will lead you to give in certain ways and from this, good will be given to the world, though it is not necessarily the good that you would want to give.

It is like being in marriage. Marriage tells you what you need to give, and it usually requires far more than you, personally, would have planned to contribute, which is good. It provides an environment that demands much from you and brings you out of yourself.

So, the Community of Knowledge must be small, and from its own inner cohesion it yields something very important for humanity. It is very rare that the participants within that intimate little group will see how this is being done. For those of you who have felt an inner opening in life, could you trace how it came about? Could you account for the forces that prepared you without wild speculation? It is profoundly mysterious.

We have spoken of God as a great attraction, as a force pulling and drawing people. That is a good analogy because it allows God to be as great and as mysterious as God is. That is to acknowledge that God in the world is a force in motion. It is here to do something. It moves people to go along at its pace. It ignites people, sets people in motion and cares for people.

Yet, people who begin to feel this movement can make some very dangerous mistakes. That is why they need community because it is very difficult for the whole community to make a mistake, if it is a Community of Knowledge. Someone is truly looking at every moment, and this protects its members from error. As you begin to feel true direction in life, the errors you make are very consequential because you will have power over other people. You need others who are wise enough to counter your errors, which will surely arise.

The Plan accounts for error. That is why the gift that is given to you is given to others as well. We give a certain gift to ten people, and if it germinates and sprouts in two people, we have done well. Then the other eight can live their lives and not feel a dreadful sense that they have failed.

So, you must find community, and it can be a community with one person because that is the beginning. If you are to join a larger group, your Knowledge will indicate this. The value of community, truly, is that you begin to live life not necessarily on your own terms.

There are three stages of personal development. There is not getting what you want and being angry about it. There is getting what you want and being angry about it. And then there is following something that you're not sure you want and finding out that it produces happiness.

Now, most people are in the first stage, so they cannot appreciate the other two at all. When you are in the second stage, you are so committed to getting what you want and so defended against anyone taking it from you, that it is very difficult to appreciate what comes next. But the fact that getting what you want is so completely disappointing is what drives you on. It leads you back to "I don't know." "I don't know" is when things open up. That is when inner striving ceases for a moment and you begin to feel there is a Presence with you.

I tell you, this work is going on everywhere in the universe. When I speak of community, I am speaking of something that is extremely universal. You see, for a Community of Knowledge to exist in physical life, it must be very secretive. Why? Because Knowledge and ignorance do not co-exist very well. For community to be meaningful, it must be very, very pure because everyone who is drawn to true community has other designs as well. So, we must be very sober about these things. Then you can participate without much disappointment.

Why would anyone become violent in life save that their idealism has been dashed by something? The man and woman of Knowledge do not expect much from the world because they did not come here to take things. They came here to give things. They realize that the world is in profound distress and in profound misery, and so they do not require it to produce much. You do not walk into a hospital and say, "OK. Everyone on their feet. Attention!"

So, learning to give is very important. The way your Teachers give to you will convince you that true giving is alive in the world. It is a relationship of such depth, power and grace that to open to it will solve your intimacy problems with other people. Why? Because it is a greater intimacy. The other person is still over there. You are still over here. You can withdraw. But your Teachers come to you within yourself, in the most sacred of your sanctuaries. They demonstrate that your life is extremely open by entering through a back door that you are unaware of. It is because of their grace and their teaching that you learn to see that you are safe in such a situation. It is only when people are reckless and ambitious that they get into trouble.

You are looking for community and Knowledge because they are life giving. Community does not necessarily have to have any certain appearance. It is the force that drives it that is the significant thing. Do you know what happens to people who want to find God alone? They become extremely isolated in their thoughts. God enrolls you completely with other people through engagement. Do you want to prepare for a greater life beyond this world? Then you must learn how to engage because when you leave this life, you go back to your enclave where engagement is given. It is so fundamental.

You will not have a personal mind to aggravate you then, but you are not yet complete. Your Group has not advanced completely, for your Group must join with other Groups. You are here not only for your personal development or fulfillment. You are here for your Group and you are accountable to this Group. Some of them are in this world with you. If you graduate from this life, your whole Group moves forward. How do you graduate from life in the world? When your contribution has been completely given, then you will be complete here. But you will be here until your entire Group is complete, and then you will move on to a whole other dimension of life. So, you see, it is group learning all the way, community all the way. What is Spiritual Community in this life but a mere extension of your Spiritual Family? Life beyond this world must be reflected here and yet only in a very small context to be complete.

When Knowledge becomes strong in you, you will be moved to do certain things, and other ambitions will fall away. You must relinquish them because you are now a component of something so great and so vast you can hardly describe it or define it, but it is moving you.

Let us talk about marriage. I want to give you this suggestion, and it will be very challenging to actually do it: Do not try to make a marriage happen with anybody; marriage will happen to you. That ought to take the wind out of that sail!

You are not cause in the universe. You are only cause in your personal universe, which is not the universe. Let marriage happen to you. It will overtake you, as if someone were chasing you and finally ran you down— probably because you stopped. That is comprehending the way of things, the movement of things. Then marriage, if it comes to you, will be so natural. It will not be this great frenzy of emotion that people call love. You will not be dazed by it. It will calm you down inside. That is marriage with something very special.

You do not need to look for marriage; you need to look for Knowledge because that is what will bring your marriage to you. You are free to make marriages in the interim as much as you like, but at great expense. God knows what you want. Your Knowledge knows what it wants.

There are people in life who demand marriage with another and it is not meant for them, so they are condemning their lives to disappointment. What can we do? "I will not be happy until I have marriage!" How about if marriage cannot come to them? They have established a very difficult learning situation which only their disappointment can reveal. So, do not look for marriage. Marriage will happen. You will be drawn and it won't be so difficult.

In true community there are rules, restrictions and limitations because a community of people needs these things to funnel their energy constructively together. The only way that this can be real is if Knowledge is the binding force. Then you welcome rules because they help you contribute more effectively and provide the way to get things accomplished. If you are not participating with the force of Knowledge, then you will respond to the rules and not the cohesion itself.

Spiritual Community is quite distinct from society. Do not confuse the two. They are entirely different. One is for survival, and the other is for advancement of a very special kind. You do not need Spiritual Community for survival. You need Spiritual Community because your Knowledge is pulling on you to let it out. Knowledge is emerging like a pregnancy, a lifelong pregnancy. It labors and it delivers, and it labors and it delivers. It has contractions, and you have to open to let it out. Sometimes it is difficult, but it yields life into the world.

*If you are
with
the world's
evolution,
you will
comprehend
what needs
to be done.*

Fourteen

WORLD EVOLUTION

*L*ET US BEGIN WITH A LITTLE PRAYER:

> *"We honor the Presence of the Great Teachers*
> *who oversee the well-being of this world, its promises and its difficulties.*
> *We acknowledge as well the great care that is given to the*
> *cultivation of Knowledge here.*
> *We give honor to all who can receive Knowledge and*
> *recognize its value and meaning in the world."*

We have an advantage in our viewpoint on world affairs. It is very difficult to see the world when you're in it, so predominating it is. It is very difficult to comprehend life when you are so deeply immersed in only one of its stages, so difficult to contemplate its continuance and universal aspects.

You are all very fortunate to live at this period of time. I am sure that you are aware that you are living at a pivotal point in history. Considering the accelerating evolution of your societies and the establishment of a global community, it is hard not to recognize this. Yet, we want you to think of your generation in a little different framework now.

At every major stage of development, people have always felt that that particular stage was the most important one and that its result would be the immediate and dramatic alteration of human society, leading either to some sort of holy reclamation or great chaotic breakdown.

It is normal to think like this because the changes at hand seem so calamitous, monumental and disruptive. There is much speculation that you are on the verge of either a great collapse or a great rejuvenation. Life will either end here in some terrible event or everyone will enter a great period of spiritual harmony. It is important to give some kind of resolution to the great forces that are operative now, but these speculations do not emanate from Knowledge. Knowledge passes through such eras of transition, maintaining its presence and offering its sustenance.

You have opportunities and liabilities in this age. Your generation is preparing for a new world order. It is not an easy age to live in because the old structures are falling away or disintegrating rapidly, and there does not appear to be anything to take their place that seems consistent and reliable, thus leaving you open for much speculation. This is an era of freedom and exploration. It is also an era of error and foolishness. There is a great opening in the collective mind now. For better or for worse, this is the case.

The greatest transition, however, is not in this era. It will come in the next century. Many of you are experiencing the events to come in your life now because your life is in preparation so that you may be a contributor in the times to come. You are undergoing planetary change within yourself individually, as if you were being forced ahead rapidly. You must proceed. You cannot find another comfortable place to lie down. You must keep moving forward.

Others around you may seem complacent and not too concerned with the things that interest you. You are driven forward and people say, "You are so serious and self-preoccupied! Let's have fun! Why don't you have fun?" And you say, "I cannot ignore what is happening within me. Can't you feel it, too?" And they say, "No, what? Have a good time!"

You are preparing to be a contributor in a new set of circumstances. You must have great confidence in your own experience in order to prepare because there will be little agreement around you. Perhaps you cannot define your intent, but that is okay because Knowledge is working within you. You are the forerunner of great change, but the great change will come in the next century, and it will be greater than what you are experiencing now. I will not tell you specifics, for it would undermine your preparation, but I want to give you a greater perspective so that you may perceive your current circumstances with more compassion and more trust.

We are communicating in a way that is occurring with greater frequency now because this is the era of the Spiritual Family. There will be no Messiah. The Messiah was a forerunner of the Spiritual Family. As this past age has heralded the age to come, so will the age to come herald the age to follow, as if each is a stepping stone that opens up as humanity begins to take the next forward step.

This is not a great ending or a great beginning but a continuation. This next great step, which in many ways will happen beyond your own lifetime, will be successful based upon the contribution that you make now, but whose results you may not see in your lifetime here.

People often say, "If there are so many Spiritual Teachers around, why don't they come and make this a better world? Feed everyone! Make all war go away! Calm everybody down! Make everyone talk! Stop all this yelling!" There is an attempt now to exert the Presence of the Spiritual Teachers. Many of them have very specific curriculums that seem different from one another and are oriented to certain groups of people that have specific needs.

This Presence that has been with you all along is exerting evidence of its existence, as if to say, "Remember. You are only a visitor here. You have come to contribute something during this period of time. Do not become so self-possessed. Do not become so intimidated by circumstances. There are greater forces at work here and you must keep this in mind, or you will become merely another adversary in a world that is struggling to keep up with the momentum of evolution."

The change that must be forged in the next century and indeed in the centuries to come—for it will take several hundred years to bring it about successfully—is that the world must unite into one community. Now, if you think about that, it can arouse both great expectation and considerable anxiety because it holds the promise of a greater ability for humanity and also the reality that humanity will lose much of the heritage, identity and meaning that it has brought with it from the past.

Why does the world need to become one community? Because that is its evolution. All worlds where intelligent life has been seeded must undergo this transition or destroy themselves because evolution is the natural progression. A great challenge it will be. You must do this if you are to engage in space travel. You cannot be a bunch of warring tribes and hope to have any meaningful contact beyond. All worlds undergo this development.

There are three factors that will generate the forging of a world community. The first factor is that this is the stage in history where your world emerges into the Greater Community of Worlds, which it is destined to do, both from its own explorations and from the timely visits of many cultures from beyond.

The second factor is that your environment will deteriorate to a very great degree, bringing about international crisis. This will require cooperation and will require citizens everywhere to become actively engaged in the maintenance—indeed, even the rescue—of your planet.

The third factor is the integration of world economy. These three factors more than anything else will bring about a world community.

Humanity is on its way to that now. The wars that are erupting now, like cancerous sores upon the world, are based upon tribes fighting to regain their identity, attempting to re-establish their former role, their territory, their spirituality, their government and their heritage. You will see many attempts to reassert the past in the times to come, but the past is gone. Many of these attempts will be quite violent and disruptive. That is why we must teach peace. That is why there is a great deal of instruction going on currently, so that people may have a greater spiritual capacity to undergo this tremendous transition.

It is very important, we feel, that individuals who hold promise to be contributors at this very important time be able to break away from the personal obsessions and engrossing dilemmas that keep them preoccupied with their own needs. This is not the time to say, "How can I get it all together for myself?" You will get it together as you are called into service. When people are needed, they rise to the occasion. They bring forth their greatness. When there is no need, people fall into trying to satisfy all of their wants. When things get better, things get worse. When things get worse, things get better. Do you see? People did not come here on vacation. Vacation is when you go Home. Then you lie on the beach—if there were a beach! No, you came here to work, to experience and to contribute. That is why your stay here is so brief.

If coming to the world were a holiday, you could come for hundreds of years, but it's not a holiday. If you think it's a holiday, you will feel empty because life here cannot give you what you had before. The world does not possess the reality of your Spiritual Family, and so the intimacy and integration that are absolutely natural in your former state cannot be duplicated here completely. Yes, the world can be lots of fun, but only for those who are contributing because they are enjoying their own presence in the world. The world is bringing forth the value that they have brought with them. This is entirely natural and is no sacrifice.

The world is moving you forward in its relentless evolution. If you are with this, you will feel the movement of things. You do not need to figure everything out. You will *know*. You will look and you will see the movement of things that permeates people's lives and events. You do not need to make things right or wrong, give them a terrible aspect or a positive aspect. In Knowledge there is no negative and positive. There is only recognition and action. There is no loving and hating. There is only giving, which is true love.

If you are with the world's evolution, you will comprehend what needs to be done by you individually, and you will not condemn the world for its inevitable course. There are many people who think, "I want the world to be fun for me, and I hate the world because it is not fun for me! I will not be happy until the world is fun for me!" So, you have another miserable person in the world, blaming the world for being itself.

You are the architects of the next century. The results of your labors will be experienced by your offspring. That is how each generation builds for the next. This has a very important spiritual meaning because you are at work reclaiming Knowledge for a long time, in time.

The transition to a global community is the most important step any race can take and the one that holds the greatest risks. You see, it is like Knowledge. People want Knowledge, but they are afraid of it. They do not want to give up anything. They want more, but they do not want to give up anything. They are like a person who holds two grocery bags and wants four more. And you say, "Well, you must put down the two to get the four." "But no! I will not put down the two because if I put down the two, I will have none, and how do I know I will get four more?" And so this argument goes on and on internally. "Put down the bags." "No. Simply give me four more." "But you cannot hold six bags." "I don't care. I can because I am a magnificent being and I can hold as many bags as I can conceive of."

Knowledge simply holds the next step for you. It does not deliberate. It has no choice. Your great redemption in this world is to allow your Knowledge to come forth and take control of you. It is *your* Knowledge. It is God within you. All attempts to plan the world to be a wonderful place, all attempts to be a wonderful person and all attempts to rearrange things to look better become eclipsed by the emergence of Knowledge.

The man and woman of Knowledge are not attempting to do anything and thus everything can be done through them. Yet, they are hardly passive. In their non-interference, a Greater Power emerges and acts with tremendous strength through them. It is the preparation for this emergence that we teach because this keeps Knowledge alive in the world. It is our function to keep Knowledge alive in the world.

It is possible for human beings to live without Knowledge. Is this not evident? God is undertaking a conspiracy to keep Knowledge alive, for this creates the assistance that is available to the world. God cannot interfere. God can only send the Emissaries and ignite those who dwell here. That is the way of things here and everywhere.

Knowledge is quite different from personal ambition, even personal ambition for good. Knowledge does not assault things and make them better. Knowledge simply attracts. God does not come with a sword and cut your world to pieces. God does not come and punish sinners. Sinners punish themselves relentlessly. God attracts. We keep Knowledge alive in the world and from this, all important contributions are made.

We have often spoken about relationships, wishing to encourage people to step out of the relentless dilemma about relationships. We have given an important promise that is quite genuine: Discover your purpose and fulfill it, and all important relationships will find you.

This is no idle promise. It is entirely natural. Here you are a force of attraction yourself. Thus, you are given what you need personally while you carry out a greater purpose. You cannot fulfill yourself personally first and then have a greater purpose, for it will never begin. There is no fulfillment for your personal side beyond the emergence of your Knowledge. You must complete what you came here to do individually. As that grows stronger within you, you will be stronger. Then you cannot go out and play all the time. You must attend to something that is calling you, and that is good.

The world will be a much worse place without your contribution. You are contributing to your race and to the generations to come. Like plants and animals, you give for the generations to come. You give all and you are spent at the end of your life. You gave all! Now you leave, happy. There is nothing else to do. But that giving cannot be natural within you until you have reached a certain threshold. It is both an empowerment and a surrender all at once. You are more self-directed, more in control of your own thoughts and behavior, but on the inside you are opening up. This can seem very contradictory, particularly to observers, but it is natural.

Now, let us talk a little bit about some specific events in the world. First, the great powers in this world will become far more like each other out of necessity. Their opposition to one another will become increasingly theoretical and less meaningful in reality, and they will find that they need each other a great deal. They are like a husband and wife who cannot leave each other and must learn to get along because they love each other. Russians love you; you love the Russians. But when you love someone and you do not communicate, you harbor hard feelings and you become estranged. Along with this, the developing nations in your world will have increasing power in the years to come, and this will complete the requirement for a global community.

There will be a tremendous breakdown in societies. This will also generate cooperation. Those who have will be forced to give. It will not be easy, but it is good. You see, when the whole tribe is in trouble, everyone pitches in! The whole tribe will be in trouble, and that is not bad. If you understand the movement of things, then you can give without condemnation. The world does not need condemnation. Do not expect it to be a wonderful, glamorous holiday resort. It is a hospital and a school, all in one. It is where people get better and help others. Then, when the hospital work is done, you go home and rest—for awhile.

Nuclear arms? I know that what I am about to say will get some of you going, but there will not be nuclear disarmament completely for a long time to come because people need something to hold themselves in check. People have given a greater authority to their creations than to themselves to keep themselves from attacking their neighbors.

So, nuclear arms will be with you for awhile, but they will decrease. It is part of the evolution of your world that humanity keep itself out of major warfare until its societies can unite. The world cannot afford another major war here. There cannot even be a local war anymore. This seems strange, but you see, it is established to allow things to come together. It is not good. It is not bad. It is foolish, but it is what humanity prescribes. There will be nuclear weapons in your life for a long time to come.

It will be required in your world that you become more responsible and prudent about your relationships and sexuality. That is forced upon you now. It is not bad.

Do not worry about loss of life. It is only loss of opportunity. People are entering the world and leaving at every moment in great numbers. Your role here is to limit suffering and to teach compassion because compassion emanates from Knowledge.

You must realize that a world community will offer less personal freedom than you have been used to in your very happy times. It will not be a society of Knowledge because it is too large. It will be a society of law because it will require laws to maintain it because of factionalism.

That is why Knowledge must be kept aglow within you and in your relationships. That is what keeps everything moving and what generates all important ideas, creations, inspiration, and so forth. That is what nourishes humanity and keeps its life functional. Yet, Knowledge itself is beyond definition and beyond concept. It is even beyond its manifestations here.

Therefore, to be happy and to have meaning in the world, you must concentrate on developing Knowledge and allow it to contribute itself where it knows it can be of the greatest benefit. This will fulfill your need for relationship and community.

As I have indicated, your world is preparing to emerge into the

Greater Community of Worlds. This is a community you know almost nothing about. It is not a community of enlightened beings. It is not a community of barbarians. It is a community of evolving societies, many of which are very different from yours, yet because they are living in the physical universe, they have undergone a similar evolution to your own. Their environments, societies and values may vary greatly, but the requirements of physical life provide a uniform experience. Here in this world it is hoped that technological advancement will erase all difficulties in life, but that is not the case. Technological advancement only translates old difficulties into new expressions. You will have new problems to contend with.

In our former discourses, we have talked about the establishment of a Community of Knowledge and what it must do to survive in the physical universe, whether in this world or in any world. In the Greater Community, the most powerful and advanced groups and societies are hidden and do not show their power. It is also true in this world that the most advanced amongst you are hidden away. You do not see them, yet you may in your life encounter them if it be necessary for you. The Wise are hidden. The foolish appear.

You will be visited and are being visited now by races from the Greater Community. Indeed, there is more visitation than is generally acknowledged. You see, this can occur because human beings are so self-preoccupied that things can go on around them without their being aware of them. We do not want to bring this out to alarm you or to intrigue you. It is simply a fact of your time. It is a contributing factor to the accelerating evolution of your society.

Many people are now thinking about extraterrestrials. Your grandparents weren't. It is not because of movies. It is simply that it is in everyone's mind because it is evident. It is a part of your time and it is part of your orientation to prepare for your encounters with other intelligences who have entirely different sets of values than your own. Then you will find that God is not a human, that human values are not universal and that those things you hold to be absolute are quite relative to your own perception. This is very healthy.

You see, Teachers such as myself and my group are not Teachers for this world alone. We would not have come here a hundred years ago.

There are Teachers for humanity alone and they are human in their orientation, but we are Teachers of the Greater Community. Our heritage, background and specific function address themselves to this, for it is given to us to translate into human understanding Greater Knowledge as it truly exists because this is a period of preparation.

You are part of a Greater Community. You are not merely human beings. God is not for humans alone. The Plan of God is not for humans alone. God is at work in the world, and the work seems mysterious because you think with a very fixed frame of reference that limits your perception. God is at work everywhere, reclaiming the separated through Knowledge. That is The Way.

You are not
the giver.
You are
the medium of
the giving.

Fifteen

GIVING I

WOULD LIKE TO TALK ABOUT GIVING in the sense of what has been given to you. Each of you has come from your Spiritual Family into this world to play your part in this era of human evolution. You have come with problems to solve, but more importantly you have come bringing the memory of your True Home here, so that the distinction between the world and the Ancient Home from which you have come will lessen and disappear in time.

You see, only those who know that they have come from their Ancient Home can give. If you do not know you have a Home beyond the world, how can you give? You are bereft. You are poor. Poverty is your state even if you have money, drive cars and live in luxury. The sense of poverty is your companion.

Because everyone here has come from this place bearing gifts for the world, we share a common heritage. And yet we are distinct in many important ways because we are in a state of evolution. We are moving towards something. Life here is moving towards something. Everything in the universe is moving—planets, stars, galaxies—all moving towards something.

We all have come from the same place. We are all returning to the same place. But we are following different ways and using different means. Now that you have come into the world, there is great assistance available to you. There is tremendous assistance, my God! It has taken a great deal of planning to get you this far because you have come from your Spiritual Family. Thus, you are a representative of your Family while you are in the world. The world is a lonely, poor place. Therefore, it is important that you who come bearing gifts not only feel that you should give or that you must give but realize the extent to which you are given to.

You see, when you are not tyrannized by your own thoughts, you begin to feel the Presence that is with you, the Presence of your Spiritual Family. You can feel their Presence here. So powerful is their Presence! If you persist in your development, then not only will you feel it, you will receive it and it will move within you. It is a very great process. Very powerful!

In studying The Way of Knowledge, people learn to become disengaged from their own thoughts so that they can enter the realm of pure experience. Along the way, they learn to refine their perception, develop their sensitivity and organize their thinking. All this happens from giving.

We are here to give. You don't have anything here that we need. We do not need cars and money, holidays or vacations. We do not need a trip around the world. We can go around the world anytime. Like that! We can be at the far side of the world in the next moment. So, it is not that we need what the world possesses, but you do have something we need. What we need is for you to give what we gave to you when you came here. You see, you need your Spiritual Teachers very much, but they need you as well. It is a perfect complementary relationship. You could not be successful in your development in this world if you did not have your Teachers with you. The world would consume you completely. You would be lost here with little hope of regaining any memory of your true existence. It is because of your Teachers and because of your true nature that this is not the case.

So, let us talk about what it means to give because giving has many ideas associated with it, and some of them are not helpful. First, it is very important for you to realize that you do not know what you have to give. It is not what you think. Intentional giving often leaves you bereft and empty. It leaves you weaker and more depleted than you were before.

It is not you who does the giving. It is your Knowledge that does the giving through you. Something moves in you that gives. That is the true source of giving. It is your life that gives. It is not you. What can you give? You have a little money, a few possessions, a little bit of time, a little bit of love, a little bit of compassion. Yes, you can give these things beneficially, but you have too little.

It is something in you that gives and feeds others physically, spiritually and emotionally. As a result, you become more powerful, stronger and healthier. Why? Because your Knowledge gives where it must give, and it gives to the right people in the right circumstances in the right way. And you, as a medium of the giving, benefit because you receive the gift as well. Here, giving is a spontaneous and natural exercise.

Can you take your Spirit and make it give something? Now, you can give ideas, thoughts, emotions and beliefs, and these can be helpful, but there is a greater giving that gives *you*. This is very important because many of you feel you must give more than you want to. This creates conflict and then you think, "Well, if I give, I will get more. If I give what I want, I will get what I want." And there are all of these ideas about giving that are nothing more than bargaining. "Well, I will give a little bit here and a little bit there."

That is not the giving I speak of. What I speak of is Knowledge emerging and expressing itself within you. It is the power of your True Being, and at some point it gives you. Something takes over inside, and it is so natural and so gracious. You find yourself saying something or doing something that you never would have planned to say or do. Afterwards, you say, "My God! What have I said? What have I done?" It is as if life pulled it out of you.

So, you are not the giver. You are the medium of the giving. This is a very important difference. Those individuals whom we honor for their great contributions in the holy days, both here and abroad, did they figure out what they wanted to give? No. Did they figure out how they would do it? No. They gave a lot because they gave more than they had planned to give because their Knowledge did the giving.

When Knowledge gives, everyone is at ease. There is no guilt or blame because you did not give enough in that situation. "Oh, I should have helped that person, but you know, I really did not want to," or "I should go see this person, but you know, I really don't want to." And there is terrible blame for not even wanting to because you're supposed to.

You don't go Home because you are supposed to. You did not come into the world because you are supposed to. There is no "supposed to" in the universe. That is not what moves things. The earth turns not because it is supposed to. Does it have a choice in the matter? Is it not moved by something greater? And is not your giving moved by something greater as well?

The Greater Community Way of Knowledge teaches people to receive their greatness. Then Knowledge can move them more powerfully. Then there is less obstruction. There is less in the way. There is less refusal. There is less indecision. There is less preference. That is why this Teaching is so mysterious, you see. It is not philosophical in nature. We do not give a whole new philosophy of giving.

So, how do you do this mysterious kind of giving that I am talking about? You have to prepare. That is essential. That is what distinguishes the true initiates from the pretenders. Those who are willing to prepare in a curriculum that they did not invent for themselves are the ones who will surpass their previous capacity. The training has already been prepared and is established. It is given in many different forms, and it always takes you on a path that you would not have taken yourself. It asks you to receive something you could not give yourself, and in time it will ask you to give something you did not know you had. You will discern the power of the universe working within you, and it will not occur to you to ask questions about God, eternity, happiness, peace and evolution. You will merely be a witness to the movement of things. Indeed, you will *be* the movement of things!

Why is a holy person so powerful? Because they *are* the movement. They have prepared long for this. It is not something that came along one day and swept them away. They prepared mentally, emotionally and physically. Why? Because this is the realm of preparation. You do not prepare Knowledge; you prepare your body and your mind to be vehicles for Knowledge.

We would like to talk about spiritual practice here because it is relevant to giving. When you practice, whether it be a meditation in any form or an exercise in writing or observation, it is quite important that you enter practice with the idea of giving yourself to it. What can you get from practice? If getting is your motive, you will not have the patience, the openness or the receptivity that are necessary to receive the benefits.

If you close your eyes in meditation and you say, "I want to have contact with the Teachers. I want to have this question answered. I want to have certainty about this issue. I want to have a high experience. I want to leave my current circumstances and feel wonderful. I want, I want, I want," then of course you don't find anything. So, there is disappointment immediately and then you say, "Well, maybe if I give up all wants, I will get what I want," and so it goes on and on.

But, you see, when you practice in meditation, you come to give yourself to it, and there is a response because your Teachers come to give themselves and that is the touch. That is where you touch each other. I give to you, you give to me and we share our mutual giving. People often think in meditation that there are all of these realms and levels and all that sort of thing, but you know, there is only relationship there. Whatever experience you have, it is because you are joining your mind with another mind in some way. Realms and all that do not matter. Relationship matters; intimacy matters. This is what generates Knowledge. This is what returns the memory of your Ancient Home to you so that you can be an emissary while you are here because that is why you came. Why else would you have come here? It is too difficult a place to go on vacation. You are not here simply to repair old mistakes. There is not enough incentive for that.

Many of you already know that you should do this and that you should not do that. It is not merely that someone told you. You know what is not good for you, but you do it anyway. You should not eat these things; they do not make you feel that great. Every time you see this person or go to that place, it is not too good for you. You know that, yes? But you do it anyway. Why is that? Wouldn't it be reasonable to assume that if you saw something that would be to your advantage, you would seize upon it without delay? When you are truly motivated, this happens.

Why is there this ambivalence about Knowledge, this ambivalence about relationship, this ambivalence about intimacy? Perhaps one way of looking at this is that if you think you are going to cultivate yourself for yourself, there is not enough reason to do it. After all, life is short. You might as well have a good time. You can't be too sure of what is waiting for you on the other side.

People generally cultivate themselves because they realize their value to the world. Why else would they go through all of this development, exert this effort, expend their energy and make these little sacrifices unless they realized that they were important to the world? It is too difficult for people who are merely self-indulgent to prepare. It is too great for personal aims.

It does not take a lot of people to keep Knowledge alive in the world. Only a fairly small number who respond completely can keep it aglow here. Their lives are Knowledge. Though they are people with personal problems and personal thoughts and concerns, a Greater Power now abides within them. It is evident. They, as individuals, must develop themselves to carry this Presence, for you must be very wise to carry this Presence in the world. You must be purified and cleansed, and your mind must be whole. You cannot have conflicting impulses and will. Your behavior must express this wholeness.

Knowledge is very powerful. It has a tremendous effect upon others. You cannot be idealistic about it. If you render this Presence to those who do not want it, you give them only three choices: They can either join you, escape from you or attack you. They have no other choice. They will hardly be indifferent. You are a force to be reckoned with.

Therefore, you must develop so that your giving is done with Wisdom. This maintains you and assures that your giving will occur in the right place with the right individuals. That is why people who are destined to receive their Spiritual Family will go through a long period of development, which to them will seem to be for other reasons. You think that you go to seminars, think about things and read books so that you can become a better person, yes? No, no, no! Life does not need a better person. It simply moves you into a position so that at some point you can experience who is with you in such a way that you will have a window to your Ancient Home. All of this personal growth, what is it for? It merely moves you into position where you can experience Knowledge. That is its only value.

Your Teachers are given to you so that you may learn to give to the world. That is happiness here. Happiness here is knowing you are at Home while you are here. The only remnant of Home is your giving, which is your Knowledge, which gives itself when you are ready. You do not need to badger yourself thinking, "I must give more. I must give more. I must give more." I don't do that. You don't need to do that either. But at certain times you will be moved to give, and these times are important. It is not obligation or guilt. It is something else. It is entirely natural.

First you must prepare, and your preparation is all about giving yourself. When you meditate, give yourself. Your Teachers will only show up if they think it is important. You cannot reel them in. Insights will come to you when you are ready. They do not come upon demand. Thoughts are not insights. Knowledge is not thought in the way that you think of it. When you study your behavior or your thinking and when you read about the lives of others in a way that is inspiring to you, give yourself to that. It is all giving. And then there is a great opening in you. It is so natural, it almost escapes your attention.

If this giving is allowed to continue and you become a person of impeccable character, then the giving can happen with little risk to you personally and with great advantage to others. You will be the witness of a miraculous event inside yourself. Do not think that Jesus Christ was not marveling at his own work! It is a marvel to see that your life is a vessel for a greater gift.

Artists, musicians and athletes must train at their skill. They must practice a long time. Practice, practice. What is their reward? Their reward is that, for those moments in which their skill is in full employment, they are feeling a Greater Force moving in them. It is almost like they are going along for the ride. They are beyond effort and beyond anxiety. They are swept up. Their vehicle has been prepared, and so now they can transcend its mechanism. It is a very total experience in a very short period of time.

When you leave this world, you go back to your Home and you meet your group. You look and you ask, "Well, did I give it all? Are my bags empty? Did I deliver everything?" If your bags are not empty, you will want to come back. No one will order you back. You will say, "My God! Why did I not see it? It is so obvious to me now! I am Home. It is so obvious! Why was I such a miserable person? I was only there for a few years, yes? It seems like yesterday that I was with you all. Well, I want to go back. When can I do it?" And you find out you have to wait a little while.

It is so obvious what needs to be done. What needs to be done is you need to be the person in the world that you are when you are in your Ancient Home. That's what needs to be done. Once that is accomplished, you will not need to come here because then you will be able to give like us. You see, the world is like a garden. It is tended by gardeners. Your minds are the soil and the seeds of Wisdom are planted. We cultivate this garden because there is only minds cultivating minds.

So, you do not need to become a saint. You do not need to emulate behavior or force yourself to give what you do not want to give. That is not the preparation. It is difficult for students of Knowledge to fully appreciate the importance of their specific day-to-day development. They are preparing for a great opening inside themselves where their Homeland reveals and expresses itself through them. For that moment, they are Home and they are an extension of Home in the world, where those who are Homeless come.

Life is so short, why meditate? You are only here for a few years, then you get kicked out, sent back like a returned package! Why spend all this time practicing? You must do it because it is your nature to give. You were made to give. You are the gift. Without giving, life is miserable.

Yes, each of you has needs and at times you need a great deal, but it is only to enable you to give. This is so clear if you ever have contact with your Teachers because all they do is give. And they ask you to do things at a point in time so that you can experience giving, and they can share their joy with you.

The great lives, what did they accumulate here? Only one thing and that is relationship. When they left, whether they were penniless or rich, what did they take Home with them? They took relationship.

You see, if your life is about contribution, you will not have a problem finding people to be with you. Your problem will be choosing the right people to be with. You will not have to worry about a good career. Life bends itself to you who give, so thirsty for giving is life here. If the Presence is with you, people will come to you like magnetism. That is why you must be a person with little or no personal ambition. You must be very clean, but it is not you who cleanses yourself. Knowledge cleanses you.

Now, the world is a very tough place to give in because people are ambivalent about getting well. There is a great deal of harshness and anger here. So, how do you give in situations like that? How do you give to people who are angry, resentful and unhappy? How do you give where giving seems prohibitive? How do you give to situations that seem dangerous or violent? There are many "how to" questions about giving and they are quite legitimate, but my answer to you is very simple, though it will be a little mysterious: Do not worry about it. What gives through you knows how, when and where to give because you are not the person giving. You are the person following.

This brings me to my next important point: You must all become followers. It is very curious in your society that being a follower seems so belittling. Being a follower is something that people look down on. "Oh, you're a follower? What is wrong with you?" Everyone here is supposed to be a leader and in command—a captain or general or admiral or leader of a corporation or master artist. Being a follower is something pathetic.

You must all become followers because you all *are* followers. There are no leaders in the world. Those who appear to be leaders are either following Knowledge or they are following their ambitions. They are bound to what they follow. There is no freedom except in choosing and in following the right calling.

To be a real student, you must be a follower because to be a real student means you are learning things that you have never learned before. You are entering territory of which you know little and you must entrust yourself to your guide or instructor. You cannot lead the way. If you try to teach yourself, you will only recirculate old information. You will walk around the same territory imagining you are making great strides and after many breakthroughs, you will end up in the same place. "Well, here I am again!" You must be a follower.

The great recipients of Knowledge, those who are leaders, their lives are bound to Knowledge. They are following it. They are given to it. They are directed by it. They are nourished by it.

What can you give away in life but your independence? Is freedom a blessing if it separates you from Knowledge? The only true freedom is to live a life of Knowledge. Then you are free to truly be yourself. Then your contribution can be given maximally and you are fulfilled.

Yes, you must follow Teachers. Why? Because your Teachers follow

Teachers. That is how everyone finds his or her way Home. We don't have individuals out there looking for the way alone. Everyone is pulling everyone, following the person ahead and leading the person behind. That is how everyone files back to God.

You must give yourself in this life or you will never experience your life here. You will return Home and realize you missed your opportunity completely. e, when you are Home, it is very inspiring to come into the world because you are Home! Everything here is so apparent, and going down there for a few years is no big deal. But when you enter the world, you forget all that. Then you are a person of the world, and survival and gratification are your concerns.

The true gift in you is to contribute Knowledge and thus receive it for yourself. You must learn how to do this because the part of you that must learn is the part of you that belongs to the world. Your personality belongs to the world. Your body belongs to the world. You do not take them with you when you leave. We don't have name tags at Home! The personality and the body must be cultivated or they will not have the capacity to carry Knowledge. You will be a seed that never germinates, and you will go Home with your seed unopened.

It is very important to think of yourself as a follower because you are always a follower of something. You can be a follower of your own indecision, a follower of your own beliefs, a follower of your own emotional states. The only thing you can command is the decision about what you will follow. That is the point at which you can take charge.

If you say, "I will follow Knowledge," you cannot lead it. It is so powerful, how can you lead it? Where can you lead it? It has its own place to go. It will take you to the people who really need you. It will find you a husband or a wife if that is what you need. It will give you children if that is what you need.

It is difficult for students of Knowledge because they are still trying to go somewhere with their Knowledge. "Well, I am going to use Knowledge to be this or to have that." But maybe Knowledge has a little different idea. You cannot bargain with it. It is a force. It does not negotiate. It does not compromise. It does not talk things over. It merely goes where it has to go, and if it cannot go there, then it is latent within you.

Therefore, we who are cultivating this world wish for you to be very kind with yourself. You cannot purify yourself. You cannot cleanse yourself. You cannot lift yourself up. Entering true preparation is entering a process with your Spiritual Family beyond the visible and with individuals in life here in very specific ways. You enroll in these things because you must. Is it right? Yes! That is it. You don't know what you are signing up for. Goodness, if I were to tell you what you would do if your Knowledge were fulfilled, everyone would run away saying, "I had a different plan for myself!"

But what if I were to say, "If you do this, you will be a person of tremendous happiness. Your nature will be complemented. You will no longer be attempting to be in an idealistic state, to be a perfect person. You will be able to be in the moment because there is no future that you must negotiate. You will see beyond images. You will hear beyond words. You will sense beyond appearances. Life will become transparent to you in this world, and you will begin to see your Ancient Home through the transparency."

This leads me to my next point. Part of your preparation in being a student of Knowledge is that you must comprehend your nature. This is very important because you must realize your limitations. It is very important that you realize your limitations because you have them. That is when you become honest with yourself. That is part of growing up. If you are to be a true contributor in life, you must know your limitations. You must understand how you work, without all of this value judgment, and then you can work with your mechanism most effectively.

Your body has a certain shape and certain physical characteristics. Your mind is like that, too. It is not your function to transcend your nature. It is your function to use it as a vehicle for contribution because your nature here is temporary. Why perfect the temporary? You don't have time to perfect it. You lose it long before it is perfected. It is like preparing a meal and taking too long. By the time you get to the end of it, everything has spoiled! Your mind, your body and your personality—their highest option is to become vehicles for Knowledge.

Yes, there are corrections to be made. Yes, you must alter your behavior. Yes, you must be able to restrain yourself in certain ways. But how can you have appreciation for yourself if you are always attempting to be an absolutely perfect person? Of course you will have fears. Of course you will have certain ways that you do things. You do not need to be limited by this, but you must understand that it is your nature.

You see, the function which you will be given once your Knowledge is cultivated to a certain point will give you a role in life that is completely complementary to your nature. It is a very great blessing that God wants you to be exactly the way you were made. It is absolutely perfect for your function. It is hard to understand your nature because you do not see its relevancy to your function. You are custom-made for something that you have not discovered yet. When you discover your function, your life becomes more about honoring your nature than attempting to change it. You will have to become a master of it, however, for there are liabilities as well as assets, and you cannot justify the liabilities. You must learn to accept and to use your nature wisely.

So, let us honor those who gave beyond choice, those in whom giving gave itself. And let us be thankful that it did so, for Knowledge has been kept alive in the world. Knowledge is the oasis in a dry and thirsty land. It does not matter that the theologians came and constructed wonderful belief systems for their own survival. It does not matter that the thought system that was a result of that giving calcified and became a restraint for people. That always happens. When Knowledge disappears, thought begins. When people can't know, they invent things to give themselves temporary stability to allay their own anxiety. For without Knowledge, all there is, is anxiety.

Let us honor those in whom giving gave itself. They had to develop themselves so that they would not stand in the way of the giving. They did not attempt to use it for other purposes. They honor why we have all come here. What a great blessing it is to leave the world and say, "Ah, I brought nothing back with me but these people. I came back with a full heart and empty hands." Then, Home is established here as well as there. And do you know what happens next? Well, when everyone in your little group that you are working with is complete in this world, you all move on to another place where Home has been denied, and then you re-establish Home there. Then you save that world. What needs saving but a place where Home has been lost temporarily? When all places have been reclaimed, then the work will be over and the fun begins. When you are

Home, your experience of Presence is magnificent, but even there your experience is not complete, for it is evolving as well. Yet, it is as great as your capacity, and as your capacity grows through time, so will the experience of Presence be ever greater and more inclusive for you. It will be your supreme joy to contribute this wherever you go.

So, let us give thanks for those who gave, for their giving is a reminder of our own purpose here. And as we become contributors to life, we will see that life gives contributors to us to make sure that our needs are met and our hearts are filled.

*You are literally
walking on the ground
that was built by
the giving
of others.*

Sixteen

GIVING II

NOW I WOULD LIKE TO TALK ABOUT GIVING, a
particularly appropriate subject for this time of year when
there is a tremendous sense of obligation to give, anticipation of
giving and the reminder of the value of giving itself. It is also a time for
people to take inventory of their ability to give, their desire to give and
the problems and opportunities that arise.

There is an opportunity now to celebrate holidays as Holy Days.
What makes a day holy, a commemorative day, is not merely a mysterious
or miraculous event. It is the giving that occurred in the past that has been
brought forth into the future.

In holy times we remember individuals who made great contributions, and that is what makes the events holy—holy days. It is not just that
some great event happened that was out of the ordinary, or that people
saw something they had never seen before, a miraculous event. These do
not signify a holy day. A holy day commemorates the lives of those who
contributed a great deal.

In these holy days the giving we commemorate is not an intentional
giving. It is not giving with a motive. It is not giving to produce a result. It
is not giving to reciprocate. That is not the essence of giving. The essence
of giving is that you give yourself, unsure of your motive and unsure of the
result. You give yourself to something. That has a lasting effect.

You must realize that you do not know what you want to give. You
really don't. What you want to give is not your greatest gift. Your greatest

gift is brought forth out of you by life. You prepare for this by becoming very honest and by making important decisions about where you need to be and what you need to do.

When you put yourself in an environment where life draws from you, this activates your Knowledge. Here something very powerful in you gives, and you feel moved to do something you had not planned to do, and you do not know the consequences. That is when you come alive. That produces a holy day—the day someone fully came alive, the day their Knowledge was activated and their life was given completely in a specific area. That is a holy day.

To graduate from this world you must have this experience. To go to the next step beyond being a participant in the physical world is to be a participant in the spiritual world. This is a position of profound giving because what can you profit by giving then? You will not need the usual kinds of things: food, shelter, praise, security, survival or romance. So, there is nothing really to bargain for. At this point you give because that is all that you can do. That is life expressing itself.

Receiving is not your concern in the next stage. Your concern is that your gifts will be given by those who receive them. That is the concern. You are concerned with the well-being of those who receive your gifts. If they do not discover what you have given and what you are prepared to give, then they will continue in misery, trying to secure all manner of things for themselves, and yet feeling very cheated because life cannot give them their Spiritual Family. It cannot give them the sense of inclusion that they yearn for so greatly.

Therefore, to graduate from this life, which is the greatest experience of holiness available to you, you must give yourself completely. Then, when you leave this life, when you return to your Spiritual Family, you bring nothing with you except relationships. Those you bring that remain behind are in your heart permanently. You have reclaimed them as part of yourself.

All of the giving you do is valuable because it paves the way for this great turning point that I am indicating, where Knowledge gives your life. I gave my life. I did not do it for a motive. I did not do it because I thought that it was a good thing to do or that it would get me some-where. When people give themselves in this way, in the appropriate place, a great turning point has been reached. That is a holy day. The day that it happened will be forgotten, but the result of the giving will continue.

Christmas time commemorates the birth of Jesus. Now, there are some stories about Jesus Christ that are very popular and cherished which really obscure his contribution. He was a forerunner of the Spiritual Family. He was speaking about the "Kingdom" and his relationship to it, and he was including others in his experience of it.

Did Jesus Christ determine what he would give? Did he decide how much he would give? For him, it took over completely. His demonstration was a very singular act, but his example is important because it exemplifies giving beyond choice. Does it matter if he felt like it on that particular day? No. He was moved by a greater force than his wishes and his wishes were fulfilled as a result, for his wishes were in harmony with his nature.

This kind of giving is magical, wonderful. You become the witness of the giving. Instead of being an isolated and pathetic event, your life becomes something that you marvel at, a holy event. It is not like you give something, and you get something back, and you weigh it at the end of the day to see how the scale tips one way or the other. You are now so happy to have a life that is important. That is what you all want—a life that is important, not a life that you think is important or that you can justify, but a life that *is* important. That is when you get your life together, take good care of your health and really value yourself as a vehicle. These are all important. Your life now is not only about your satisfaction. You have come here for a purpose that you can now feel because you see this purpose being enacted.

Therefore, it is so valuable to think of the giving that has happened. There has been so much giving that has made your life possible, even in a very physical sense. People gave their lives to invent the conveniences you see about you, to build these things and to make these things available.

Keeping religion alive in the world, despite its errors, took tremendous giving. You see, religion dies the minute after it is born. It is something that spoils very quickly and must be reborn every minute. If it is allowed to die, it becomes merely another thought system, a constraint now and not an apparatus for freedom. It must be renewed. What renews religion in the world is Knowledge, this quality of giving where individuals render their lives naturally. They infuse so much life into the idea of God that God comes alive. Without this infusion, God is dead. When people say, "God is dead," they say that because God has become merely an idea. The life of God is dissipated. Then someone comes along and gives his or her life and that is God. And you say, "Oh, my. *That* is God!"

How do you achieve this kind of giving that reveals to you your Spiritual Family while you are here in the world and that fulfills you and completes your purpose in time? Well, one of the things that makes this giving possible is that eventually all the other reasons for being here fall away. This is very confusing to understand because often it seems like things are leaving you or you are losing them. You become less certain. Your assumptions fail you. You lose interest. It looks like things are coming to a standstill. All your ideas about how life should be for you seem to be breaking up, and you are becoming confused. This confusion is the beginning of a true opening.

It is hard to understand this philosophically, but students of Knowledge have this dual experience of becoming less certain and more certain at the same time. They are less in control of the specifics of their lives, but they are more in charge of the direction of their lives. What happens today is not as important as what today is for. Before this, however, they were very concerned with the particulars of their lives and with having their desires fulfilled. Beyond basic survival, they wanted to fulfill their wishes because they believed that this produced happiness.

Students of Knowledge, however, start to lose interest in these forms of stimulation. They have other interests that are more mysterious and more compelling. All of the other incentives for being in the world begin to wear down and in their place something begins to arise. At the beginning, it is ill defined. It is just a conviction that you have a purpose and a direction in life and you can feel it. But you cannot justify or explain what is happening. When someone asks you, "What is it you want to do in your life?" you say, "God, I don't know anymore!" But you *do* know. "I'm going to do something very important, and *that* I did not know before."

So, there is this loss of explanation, but what you gain is so much greater. What you gain are purpose, meaning and direction. Here your life becomes increasingly inexplicable. When you view this positively, it is very exciting. When you view it fearfully, it looks disastrous because your former incentive to be someone is breaking up, and yet the person you truly are has not yet fully emerged.

The person you truly are, once you are prepared, will give your life. You will be a follower and a leader all at once. This is profoundly different from your former state where you were primarily concerned with your own thoughts. Now you are moving with life itself, and your experience of life is greater than your thoughts, and you are able to view your thoughts much more objectively. They do not harness you so much, and your life becomes a holy event, an event that individuals around you will begin to commemorate.

With the emergence of Knowledge within you, you begin to attract others who are experiencing the same thing, and the quality of your relationships begins to deepen a great deal. Those individuals who cannot keep pace with you begin to fall away and others come to take their place, for your relationships now have a new basis.

A person who has direction has the power to create effects and events in the world. Direction is power here because most people are without direction. They are merely governed by their circumstances and do not experience that their life is *for* anything that they can truly feel. So, a person with direction, good direction or bad direction, has a strong influence.

People who are truly giving do not know why they are doing it because why is not important. They have not figured it out. It is too powerful. God is using their lives to write God's signature upon the world.

You individually must prepare your mind and your body for a life of giving. It is not merely that old things fall away. It is that you become stable, and you are able to weather your own internal storms without losing your vision. You see, Knowledge is a very great thing to carry, and you must be stable to carry it. This is capacity. You must have a great big empty space inside of you to experience Grace.

Now, people are always trying to keep themselves filled up to the brim. There is not much you can fill yourself with but sensation and concern, happiness and sadness, and so you try to keep it full all the time. Full, full, full. If it starts to run out, it becomes very scary. "Oh, my God! My life is becoming empty. Quickly! I must do something! I must find a relationship! I must get a new job! I must build a new house! I must travel! I must, I must, I must . . ." Keeping it full all the time.

But students of Knowledge begin to let the stimulation run down so that what it conceals can come forth. This is the great faith—that you truly *are* sent from God! Letting the stimulation run down is something that your Knowledge indicates simply because you are losing interest in things. Instead of stimulation now, you seek quiet. Instead of feeling all filled up, you want to let yourself open up.

This shift in emphasis in life is very natural and signifies a spiritual emergence. It is academic to analyze it. It is something that is entirely natural. If it is not yet occurring within you, you will not understand its meaning. You will think it is a psychological process, or a spiritual process, or some other kind of process. If you have not undergone it yourself, if it has not happened in your life, how can you really know?

Your life is a gift. If it is not given, you will return Home like an unopened package, like return mail! "Oh, package returned unopened!" And you will not be happy because when you return to your Spiritual Family, you will see that you are an unopened package and you will say, "Oh, my God! How could I forget you who are here with me now? I must return. I want to go back! Please, can I go back? It is so obvious to me now!" And you will want to come back. You have to come back.

If you look at the animals and plants in your environment, you will see that they give everything so that at the end of lives there is nothing left. They exhaust their life force according to their nature and their role. You have a nature and a role, too, only they are greater.

You see, it is very important to understand contribution in your life because the contribution that you are really making is for the generations to come, and you cannot see that. You can say, "I am not making a contribution in my life. I do not see the results." Yet your true contribution is to lay the foundation for the possibility for life in the future, not only physically but for the promise of redemption.

We celebrate Christmas because a life was given for the promise of redemption. Knowledge was kept alive in the world. Religion was infused with Spirit. A very unique life was completely given and religion, which at that time had become dead, was infused with life and began to breathe again. God is always pumping life into life, essence into form. When things begin to die, individuals are sent into the world to bring new life. This keeps life going. This makes your redemption possible.

Your contribution will not be fully felt for many years, even beyond your passing from the world. It is very hard to justify your contribution while you are here. How can you? You can build buildings and empires. You can have medals and commemorative things. You can have everyone saying you're wonderful. But they will all forget you. The buildings will fall down. The justification for giving cannot be found in that way.

It is very important that everyone here find something that they can marry in life and give themselves to completely. But you must be prepared to give and you must give wisely. If you give with a motive, you will make many mistakes in where you give. You will try to prove things with your giving. Your giving will then be a desperate attempt to justify your existence, and you will give to people who cannot give back. You will give to situations without promise, and you will be used by others. This will leave you bitter and confused.

When you come to that place where your life is to be rendered and given, it will be given back to you even greater than before. This is natural. If you come upon this place, do not hesitate, for you have promise.

For those of you who know you are true givers, you have realized thus far that you must be very discerning in where you give. When you find that to which you truly must give yourself, your Knowledge will indicate it, and you will not need to justify it. You will know you have hit upon the right place because it will ignite your Knowledge, and your Knowledge will want to give itself. This is a different experience. It is so different from trying to give to get something.

Contact with your Spiritual Teachers is very meaningful here because it honors relationships that are for giving, and if you receive that gift, it will ignite you to give. That is why in our work here, we encourage students of Knowledge to allow their Teachers to demonstrate their reality so that you can witness giving and receive its benefits. This will ignite you to give because you only came here to give.

Now, the problem is if you are trying to rule your own life, it is very hard to give because there are so many things you must secure for yourself to be the master of your life. Your preoccupation is to keep people from taking things away from you, to keep what you have, to try to get more and to exert dominion over your life and affairs. What threatens you are people who have given their lives completely, for it burns in your heart how much you suffer in your own kingdom.

If you try to seek dominion over your life and establish your personal kingdom, you will feel very cheated by life because it is always taking something away from you. It is always eroding the foundation of your castle walls. It is always depriving you in one way or another. Circumstances attack you. Illness attacks you. Personal greed from others attacks you. Time attacks you. So, this insistence that you must be the master of your realm and that no one can tell you what to do —"I am in charge!"—is a very sad state. Being in charge is meaningful when you are following something that is real. Then you must exercise true discipline and capability in managing your mind and affairs because you have something important to do. This is real mastery on a personal level.

Being the king or queen of your kingdom is very tragic because it leads to despair and failure. Why? Because you will get called back. Your life is not of the world. You are sent here for a purpose. You have a little bit of time, and then you get called back. What difference does it make if you bring your kingdom, your personal kingdom, to your Spiritual Family? It would be completely irrelevant. It is only a device for your own personal survival.

That is why we say those who follow Knowledge will become masters of their lives, but their lives will be completely given to life, so there is no conflict. They are here to give, not to take, because they are richer than the world. The world merely renders those things that allow them to give. Thus, they have things and want things only so that they may give their lives. They are the rich ones now and the world is the impoverished place, instead of the other way around. There is a complete reversal in your experience of the world when you make the transition from personal fulfillment to personal surrender. Giving is surrender. My God! The flower opens, gives it all away and dies. Surrender! You reap the benefits. Complete surrender: complete accomplishment.

People think surrender is a passive state where you lie down by the side of the road and sort of give up. That is a very pathetic view!

Surrender is allowing Knowledge to take over your life and give it. This is the greatest act for any person. Up until this time, you will need to prepare your abilities. You will need to reduce the harmful tendencies in your personality. You will need to establish a new foundation, and that is very important. Not many people are yet at the threshold of Knowledge. Yet everyone has the opportunity to provide a foundation for Knowledge, so that when it emerges, it will be able to stand in the world. The person who is honest, consistent, dedicated, contributing and open has already developed a foundation for Knowledge, so when Knowledge takes over, it will stand. It will not crumble and the world will not be able to assault it.

Therefore, working on yourself personally before Knowledge emerges prepares you for a greater opening that is incomprehensible. The dam will break. Eventually, one of God's arrows hits the mark, and you fall apart and are a mess for awhile. All of your attempts to fulfill your ambitions fail and something begins to stir. That is when you are born again. That is Christmas! Christmas is not the birth of a child who later became Jesus. Christmas is the birth of Knowledge in the individual. That begins true giving, and that is what we commemorate in the holy days. All individuals who have done this have laid the foundation that has made your life possible—physically and spiritually. You are literally walking on the ground that was built by the giving of others.

The trees grow from the ground that was prepared by earlier generations. When a tree dies, it is fertile soil for new trees. Knowledge is like that. Knowledge gives itself in the world so that there will be fertile soil for Knowledge in the future. You see, God is pumping life into the world. The more developed you become and the greater you are, the more inclusive your life will be and the greater will be your contribution in this respect.

So, to be a student of Knowledge, allow your life to have its mysteries. Do not try to explain everything and justify everything. Knowledge will emerge within you once you have chosen that this be your life. You will become less certain about particulars and more certain about your purpose, meaning and direction. Then you will begin to find freedom from anxiety and ambivalence, and that is the greatest gift of all because a life without anxiety or ambivalence is completely rendered into the world.

*Mastery
is something
that works
through you.*

Seventeen

MASTERY

I WOULD LIKE TO SPEAK ABOUT MASTERY—about learning, preparation and cultivating the experience of Knowledge. Mastery has become a very popular subject. It is promised as the result of many spiritual study programs that are available now, and people have great expectations of themselves, of the educational processes and of their teachers in this regard. This is unfortunate because you approach relationships with teachers with very grandiose ideas about them, and part of your learning is your disappointment when you find out that they are real people like you. Mastery is very relative in this world. It would be wiser to become proficient rather than masterful because a master in the world is a profound beginner, a novice, in the life to come. So, how do you determine who is the master, who is more learned and who has greater skill if mastery in the world makes one a novitiate in the world to come?

The great gulf between you and God must be filled in with reality. The assumption is always made that there is you and there is God, and you are small and God is great. But between you and God is all of life's evolution—a vast expanding network of relationships. It is through this network that you must pass. It is within this fabric that you must become entwined. God is not waiting to meet you when you get off the train. "Welcome Home!" It is not like that. It would be more accurate to say that you go on to your next assignment, and yet that sounds too formal. In essence, you simply take the next step. You then begin to comprehend life on a greater scale than you can perceive here, and you have teachers and students along with you to help you accomplish the next tasks.

So, what does becoming a master mean? Why become a master? Who is more masterful amongst you? These are valid questions. One of our first lessons for you is to learn that there are no masters living in the world. This is very important! There are no masters living in the flesh. There are great students, there are proficient learners, but no masters. Give up the pursuit of mastery. Become proficient. Do not discourage yourself by trying to grasp what is beyond your realm. The world is a place to work, to give and to receive. It is not a context for mastery. Much of the mastery of the world will be useless when you pass beyond, and because this life is preparation for the life beyond, it is important to have this perspective about these things.

The pursuit of mastery leads to disappointment. This disappointment can reveal a greater truth or it can discourage one entirely. Since we do not want to discourage you in your pursuit of Knowledge, we wish to make your pursuit more genuine, more compassionate and more kind. We are masterful compared to you, but there are greater masters than we who do not serve this world. They simply have a greater realm of responsibility—that is mastery.

Along with the desire for mastery is the quest for power, the escape from pain and the permanent acquisition of pleasure. You will not master the world, but you can give something to it. What you bring, you bring from beyond this world and what you bring, the world cannot spoil. With your gift to the world, as it finds its expression through you, comes your memory of your life beyond this world, and this begins to free you from fear.

This is Knowledge. It is the aspect of mind that you have brought with you from beyond. It has nothing to do with your past lives. It has nothing to do with your memory. It is simply the part of you that has never become separated in life. It is dormant now because it cannot be activated before you reach maturity in this life. Therefore, the primary emphasis for human beings is to become mature enough to build a foundation so that Knowledge can emerge and express itself. That is worth thinking about.

Mastery is not having information about all things and all people. Mastery is not about being completely free of fear. Mastery is not about having no anxiety. Mastery is not about wealth and power. The truly advanced may not appear to have wealth and power. They may not appear to have exemplary behavior. They may not appear to be free from fear. Indeed, they will rarely appear at all! They do not seek glory or confirmation from others.

We wish to open up this whole issue of mastery because then something important can happen. If you are certain that what you are pursuing in life is mastery, then your first task is to become confused because your objective is not true. Even though you may never have thought of being a master, it is still part of your ambition. You may call it something else. At its core it is the desire to be God without God, to replicate God's Kingdom in exile, an exile that you have chosen. This is your intent, but it is not your Knowledge, for your Knowledge has brought the Kingdom here. The world is predominantly a place where people want to be God without God. Yet once Knowledge emerges, all other ambitions simply begin to fade because they are unnecessary and cause conflict. Knowledge is the unifying factor in you. It is God working in your life, and it is you, too.

Mastery is something that expresses itself through you when you are not trying to do anything with your life. Mastery has its own design and direction and its own time of expression. There are no masterful individuals. Do you see? There are no masters. There are only vehicles of expression. Mastery is something that works through you. Your preparation is to become a vehicle for it, to build a foundation to let Mastery build something upon you and within you. Then there is freedom from perfection. Many people are killing themselves to become perfected, trying to have perfect minds, perfect bodies, perfect affairs, perfect relationships—everything perfect. Not a flaw, nothing to disrupt perfection. These people suffer very much because they live in a world that is very involved in error, is constantly changing and has very gross appearances. Most people don't give a damn about perfection anyway, so there is very little agreement, and life is always eroding their perfect establishment.

Life is not about becoming perfect. It is about becoming real. It is about stabilizing your mind and affairs and beginning to open yourself to a Greater Reality that wishes to express itself through you. You cannot control the mechanism for doing this. You cannot determine its outcome. You do not know where it is going to take you, who it will bring into your life and who it will send away. It is mysterious, yet with Mystery you will be able to participate in life with such certainty and confirmation. You will be far more certain of this Mystery than of anything you can perceive around you—your society, your economy, your physical health. All of those are so changeable, but the Mystery of which I speak is firm and established. It is in perfect peace because it is not changing. It is only expressing itself in changing conditions. It is without change, and yet it is moving things along. It is not growing. It is not becoming. That is why it is so still and why you must become still to have a direct experience of it.

So, we want to unburden you of mastery and perfection. This clears the way for you to become a truly proficient student of Knowledge and a true contributor in life. You will find that that challenge is quite sufficient. Then you will be able to be a real person in a real world with real feelings and honest communication with others. And your whole basis for condemnation will fall away because, you see, if you do not judge others, you love them. If you have no criteria for judging them, then it is easier to love them. But if you are attempting perfection, well then, everyone is either passing or failing your assessments.

Your energy is required for preparation, and what you are preparing for is freedom of a very substantial nature. What you are preparing for is contribution and satisfaction. So, let us put mastery aside. Let us not try to become masters. Perhaps one day someone will come up to you and say, "You are our master." And you will say, "Oh," uncertain if that is a good thing or not. People will call you a master, but you will not be trying to be one, and you will not be so sure it is a good thing they call you this because of the expectations that go with it.

Demonstrating power in the world is extremely hazardous. That is why the Wise rarely do it, and if they do, it is only under certain circumstances. If I were to say, "If you achieve greatness, you will have to hide it," does that discourage you from achieving greatness? If I say, "If you have power, you will have to hide it," will that discourage you from seeking power? The truly advanced work in the world behind the scenes, drawing as little attention as possible. On occasion, certain of their numbers will become more visible to make specific contributions. They may be in the field of education or politics or any field. They are willing to take the scrutiny of the world and all of its misfortunes because that is their calling. But they are the exception and not the rule.

At some juncture, whether you agree with my words or not, you will become very confused about why you are doing all this personal growth. You become very confused because it is not justifiable for the reasons you think. Your life is getting better in some ways and harder in others. It is getting a little harder to tolerate the aggravations of the world because you are more sensitive, and yet you seem more in control of your thoughts and feelings and more tolerant of others. At some point this becomes very confusing, and this is a very important point because here you begin to discern the reality of your pursuit.

What is being called for is the activation of Knowledge. That is what everyone is moving towards because it is the escape from pain. It is the escape from ambivalence, which is pain. It is the escape from choice. It is the escape from conflict. Here your life becomes uniform. It has purpose and direction. It has true relationships. It is moving and you can discern its direction and movement. You are a witness to your life rather than attempting to be its master.

I'll tell you a story. Long ago, when I was learning to follow, I had to receive a Teacher such as myself, who was not visible to my eyes, in the face of very severe circumstances in the world. My people were fleeing a defeat of our nation, and we were all heading for another land in the Mediterranean area. Yet a Teacher appeared and said, "No. I want you to go back into the heart of those pursuing you." I thought this was madness. It seemed certain death to me to do this, but I felt I could not deny the Teacher, not only because of my reverence for the Teacher, but because I *knew* I must follow this. I turned and returned. The pursuing armies did not even see me. I passed through them like a knife passes through water. I was not invisible; I had no magical powers, but I did not expose myself unnecessarily. It was a good thing I turned back, or I would have been destroyed, for those I was fleeing with were caught and executed. No one expected me to return. Therefore, my escape went unnoticed. I returned to my former city and took refuge and allowed things to quiet down. Then I began my preparation with my Teacher. Because I was a doctor, I could practice my craft under the new government with some degree of license and freedom. It was there that I began to teach Knowledge because I was following Knowledge.

Who would want to become a master when your land is under submission by harsh rulers? Who would want to show their power and gain recognition? Certainly not me, being a servant of that land. I was able to dwell in that country for a long time before leaving. I departed soon before my rulers themselves fell to other conquerors because I followed the same Instructor. Why was I selected and called out while others were not? I cannot say. But I was one who could receive, and I did. You see, even my life has Mystery.

That was long ago, very distant in my mind as well. But my decision to turn and to go gave me something I did not have before—it gave me confidence in an aspect of my own self. It gave me confidence that I had assistance in life, a form of assistance I had not anticipated. I was not a religious man, but I had a natural inclination to recognize and to trust something substantial.

You see, when you leave the world, you do not find out about everything—"Well, this is the way it really is!" You simply have a bigger perspective. The Mystery continues to exist. I am here at the request of the same Instructor. I have grown with my Instructor. She became greater as I followed her. I became greater as I followed her. There was no personal ambition in this matter. It was a matter of wise action. The severity of the circumstances only gave it more credibility.

So, let us talk now about in proficiency in learning. In The Way of Knowledge, we emphasize the development of Knowledge as the main focal point. We do this because Knowledge is not something you can define or point your finger to and say, "That's it!" It is the great mystery of your life. However, we can talk about its aspects, which can be directly experienced and witnessed.

At the most basic level, Knowledge represents your ability to *know*, without deduction or reasoning of any kind. It represents your ability to recognize the present, to recall the past and to foresee the future, not as a personal skill, but as an immediate necessity. If you think about it, you will realize that your life has been saved great difficulty because you have this capacity. This capacity is the major emphasis, but to conscientiously develop yourself so that Knowledge can emerge within you means that you must begin to address every aspect of your life—everything you are doing that is in violation of your nature and everything that you are doing that is complimentary to your nature. It takes a long time to develop Knowledge. You do not take the quick easy course. It takes a lifetime, but to prepare conscientiously means that your life is more perfectly utilized, with greater rewards and greater contribution to others.

Therefore, to prepare yourself for Knowledge, you must follow what you know now against advancing armies, which in your case are primarily your advancing thoughts. Those are your pursuers—your thoughts, your fears and your unquestioned requirements for your happiness. Here you give up no power; you only give up presumptions. You do not follow; you join. There is a difference. Purely following is mindless and without purpose, but joining to follow means that you are participating and cooperating. Here your action is complementary to the action of others. Here your ability is required, acknowledged and strengthened. It is an immediate gain to you.

So, you do not become perfect; you simply become available and disentangled. Then your life is no longer held back by extenuating circumstances that are in violation to your true purpose. You have reached a place of simplicity. When I was requested to return, I did not sit and think about the consequences. I just did it, and it was a good thing. If I had thought about it, well, there would have been a different outcome. The Teacher appeared. "Go back!" I went back. The Teacher appeared again. "Do this!" I did that. The Teacher appeared again. "Do this!" I did that. I did those things not because the Teacher was grand. I knew almost nothing of the Teacher. It was because I responded. It was my heart that said "Yes." I did not change the winds. I did not bring the rain. I did not black out the sun. I did not destroy my enemies. I was not a master, and so the world left me alone to do my real work.

Being a student of Knowledge means that you learn to become a uniform person, not a whole group of people anymore. You will have one frame of reference within yourself and one true response to that frame of reference. This is entirely natural. There is no imposition of structure upon your true nature. There is only a temporary structure in your external life to help you reclaim this ability. Knowledge re-engages you with life as it really is. It re-engages you with your purpose for coming into the world. It is a new experience of life, truly.

Becoming disentangled will take great effort. Here you do not give up everything and go sit on a mountain. No! You simply begin to tell the truth about your life, follow the truth to the best of your ability and allow your life to open. It is not a passive state. Then maybe one day someone will come along and say, "You are a great master!" and you will say, "Oh," not certain you like the sound of that. You can become a master teacher because you are proficient at speaking or engaging with individuals. You can become a master musician because you are proficient at your instrument. You can become a master athlete or a master this or a master that. That is different. That is simply being proficient with a specialization.

The primary difficulty here is that people are afraid of their own Knowledge because they have built a life without it and against it in many respects. They do not want to really know. They are afraid their Knowledge will rob them of their happiness, take away their securities, take away their control, their goals and their ambitions and take them into some dangerous and risky situation. It is all fear, fear, fear. It is all the fear of God—that is all it is—but people do not say, "I am unhappy today because I am afraid of God." You do not say that, do you? "I am depressed. I am afraid of God."

Knowledge is so graceful. It is so beautiful. It is so pervasive. If you open to it even a little, it will begin to emanate from you like a sweet fragrance. It feeds everyone around you. People come to you, and they do not even know why. You don't look any different, necessarily. Maybe you stopped wearing those funny shoes, or you fixed yourself up a little bit. You don't know why they are there. They don't know why they are there. You are host to something greater. Your life is about that now, not because you planned it to be that way but simply because you allow the space for it to enter.

People who are trying to get everything from life may get what they want, but they will not be satisfied. Then, their only means for freedom is disappointment, profound disappointment. Becoming a student is a very great thing. It is very important. There are very few true students around. Lots of people want immediate results. "I want it now!" They don't know what they want, but they want it immediately. At least they know they do not have it, even if they do not know what it is.

Becoming a student means that you are willing to follow and be responsible for being a follower and to orient yourself towards your preparation. This takes discipline and consistency. It is a commendable state. Your role in your own development is quite small. You only have to follow the preparation as you discover it. When the preparation says, "Turn right here," you turn right there. And if you open a page and it says, "Better to get out of this situation you're in," you do it! Not because the preparation is a holy book but simply because within yourself you know it must be. If Knowledge is exercised, it becomes powerful and pervasive. It is not *your* Knowledge, however. People say, "Well, I have my knowledge and you have your knowledge." What they are saying is "I have my interpretation and you have yours." There is no individual Knowledge.

The important thing is to learn how to learn. If you can do that, you will graduate from this life with true accomplishment, learning how to learn. Our preparation for students is very specific. It develops essential qualities in the individual and provides guidelines so people will stop hurting themselves habitually. It gives you an opportunity to come into the clear, to become unfettered long enough to value your freedom.

Your Knowledge is called upon again and again as a resource for you to discover and to develop. Your ability to express Knowledge in the most common situations is encouraged. You have to be a person who is consistent enough to maintain a practice on a daily basis, which has a stabilizing effect on the rest of your life and affairs. You begin to listen instead of talk so much. You begin to look instead of project. You begin to feel instead of think so much. You are presented with relationships of true value, and you are encouraged to take action where action is needed in your life. You learn to lead and you learn to follow, for any leader is a profound follower. There are no leaders in the world, you see. If you follow, you will lead. If you will not follow, you will follow and not know you are following. There is someone pulling you along, and you are pulling someone else along. That is the way of things. You have a great amount of assistance available to you, if you begin to go in the direction your life is intended to go. If you attempt to go in another direction, it will seem like you are doing it alone.

There are things you must apply yourself to very specifically because there are two aspects to life: There are concrete accomplishments and there is Mystery. You must approach both. Mystery opens you to a greater assistance than you could provide for yourself and saves you from condemning circumstances. Applying yourself to tangible things enables you to reclaim your self-respect and to build a foundation that is sound and firm. That is what personal growth is for—to build a foundation for Knowledge. What other value does it have? The person you are attempting to improve will be shed like a garment when you leave. As you become stable, then you can represent something greater. Without Knowledge, you are still profoundly confused and subject to miseries. Without purpose, meaning and direction, your life is still a desperate event.

When you think of your spiritual preparation, think not of mastery but of proficiency. With proficiency, you are able to function and to be involved in life on a day-to-day basis, whether you are happy or sad, whether circumstances are good or difficult. It is like the difference between a honeymoon and a marriage. When people discover their Inner Teachers, often they go into a kind of honeymoon phase for a long time. It is all about having wonderful experiences and romantic interludes! Of course, the Teachers simply give their blessings on occasion, while the students are enraptured with themselves. But if students persist, they begin to settle down into a true relationship with life and start working together over a long period of time. This is called building a foundation. It is not glamorous, but it is so vital and so invigorating to your life. If you have a foundation, then you can provide a foundation for others because what most people seek is a foundation. Then, upon this foundation something can be built that is not of your own design. You must build the foundation, but what is built upon it, God builds.

We teach a very practical approach to life and often, even though this is a spiritual training, it is necessary for us to despiritualize people. Your pursuit of God must be built on a successful life in the world. By successful I do not mean that you are rich and famous. It is simply that your life in the world is sufficient, and you build upon this. The Plan of the Teachers calls for the development of students who have a foundation, for they are in a position to give. Their lives are not about attempting to fulfill all of their great needs because there is no fulfillment there. Their needs are met sufficiently, so they are in a position to contribute something greater. As a result, they are in a position to receive something greater.

Now, it is very difficult to approach Knowledge and Mastery from a logical point of view because when you try to be logical about Knowledge, you do not have Knowledge anymore. You have your logic. When you apply a certain perspective to Knowledge, you have your perspective. You individually experience Knowledge according to your perspective, but Knowledge is beyond your perspective. The great turning point in life is when you allow your life to be guided by something that you cannot understand but that you can follow wholeheartedly. That is what renders greatness into the world.

*Knowledge
is knowing
what must be done
&
Wisdom
is knowing
how to do it.*

Eighteen

HIGHER EDUCATION

I WOULD LIKE TO TEACH YOU A FEW WORDS to say with me. The words are RAYE NAVAR. Please say them with me now. RAYE NAVAR. This is an appropriate invocation for our subject. RAYE NAVAR means, in a rough sense at least, "to shed the mind" because it deals with a level of education that is beyond what is normally considered to be education here. It also translates to mean "to part the mind" because the mind has a center line between the rational and the intuitive. There is a seam that joins the two aspects of your personal mind, and it can be parted. What this reveals is a seed of light, not the kind of light that you see in a light bulb, but a seed of Presence, a greater expression of your being in the world.

I would like to talk about education to stimulate your desire for Knowledge and to give you a new perspective on things that will be very helpful. I will speak about education as having three levels: The first is survival in the world; the second is development of your personal self; the third is the discovery of Knowledge. RAYE NAVAR relates to the discovery of Knowledge.

Now, you have all been learning since day one, yes? Your early training was primarily for survival in the world and the development of your personal self. Well, you have survived in the world. Congratulations! And you have a personal self. Congratulations! Now, there is only so much survival training that is required, and there is always a little bit that is ongoing because it relates to your need to provide income for yourself and to get along with other people. You live in a social setting as well as a biological one. You must survive physically and you must survive socially. To do this, you must develop your personal self so that you can communicate and participate with people effectively and be able to manage the simple affairs of your life. This is ongoing because even with a greater emphasis in life, you will have to develop and cultivate your personal self to accommodate this greater emphasis. Do not expect God to come and give you a great mission in life until you have the capacity for it.

So, as we enter the third realm of education, which I will concentrate upon, we must also keep in mind that your ability to survive and your ability to develop your vehicle—which is your mind and body—must be ongoing as well. Your mind and your body are never sacrificed because the more you develop your capacity to experience Knowledge—the profound ability to know the truth—the more you must become a person of strength, consistency and direction, and you must learn how to survive in a changing world. So, survival training is not over, but it is not the primary emphasis now.

Knowledge is not only your ability to perceive the truth and to resonate with the truth, it also contains the memory of your life beyond this world and your reason for coming here. Everyone has come into the world to contribute and to learn to contribute; everyone has come into the world to learn more about the world. A few who have come into the world will graduate from it. By this, I mean that they will not need to come back here again. You do not need to be a master to graduate from the world. That is very important to understand, particularly since mastery is such a relative term. Mastery in the world does not necessarily mean mastery beyond the world. We must think of mastery as relative to your situation now because this life not only is an experience in and of itself, it is preparation for your life to come and for life beyond the world. That is why much of your education will seem mysterious. If you can enter into the Mystery, you will enter a far greater range of participation that will make you more effective, more capable and much happier in the world.

It is very important in considering Mystery that you allow Mystery to be mysterious because no matter how much you survive and no matter

how capable you seem to be on a personal level, you are profoundly ignorant of who you are, where you have come from and where you are
going. You are like a person who has learned to sail a ship, but you have
no idea when you departed or where you are sailing to. That is a Mystery.
Theories and philosophies about your point of departure and destination
must fall considerably short of the reality. You do not need to define what
awaits you, for that would disable you from being here now in a productive way. You shall discover that as you proceed.

The third level of education is the discovery of Knowledge. Here you
begin to remember your point of departure and anticipate your point of
return—not because you are anxious to leave the world, but because the
meaning of your being here is entirely defined by where you have come
from and where you are going. It is as if you went to school one day and
you stayed there for eighty years and never left the classroom. Well, after a
while it would be very difficult to remember what life was like outside the
classroom. But when you leave the classroom after eighty years, more or
less, you go home to your "parents," who are your Spiritual Family. It was
just a very long day in class, that's all—so long, in fact, that it allowed you
to concentrate on the classroom entirely. If you penetrate the membrane
that separates this world from the life beyond, it becomes very difficult to
concentrate on being here because the life beyond is so alluring. It is so
attractive. It is easier to be yourself there than it is here. That is why you
must enter the world in an amnesiac state to enable yourself to concentrate on being here.

Now, The Greater Community Way of Knowledge takes people to
the third threshold of learning, which is the discovery of Knowledge. It is
very essential here to keep in mind that this discovery will make you far
more capable in personal survival and personal development, but it is
extremely mysterious. At the third threshold, you are beginning to have
access to life beyond the world, but in such a way that it renders you more
capable of being in the world rather than less.

If you were in a classroom for eighty years and you were thinking
about home, you would have a hard time being in the classroom. "Can't
wait to get home!" You can remember how it was when you were a little
kid, waiting for the time to come around when school was out. Couldn't

wait, watching the clock, couldn't hear the teacher. Just waiting for the time to pass.

It seems when you enter Mystery that you leave behind all rational, responsible and objective approaches to life, but that is not true. What is true is that you now have a foundation for true objectivity. How can you be objective if the world makes up your whole reality? It is so temporary and changeable with so many threatening appearances, how can you be objective here? How can you have equanimity if the world is all you know? It is like putting someone in a washing machine and asking them to meditate. If the washing machine is all there is, all they will know is tremendous revolution. Well, the world is like a very slow washing machine. It kind of tumbles you around, yes? It is very difficult to have any perspective here.

There is so much Mystery everywhere! Your relationships are mysterious. You can identify the physical qualities of a relationship—the behavior involved, the physical interaction, the personal habits, and so forth—but the attraction is really mysterious. It is magical because it is mysterious. The fact that you can breathe without thinking about it is mysterious. The fact that everything happens is mysterious. It is all mysterious! It is wondrous, as a matter of fact!

The first two levels of education, which account for about ninety-nine percent of education in life, do not deal with Mystery. Mystery is a nuisance, something not to deal with, yes? It makes you a dreamer—less capable of surviving and developing your personal self. Much of the education that is happening now in human potential is for personal development. It is to talk better. Think better. Look better. Act better. Have more. Suffer less. Yes? These are important, but there is something more important.

Our Presence represents the Mystery of your life because we live where you have come from. That is why when you receive our communication, you receive an aspect of yourself that is very much alive, but which is perhaps beyond your reach as an individual.

You have brought the vast majority of your mind, which is Knowledge, into this world. This is not your personal mind. It is not the *you* who is trying to survive, get things, keep things away, acquire pleasure and avoid pain. It is not struggling. It is not changing. It is not even growing. The first two stages of education deal with growth. The third stage deals with discovery. Knowledge is not growing, but your awareness of it is.

There is a great deal of discussion these days among people who are involved in higher forms of education who say that all the answers are within you. "You can find the answer in yourself. All you have to do is a little digging or become very still or ask with enough sincerity, and it will come to you." But the fact of the matter is, you cannot reach these answers. You cannot dynamite your insides to try to find a way to them. You cannot hammer and drill your way down because the answers that you possess are not for you alone. They will emanate naturally as you are prepared to receive them and to render them to others. Your message is not for you. It is for others. It is the giving of the message that restores Knowledge to you as a living reality.

When you have graduated from this world and it is no longer a place to hide from God, then you will begin to help those who remain behind—not everyone, but certain individuals who are part of your group who are still working down here. Being in the world is like being in the bottom of a mine shaft. You look around and all you see is a mine shaft, yes? So, you're down there long enough and that is all you know. But when you go back to the surface, you say, "Ah, I forgot all about this!" You breathe easy and there is room and you have perspective.

Knowledge gives you the experience of being outside the mine shaft while you are still in it, but in such a way that you are rendered more effective at being in the world. There are certain individuals who become monastic in life, but they are the exception and not the rule here. Think not that if God calls you, you will become some kind of novitiate monk or something. Your first job is to become a sound and reliable person in the world. Then something important can be given to you. If you are not sound and reliable, your true gift will be a greater burden than a joy to you and will, in fact, be very dangerous for you. You will not be able to carry it effectively and you will not be able to render it effectively.

Ambition in this is quite unfortunate. That is why there are limits to personal growth. We don't want you to try to become a perfect, flawless person because you will not be honest. It is wise to know what can be done and what cannot be done by you. There is a great emphasis now in many teachings that if only you would get out of the way and stop being such a dummy, you would be able to have everything, do everything and be everything. Well, it is the "if only" that is the constant bugaboo in this situation. "If only I were not so impaired, I would be this magnificent person." "If only I did not have obstacles and barriers, my life would soar! I would be like a shooting star!" It is true! You would! You would last about one second and fizzle out. You have not come here to last one second and fizzle out like some kind of holiday sparkler.

In personal development, there is a great deal of motion but not much real movement. There is a great deal of splashing about, having high and low experiences, great insights—"Oh, I realize why I have been a nut!"—and then you go from there to being a nut again. It does not matter that you know the reason why you are a nut. It is not true that if you know the reason, the problem disappears. People are always searching for the key answer. All they want from life is answers, and they are not alive because they are missing the whole picture. Life is passing them by, and they are looking for an answer. "If I know the real reason why I am a nut, I will not be a nut. Then I will be this magnificent creature that will be a blazing light for all to see."

The advanced ones in this world are not like that. They are hidden. You don't find them very often, and if you do, it is for a reason. Why is this? Why do they not make a public display and share their radiance with everyone? Why are they not out there proclaiming the majesty of God through their own life? Why is this? Is not the purpose of personal growth to be a blazing, majestic demonstration? Then why are the advanced ones not doing that? Why are they hidden in the recesses of the world?

It is important that you learn about survival and personal development because Knowledge must be accompanied by Wisdom. Knowledge is knowing what must be done and Wisdom is knowing how to do it. You must be a person who knows something about life and can actually carry through activities and maintain yourself in doing so. That is Wisdom: Wisdom is knowing how to do things. It is the result of real experience in being in the world. That is why the first major portion of your life is all about survival and personal development. Here you will hopefully learn how to do things effectively. You still have not found out what your life is for, but once you do, if you are developing in the first two stages, you will be able to do something with it without creating catastrophe for yourself or others.

The reason why the advanced individuals who are in this world do not walk around displaying themselves is because they have Wisdom. They do not want to be shooting stars. They would rather be an abiding Presence in the world than a momentary sensation. They are seeking for students who are ready for Knowledge, the third level of education. They may disseminate information to others to help them in their personal development and in resolving personal dilemmas, but they are looking for students of Knowledge. They understand that God works secretly in the world because people are afraid of God.

Do you want to know why you are really sad and depressed and why those emotions come to you? It is because you miss God. That is the reason for all unhappiness and it is also the seed of all joy. God works mysteriously. God is like a great attraction without a marquee or a billboard. God is pulling you along incessantly. Hopefully, the excess baggage in your life will be left aside sufficiently so that you can begin to experience the attraction itself, for this is the call of love to the lover. This is what you try to recreate with one another, this profound love and attraction.

Knowledge takes you back to God while you are in the world, but it does so in a very specific way because its emphasis is practical, not magical. It is not about metaphysics, learning all about the sixteen million levels and the cosmology of all of the universes. That is for people who think and do nothing. The man and woman of Knowledge is not concerned with these things unless they have a specific relevance to their function in life, and even then they are a temporary expedient and nothing else. If you want to know about mystical cosmology, then perhaps a teacher will tell you about these things to get your attention while he or she gives you something far greater. Mystical cosmology does not get you through the day. It does not attend to you when you are alone and miserable in your thoughts. It is simply a broader range of speculation. It may be a reprieve from your personal difficulties, but it is not the key to your freedom.

So, the third level of education requires profound honesty. It asks that you become a person who can look at life objectively with honesty and consistency. You are not trying to be a wonderful person now; you are not trying to be a villain, either. You're not even trying "to be." You are freed from the attempt to be someone. This is the greatest freedom you can experience in life. In a way, the quest to be someone has to be relinquished before you *can* be someone. Knowledge does not require that you become exemplary according to your standards. You cannot say, "I am going to use Knowledge to get more of this or less of that," because Knowledge *is* the Master in your life. It is moving you. You have set sails, and God is now blowing you across the world.

Jesus Christ is a person who has set sail. He is not in the shipyard doing repairs. He is on the water. He is moving. He does not have to be concerned about what he has to be in life. His only emphasis is to maintain his sails and to adjust them according to the movement that is moving him.

In the *Steps to Knowledge* Program, there are two aspects that the student must concentrate upon: the first one is for you to discover what you know now, what you don't know and what you cannot know. The second is contact with your Inner Teachers. You need a guide into new territory, and you must rely upon this guide with great emphasis. Your Teachers will not let you rely upon them too much; nor will they allow you to hold them as great heroes or heroines. This is not appropriate. Like all true teachers, your Inner Teachers are here to render their presence unnecessary. They help you to set sail, to strengthen sails, to learn to mend your sails when they break and to follow the wind that is God's movement in life. They teach you to sail.

This is a good analogy because people who are in charge of their ships have to exercise tremendous ability and responsibility. At the same time, their movement is guided by greater forces. They are in profound awe of the forces that move them. They are not claiming mastery over the world. They are simply using the world to accomplish their task. That is why we are not very excited when we hear people talk about mastery in life because most people think of it as perfection of their personal self to the exclusion of life itself. How can you be happy in the world if you are attempting to use everything to show off your own sense of perfection, trying to make everything wonderful and trying to make everyone agreeable, while life is eroding your creations at every moment. This cannot be a happy life.

You know you need to set sail. We can ride with the wind. We are not bound to the shore. We do not drown in the waters of life, so we go with you. Exposure to your Teachers stimulates your sense that there is true assistance and that your life is not dependent upon your efforts alone, for you cannot do anything great alone. As a matter of fact, you cannot do anything alone. That is why people find the pursuit of Knowledge personally insulting sometimes because they see how small their part is. "Well, gee, I thought I was supposed to be a Master!"

And yet you cannot give over your responsibilities. Your Teacher asks you to claim your responsibilities but not to claim responsibilities that are beyond your role. You learn what can be done and what cannot, what is your function and what is not your function. Even on a personal level, part of becoming mature is finding out what you are *not* supposed to do in life. A very big part of becoming a mature person is realizing that you can only be really good at a few things. Then you can begin to relax and learn to claim your true role without trying to claim others.

Life is very fair and honest, but it can be a very harsh experience for those who are not. Likewise, if you set sail on the open sea, you will find conditions difficult if you are not prepared and you will find conditions dangerous if you cannot sail. Knowledge takes you into the open sea; it allows you to enter new realms and have greater perspective and Wisdom in the world. It tempers ambitions that are inappropriate and it encourages ones that are. It is the great equalizer in your life, and that is why it is the foundation for peace. It sets all things in right proportion. Here you realize that you have been fighting yourself, trying to be a perfect person, without realizing that you have a nature. Then you learn to work with your nature, rather than trying to change it. Life will change you accordingly. You do not need to change yourself on top of it. The way life changes you is quite maximal.

I want to be very clear with you that the third level of education consummates the first two; it does not replace them. It simply gives them a greater context in which to be truly meaningful. Then you see why you are surviving in the world. Then you see why you are doing personal development. Now there is a reason. Your life is more important than your own ambitions.

When you realize that your life is important for everyone, then you will value your presence in the world. If your life is only valuable to you, well, you are not so sure it is worth so much effort, yes? The price seems too great. Yet, if your life is important both for you and for others, then you will see that there is real merit and real cause to do those things that are very good for you and to set aside things that belittle you or hurt you. Then self-love is possible. Besides, if your life is about contribution, you don't have time to go out and hurt yourself, do you? You are all very important people to life.

You all know you should eat certain things and exercise more often and probably not go to those kinds of movies, yes? But you don't listen! Why? Is it because your childhood was so difficult? Why don't you do things you know are good for you? Is it because you do not love yourself enough? So you love, love, love, love. "I love, love, love, love and I still don't do what I know I should do. I still fall in love with someone who is not interested in me." Kick in the face. "I still eat food that gives me an upset stomach." Why? Animals will do what is good for them. A bird does not eat stones, unless it is necessary for its digestion. They are discerning. Why are you not discerning?

It is amazing what people can do when they are guided by Knowledge, and yet they will remain hidden, working only in the area that is theirs to work in. If they have progressed, they have learned enough not to display themselves to the world, for the world is quite confused about Knowledge. It wants Knowledge for the power it can seem to provide, but it hates it for the memory of God it seems to render. That is why you deify and crucify your great teachers. They are too wonderful to forget, but too challenging to live with. So you kill them, and then you can keep a wonderful memory of them. That is why the Wise remain hidden. They work behind the scenes. That is mastery. That is a form of practical mastery.

The reason that the third level of education is difficult to approach is because it is mysterious. It does not conform to your personal ambitions or your desire for perfection. You are not sure you want to enter that door. It cannot guarantee you more of everything you want. You enter that door because happiness is there and confirmation of your nature and your Being. That is why you enter. When I entered preparation with my

Teacher long ago, I did not say, "Well, let's see. I'm going to make sure that I get everything I want before I invest." I was called. I responded. I was called again. I responded again. I was called again. I responded again. It is this call and response that is Knowledge in your life. It is not your planning out how you are going to profit by the situation.

People who enter the *Steps to Knowledge* Program, or any similar educational process, know they have a calling in life. They are not shopping around now for new methods to become a greater person. Their decision to participate is from a deeper place within them. It is from Knowledge. "I am not so sure why I am here, but I *must* be here." That is a statement of incredible value. It is this same ability to respond to a deeper force that will save your life and has saved your life over and over and has kept you away from certain things or pulled you out of certain things that were dangerous for you. Only afterwards did you look back and say, "Oh, my God! I am so glad that relationship did not work!" or "I am so glad I did not go to that place with those people."

No one is at home here. This is a beauty school. Everyone is using everyone and everything to enhance their appearance. Very lonely this is. There is a certain wonderful resignation that comes with landing on your true foundation. It is the comfort of a loving parent; it is the comfort of a loving God that you do not have to be all the things that you think you have to be, and you cry because you are so relieved.

What I offer is that my life is Knowledge. I have no other life. I have come from where your life is more abundant to help you in the world.

There is a
happiness
of an enduring nature
which is born of
your satisfaction
that your life
is
truly engaged.

Nineteen

FULFILLMENT

THERE IS A GREAT DEAL OF SPECULATION on what produces fulfillment in life. But I would like to talk about what fulfillment itself produces because, you see, you cannot produce fulfillment. It is something that naturally arises when you are engaging with your True Mind, your Knowledge. Here you have united with yourself internally, and you have united with others around you in a meaningful way.

People often think of fulfillment as the end result. It is the thing that you receive after all has been said and done. That puts it far out of your reach because your life is not over. We do not want fulfillment to merely be a future possibility but instead something that you have access to immediately in your life. It is not complete fulfillment, but it is not necessary that you have complete fulfillment because the fulfillment that you will have in life will lead to greater fulfillment, and so forth. It is an experience you will begin to honor within yourself because it renders peace to you and a sense of purpose and effectiveness.

Your life is far from over, so let us not think of fulfillment in terms of an end result. Because it cannot really be defined, fulfillment is something you must think about in terms of your own experience. I encourage you to work with the ideas I am presenting here and to consider them seriously. Do not think you know everything about them, even if they are familiar to you. What I have to say is meant to be helpful.

One of the results of fulfillment which I would like to emphasize at the very beginning is gratitude. The experience of gratitude is a very great part of fulfillment. Gratitude opens you to a sense of inner peace and greater association while you are in the world.

Fulfillment is possible for you regardless of the state of affairs in the world because the world is not your Ancient Home. You are a visitor here and because you are a visitor, you have the ability to overcome the tribulations of this life and to become a true contributor. You have the ability to rise above the misery and the confusion that you perceive around you and in so doing, you bring something with you from your Ancient Home that the world needs a great deal. Our presence here brings with it the reinforcement and the memory that this fulfillment is real and possible. It is meant for you.

First, let me talk a little about Knowledge, and then I will address the experience of fulfillment itself. As I have often said, you possess within you your True Mind. It is not a mind that has been created in this life. You have not acquired it from your environment or relationships. It is intrinsic to your Being. It is the Mind behind your mind, or underneath your mind, depending on how you want to look at it. It thinks in its own way, which is quite specific and very different from your conscious mind. It is very quiet and very strong. It is very still and yet when it thinks, its thoughts have great impact. You must approach this quality of intelligence gradually because it is so powerful. You must learn to receive it, to trust it and to use it properly. You must learn how it affects other people around you in order to become wise in its service. Its power is very gracious, but it has tremendous impact on others. It is within you and is quite protected from your own interference. You cannot spoil it, but you can have incorrect ideas about it and think you are using it when you are not and thus make some serious errors. But it is beyond error because it is intelligent.

It is called Knowledge because it is intelligent and it also contains your part in the Plan. This idea of a Plan is very difficult to comprehend fully here. It obviously indicates that you are a part of something greater, that you are not only an individual, not completely, and that you are not an isolated, unrelated living event in the world. You are part of a Plan. It is not a Plan that you are meant to fully comprehend because this is not possible. You do not have the perceptual range or the capacity, but that is not important. What is important is that you can discover that there is a Plan, that you are part of it and that your inclusion in it is entirely natural and inbred within you. It offers a promise for your life that is very real.

Because Knowledge is intelligent, it is also thinking spontaneously every moment. It is not like a computer program that is all preset. It is alive and is thinking now. It is responding now. It is meant to be your guide. When we speak of Inner Guidance, we are talking about people becoming students of Knowledge. As you begin to experience Knowledge, it will become greater and greater, and its greatness will always extend far beyond your grasp. So, think not that you can define it or hold it in a thought system, for it is greater than that. As Knowledge is the Mind behind your mind, so there is a Mind behind your Knowledge, and this Mind is God.

Knowledge can be looked at in many different ways, and I want to give some illustration of this so that you can relate to it within your own experience. People's first experience of Knowledge is profound intuition. Profound intuition is usually stimulated by very demanding circum-stances—danger, a difficult situation or extreme circumstances. This is important to understand because everybody in the world wants to become safer and more comfortable. Everyone wants to escape difficulty and tra-vail. Yet, the more you escape difficulty, the farther you are from Knowledge. Why? Is Knowledge supposed to be difficult? No. It just usu-ally takes these kinds of circumstances for you to penetrate your conscious mind and reach deeper within yourself. There is now a necessity. You *must* know something.

In the future, you will not require difficulty to gain access to Knowledge. It is not intended to be this way, but because you are apart from Knowledge, you will create the circumstances that make it necessary for you to reach it. You will make sure that your life will bring you to this threshold. That is why people let their dilemmas go until they become extreme. They commit the same self-violations until they become intolera-ble. They stay in the same situations until they cannot stand them any longer. Then they *must* know something.

Do not think that pain and Knowledge are truly associated because this is not the case. Knowledge is natural knowing. It is not thinking in the usual sense. It is not the result of deliberation or choosing. It is truly God's gift to you. You may demand from God a prettier world with less grievous circumstances, nicer appearances and happier times, but I assure you, no greater gift could be given you than your own Knowledge. Your dilemma is with Knowledge.

Knowledge will show you whom to marry, what work to do, where to go next, whom to engage with and whom to avoid. It does this without judgment and without condemnation. It solves the authority problem with God because you know it is something within you leading you, but you know it is something that is much greater than you, and so it cannot be you personally. This is very important.

People treat a greater authority in life in very peculiar ways. For instance, they either avoid any greater authority other than themselves—which is very foolish—or they succumb to a greater authority mindlessly—which is also very foolish. So, within yourselves, each of you, there must be a way to reconcile this dilemma, to heal this primary relationship with God. I assure you that if you heal that relationship, you will not have problems with each other. This dilemma is the source of all of your guilt and anxieties and as a consequence, it produces the world that you see.

Knowledge speaks of intrinsic relationship. That is why at certain times in life you meet an individual, and there is a sense of recognition that is profound, even frightening. If you are observant of this recognition, you will realize that this is not karmic. It does not have to do with "past lives." Past lives are very superficial compared to this, for these relationships were established beyond the world. You may even have difficulty with this person because their personality and yours do not get along too well. But still, there is a great recognition that is beyond description. There is no need for introduction. Indeed, what you want to do is simply get caught up with each other. "How did *you* get here?"

You see, so much of you has nothing to do with the world. And part of you has everything to do with the world. It is meant that the part of you that has nothing to do with the world guide the part of you that has everything to do with the world.

Now, in times past we have spoken of the importance of Inner Teachers. Part of the value of this discussion is for people to recognize their problems with authority. Some say, "No, I do not need any kind of teacher. Why do I need teachers? I will go to God directly!" And others say, "Ah, a teacher! I will not live my life for myself. I will live my life for my teacher!" These are two extremes. Most people fall somewhere in between. It is very hard to comprehend what a real teacher is to you when you are thinking with your personal mind, which is your worldly mind. Someone always loses in this approach. Either your teacher is belittled and neglected, which is a loss for you because your teacher brings gifts to you, or you succumb to your teacher, which is a loss to your teacher and to you because it is your teacher's purpose for you to reclaim your abilities and with your abilities your sense of Self. These difficulties are anticipated. That is why, in most cases, your Inner Teachers work behind the scenes, contributing to you in such a way that you will be able to re-experience your abilities and learn to use them effectively.

It is Knowledge that is important. Each of you will have a unique way of finding it within your circumstances in life. Your Knowledge is profoundly wise, even concerning your worldly state. That's what makes it so effective. Since it did not originate here, it can be truly effective in the world because it is not infringed upon by fear. It activates Knowledge in others and thus leads others to act nobly in difficult situations.

So, people say, "Why do I need a teacher when I have all of this Wisdom built in? I'll just go to God and bypass all teachers. Teachers are a nuisance, an impediment." That is fine. You can think that. But it does not change the reality of the fact that your Inner Teachers are initiating you into Knowledge. It just limits your access to them. They are initiating you so that you can become one of them. The reason for this is that this life that you are living is preparation for the life beyond as much as it is an experience in and of itself. That is part of the difficulty in understanding your circumstances because many of your learning experiences have nothing to do with this life. They have to do with the life to come. And so people create wonderful metaphysical justifications and explanations for everything that is happening. That is okay. It is all preparing you because your life extends so far beyond the world. The world is a midway point in your journey Home. There is a great range of experience between the world and your Ancient Home.

Now, in talking about fulfillment I would like to use an analogy. The analogy I would like to use is that of the surgeon working on the patient. You are the surgeon; the world is the patient. Now, when the surgeon is working on the patient, the surgeon is not suffering for the patient. No. The surgeon is simply working on the patient. If the surgeon is performing his or her task, neither the future nor the result is totally predictable. They are simply working on the patient. They are not stopping to have discussions about how terrible it is that the patient is sick. They are not concerned unnecessarily about the history of the patient, except insofar as it affects their performance in the moment. The patient's history and future are not important, only the work at hand.

The reason that this analogy is useful is that the surgeon can experience fulfillment while working on the patient even though it is a critical situation. This means that you can be in the world and be fulfilled while you are working in the world. The surgeon knows that the patient is in distress, or there would be no need for surgery, so there is not a complaint in that regard. The surgeon is simply working on the patient.

Because your fulfillment has to do with your reason for coming to the world, it is related to your work. You did not come here for a vacation. There are better places to go for a vacation. You also did not come to the world to work on yourself because how can you work on yourself? You only have access to your personality, and it does not require that much work because it is a personality. And you certainly cannot work on your Knowledge because it is working on you! All you can do, really, is make adjustments in your perception, behavior, attitudes and expression as you proceed along.

The other quality of the surgeon that is very important is that the surgeon is not working on himself or herself. The surgeon is working on the patient. It is this total attention to the patient that makes the surgeon competent—this and the surgeon's preparation. If the surgeon is thinking about other things, well, there can be a mistake. It is this single-minded approach that makes fulfillment possible. The surgeon is concentrated on the duty at hand. For the surgeon, it is not a matter of happiness or sadness, heaven or hell. It is that kind of concentration that God has on the world. Why is the surgeon so effective? Because the surgeon is thinking of only one thing. This is having power in the world. The less magnified your mind is, the less powerful it is; the more it is swayed by circumstances, the less it affects circumstances. Anyone, for good or for ill, will exert tremendous power if they are concentrated. Why? Because when you are concentrated, you are not dealing with conflict within yourself, and so your mind is more powerful. Your efforts are more uniform and more directed, and you have greater influence over the weak-minded who are not concentrated in their approach.

It is very important to see this. Do not think you cannot be influenced by others. Your Knowledge cannot be influenced by others' personalities, but your mind can be greatly influenced. If they are more concentrated in their approach than you are in yours, they will exert an influence upon you. I do not say this to frighten you. It is simply a fact. If you are with Knowledge, this is not a problem because Knowledge is more powerful than any personality could possibly be.

So, the first aim in your true development is to simplify and unify your life, and the unifying factor in your life is Knowledge because it is united in its purpose and thinking. That is why it does not think like you think. It does not deliberate between choices. It does not discuss things. It does not deduce things. It does not induce things. When it comes time to act, it acts. It is like a very, very deep spiritual instinct. It does not come to you upon demand.

Now, it is very important that you become observant of yourself, your thinking and your behavior and that you have skills for doing this because to observe your life objectively gives you far greater perspective on what you are doing and what can be done through you. But this has its limits. In fact, it is not the most important part. When you are experiencing Knowledge, you are not aware of yourself, but you are profoundly aware of things around you. Does this not seem contradictory? After all, isn't this all about becoming more aware of yourself? Isn't that the way it is supposed to be? You are becoming more and more aware of yourself all the time. It is very mysterious, and I am not sure I can explain this effectively in words, but when you are experiencing Knowledge, you are like the surgeon observing the patient. You are completely present to the situation. You are not conscious of yourself. You *are* yourself. That is the difference. An observer is still separated. In this case, you *are* yourself. This is fulfillment.

How do we achieve Knowledge? How can we uncover Knowledge? Don't we have to become pure first and be without fear or anger? Don't we have to have greater thoughts than we have now? Well, not necessarily. Yet, choosing Knowledge is a conscious choice, and it requires some very fundamental premises and beginning steps that are easily forgotten, so they must be reinforced constantly.

There must be a great honoring of Knowledge within you, even if you do not know what it is or what it will do. This means you must allow Mystery in your life, and this Mystery calls for reverence because it is beautiful and meaningful. This requires that you acknowledge your ignorance without self-condemnation. This means that you allow yourself to be a student by not assuming that you know too much. This requires that you honor and claim those things you do know and that you not doubt them. You are open to having your viewpoint amended, but you are very certain in your claim to Knowledge.

Knowledge will prove itself to you, but first you must follow it. It has saved your life before and this, perhaps, is the experience you can think of when I speak of Knowledge. It is that thing that turned the steering wheel away from the oncoming vehicle. It is that part of you that overrode your mind and changed your course dramatically, beneficially. It is the part of you that said, "I cannot commit myself in this relationship," a decision for which you felt shame and anxiety but which later saved you.

As Knowledge begins to emerge in you, you will have a tremendous sense of Spiritual Presence in your life. You will know there is a Presence in your life, within you and around you, and though it is inexplicable, it is so abiding and so firm that it will give you courage in the face of all manner of uncertainties. Your friends will say, "You have changed. What is going on with you?" And you will say, "I do not know." You will start to feel certain things very deeply, and you will start to avoid things that are aggravating. You will select new people to be with and new experiences and leave aside old ones.

Knowledge has a purpose to fulfill, but you cannot define this because it has not yet come to its fruition. It must show you itself. That is how the reality of God is proven to you. That is how you find your value. Like a surgeon in surgery, you can contribute to the world, for that is your purpose in coming—without concern for yourself or concern for the world. If you become concerned for the world, you will become frightened and angry, and this fear and anger can overtake you at any time.

The value of the analogy of the surgeon is that surgeons are profoundly aware of their limitations. They are not healing anyone. They are performing a technical task. If there is healing, it is happening in conjunction with their efforts. They are participating in a greater event in which they are a principal participant.

Now, our teaching method is very practical, and that is why we discourage people from becoming too metaphysically-minded to the neglect of their real responsibilities. Yet, there will be much Mystery in your life as you begin to follow what you know. What you know will join you with other people meaningfully because Knowledge is the great joiner of life. You will become a part of community because you were made to be a part of community. Your community may be a group of students. It may be a marriage. It may be a business. You will naturally give yourself to that place you are intended to give yourself, and then you will understand why you did not give yourself before. It was not because you were a bad person; it was just not the time and place. Knowledge is very mysterious for people because they know there is something there, but it is so elusive. They cannot grab onto it.

So, what about happiness? Happiness is of two varieties: There is the happiness in the moment which is the result of fun and play and, on rare occasions, true recognition of another person. Then there is happiness of an enduring nature, which is born of your satisfaction that your life is truly engaged. It is perhaps not as spectacular a happiness. You do not go around laughing all day, but it abides with you. No matter what happens to you or to the world, you have found your place; you have found your way, and there is a very great certainty that your way will lead you on.

Like the surgeon, you are neither the leader nor the follower now. You are both, for you are leading others and you are leading your own senses, yet you are being guided by something very great. Your Teachers are there to help you prepare for this, for they represent intrinsic relationship, and they have come from where you have come from. They are the evidence of your life beyond this world. They are not perfect, for a perfect teacher you could not receive. Actually, a perfect teacher is hypothetical, for all teachers are in various stages of development. Thus, teachers have teachers, and so forth.

So, do not be concerned about the perfect teacher. That is like a perfect person. It is in the imagination of therapists. You are a teacher for those who need you and can benefit from your experience and your abilities, and there are teachers for you. That is how everyone progresses. People say, "Who are you to tell us these things? Where do you come from?" I come from where you come from. I just did my homework earlier, that is all. I grew up in times more difficult than yours, but simpler in some respects, I suppose, because there were fewer decisions to make. But I have learned what I am speaking of, and I am very, very involved in this world. There are no Teachers possible for you who have not traveled this path, for they cannot relate to your experience, and you must have this sense of relationship, or you won't give yourself. There are Teachers who have never lived in the world, certainly, but those who are with you are from your Spiritual Family, and they have traveled a similar road to this, in this world or another. Therefore, they understand your difficulties in trying to apply your life from beyond to life here.

So, it is important to ask now, "How can I be in the world and cultivate Knowledge?" Certainly not by changing the world. No. There is a time to step into the world with your true abilities, and you will not need to predetermine this because it will move you itself. Then you will be able to enter the world with greater certainty and power because it will not only be you who is doing the work. This is very important.

You have come here to do something. If you do not do it, you will feel very confused and frustrated. This is difficult to comprehend because you tend to blame your circumstances for this frustration. You have not become engaged with your Self, and that is what is making you upset. It is not because people do not understand you or things are not going your way. When you see this, you will begin to extend your efforts where they can be truly effective because no matter how much you balance or harmonize your external affairs, this yearning continues. If you address this yearning directly, it will balance your affairs. That is the Kingdom you must seek first.

Inner Listening
makes you able
to respond to
communications
from your Teachers,
from others
in your life &
from your own
Knowledge.

Twenty

INNER LISTENING

NNER LISTENING is a subject that is very relevant to everyone. It has practical application in every circumstance and with every person you might meet. In fact, if you become proficient in practicing the things that we will speak of, you will have an opportunity to be far more effective in all your engagements and will be able to perceive things that are extremely useful beyond the realm of normal perception. When you listen within yourself, you must remember you are practicing becoming a listener. Over time you can then become far more responsive to messages that are coming both from within you and from without.

This is a very intentional form of listening. You are not trying to get anything. You are not trying to fill up the emptiness. Listening in this way is becoming very alert to everything that is occurring within you and around you. If you have witnessed other people, you will see that there is a great deal of conversation and very little listening. In fact, it is quite rare that someone can actually hear you when you are communicating.

You always communicate simultaneously in two ways: You communicate verbally with your thoughts and ideas, and you communicate nonverbally with your overall feeling and intention in life as it exists in that moment. Of the two, the latter is far more important. It is rare indeed that you can verbally communicate the depth of your own experience. This is not an easy thing to accomplish.

The adept listener, then, is able to receive people very directly. This skill is quite important for those who are counselors and teachers, but it has tremendous advantage for anyone. Every time you are with another person, you are engaging in a very complete communication experience, much of which is still beyond your range of perception.

When you are communicating with someone and you realize that you are not really communicating and it is uncomfortable for you, that is the time to start listening to the other person. It is the time to stop talking and start listening. When you are ill at ease in any situation, it is a time to stop talking and start listening. Here you must listen without judgment because you want to hear what is there. You want to be able to feel how you feel while you are hearing what is there. You want to listen inside and outside all at once. Then you will know if you should be in that situation or not. So, this is a good rule of thumb: When you are uncomfortable with someone, start listening. If having quiet between you is too uncomfortable, then ask them a question and start listening. It is very good in relationships to listen to each other. You learn a tremendous amount. You know when you meet people, they tell you all about themselves right at the beginning. Many of you, after a long relationship ends unhappily, think back and say, "Well, I saw the signs way back at the beginning. I felt restraint in myself at the beginning." This is very important. This is why listening is so valuable.

It is very valuable to listen to other people talk about their relationships because you can learn from them. You cannot have all experiences yourself. You do not have enough time. Besides, it would wear you out if you did. But everyone around you is having all kinds of experiences, and you can learn a great deal from them. They are acting out your fantasies and you can see the result. They will teach you about what is real as distinct from what is hoped for, and this will save you time. That is very important.

How does this relate to inner listening? It is very significant because as you learn to listen inside of yourself and are able to penetrate your own thoughts, you will begin to experience the core of your own Knowledge. This takes a great deal of time, of course, not because it is difficult but because there is a great deal of ambivalence. People are quite afraid of what they know.

So, you must first establish relationship with Knowledge, which represents your True Self. This is the very heart of you, the very core of your experience. If you are not afraid to penetrate your own Self, you will not be afraid to listen to others, for what they tell you is about your own Self.

To become a true listener, you must learn silence and feel comfortable in silence. This is natural for those who are beginning to practice meditation and are beginning to be receptive within themselves. They will seek out quiet more and more frequently, seeking refuge from the noise of the outside world.

There are very important qualities that a listener must develop, qualities that have tremendous benefit in all aspects of life. You must become used to silence. You must become very courageous, which means you are willing to see things and hear things that have direct bearing on your life. You must learn to be very patient. You must learn to trust your own experience to a high degree. You must learn to be discerning, for much of what you hear will be quite useless. You must be determined to penetrate your own thoughts. You must be persistent, have great regard for yourself and treat yourself graciously.

These qualities are developed naturally because what you are attempting to do is so important. It is so valuable for those who know you. We would never expect anyone to undertake this quality of development for themselves alone. There are very few people who feel they would deserve the benefits. But when you think that you will be able to serve others in a very direct and meaningful way, this gives great impetus and encouragement, for your gifts are meant for others. You are merely one of the beneficiaries of your own gifts.

When you begin to listen within yourself, one of the first things you will encounter is the noise of your own mind and your own chaotic and inconsistent thinking. This can be very shocking and perhaps discouraging. But the thinking that you are aware of as you begin to listen to yourself does not represent your True Mind or your true communications. It is merely the automatic response of your mental state carrying on with itself. What unifies your mind is the Greater Power within you, which we call Knowledge, and that is your goal.

When you begin to practice inner listening, your first objective is to become a good practitioner. That is the most important aspect. It is learning to practice. It is learning to listen. There are many things within yourself which will discourage you, but your desire for peace, harmony, love and grace in your life are far more compelling than any restraints you may feel.

Within your mind is a great terminal of communication because you are part of something far greater. This is the core of your own Self, which is Divine and has lived forever. This Self is in communication with others and it has direct bearing on your life in this world. This True Self that exists within you is specifically seeking out other individuals with whom it can relate and communicate directly. It seeks to develop you so that it may contribute to the world you see around you.

If I stop momentarily, we can listen together. Listen outside. Listen to all the noises in the room and to the noises outside on the streets. Listen just to listen. Concentrate on the noises, not on your thoughts about them. Good. Now, as we listen a little while longer together and practice together, I would like you to listen with your whole body, as if your entire body were a membrane that can hear and feel. Listen and feel, as if the sound waves can strike your entire body, which they do. Your whole body is a beautiful listening instrument. Let there be no judgments in your listening. It is purely an experience of listening. You have had this experience before when you tried to overhear a conversation in the distance. You listened very intently. You simply wanted to know what was being said. So you really listened. Or someone pointed out a distant sound and said, "Listen for this sound," and you listened very intently. Exercising your listening ability in this way allows you to become truly able to respond to the truth within yourself and to be far more receptive to things outside.

God has given you a perfect guidance system within yourself, which we call Knowledge. You may also call it the Holy Spirit, if you wish. It is an inner guidance system. In a very pervasive way, it is exerting its influence on you continuously, and on rare occasions it will actually move you to do something and motivate you in a very strong way. The power of your Knowledge is tremendous, and it is safely hidden within you in such a way that you cannot meddle with it. It is more powerful than you are, but it is actually who you are. If you did not have a personality, if you did not have a body and if your mind were completely unified, you would be communication itself, which is actually what you are. But in this life you are like a communication that is tightly wrapped and sealed inside a thick shell.

I am being truthful when I say that you are sent from God to be a message. Your life is a message, but it is concealed from you and from others as well. This is the source of all of your anxiety and discomfort within yourself. No matter how you may identify your problems, no matter what aggravates you on the outside, this is the source of your discomfort: You are not being your True Self.

When you begin to listen inside of yourself, you hear the chaos of your own thinking and begin to feel your discomfort. If you are patient and observe these things without running from them, you will pass through them because they cannot keep you from what lies beyond. What keeps people from being free is not their external circumstances. It is their own mind and their own thoughts. They are prisoners to their thoughts. They cannot stop watching their thoughts. It is as if you were watching a movie on a screen and you could never tear yourself away. The screen then becomes ever more real to you, for you have no contrast. You have no experience to remind you that it is just a movie you are watching. As a result, it has greater and greater impact upon you, and you become a more captive audience with every moment.

These things which make you suffer, cause you pain and drive your behavior are only thoughts. They are vaporous things. They have no substance. But for you to look beyond, you must not be afraid of what lies beyond them, for what lies beyond them is a wellspring of tremendous love. What lies beyond them are your true Teachers.

Hidden deep within you is your calling in life, waiting to be activated, waiting until all the internal and external conditions are ready for it to emerge and express itself. The change you are feeling in your life is largely to prepare you for this emergence. Happiness and disappointments both open the way for you here. When you begin to really feel Knowledge working in your life, your life will begin to make sense to you. Your past will not be a record of painful encounters. It will be a demonstration of the importance of the way you are truly meant to go.

Inner listening is such a major part of your development. It enables you to respond to communications from your Teachers, from others in your life and from your own Knowledge. It takes time to develop this, indeed, yet it is time well spent. Every few moments you spend listening without judgment save you such great amounts of time and bring you so much closer to your goal.

It is this great meeting place between your conscious mind and your deeper, impersonal mind that unifies you and makes you a force of unification in life. This is what Christ means. Christ means that your personal life has been anointed with Knowledge. You have touched yourself. God has touched you. And now you can touch others. Yet, this anointing has various stages. It does not happen all at once. When you feel truly touched within yourself, you will realize that there is still much fear within you. There is still much ambivalence. You are still afraid of what you possess. And so it takes time to resolve these matters. It takes time to resolve the distrust you have for yourself and to learn to relieve yourself of judgment.

Inner Listening is very, very simple. It is simply sitting and listening. Because it is a practice, it must be mastered as such. You have opportunities for it frequently. When you start to hear beyond your own mind, you will begin to encounter things in your environment and in other people and even things that come from beyond your visible life that are very profound. With listening comes seeing, and when you can see and you can listen, you are in a position to engage in a more powerful form of communication with others. This expresses your Knowledge and makes it more available to you.

It is important for you to know that you have a relationship with yourself that yearns to be consummated. This is when your Knowledge becomes conscious. It is protecting you and guiding you even now, like a great force that you cannot see but you can certainly feel. In times of distress or great difficulty it will manifest itself more sharply to you, and you will know that there is a guiding Presence in your life. As you become closer to it, you will start to feel it every day—unifying you, keeping you from error, orienting you towards people and situations that are truly nourishing and beneficial for you, bringing helpful change and making your encounters with others truly meaningful.

Perhaps you can practice with me. Let us practice together. Just breathe deeply and listen for sounds. Imagine you have great huge ears that go all the way to the floor. You are like a radar antenna.

Practicing in this way is very much like physical exercise. When you begin to exercise, the first thing you encounter is how bad you feel physically. But then, if you persist in your efforts, you will begin to experience the benefits of your activity and will increasingly leave the discomfort behind. How free you will feel when you are not afraid to listen, not afraid to see, not afraid to forgive and not afraid to be quiet! God is here. Yet no one can be still. Relationship is here. Yet no one can feel it. Your Teachers are with you, but your eyes are moving too fast.

Students of Knowledge, who are learning to become receptive internally and externally, will value inner quiet increasingly and will adjust their outer circumstances to give them this freedom. As a result of this practice, you will begin to have insights into how to resolve the dilemmas that are impairing you now. Your mind will open and into that opening will come ideas, insights and direction. These things will help you to unify your life, making it simpler and therefore more powerful. Increasingly, you will have a sense of relationship within yourself that abides with you regardless of the circumstances around you, a source of strength greater than the world.

Now I must tell you something that is a problem here. It is not an obvious problem because everyone thinks their problem is something else. What I am going to say will require a great deal of thought. It will not be immediately apparent, but if you contemplate it seriously, it will turn all of your problems into one problem. Then the solution becomes far more available and recognizable.

People want to be God without God. That is what has produced the world. So, when you practice inner listening, you find out that you cannot be God without God. This is very disappointing. It is also a tremendous relief. The more you try to be God without God, the more isolated, alone and estranged you are. What surrounds you, then, instead of relationships are your own thoughts. You are caught in the middle of a web of your own thinking, and this is the great entanglement.

When you listen, you will hear things that come from beyond the web itself. You will realize, in time, that your thoughts and your thinking are no more than a web that you are caught in—a web of your own design, a web that you have designed with others and that everyone is designing and reinforcing constantly. But the web is transparent. You can see through it, you can hear through it and you can feel through it. But you must become very still to do so.

So, I want you to realize that it is no fun to be God without God. It is a very great challenge, though. "Be the source of your own life! Determine your own life! Direct your own life! Control life around you! Have influence over others! Command your body! Command your mind!" This is kind of a little god, you know. A tiny little god. But it is no fun to play god because you are alone.

When you begin to open inside yourself, you realize that God is with you and that God's messengers are with you. You realize there is a realm of relationship that is uniform and gracious which has bearing on your relationships in this world and your perception of the world. The world, like your mind, can be a terrifying place to be. Its appearances are frightening and threatening, and it is in chaos with great, insurmountable problems—just like your mind.

When people begin to practice inner listening, the first thing they encounter is all these terrible things, these thoughts they could never think. "God, I had this terrible thought! Only crazy people think thoughts like this!" Or they have terrible images. "Oh, God! I am the source of these images! I must be an awful maniac!" Your thoughts reflect what you see outside, the best and the worst, the most loving and the most hateful. But your Knowledge is beyond all of it and you are not apart from God.

You have been sent into this world to allow your Knowledge to emerge so that you can contribute your specific gifts. The beauty of this is that the gifts you have to contribute will honor your presence as a human being. You can really be yourself as a human being. This generates tremendous self-love. Finally, you do not have to change all the time—to become good, to become better, to become the ideal person! Everyone wants to become an ideal person, secretly perhaps. Now you can honor your nature and work with it. Instead of trying to erase all of your limiting qualities, you begin to use them purposefully. Of course you're in a limited state. Being in a body is a limited state. It's a great nuisance carrying around this hunk—feeding it, housing it, keeping it clean, clothing it, making it beau-tiful, keeping it comfortable and attending to its many aches and pains. A nuisance, my God! Don't you just want to fly away sometimes? But the body is the garment you wear in being in this world, and it enables you to communicate here.

You don't get much attention if you don't have a body and you want to communicate. Then it is hard to get people's attention. And if you do get their attention, you scare the daylights out of them, and they never want to have an experience like that again! So, obviously, our ability to communicate with people in the world seems very limited. We still give them something, but it will arise from within them and they will think it is from themselves. That is okay because we do not need the recognition, but you do. It is very important that you realize that you have great friends beyond this world. They are not intimidated by what you see, and they have traveled this way before, so they understand your situation very, very intimately. And they know the way out of it.

Your purpose in life is to discover your Knowledge so that you can be your Self. As your True Self, you can contribute specific gifts because you have come here to give something, not to take something. People who have begun to recall their True Home and their associations beyond this life are in a position to truly contribute because they are being fed so richly. Their memory, which is now returning to them, enables them to contribute to life without being thwarted by it. That is the source of great happiness.

*Enduring happiness
is an abiding sense of
purpose,
meaning &
direction
in life.*

Twenty-one

ENDURING HAPPINESS

THERE ARE MANY DIFFERENT PURSUITS OF HAPPINESS. There is such a great investment in trying to avoid pain and achieve happiness. When you think about it, there are so many occupations, interests, hobbies and pursuits aimed at achieving happiness that it seems like a very big subject. But it really isn't. Achieving happiness is very simple and very specific, but you have to think about it a little differently.

There are two kinds of happiness available to you in this world. The first kind of happiness towards which all of these interests and pursuits are oriented is a very temporary happiness; it is momentary and carefree. People do all manner of things to experience this kind of happiness, and when they are experiencing it, it seems like a true refuge from pain and conflict. Indeed, it seems to be a desirable state to attempt to achieve at all costs. You remember the time you were so happy and you want to feel that way again, so you try to recreate the same circumstances, follow the same course of action or have the same kinds of stimulation to recapture that wonderful moment.

The first kind of happiness is momentary happiness, and it can be good, but I am going to talk about enduring happiness—happiness that endures. It is not quite so gleeful. It does not always possess the kind of self-abandonment that temporary or momentary happiness does. It is not the kind of happiness where you go around laughing all day, not thinking of any concern or responsibility in life. It is a happiness that is far more pervasive, has greater depth and is more difficult to lose. It is not based upon stimulation from visible objects, and its wellspring is within you.

Now, enduring happiness is not the greatest happiness, but it is the road to the greatest happiness. We cannot talk about the greatest happiness here because you do not have the capacity for this. No one in the world has the capacity for the greatest happiness, but you do have the capacity for enduring happiness, which leads to greater and greater happiness as your capacity, vision, clarity of mind and purpose become strengthened and deepened. But we must have a starting point. Ultimate happiness is so far beyond this world, so all-inclusive in life, that it is almost without any kind of reference point in your worldly experience. It is incomprehensible to you now, but it is your true destination.

Therefore, enduring happiness is the happiness I would like to talk about because it is available to you now. I would like to talk about it in terms of purpose, meaning and direction in life. Happiness, you see, is often thought of as an emotion or an emotional state. "I am very happy because I am laughing." Enduring happiness is not like that. It has more to do with satisfaction and fulfillment, which come from a deeper resource, a deeper wellspring within you. It is not a momentary relief from the burden and strain of being in the world. Therefore, enduring happiness must be very comprehensive. It is not an emotion. It does not mean that you wear a big smile and tell jokes all day. It is something that you can carry with you into any situation. It can abide with any emotional environment in which you find yourself. It is completely adaptable to the world. It permeates everything.

You see, ultimate happiness is incomprehensible here because it is so different, and yet it is your goal, ultimately, because it is natural to you. To comprehend the contrast between your true happiness and your life in the world you must understand profoundly why you are in this world and what the world really is. This must come through realization. Though my words can perhaps be helpful as a framework, they are merely controversial until they are fully experienced and realized.

Enduring happiness is something you bring with you into the world. The world cannot give it to you. Perhaps you have heard this before, for it is a spiritual truth that has been restated in many ways with many references, stories, parables, and so forth. Enduring happiness is something you bring to the world. Now, to accept this means you must have come from someplace where there is a great deal of this kind of happiness. You brought it with you, and you have come here for a purpose to give it to the world and to discover it for yourself while you are in the world.

You can be fully present and find temporary escape from your worldly burdens and conflicts. But difficulties will continue. That is not the problem. Trying to have a life without problems is not the goal. Trying to discover what you have brought with you is the goal because it is greater than your problems. It is greater than the world's dilemmas. It restores your true value to yourself and teaches you the meaning of relationship because happiness is something you find together and not alone. In the pursuit of momentary happiness—in which there is great investment here—people attempt to join and establish relationships to achieve this purpose. However, you can also join in relationship to establish enduring happiness as well.

Enduring happiness is very quiet. One of its qualities is stillness. It has a calming effect on you because it relieves you of fear. It has a calming effect on others as well. It brings ease into the world, but it brings far more than this. It brings with it Knowledge and memory, for together they are the true redemptive force in the world. It is because of your origin and your purpose in being in the world that this is the case. It is not the kind of memory where you try to remember something. It is simply a memory that comes to you when your mind is opened—a sense of relationship and a sense of purpose. The amnesia of being in the world has worn off temporarily and you have a sense of continuity in life. This produces enduring happiness.

Enduring happiness is very relevant to your interests. You cannot escape the fact that happiness is a natural radiant aspect of who you are. You will keep trying to reclaim this for yourself. When you truly give this up at any time in life, you will begin to die. The possibility for success will be over, and you will begin to leave the world, slowly perhaps, but you will begin to die. As long as you are not preparing to die, then, you are still seeking for enduring happiness—for yourself and for others. Happiness seems like an emotion because that is how everyone is used to thinking of it—lots of laughter. But I am speaking of something that is an abiding sense of purpose, meaning and direction in life. It gives you a sense of satisfaction and makes it possible for you to truly relax.

So, let us talk about purpose, meaning and direction. Meaning is born of the fact that the world is a place for something to be done, and you are part of the effort in doing it. You came here for a purpose. You came from someplace else and you are going someplace else. You must entertain this possibility to be able to embrace the ideas I am giving you and even to accept my presence because I have come from where you have come from. That is why we are so much alike. Yet, I am more like you than you are because I have nothing added at this point. I added everything like you, and then I subtracted everything. You have added but have not subtracted very much, so you are yourself with all the additions—everything you think you must be, everything you think that you are, everything you think others are and everything you think the world is or should be. It sounds like a great deal, does it not? It is a lot of extra baggage, but there is the belief that without all these things you would be nothing. "What would I be? Does not my purpose, meaning and direction derive from all these things I strive for? As a person, do I not derive my value from who I think I am and what I think I do and what I think I have done? What would I be without this?"

So, it takes a little bit of faith to accept that there is actually something there when all these things are taken away, even for a moment. We, of course, do not want to take away anything from you that you want and because you live in the world, you are free to try to have whatever you want. You can pretend you are anyone you want to be. You can pretend you are the person you have been calling yourself all these years or you can pretend you are someone else, and most people believe you unless you take a position that is untenable. Then no one can believe you and they lock you up! If it gets too outrageous, people become uncomfortable with you. Well, it is fun to masquerade unless you cannot take off the mask. Then it becomes grave and serious, and you feel trapped and burdened.

Yet, you have cause for enduring happiness because your identity in the world is only a temporary expedient. It actually has value, but only in relation to your true purpose in coming here. You see, if you did not have a mask, you would look like me and how many of you can see me? I am as much here as you are, but I am like a naked person. I have passed through the training of the world, as all true Teachers have done, and that is why I am a Teacher of the world. All true Teachers have added everything the world has to offer, and they have subtracted it as well. If you can become your True Self while you are in the world, you will graduate from the world. Until you do this, you will need to come back and do this again and again. As you become more aware of this, you recognize that it is really very burdensome to do that. Your desire to reveal yourself and to contribute your gifts now begins to become greater than your desire for separation, refuge and hiding.

So, enduring happiness is a quality of your entire life. It is not an add-on feature. You do not put on a happy face or a spiritual face or any face now. It is merely beginning to radiate from you like heat from a radiator. You are feeling it, and others are feeling it because you are feeling it. You are the first recipient always. You are the first student of your own training.

Because you have a purpose, you have meaning, for meaning in this world is related to purpose. Anything that has meaning has purpose. Purpose is its meaning. Ultimately, this is not true, but in the world of tangible objects, in the world of time, this is actually the equation that generates meaning. Objects in the room around you have meaning because they have purpose. If there were something in the room that had no purpose, it would be meaningless and you would probably want to get rid of it. You would not want it around if it did not have a purpose. So, purpose in the world is meaning. Beyond the world, purpose is also meaning, but it is a little different there.

You see, God has to be a God in action to be meaningful in the world. God has to move because you are moving. In the world you see, there is nothing staying still. Everything is moving, dynamically. So, if something is not moving, you will not be able to experience it. Can you experience anything that is not moving? Even the stars are moving, rapidly. Everything in the room is moving, rapidly. The only thing in life that is not moving is God. That is why you cannot see God. Your eyes were not made to see something that does not move. Even with the refinement of your vision, which will give you a greater sense of Presence and the ability to discern that which is moving less than you are, you still will not see that which does not move.

God does not move because God does not need to go anywhere because God is everywhere, so there is no movement. But God's Presence and Thought generate movement in the world of moving things. This is a very important idea I want you to think about, please. It is a little mysterious, but it allows you to have a sense of abiding Presence with you wherever you go. When you are out in the world or even at home, you are interacting with moving objects. People, objects, things. Even your thoughts are moving. If you think about it, did you ever have a thought that did not move? Those of you who are practicing meditation, have you ever engaged with a thought that did not move, that did not change to something else or was not dynamic? A thought that does not move is pure Knowledge. It is the most powerful thought in the world. It is the thought that gave birth to the world. Only those who are very advanced can be fully aware of this thought. This sounds a little far out, but after all, this is all far out, yes?

Therefore, your purpose and meaning are the same. You do have true purpose in the world, but you have to become a mature human being to discover it. Until you find your true purpose, you are living with the purposes that you have created. You have adopted them because you cannot live without purpose because purpose is meaning, and you cannot live without meaning. Without meaning, you would end your life. Because life in the world is temporary, it must have meaning and purpose. Because it is all moving, it must also have direction.

So, the reason you are unhappy is because you are not experiencing purpose, meaning and direction. These are what give value to everything. God is moving things, like a great gravitational pull, moving things, often imperceptibly—a great attraction. You are free in this world to not follow this attraction, but you cannot eradicate it from your life. That is why people are afraid of letting go of things and having a little openness or emptiness in their lives. It is that attraction of God. Something may be very painful for you, but you still hold onto it. Why? This is a very important question.

We want you to consider happiness in terms of enduring happiness, where you experience purpose, meaning and direction. Definitions are inadequate. You do not need definitions. You need experience. You experience your purpose, meaning and direction. Then, an abiding sense of well-being begins to generate within you. This does not mean you do not have bad times and are not afraid or upset or angry. It is something that is growing within you. You have a sense that you are not alone now. It does not matter if you are in relationship or not. You can discover enduring happiness in any circumstance. Often the worst circumstances are the best for this because they challenge you to escape your own thinking and deal with life directly.

The problem with momentary happiness is that you are always losing it, and you cannot control life to create those perfect circumstances to give you that wonderful experience again. And so, the relentless pursuit of momentary happiness produces the misery you see around you—the addictive circumstances and the addictive substances.

We are primarily concerned with engaging you with your true happiness, which is engaging you with your purpose in being here, your meaning in being here and the direction which you must follow now. You have the capacity in your mind to respond to what is real and true because you have a True Mind. It is not the mind that you made. It is the mind that you brought with you from your Ancient Home. It is the real you. It is very great, but it is quite hidden. It will not emerge within you until a way has been made for it, until you desire it. Because its effect on you is so powerful, you must be truly present for it. Momentary happiness only reaches you at the very surface of yourself, but enduring happiness engages all of you—parts of you, you are aware of and parts of you, you have not yet reclaimed.

The pursuit of true happiness, or enduring happiness, requires true preparation. One of the qualities of this preparation is simplicity. You see, human beings are very simple, extremely simple. They pride themselves on being complex because being simple seems to be stupid. Being simple is like being an idiot, not a very interesting person. Only people who are very complex seem interesting. But it is not like that. You are very simple. Your nature is very discernible and your true inclinations are very direct. In your true nature, there is nothing clever or sly about you. You are child-like, but you are also powerful because with simplicity comes power and Presence. As your mind becomes more simplified and directed, it is more powerful. So, with simplicity come power and true ability. With these also come the necessary requirements of understanding your limitations and having humility.

In this day and age in which you live there is a great deal of spiritual psychology and spiritual philosophy. Many of you have been exposed to a great deal of it. There are many different ways of looking at this issue of happiness, God, purpose, meaning and direction. Because people think they are wonderfully complex, they are afraid to take a position. The Way is really simple, but it does mean that you have to let go of those things in yourself that are non-essential to your purpose. This is maturity. With this comes enduring happiness because purpose, meaning and direction are already built in. You do not need to add them to yourself. You do not need to make up a wonderful purpose for your life and then try to live it out. It is a process of reduction, not addition. You are very burdened with your own mind and with the troubles of the world because of all you have added. I am talking about reduction—losing weight! It does not mean that you become an ascetic and give up all things. That is ridiculous. That is only for very specialized individuals. It just means that you allow your life to become oriented towards those things that are truly meaningful to you.

When you leave this world, you also leave all you have added to yourself. It is very useless in the beyond. When you go back to your Spiritual Family, what do you do with all this? It has no place there, no context. After all, if you don't have a body, there isn't much to do, is there? It is lots of fun not having a body! It seems terrifying to you because the body is such a refuge, but being without it is marvelous! You can still make appearances, you know, but you do not have this heavy sack to carry around night and day. You have to feed it all the time, make it beautiful and keep it comfortable. It is like caring for an infant that never grows up! Anyway, you will all find out what I mean at some point.

In The Greater Community Way of Knowledge, people begin to discern their Knowledge, to the extent to which they are aware of it, from other motivating factors in their mind and in their environment. This process takes a great deal of time, but the results are very immediate. Here you are able to make very intelligent decisions at the outset which reflect your Knowledge. The only difficulty is when your Knowledge is in conflict with what you want. Then Knowledge must wait.

You still feel that you must have what you want in order to find out if you really want it. It is very confusing to have what you want if it is not in true alignment with your Knowledge. It produces great discomfort. As you begin to have experiences of Knowledge, you will begin to see how uncomfortable it is to want things without Knowledge. This contrast between being at home in yourself and being estranged from yourself is very, very important because it illustrates everything I am speaking of purely within the realm of your own experience. You cannot miss it. In time, you will see that your happiness increases as you come closer to Knowledge and decreases as you go away from it. Then, naturally, you will want to be closer to it increasingly.

Knowledge is your True Mind. It makes decisions, important ones. It moves you to do things. It does not think like your personal mind thinks. It is very quiet. When you become quiet, you will be able to experience its greatness. All intelligent beings in physical life, both here and in other worlds, possess Knowledge. When Knowledge and relationships begin to make sense to you, you will not get together with others out of ambition or for temporary happiness. You will allow your natural alignment with others to occur. You will become engaged with each other very, very naturally and you will have relationships of an enduring quality and depth which reflect the kind of happiness of which I am speaking.

The pursuit of that which endures is very different from the pursuit of that which merely stimulates or excites. As you seek for that which endures, you realize that you endure with it, and the fear of death begins to leave you. You begin to value different things. You seek intimacy. You seek quiet. You seek inspiration. You seek companionship. You seek community and family. You seek health.

Anything of value will require a lot from you. You cannot want it casually. If what you seek is something of real significance and substance, you cannot want it one day of the week only and have any hope of success.

Students of Knowledge who are in the process of reclaiming Knowledge realize over time that it is the only thing of value because it is the source of their true relationships. It is their source of inspiration and the source of their sense of purpose, direction and well-being. It is a gift that gives continuously.

Now, students of Knowledge often think, "Knowledge is something you only use when you make important decisions, so I have to remember to use my Knowledge." And so, they try to do that. "Must use my Knowledge! Important decision at hand. Let's see, what do I know about this?" There is a great deal of effort to know the truth and then they finally give up. Then they can know the truth.

Knowledge is not something you simply use when an important decision is coming around. Knowledge is an abiding Presence within you. It can counsel you every five seconds. It abides with you. If you are not a religious person, well, you can just say, "I feel very good." And if you are a religious person, you can say, "Well, I feel God is with me or Christ is with me or Buddha is with me or the Presence is with me." It does not matter if you are religious or not. God does not care. God does not understand religion. God did not create religion. God only knows God. And because God only knows God, then God attracts you because you are part of God.

This enduring happiness I speak of leads to greater and greater happiness. If there is more room in your life for happiness, there is more happiness. You cannot put happiness on top of a life that is filled to the brim with old things, like a closet that is filled to the ceiling. You can't get any more in there. Your mind is like an old closet full of old things. "This might be useful someday. I shouldn't throw this one away. Need this one for sure!"

Our teaching is very compassionate because we ask only one thing. It is the one thing that brings all goodness with it and sets you on your true path. When you are not on your true path, you are not really going anywhere. You are simply standing by the side of the road entertaining other things. But when you are moving with Knowledge, you have direction. You know you have purpose, even if you cannot define it. And you do not have to wonder if you have value because life will be demonstrating to you that you do. It is up to other people to show you your worth. They are the witnesses to it. It is not enough to love yourself, as people often think. "Well, I must love myself or I cannot love another." It is watching other people love you that makes the real difference. Then you will know what is happening. That is what melts down fear and shame. You watch someone else loving you, and you know they know how crummy you are. They don't care, so your being crummy must not be too important.

Our teaching is very simple. It takes time, it has many steps, but it is very unified. You can always come back to it. It is like an old friend who waits for you while you stop by the side of the road to ponder and think and imagine and dream. Then you come back and say, "Okay, let's go on together." And you go on together.

All you can do in life is move with the purpose of your life or hesitate. Hesitation is unpleasant if it is prolonged, but Knowledge waits very patiently. Believe me, when I say you must wait for Knowledge, think how much Knowledge must wait for you! But because Knowledge is not trying to become anything, it can afford to wait.

Your purpose here is to discover Knowledge and to allow it to guide your life. That is one way of saying it. Knowledge contains your true identity and your specific function in the world—what you are really here to do. It contains the Wisdom and the love that you have brought with you. It is not the Wisdom you can personally claim for yourself because it is not only for you. It is for others, and it is hidden deep within you. You cannot find Knowledge yourself. You cannot misuse it. You cannot discover it prematurely. Knowledge arises when you are ready, and it arises gradually so that you have time to learn about it and to distinguish it from the other aspects of yourself which you have acquired. You learn to give it, to receive it, to abide with it and to accept it. It is a burden until it is recognized for what it truly is. Knowledge has the assurance of your True Home. It is not frantic. It is not intimidated by the world or disappointed by the world. That's what makes enduring happiness possible. No matter what happens, it is still there.

*What is
meaningful
is lacking
&
that is why
people suffer.*

Twenty-two

ESCAPING SUFFERING

HERE ARE THREE DIFFERENT CURRICULUMS for ending suffering, three different remedies. There is the remedy for those who wish to give up a little bit of suffering. There is the remedy for those who wish to give up a lot of suffering. And then there is the remedy for those who wish to give up all suffering. They are very different remedies—prescriptions you might say. I would like to talk about the prescription for giving up a lot of suffering.

You are already quite aware of the prescriptions for giving up a little suffering. They are very, very simple and most of them simply mask your problems. Some of them give you temporary relief for very brief periods of time and make life a little more tolerable. This first prescription is by far the most popular.

People are not aware of how unhappy they are unless something very wonderful or mysterious happens to them. Only a profound experience of happiness provides the contrast necessary to illustrate what is truly possible and meant for people. You are here because you are seeking a greater remedy, a greater happiness and a greater fulfillment in life, and that is why we must talk about suffering.

There are two kinds of suffering. I would like to make this distinction. The first kind of suffering is the kind most people think of when they think of suffering and a simple definition could be: Suffering is the recognized or anticipated loss of something you value temporarily. Yet, there is another kind of suffering that people rarely consider that I would like to concentrate on because it has a great deal to do with your understanding of how happiness can be achieved here. The second kind of suffering is your yearning for your Spiritual Family, for God. It is a very different kind of suffering from suffering because of the loss of temporary things.

The first kind of suffering deals primarily with your mind. It is not pain. We must make that distinction. It is not physical pain, though physical pain can result from it. I do not want to analyze the first kind of suffering, for there is too much of this already—"The Psychology of Suffering"—but I would like to talk about what really motivates people in life.

The first kind of suffering is something that you experience daily, even every hour—the loss of things and the anticipated loss of things. Loss of experiences, loss of objects, loss of friends, loss of abilities, loss of opportunities, loss of securities and loss of pleasures. Loss, loss, loss! This is very dominating, this "loss" phenomenon. It is the down side of happiness. It is like a great shadow that follows you about, for whatever you hold dear today, yes, you can lose tomorrow. It can be gone. Many things you cannot even consider losing because it would be too terrifying and painful.

So, there is this problem of suffering. You cannot avoid it because it is such a constant companion. If you begin to observe your thoughts, you will realize how your mind goes from one loss to another, and the only way it can mask this emphasis is by hoping for new and exciting things, for whatever you hold to, you keep losing it, and this gets very tiring. You spend a lifetime accumulating and giving it all up. It is a very tenuous state to live like this, but it is the state of the world.

Traditional religion in its very pure forms has said, "Give everything up now that you anticipate losing and you will undercut the source of your suffering." Well, for most people that increases their suffering right away because they must give up everything they want even before they lose it, and it looks like a terrible prescription. Not a lot of people are very excited about this approach. Not much enthusiasm here. "Oh, boy! I'll give it up right now. Then I won't have to worry about it anymore!" This prescription plunges you into the heart of the dilemma, but it is only half of the picture and of the two halves, it is the less important.

Your happiness, your healing and your well-being cannot be born of a negative influence or emphasis. What motivates people to look beyond their pain? What calls people out of conflict? What carries people forward in life? What encourages them to give up a painful situation for a greater opportunity, however uncertain? What is this power that calls on you and why do you respond to it?

Many of you have specific questions on how to make things better in your life, but I will give you more than that because you need more than temporary relief. Now, there is a problem here because if I tell you what is true and you are not ready for it, you will argue with me because knowing what is true is always dependent upon how much you want to know it. This can be difficult to ascertain sometimes within yourself because you may be eager to give up suffering, but you are not always eager to embrace the change that is necessary.

What is this power that calls you forward in life, keeps moving you, keeps you out of stagnation and keeps reminding you that there is something greater for you to do in life than simply suffer? What is this power, this great attraction, this great response within you? Yes, it is true that people suffer over loss—whether recognized or anticipated—but there is a greater yearning that is in the very heart of all people. It is in such an intimate place within them that it is rarely discovered either by themselves or by others. In this place are the greatest tears and the greatest laughter and the greatest happiness. Here suffering is like a shell or a very thin wall. It is not deep and cavernous.

This power does not itemize everything you must give up in life. It speaks of what life is bestowing upon you. Its emphasis is giving, not losing. It is an attraction in and of itself. When you recognize it, you just begin to simply drop everything and go for it. Who cares about losing anything? And because you cannot take everything with you to find this power, you naturally let things go along the way. They simply become burdensome to you. They are recognized as complicating your life, holding you back and making you unhappy, and you simply drop them.

This great attraction, this yearning you have, is for God. Without God, about the greatest yearning you could have is for romance. It is about the only other thing that you would abandon yourself for. Falling in love, head over heels, who cares about security in the world? Who cares about what happens to you? "Oh, I don't care! I only want my love!" You can only think of your love night and day, day and night, and you notice your life keeps working out for you, miraculously, even without you managing everything. But romance is only a very, very small and temporary experience compared to what is really moving you in life. Until you find out what this is, you will keep yearning and trying to fill your yearnings with people, things, new experiences, new sensations or new stimulations—constantly new things, new, new, new! You don't really want most of them anyway, so you end up giving them up for other new things.

When you stop stimulating yourself, you begin to feel this great yearning, and this is the beginning of your Self discovery. This yearning is not terrible. It is simply very deep. It is like remembering how much you love your parents, in spite of everything that has happened. It brings sadness but gratitude, too. It is too deep to be sentimental.

You are endowed with the source of happiness, and it seeks to be used each day and, in time, to be relied upon. That is why we teach people to begin to use Knowledge, the greater capacity of mind they have for knowing and for following what they know. People who want only a little bit of relief from suffering only go so far with it. Perhaps they try to use their intuition in the face of very complex and confusing decisions, and the rest of the time they never think of it. But people who want to give up most suffering begin to see new opportunities for using Knowledge, developing their experience of Knowledge, developing their capacity for Knowledge, fine-tuning their abilities and developing themselves. And then there are the very rare individuals who are ready to give up all suffering, and for them there is a very special curriculum which we will not speak of, for it is not relevant to your needs. They choose a path that is very expedient but not easy because the direct method is not easy. The slower method is easier now but more difficult in the long run.

If you think of solving any problem and you think, "Well, let us solve it today!" or "Let us solve it sometime soon," or "Maybe we'll solve it later," these represent the three kinds of approaches. But I must confess, there is a little trick in all this because God is very smart. If you seek to give up most suffering, which is a very great step, you begin to experience a very profound happiness, and this paints a very sharp contrast in your life. You begin to see that as you use Knowledge, you come closer to happiness, and as you neglect or avoid Knowledge, you go away from happiness. So, you learn the simple lesson that if you go towards Knowledge, you become happier and if you go away, you go back into confusion, anxiety, anger, sadness and all forms of unhappiness. And you know, eventually you will get the idea that if you spend more time with Knowledge and follow Knowledge, things will work out better. So, you start doing that more and more and then, of course, you will want to spend all your time with Knowledge because what is the point of only spending part of your time with something that renders certainty, power and relationship to you? It can take many years to reach this decision, but people do eventually. So, it is guaranteed that if you undertake the process of giving up most suffering, you will want to give it *all* up someday.

Now, I have to tell you a very important thing here. I hope you will listen to me and not to your thoughts, please. I am more interesting than your thoughts. When I say, "Let us give up suffering," people don't get excited unless they are in a very unhappy place in life—in fact, so unhappy that they will consider anything. They want out! Unless they are that uncomfortable, giving up suffering only sounds like a good idea. "I'll add it to my list of things to do this year—this month give up suffering. I'll put it on my daily goal list!" Well, if things are not too bad, who cares about giving up suffering, but when things get really bad, oh my! "Now I'm interested!"

So, the idea of giving up suffering is not enough to encourage or evoke enthusiasm from people because people ask, "Well, what do I have to give up to give up suffering?" They become very nervous about the deal! "What do I have to give up now? Maybe I don't want to give up some things. Do I have to give up those things to give up suffering?" And people think of all the ascetic, religious people who don't have anything and think, "Oh, that's not for me!" What this really means is accepting happiness and certainty into your life, and that undoes suffering.

I want you all to give up suffering. That is my wish for you because you do not need to be this unhappy. You must recognize you are unhappy to recognize the need to do something about it in your life. How people recognize they are unhappy is either by becoming more unhappy and finally realizing they are unhappy or by having a profound experience of happiness and realizing the contrast.

There is not a great deal of change you must make to become very happy. The world does not have to be a pretty place. There does not have to be no war in the world for you to be happy. You do not have to have all problems solved to be happy. You do not have to satisfy all of your great goals to be happy. That is not the requirement. Having more of what you want will not make you any happier. You have more of what you want now than you did yesterday or a long time ago and you are not much happier, correct? It is a little better, but you are still involved in trying to get things, to keep them and to prevent life from taking anything away from you. That is very desperate. There is no happiness there. There must be a different approach.

It is like a prison full of people who are all in their cells, but all the doors are open, and they are still in there because they have been in there so long, what else is there? The fact that the doors are open does not occur to them. They are still trying to make do with their current circumstances.

When you begin to experience Knowledge, you begin to comprehend some important contrasts in life. You begin to experience true certainty in the world, incrementally at first in little situations, and with increasing regularity as you begin to follow Knowledge, mysterious as it is. Learn to follow Knowledge and learn to contribute to others very directly and there will be no time for suffering. Who has time to sit around and anticipate loss when there is so much to do right now?

You see, you are very helpless in determining the course of events. I know that sounds like an insult. Human beings are supposed to be so powerful! Such great minds, they can do so much, they can achieve so many goals! But if you observe your current state of mind, you will realize how helpless you feel in the world. You live your life on assumptions and when they are disappointed, it is a crushing blow. How easily your happiness is blown away by some minor change in life. Your happiness must be established on a firm foundation, on something you brought with you into the world and not on what the world can do for you.

Because you are so often afraid and endure so much anxiety, it bears witness to the fact that you truly feel endangered and vulnerable. You can bolster up your courage to say, "I can handle it all! I will determine my destiny! Yes, I will forge ahead!" And by sheer will power, you actually can achieve more than you thought you could, but you have not resolved the problem of suffering, and the real happiness that I am speaking of will still escape you even though it is right there.

Your first objective, then, is to face your suffering directly, and by this I mean you must face suffering without judgment. If you are present with suffering, it cannot affect you. But if you are reacting to suffering or trying to change it, it can overtake you at any time. Those who fight suffering will become enslaved, for they are responding to it. It is capturing them because it is a habit and an addiction. It is something that claims people in spite of their good intentions.

Now I would like to talk about some points that are relevant to everyone. First, one of the requirements is that you stop trying to solve your problems. That is very important. Begin now to give up trying to solve your problems and everyone else's. If you are always trying to solve things, you are not in a position to experience Knowledge. You must relax about the situation. Only if something demands immediate action must you act. Unless this be the case, unless the requirement is immediate and obvious to you, then it is wise to settle down and begin to really feel where the certainty is regarding the situation. This is not a desperate attempt and it involves faith.

You cannot solve all of your problems. That is not the way out of suffering because more problems will take their place and more problems and more problems, and they will enter as fast as you resolve the old ones. You will not have a life without problems, and if you do, that would be a terrible problem for you. So, problems will always be around. It is like having to eat the next meal or get sleep the next night or go to work the next day. Being in the world is a problem, so problems are part of life here.

The second requirement is you should take inventory of those things that you feel are truly making you unhappy and see what can be done about them. Again, ideal circumstances do not provide happiness, unless you are starving to death or have some immediate requirement that is absolutely necessary for your health and survival. People have very important discoveries in life when opportunities do not look good. As a matter of fact, most important discoveries happen during these periods. When everything is going well, people go to sleep. They become less attentive and less observant. They are lulled into sort of a napping state. So, if your circumstances are not ideal, that may be very good for you.

Next, do not be satisfied with the normal state of mind. It is pathetically limited. There is much more for you. As you become more serious about your well-being, this will become more evident. So, it is very good to check up on yourself regularly. For casual students, at least once a day. For serious students, more often than that. Check up on yourself. How are you doing, really? We present a contrast in how people can live their lives from the way they habitually live their lives. This contrast is very, very important.

The next requirement is not to think that improving your circumstances will guarantee what you are truly seeking. Those who live very luxurious lives do not exemplify any greater happiness than you do. Is that correct? And if you think otherwise, you should go spend time with them and find out how disappointing it is! They are more anxious about losing things than you are! They have more to lose, and they have not found the source of their own happiness or their foundation in life.

Next, it is not the goal of life to not work. It is the goal of life to find real work in the world. It is what is meaningful that is lacking, and that is why people suffer. When meaning becomes your foundation—true meaning— then that will be the source of your happiness, and you will be able to take it with you wherever you go, regardless of circumstances.

People who are inspired are not thwarted by unhappy appearances around them. They can function anywhere to some degree, if they have adequate support from other people and if they continue to nourish their awareness and experience of Knowledge. Then, as they become stronger, they can take Knowledge where Knowledge seems to be lost, and they can contribute to people who are without Knowledge and are lost.

The more you come to Knowledge, the more the dark cloud of suffering will part for you. You see, people in life are swamped in misery. I know that sounds very negative, but compared with your natural state it is quite accurate. When you begin to wake up, you begin to realize that you have been in a very deep sleep. The world generates this kind of sleep. It is constantly feeding it and regenerating it, so you will need to withdraw from the world a little bit at the beginning of each day to find some relief and to allow your mind to settle down if it is aggravated. This is true for everyone. That is why we do not recommend that students of Knowledge read newspapers or magazines or watch television very much because this simply aggravates the personal side of their mind, which is where they suffer. If you are serious about finding a way out of suffering, you do not want to keep aggravating your problem by putting your finger in the wound. You must allow your mind time to settle down. Your thoughts are moving around very rapidly. They preoccupy you and you follow them. They are very unhappy thoughts, and if you try to put happy thoughts in their place, well, they are moving around, too.

Happiness is a quiescent state. It is not jittery. It is not trying to go anywhere or get anything. It is very still, so you have to become still to come into proximity to it. It is as if happiness were going five miles an hour and you were going a hundred miles an hour! Well, you passed it by!

Some people are very critical, thinking that they have created all this misery and suffering. Well, they have, but it is only because they did not know any better. After all, you are simply doing what everyone else is doing. Do you blame the child for being a child? Do you punish a child for acting silly or being forgetful or not having skills?

If there were only two avenues to follow that you were aware of, and they were both unhappy, it would be hard to choose one of them, yes? If you could choose between a path of unhappiness and the Path of Knowledge, well, there would be no choice. That is why our emphasis is to bring you to Knowledge. That solves the problem right there.

Why is forgiveness
so difficult
to accomplish?
Because you are
afraid to go
beyond
your mind.

Twenty-three

FORGIVENESS

I WOULD LIKE TO PROVIDE A FRAMEWORK for you to look at forgiveness and an opportunity to see its relevance to your development and happiness. There is a great deal of idealism about forgiveness these days. Many people who have developed an understanding of spiritual thought have studied books and teachings which deal with this subject at great length, even to the extent of considering it to be the pivotal area of concentration. For other people, perhaps, it is not something that they have thought of a great deal. Yet, when you begin to examine your own mind, to observe your thoughts, feelings and behavior, you realize the relevancy of this great subject.

So, we wish to talk about forgiveness because it represents a path of redemption. It is an activity, if we can call it that, which deserves your attention. It is relevant because there is a great deal to forgive. You are easily upset by the world you live in. You hold many judgments about yourself and thus about others. You are aggravated by many circumstances and events, great and small. If you are to begin to discover your true quality of mind and your true abilities, how can this be done or undertaken when you are beset by so many aggravating things? How do you start?

Well, the fact is, people don't start. They never start. They are like seeds that fall from Heaven that never open or germinate. What they contain inside such a plain exterior is a wealth of life and the possibility for life. You are all seeds, thrown upon the earth, attempting to sprout. You are in fertile soil. You need nutrients and you need someone to tend to your development. What you possess within you is so much greater than your current form would indicate—something so small and seemingly so limited that possesses such great life force.

So, what is in the way? Is it unforgiveness that is in the way? Well, it is, but it is more than this, so I would like to expand the idea of unforgiveness—the judgments you hold against yourself, others and life in general. These judgments hold you within the personal side of your mind. As a matter of fact, they make up your personal mind, which represents a very limited sense of identity. Everyone in the world has this because this is part of being in the world. Yet, beyond this limited identity lies your true reason for coming here. You cannot know your purpose from your personal mind. The value of the personal mind is to provide a medium for Greater Life to begin to express itself in this world. We call this Knowledge, an all inclusive term.

These grievous judgments you have of yourself and others—many of which seem so substantiated by life—what can they do for you, who possess the Godseed? When my little talk is over, you may protest a little because, you see, I will say your unforgiveness is not justified and you will say, "Oh, how can he say such a thing? Look at what happened over here. These people were terribly assaulted and hurt and there is destruction everywhere. How can he say my ideas are unjustified? Is not what is happening a terrible event?" For this you will find agreement in the world in great measure, but your thoughts about it are still unjustified. You may hold them as true if you wish to stay in your personal mind because what does the personal mind think of? It has fear, it has excitement and it has judgment. Take away judgment, and things begin to break up. Then, you begin to see through the appearance of things.

You were not sent into the world to judge the world. The world is a ridiculous place, so why judge it? It is a magnificent and beautiful creation, and it does not make any sense. But you did not come here to make sense of the world. You came here to carry something important that wishes to grow, and given the right environment, encouragement and, of course, your permission, it will grow on its own. That is your greater life. Your personal mind is like a shell that contains the infant. Once the infant begins to break through the shell, the shell is discarded and the life that emerges from it is so much greater and so much more natural. Judgment and unforgiveness bind you to your shell. Many of you realize the weight and burden of carrying such judgment and the pain of entertaining such unforgiveness. They are like bars across your way.

Forgiveness releases you temporarily. You can breathe easy now. You have just eliminated one enemy from your life. That produces a great relief. So, forgiveness always produces a relief, and with relief you are able to see the situation differently. It is not threatening to you now. If it is ridiculous, it does not matter. Life here is ridiculous! That is why you have come.

People come to the world and say, "Where is all the good stuff for me?" and they are disappointed. The world does not have what you want, but you have what the world needs. You make sense. The world does not. If the world makes sense, you do not. The more you make sense out of world, the less sense you make. And God certainly doesn't make any sense. How could God permit such things to occur? Either there is no God, or God is evil, or you are so bad, so criminal that God is punishing you by sending you to this place. This is all ridiculous! The world mechanically makes sense, but beyond that it does not make sense. If you can accept that, then you will stop complaining about it. You came to give something to the world, all of you. Obviously, your unforgiveness prevents you from doing this. So, unforgiveness is a burden. It makes you feel unworthy of the gifts that we present and that we remind you of.

You see, at the very core of your judgments of others and the world is your own personal shame. Why is there shame? Because you hold judgments that life does not share and you have rejected life as a result. God has made your healing very easy, very direct and uncomplicated. Life without God is extremely complicated and terribly fearful. It is always beset by anxiety and the threat of annihilation. The only way that people can live in the world is to have some kind of god. If you do not experience God, you make up a god. Everyone has a god here in the world. To live without God, life has no meaning. It is over. So, if you do not experience God, you make up a god and then try to experience the god you made. But the god you made up is not totally satisfying, and so there is disappointment upon disappointment.

Now, everyone here has judgments about themselves, yes? You are not perfect looking enough, not exemplary in the right areas, can't do this, stupid in this area, too tall, too short, too thin, too fat, too silly, too serious, and on and on! And people ask, "How can I rid myself of these terrible judgments? I see I have these judgments. They are binding me, imprisoning me, weighing upon me. They torment me. How can I get rid of them?" Well, you cannot get rid of them where you are, but you can do something else in life where they are not necessary, and then they begin to evaporate. God has a Plan and how the Plan works is that it gives you something meaningful to do in life. It gives you a meaningful foundation for relationship and participation. Can you work out these judgments? You cannot. You cannot stay in the room of unforgiveness and make it better, but you can leave the room.

People ask, "How can I get rid of this burden I carry inside? My mind is like a crown of thorns." You cannot make the thorns more comfortable, but you can do something in life that allows the seed you carry to emerge. This is the source of true healing. In this, you are not simply made more cosmetically attractive or given temporary relief or comfort. It is not enough, you see, for me to say that your judgments against yourself have no foundation. Will you give them up because I said so? "Well, the teacher says I don't need to think this way. I won't ever think this way again." Poof! The thoughts are gone! "He is a great healer! He has cast a healing spell on me!" I can see the headlines now. "The next Messiah is here."

We do not want to be too grave about this subject because you are already too grave about it. It is serious. You cannot deny it, but you need not crucify yourself for it, either. To follow Knowledge is the way. You begin by making decisions based upon your deepest inclinations, but this is only the beginning. Do not think Knowledge is only intuitive decision-making. Oh, no! This is only the very beginning steps, the baby steps. But these beginning steps are very important because following Knowledge means that you are turning away from all accusers, both internally and externally, to follow something that you now hold to be more important. Here you must value your Knowledge increasingly, which erases your self-hatred. Yet, you will not be successful if you think you are grandiose. Little seeds are not grandiose yet. Those who value their true worth are willing to be diminutive. It is no affront to them. Those who hate themselves cannot stand the idea. For them it is painful. If God could be a seed, how diminutive, how humble—no identity to protect.

Therefore, follow the Path of Knowledge. It is so simple, and yet it is so commanding. The easy way is the commanding way. It makes your life very direct. You cannot sit on the sidelines now and imagine how life could be. You need not maintain complex ideas about human nature because human nature is not complex. The only thing complex in the universe is confusion. You are not complex. Do not think of that as degrading. People love to think they are multidimensional radiant beings possessing all potentialities. You are bigger than all that. A diminutive seed of life is bigger than all that.

Why is forgiveness such a relief? Because it lets your mind open and relax. Why is forgiveness so difficult to accomplish? Because you are afraid to go beyond your mind. You would rather stay miserable with little ideas and chew on them, like hard little candies, than go beyond into uncertainty. Obviously, what I am talking about is a profound change in thinking. It is not a change that you can bring about. You cannot change your mind. You can change your habits of discernment; you can change your decisions, but what changes you is bigger. What breaks out of your shell is something you did not invent and cannot direct. Unforgiveness only keeps it in. What emerges is *you*. It has no self-consciousness because it is not trying to be anything else, so it does not compare or contrast itself with other things.

We teach people to recognize their Knowledge, to begin to use it and to begin the path of Knowledge according to the Ancient Teaching. Immediately people are faced with a few obstacles. Primary amongst these obstacles is their own self-doubt, which reflects their self-hatred. Can you trust something inside yourself when your mind has fooled you so many times, when so many times you found out you were wrong when you thought you were right, when you did such stupid things so many times? Can you trust something inside yourself that you cannot define and that you rarely experience? Can you do this?

In The Way of Knowledge we give you very simple practices. Goodness, the practices are simple! "Oh, they are so difficult!" you may say. Why is it difficult if I say, "Let us practice experiencing Knowledge thirty minutes a day." "Ah! It is difficult!" Why is it difficult? You spend more time than that in the bathroom looking at yourself! Why is it difficult? It is difficult because you do not think you are worth it. This is really an investment in yourself.

Now, let us make this very important point. People are terrified of their own judgments. That is why looking inside, at first, can seem so ominous. It's all dark in there, you know, and there are these terrible thoughts, terrible memories and images. The world has taught you hatred. The world teaches this because it does not know anything. You know something. That is why the world is not your place of origin. You are a visitor. You are not merely part of the biological machinery of this world. You carry the seed of Knowledge. Knowledge unused is a terrible burden. It is the source of everyone's neurosis. It is like having an arm that you never use. Well, it's an awkward thing to carry around all day, yes? Having this thing dangling from your body—it works, but you just never use it. It's always in the way. Try putting a shirt on with one hand. What a nuisance!

So, when individuals begins to follow their Knowledge, they are confronted with their own self-doubt and their fear of self-judgment. It is their own ideas they are afraid of. What scares them is their own ideas! Well, the only way to know that an idea is only an idea is to face it if it stands in your way. If you become a student of Knowledge and you begin to follow a deeper, more profound power within you, you will be confronted with your own doubts and your own judgments about life.

You see, Knowledge does not care what you have done. It only wishes to emanate from within you. People think, in psychological terms, that they carry all these unresolved issues from the past. "I must devote the next twenty years to resolving them and then, perhaps, I can be a human being who can be happy and can enjoy things with a fresh viewpoint." Well, that puts the resolution conveniently in the future, does it not? Twenty years resolving your past is ridiculous! You will end your life a seed unopened. That is not what we are proposing.

You will find out that you can live life very effectively without having to make these judgments. And once you have the experience of doing so, which you can have even at the outset, this will strengthen your conviction that what you are following is worthy of your complete devotion.

This will redeem you in your own eyes because you will see your value in relationship to something very great. People's value must be demonstrated to them. It is not enough for me to say, "You can forget about not liking yourselves because you are all wonderful." Now, I will say that because it is true. I enjoy you very much, but is that enough? Your value *must* be demonstrated. God will do most of the work, and you get all the credit. God does not need the credit.

The path of resolution does ask, however, that you become very conscious in the moment. Here you can begin to witness yourself making judgments and accusations against yourself and others and be present enough to check this when it begins to happen and to choose a different way. You see, the personal side of your mind is made up of habits. That's all it is, is habits. It's a whole network of habits. That is why it keeps repeating itself over and over again. The more you see your personal mind, the more you see how repetitive it is because this is how it maintains its identity. Your personal side is not to be condemned or thrown out. It is useful. It understands nuts and bolts and is very useful, but it makes a very poor god.

So, to begin to follow Knowledge, you must realize there is a need for it and feel you are worthy of it. This in itself is a step towards recognition and an important step away from self-hatred. Merely changing your thoughts about yourself will not resolve the dilemma because that does not provide for your true needs. Following something within yourself that is not based upon your judgments takes you away from them altogether. Without your attention and reaffirmation, they simply begin to dissolve. That is why God gives you something meaningful to do that has nothing to do with your conflicts. You may say, "I am here working this out and resolving that," but this is simply your way of trying to make your new life relevant to your old life.

Survival is not the main concern for the man and woman of Knowledge. They are in a position to contribute to life because they possess what life here does not have, and so they have a life that is not impoverished. They are individuals who are in a position to give meaning to the world. They are not grandiose, yet this meaning can flow from them. All people really want to do, you see, is to belong somewhere and to provide value to their situation—to be at home somewhere and to be a part of something real. Then they can begin to settle down and participate, and their value and meaning will be demonstrated over and over to them, for value and meaning can only be demonstrated.

Because you live in a world of limitations, you will always have limitations, and you will always make mistakes here. Yet now you have no basis of condemnation because you are not trying to make the world look good. In fact, you are not trying to make anything. You are active now in allowing Knowledge to direct your contribution. If you are too fat, too thin, too tall, too short, too silly, too serious, too anything, it does not matter. The desperate attempt to justify yourself, that great harness, now begins to fall away.

You see, God is like air. Everyone absolutely depends upon God, but they never think about God. People are only concerned with objects, but the very essence that maintains them moment to moment and that provides this pristine world they live in is taken for granted and never thought of. When the essence is more important than anything you see, then you will feel a great power in your life and gratitude will abide with you.

God is pulling everyone Home. That is your Knowledge—pulling you Home, reeling you in, drawing you close. Once Knowledge begins to emerge, it will seek to fulfill itself, and the whole basis for unforgiveness will disappear. What the world needs is for individuals to both find and bring their Ancient Home here. That is when the world will cease to be a place of denial.

The world
cannot provide you
happiness,
but you can give
the world happiness
because
you have brought
happiness
with you from
your Ancient Home.

Twenty-four

HAPPINESS IN THE WORLD

OR THOSE OF YOU WHO ARE BEGINNING to develop an inner life and an inner sensitivity, it can be more difficult being in the world. You are becoming more sensitive now. The harshness of physical life is more abrasive to you, and you seek retreat more than stimulation.

People ask, "How can I be happy in the world?" As we have said in previous discourses, there are two kinds of happiness. There is momentary happiness, which is the result of happy stimulation that can be very pleasant but very easily lost. Then there is enduring happiness that abides within you, and as it grows strong, it can be experienced in all circumstances. It is the very seed of freedom in this life.

We wish to speak of enduring happiness and how this can be established in life. Yet, I must give you more than simply an idea or a definition. You must go beyond making simple changes in your behavior or thinking because the world is very powerful. It induces certain kinds of thinking in people that are quite strong. You are so used to thinking a certain way that you have no idea that it is only one way of thinking. This becomes habitual. You never question it. But as you begin to open internally, you see that your point of view is simply one way of looking at things. It is not necessarily the truth. Because you see things in a certain way, you think that that is truth. People argue and fight and they suffer over what they think the truth is. They look at the same thing and they see two different things from different points of view.

When you begin to open inside, begin to have a greater sense of yourself, begin to develop your capabilities and sensitivities and begin to draw upon the higher qualities that you possess, you see that points of view can vary and that how you see things is not the truth. The truth is very hard to see, but it is not hard to feel. Two people with very different viewpoints can have very similar experiences feeling the truth. When I say "feeling," I do not mean emotions. I mean a deeper kind of experience.

You see, the world cannot provide you happiness, but you can give the world happiness because you have brought happiness with you from your Ancient Home. You must be its first recipient, however. Everyone in the world is looking for the way to happiness, how to maintain happy stimulations and how to avoid pain. It is very desperate to try and keep everything pleasant and comfortable and to have all things you want without loss. Is this not difficult to achieve? There are people who will guarantee that you can do it, but if you look about, no one is successful.

True happiness is something that you bear with you, but it is deep within you. It is the result of experiencing purpose, meaning and direction in your life. This is not a purpose, meaning or direction that you invent for yourself. It is something that arises in your mind. You realize it. It is not merely your thoughts or beliefs or philosophy or religion. Though the experience of happiness can find expression in these, they are not its source. The source of true happiness is inexplicable and beyond your realm and range of experience. The result, which is happiness in this world, is something that you are meant to have, but you must cultivate yourself to be able to gain access to it, to have the capacity to live with it and to carry it into life.

People are very anxious, you know, to have great experiences. They want to experience Jesus. They want to have God appear. They want proof. They want answers. And yet their capacity for experiencing these things is extremely limited. You cannot experience something if you do not have a capacity for it. Only momentarily in your life will you perhaps have a glimpse—a new experience of looking at the world without an old viewpoint, a feeling of Presence abiding with you that is powerful or a feeling of empathy with another that is beyond words. These are reflections of the happiness that I speak of.

Why is happiness important? Happiness is not going around all day laughing about things. There are people who do that, and underneath they are often very unhappy. Happiness is a sense of peace, a sense that you are at home in the world, and from this comes comfort, contribution, direction and good counsel for others. With it, you are like an oasis in a very desolate place. If you look about at the people that you have contact with, you will see that there is very little happiness in the world. It is very good to tell the truth about this and not simply dismiss it by saying, "Well, that is the way things are. That is life."

You see, a truly happy person, a person who is honestly happy, gives the evidence of God. God wants to give to people because people are poor. This happiness that I speak of is something you discover in yourself and in your relationships with others. It is an experience and not an idea. Do not be satisfied with ideas. Do not think a whole new list of definitions is going to make your life miraculous and happy. You already have lots of definitions, a mind full of them. It is the experience that I speak of, and here my words can only be approximations.

You have within Knowledge, your ability to *know*—profound it is, great it is, beyond definition. Rarely do you experience it, but as you develop yourself to experience it, it will become greater and greater. This will give you a sense of meaning in the world because the world cannot give this meaning to you. Everything here is temporary. You are not temporary. Everything you see is passing before your eyes, but you who are watching it are not passing. Yes, your body is passing. Your ideas, they are passing. All are temporary. Yet, if you think that that is who you are, you will feel you are dying all the time, and happiness will be beyond your reach.

That is why our meeting with you is meaningful. You see, we represent your life beyond this world. We do not live here, not anymore, but we are very close to the world. We are like a bridge. Our existence is the demonstration that you have life beyond the world. The minority is here now while the majority is on the other side—in various states of development. It is like being in and out of the fish tank. When you are in the fish tank, it is an all-consuming experience, yes? Yet, when you are out of the fish tank, you can see things in the fish tank very clearly, but you cannot easily interfere. We are out of the fish tank. You are in. You are underwater in your world, but only for a little while.

The source of all fear is the belief that you are temporary, that death awaits you and that everything you value and everything that is meaningful to you can be taken away at any moment. With this belief, you are extremely vulnerable. Your happiness, then, can be ended in the next moment. Terrible things may happen, yes? With so many fears and so many threats to your well-being, real and imagined, how can you be happy with all these conditions, with trying to save a little piece of life for yourself alone while time is eroding everything away. Yes, there can be happy moments, fun times and recreation. That is good, but it is not enough. You cannot play all day long and be happy.

When you begin to develop your awareness of God's Presence in your life, within yourself and within your relationships, then a greater sensitivity begins to arise within you. Here you will see that there is a very great distinction between this experience you are having and the world that you see with your eyes and hear with your ears. If you live only in the world, well, you are worldly-minded. You may be very practical. You may know all about things, how things are and should be, and so on. We call that being worldly-minded. Being worldly-minded is being intelligent about only a few things. But now you are becoming aware of something much greater. It is not easy to talk about it. Language was not made to describe it. It is more than a feeling, but perhaps that is all you can say about it.

You are beginning to experience the presence of Knowledge in your life. Very deep in you it is, so you cannot misuse it. It is in safe storage at the very center of you, like a treasure at the bottom of the sea. You cannot get at it because you live at the surface where everything is turbulent and changeable. Like the surface of a great ocean—one day life is calm and peaceful and the next day there are raging storms! But deep down inside of you God has planted a seed. If that seed is allowed to grow and to develop, to germinate and to take form within the world, it will be a source of purpose, meaning and direction for others.

On occasion great teachers are sent into the physical world, but this is quite rare. Why is it rare? Because people cannot tolerate having someone like that around. Would you want to go share a household with Buddha or Jesus? It would make you very uncomfortable! The problem with people like that is you cannot stand to have them alive around you, but you cannot forget them either. So, you prefer to worship them after they're gone. They are rarely tolerated in their own lives, except by very few people.

That is why God always works behind the scenes. God works in your relationships. God doesn't think and scheme and plan like a little spy agency. God is like a great attraction pulling you Homeward, and this attraction stimulates your Knowledge. Once Knowledge is stimulated sufficiently, and once you are prepared and your outer life is open enough, then Knowledge will emerge within you, and you will begin to discover real happiness.

This emergence will not be easy at first. You will be very distrusting of it, and all of the terrible things you think about yourself, the shame and the guilt you carry for so many things, will stand in the way of you accepting your deeper inclinations that will be emerging from Knowledge. Here you are not pure; your inclinations will not always be reliable, but it is a beginning. You are learning to walk, and there are forces beyond this world and forces in this world to help you learn, for you cannot do this alone. You are like a little baby learning to walk who needs great assistance and care night and day. You don't throw the baby out into the world and say, "Survive!" You care for the baby and teach the baby all the necessary things.

So, on the Path of Knowledge you are like a baby. You must have constant care and someone must be watching out for you, for you are learning to do something very few other people can do or will do. This is a beginning. This is experience beyond belief. If this is allowed to grow and you take the steps, one by one through the stages of development, you will become a source of happiness in the world. You may have no religion at all, and people would feel God in your presence. It is not you who are God. You are just a window into the world through which the Greater Life can shine through.

You see, historically people always want to make the messenger of God the object—after they kill him, of course. They worship the person because it is easier to deal with a person than with God. It is easier to worship Jesus on the cross than God. God is very big. Jesus is very finite on the cross—pathetic, even. Jesus is part of a Greater Order, greater indeed. Think not his presence in this world was a singular event long ago. But now, your society has become open enough and developed enough so that we can speak in this way to you. Never before has this been the case in this world. A rare and wonderful freedom you have. We most certainly hope that you can appreciate it in light of what humanity has endured. This is a very great opportunity from our perspective.

If Knowledge—this profound state of mind that you possess buried within you—is allowed to emerge and if you become its student and can follow its direction, you will experience it ever more clearly and will become like a beacon to other people. If you allow yourself to develop and open through all the stages, you will become a source of happiness. You are carrying it with you. This does not mean that you will be a person who is pure and beyond all reproach. That does not happen in this life. You might as well give up perfection altogether. Even Jesus made mistakes. It's part of being a human being. Perfection is not the issue. Being in this state does not mean that you have no bad habits and are happy all day long with not an angry thought. What this does mean, however, is that you carry the Presence with you. It is this Presence that people instinctively respond to. It is not personal charisma. That only sways people momentarily. What I speak of affects people for the rest of their lives.

If Knowledge were expressing itself through the person who works in your yard as a gardener, he or she would be teaching God's Presence to everyone he or she came in contact with. Some great teachers actually hide out in these kinds of disguises, so that no one knows what they are doing. There is still too much fear of God in the world for any messengers to appear without protecting themselves. Fear breeds hatred and distrust, anger and retribution. That is why when Jesus was taught of his ministry, he had to be informed of what would happen to him personally. That is the price of complete exposure. That is why true teachers must give up all personal ambition, for that is counter-productive to their true mission and well-being. This, of course, is very difficult to achieve.

The world is a tough place. Why come here? It would be better to go to the beach somewhere, yes? Why come here? It's hard work! You see, you are all like acorns from Heaven, possessing the germ of life within you. If given the proper environment, assistance and circumstances, you will become a great tree. Humanity has been improved and developed by the efforts of a relatively small number of individuals who carry your race forward in all respects. So, you are like acorns from Heaven. Do you know what I mean? Many do not open. That is why there are a lot of them. Not all of them open to become seeds for great trees, but that is their promise. That is why I am here. I am a gardener. My regard for you is much higher than yours is for yourself, for you see only your difficulties, your wishes, your fears and your ambitions. But that is only the shell, the very outer part of you. I see that too, but I see the seed that you carry. You have free choice in life. You can either be an acorn or a tree. Not everyone needs to become a tree, but if you become a tree, you will regenerate your race.

You have happiness. You have it! It is way down inside. Go outside and you will not find it. You will find lots of stimulation. Having no pain, having fun all day long, having lots of money and a wonderful wife or husband—these are all promises with little promise of success. The hunger for happiness, which is the hunger for peace and inner resolution, burns hotter than ever.

Often, people say, "All I want is a true partner in life, a true relationship. I want to be married. I want to have a family. That is all I want." And I say, "Well, that is very good. Go spend time with people who have that and ask yourself if you want to have their level of satisfaction." I do not want to deprive people of what they want. After all, relationship is very important. But having a marriage or family does not guarantee success.

In the world, people live in a state of amnesia. Like fish in a tank. Your world is that tank. Rarely can you see beyond the waters of your little world. But knowing that you have life beyond your confinement and that you are representing it here, that is very great! The worldly-minded will accuse you of being ridiculous. They will accuse you of being a dreamer, or something even worse than that. You must discover your happiness, which takes time. You must let it grow, which takes a lifetime. And you must learn to carry it and still be a responsible person in the world.

Many people think that spirituality is a great excuse to take a holiday from life, but that is not our intention for you. That is not what brings about success. There are very few individuals in this world who become true renunciates. Humanity could not continue if everyone became a renunciate. Only a few are meant for this, and they know who they are. Yet, that is not the model for spiritual life. The model for spiritual life is someone who is capable and responsible, someone who is carrying inner Wisdom into the world and letting it grow. This inner Wisdom will never reach its full maturity while you are in the world. It will always be in stages of development because it is greater than the world. Our life is proof of this, if you can experience us.

Becoming a student of Knowledge requires that you begin to claim those things you know and to distinguish them from what you think or want. It means that you enter preparation. You must learn how to do this. Some people think, "I'll read enough books and I'll invent a way for myself. No classes, no teachers." And you know what happens? They merely entertain themselves. How can you lead yourself into new territory? Can you take yourself beyond where you have been? You need true relationship in the world to do this, and you need guidance from beyond the world.

The Great Way in the reclamation of Knowledge is totally successful because it will attend to all of your needs and to every aspect of you as a person, bringing complete harmony to you. Its emergence in your life is so natural.

I spoke of Jesus because he is very popular, yes? As a person. But very few people have any sense of who he is or where he is or what he is. Jesus is a window to look into the world and a window for you to look out. After all, if you knew when you left this world that you were going to a happy place, wouldn't that lessen your burden? You don't have to worry about going to hell. You are already there. This is it! Being alone in your thoughts, what could be a worse form of isolation?

Your first experience of Knowledge will probably be in the form of profound intuition, something that you sense or know about yourself or another. It usually takes very trying circumstances to bring this forth. When people are very comfortable and everything is going along fine, rarely do they have experiences of Knowledge. When things are being challenged or upset, well, often people have this experience. The first experience of Knowledge as profound intuition can be used in your decision making increasingly, if you enter preparation. However, Knowledge itself is much greater than this. Very few people in life will discover it completely. Not many need to. But many of you do need to because it is the answer to your questions, all of them. All the why, why, whys? When you are experiencing Knowledge, they do not matter.

Your capacity at the beginning will be very small. You will only be able to experience it for moments here and there, but this will become more frequent and longer lasting. Through these experiences of Knowledge you will also be receiving grace through your Inner Teachers, who guide you and look after you. Very little of this will be conscious because your mental awareness is only activated at certain levels. Beyond that, you will not be able to see things or hear things. Yet, as your mind develops, you will experience living in a greater and greater universe. You will have more sense of Presence in life. Life now is not just a bunch of moving objects. You will be able to see beyond your own thoughts more and more regularly and be able to look without interpretation, which will enable you to see things as they really are. There are many specific skills that you individually will need to cultivate to do this, and they are all very worthy of your attention. You are all students. You may not know it yet, but you are.

So, obviously, we wish to encourage you to develop your experience of Knowledge, which yields for you a real sense of purpose, meaning and direction. Here you will see that there is a way to resolve the kind of issues that you are facing and the serious decisions that you must make. You cannot resolve all of them at once because you are not ready at this moment, but the answer is there because Knowledge is answering for you.

Many people ask, "Why do I need Teachers? I want to go to God directly." You can go to God directly, yet who you will encounter there are your Teachers. You cannot change that. The Mind of God is beyond this world. God does not speak. Teachers speak. God does not counsel. Teachers counsel. Do you think God knows how to speak English? God does not have a voice. God cannot not be God. That is the one great limitation upon God. I can speak to you. You can understand my words. You are free to discard me if you do not want to believe me. That is fine. It simply means we have to wait longer. God always speaks through Teachers, you see, because they translate God's Will into an experience and into a form that you can understand. They are like mediums. You see, I have Teachers, too, translating to me. I translate to you, you translate to other people. Everything gets translated at all levels, all the way down the line! Everyone is taken care of. No one is left out. God is made comprehensible to you here within your range of experience, and as your experience grows, you will begin to experience God in new ways. Eventually, you will not need words at all. I am a speaker. That is my special function. So, I am here to talk to people, but there are other Teachers who do not speak.

It is possible to be truly happy in the world. It is not only possible, it is meant to be. When you are truly happy in the world, you will not need to come here again. Then you can serve the world and be outside the fish tank. Things do not look so frightening when you are on the outside.

Your calling is the work that you are here to do specifically. You not only brought happiness with you, you also brought a blueprint for the best ways you can serve the world. That is also buried within you. Being in the world is action-oriented, and your work here is a source of meaning for you. Here you do not find your purpose out first. It simply emerges when you are ready to act upon it. After all, if I say, "Your purpose is to be a this or a that," it is merely another controversy in your mind, is it not? But if I said to the man or woman who is truly ready, "Your purpose is to do this," they would know instantly it was the truth, and their lives would change instantly. It is not because I have special powers that I can initiate people into their Knowledge and purpose. It is because they are prepared. I am only a confirmation of their preparation, yet I or someone like me has worked with them. It is like graduating from school. Graduation ceremony only takes a few minutes, but you go to school for a long time.

We often speak of people's decision-making process. We want you to learn to be wise decision makers because that is a very good way to discover Knowledge within yourself. The source of a wise decision is not something you made up. The decision is there already. You simply get ready to receive it and to accept it.

Sometimes the word "happiness" seems to be a limited term. Yet, that is what people are seeking for desperately—in their relationships, in their hobbies, in their work, everywhere. We are talking about a happiness which is more a resolution leading to peace. This happiness and content-ment are truly rare commodities in this world, and anyone who has found them is a gift to humanity.

Fear is escaped
because
there is something
more important
than fear
that takes you
out of it.

Twenty-five

ESCAPING FEAR

W E WOULD LIKE TO TALK ABOUT ESCAPING FEAR because fear is so much a part of your experience. There is a way to escape fear so that you may become much more effective and present in life. It is not an empty promise to say that you can escape fear, but you must enter a different state of mind. You must enter the state of Knowledge, a state of profound knowing. You cannot escape fear when you are living in your personal side, or personal mind. There are many attempts to do this, and they end up being extremely difficult, requiring great amounts of energy with little success.

To understand how to escape from fear you must understand something about fear itself—where it comes from and how much it governs and determines your thinking, actions and experience. It is very difficult to define fear, although there are many definitions. Definitions are limited. You cannot simply have an explanation that will really serve you because this is something you must recognize in your experience. When you are very upset, very distressed or very angry, stop and say, "Ah! I am afraid right now." It is this recognition that is important. "I am afraid." Often this is enough to disengage you from your distress or to give you a greater perspective while you are in distress. You recognize you are afraid. "At this moment I am afraid." Having this recognition brings you into your experience. Otherwise, you will simply demonstrate the results of your fear because fear is very captivating.

Why can't you give up fear in a normal state of mind? Does that not seem like a worthy objective? When you are in a normal state of mind, you are identified with temporary things that are easily lost or destroyed. You want to protect what you have and acquire more and at the same time give up all the discomfort of doing this. Protect this body. Protect this mind. Protect these ideas. Protect these beliefs. Protect these possessions. Protect these affiliations. Protect this wealth. And protect all the things that will lead to further security in these areas. Can you achieve this without anxiety? Can it be done? You are not a monastic. You do not give up all things and live in a monastery. Only very few people can do that. You are a person in the world. How can you escape fear? That is what we will be addressing.

What about fear itself? So prevalent it is, so much a part of your thinking and your behavior. Your priority is fear. It is so fundamental to your experience here that only through self-observation can you begin to realize what a dominant force it is. So, even my words can arouse fear. Something new? Fear! Your first response? Fear! My words, if they are true, what will they challenge? This response is very important to understand because if you undertake the reclamation of Knowledge—the very essence of all true individual development—you will begin to have a new relationship with fear. As a result, you will begin to understand the impact of fear on your life in the world.

This is not something that can be accomplished only with definitions or explanations. Fear is too prevalent. It underlies most of your thinking, even your desire for a better world and your desire for peace. Many of your efforts to improve humanity's situation or circumstances are governed by fear. Your longing for relationship, your anxiety about death—it's all fear! So, when you begin to really encounter all this, it becomes ominous. It seems like too much.

When people begin preparation in *Steps to Knowledge*, they learn to become objective about these things and as a result are able to see them more thoroughly. This is important in enabling them to experience their true nature. They become observant in their lives. All true religions must teach this, for you cannot attain greater skill or ability or have access to greater intelligence if you are thoroughly identified with your emotions or your ideas.

You have your experiences of fear, and if you have been observant of yourself, you will see how much fear impairs you and how much it holds you back. You begin to see what is possible and necessary and you say, "Ah, I could do that, but I am too afraid." However, it is not enough to say that all that is standing between you and your goal is your fear.

People often think that without fear they could be magnificent. This is not true! It is a very prevalent idea in many teachings on personal growth that without this demon called fear or early childhood memories or society's programming, you would be such a great magnificent being, you could do anything and have anything. This is a very prevalent idea and very stupid. It is not based on Wisdom but on idealism. So, people attempt to attack their obstacles like great warriors and slay the dragon that stands on the bridge. And, of course, they wage war upon themselves. This is not the way.

Fear is indigenous to your personal side. It is like trying to have a body without aches, pains, bruises or cuts. You need to have compassion so that you do not place impossible demands upon yourself or upon other people. This is very important if you seek to become a teacher. People can become fiercely involved in improving their personal side, but this is not the way.

Fear is escaped because you are cultivating Knowledge. There is no place for fear in Knowledge. Knowledge, then, must become your focal point. Here you are not at war with the world or with yourself. You are cultivating something greater. You see, your mind and body are like the house, and Knowledge is like the garden. So, you go out in the garden to grow your food and you bring it back into the house. You cannot sit in the house saying, "Where's the food? Where's the food?" No food arrives. So, you look all over the house and you decide, "Let's change the house." But the garden is outside. You must bring the food in.

It is like serving the world. People are very indignant that the world is the way it is. Yet, how could it be otherwise? It is exactly the way it is because it is the product of where people are in their lives. So, to say, "The world should be very different than it is," means that you intend to declare war on the world. This is not the way because sooner or later, you will become an adversary in the world, and you will become violent, governed by fear and not by Knowledge. "If the world does not change soon, it will blow up!" Can you teach peace if that is your motivation? Can you be a force for peace or reconciliation if your motivating force is profound anxiety? Can you raise a child thinking, "I must protect this child from becoming a criminal"? Can you raise a child effectively with that point of view? You cannot tend the world with this point of view and hope to give a true benefit. Besides, the world is frustrating to change. People are very entrenched.

There is one way to escape fear and that is by cultivating Knowledge. In this way, you do not declare war on yourself. You do not dissect yourself with a knife. You do not become cruel towards your personal side. You do not cast out your feelings or your little thoughts. You have compassion for that which is weak and respect for that which is strong.

Here we take a complex situation, and we provide a simple direction. Yet, to cultivate Knowledge, you will go through a lot of fear and by going through it, you will weaken it. Fear is a master. It is the master of the worldly mind. I do not call it an entity because that gives it a significance that it does not have. Yet, it is a force that people share and generate. When people stop doing that, of course, fear will disappear. You cannot say the same for love because you are not the source of love. But you are the source of fear. If everyone stopped loving, love would still permeate the world. That is why people have been unable to get rid of it.

We do not recommend, then, a prescription for removing fear by simply saying, "I will get rid of the fear and all there will be is love, happiness and peace of mind." You know what? It does not work! Fear is too strong. You cannot say fear is nothing if it dominates the world. In a Greater Reality, fear is nothing, but in your reality it dominates the world. It is quite wise, then, to give due respect to the strength of something you must face. When I say you must go through some fear to reach Knowledge, well, that is true. In doing this, though, you will find out what the source of fear is because Knowledge takes you directly to God. Then you will begin to understand why people hold onto their fear, as painful as it is. But this is a mystery you individually must discover for yourself. Definitions and explanations will not carry you through.

In the reclamation of Knowledge, you will have to override your fear again and again. You are not at war here. You are simply choosing another way. "I choose to go this way, afraid or not. I follow Knowledge in this situation, no matter what." Then you pass through fear as if you were passing through a great black cloud. To do this, you must realize that your fear is not you. There must be some objectivity here. "This fear—it is not evil, it is not bad, but it is not me. I will be attentive to it, but it is not me."

Now, we must make a very important distinction here that many people forget: Caution is different from fear. Caution can arise from Knowledge. Caution means that you are being very attentive because there is a possibility that something may go wrong, or you may have to make an important decision, even if nothing goes wrong. So, you are very attentive—like a mountain-climber, very attentive. Mountain-climbers are very attentive to where they put their hands and feet. Would you call that fear? Mountain-climbers would become very afraid if they thought about falling off the mountain. They would panic; they would make poor decisions. That is why people like to climb mountains—they become very fearless and they can experience Knowledge, momentarily.

So, you must learn the difference between caution and fear. They are very different, but you must have the experience. To be able to experience caution in its real sense, you must separate yourself from fear within yourself. You must be able to identify it increasingly because fear is very blinding. It dominates your perception. You must see that reality is not based upon your perception.

Now, you do not need to become a therapist with yourself to do this because the emphasis here is on keeping your eye on Knowledge, not on the obstacles to Knowledge. Here I must make another very important point: If you become concerned with fear or any of its manifestations, it will dominate you. If you study evil, it will claim you. Why? Because without Knowledge, it is more powerful than you are.

Therefore, Knowledge must be the emphasis. It starts with recognizing what you truly know about your life and about the decisions that you must make. It requires that you develop the ability to be still internally through practice. This is important because with a certain degree of stillness, you are able to become observant. You cannot be observant if your mind is always on the go, running from thing to thing and going from thought to thought. How can you be attentive? How can you see anything? The reclamation of Knowledge requires stillness of mind, it requires cooperation with others, and it requires the development of true discernment. This is all extremely practical and will have a direct bearing on everything you do in life. Because there are so few people who can demonstrate Knowledge in life, if you have even a little bit of ability, you are a tremendous asset.

You have things that you can lose that you feel are truly yours. There is so much regarding your social and physical survival. I can say, "Well, give it all up! It is not worth anything, anyway! You'll be out of this world in a few years, and what is it worth then?" But it is not enough for me to say that because you are meant to be in the world. You have a purpose in being here, a purpose that you cannot find either in your personal mind or in your fear.

Knowledge is planted in you like a seed. If you begin to cultivate it, it will begin to grow and take its own form. It has its own life, like a seed in the ground. You do not need to tell it how to grow. Just provide the necessary environment, nutrients and conditions, and it will grow. While this is happening, you are a person in the world who is still concerned about physical, mental and social survival, but there is something else in your life now, and you are giving it increasing attention. You cannot neglect the world because you have to live here, and you must be responsible. You cannot neglect the world to become a student of Knowledge. "All I want to do is practice all day long and have great experiences!" That is not a good idea. It will cause much distress. So, you must be responsible as a person in the world and also develop your capacity for Knowledge. Knowledge develops very slowly because people are very afraid of Knowledge. They are very afraid of the one thing that will take them beyond pain.

Someone will ask, "Well, that is all very good, but what do you do about the world in its difficult state? I feel I must do something." What do you do about the world? Well, there are two motivations for serving the world: one is where you are moved by Knowledge and the other is where you are moved by fear. For this reason, many students of Knowledge must temporarily withdraw from political or social involvements because fear still captivates them, captivate their minds. They do not permanently withdraw; they only need time because they must learn to become observant and discerning. They must develop some very fundamental and useful abilities.

Sometimes my answers seem rational and people say, "Oh, this is very good!" And sometimes they are not rational and people say, "I do not understand this." But answers are temporary expedients. Not everyone wants to become a person of Knowledge. Very few do. Yet, the person who will help your life to be beneficial is the person of Knowledge, whom you may never meet.

Why has the world kept going in spite of all of its tribulations? Twenty years ago, people were saying, "My God! We are on the verge of total destruction." Today people say we are on the verge of total destruction. Twenty years from now, people will say, "We are really on the verge of total destruction! We must do something quick!" Who is holding us all together? The animal nature in people is quite capable of destroying the race, yes? Any of you could be murderers or criminals! So, who's holding it together? Why have human beings persisted? There must be a force. Something is doing this.

You only need relatively few people with Knowledge to preserve life here. Everyone drinks from their wellspring, yet only a few know where the water comes from and who brought it here. That is why the Wise go unseen. If someone of true ability pronounces themselves, it causes a lot of trouble. That is why advancing students of Knowledge must give up all ambitions, even to save the world, even to use their newfound skills to bring good to a suffering world. A few individuals will need to make a presentation to change the course of religion or history or to effect change in human thought, but for the most part, the truly adept individuals in the world remain hidden. In this way, their work will be unimpeded.

What we are doing here, you see, has been done for thousands of years. It is not a new phenomenon. Yet, for thousands of years it was done in extreme secrecy. You have such freedoms now! Of course, the disadvantage of your time is that people respond without a great deal of intention. In earlier times, you risked your life to receive a teaching such as this. Therefore, it would have been very important to you and not a casual curiosity. So, in your world now, you have greater freedoms, such great freedoms. Few of the advanced worlds in this part of the galaxy have such freedoms. But along with such freedoms, people suffer from very poor motivation. People are without direction.

Everyone of course wants to minimize difficulty and conflict in their lives. "I don't want trouble! I don't want to run out of money or have anything bad happen!" You want to be comfortable so that you will be free to enjoy your personal pursuits as much as possible, yes? However, it is usually the uncommon and even extreme circumstances that spark Knowledge in people. Not that pain should be a prerequisite for Knowledge, but sometimes when things happen that are really different, people have new experiences.

Sometimes I must talk about the "house on fire." If the house you were living in were on fire, everyone would forget their personal reasons for being here and pitch in and do what is necessary. This situation would put you in a different state of mind. And you know, when these kinds of things happen, people sometimes respond without fear. But after it is all over, they become very afraid. "Oh, my God! What could have happened! Oh, I just barely escaped!" But in the moment, they were without fear.

So, while people are trying their very best to make all their circumstances very agreeable, at the same time they are also trying to make circumstances very severe to give themselves an opportunity to experience Knowledge and to wake up. Isn't that interesting? I think that is very interesting. Why do people do such stupid things? To wake themselves up. If everything were wonderful, if you had Heaven on earth right now, wouldn't that be grand? Wouldn't it be beautiful with everyone loving and no one having to work unless they wanted to? But how long would it last? If you did not return to Knowledge, it would not last but a moment.

You cannot have stillness in your environment if you cannot be still within yourself. You could not tolerate it. How many of you could sit quietly for eight hours and not move? How many of you can sit still for twenty minutes and not move? Being still. Everyone wants a world that is still and lovely, but who could tolerate it? That would be the most fearful thing of all. That is why Heaven is not wanted. Who wants Heaven? People want to know there is a Heaven, just in case the world does not work out, but who wants it now? I am not saying this to frustrate you but to allow you to have compassion for the world. The world is doing pretty well, considering that human beings are only a few years away from being tribes people and that you have so many newfound skills and abilities. You are doing fairly well, as far as societies at this stage of development go.

Now, the man and woman of Knowledge are concerned with Knowledge, but they are also concerned with what Knowledge is directing them to do. This is where your calling in life begins to arise. People, of course, want to find their calling without Knowledge, which means they simply want a new definition for themselves. Your calling in life emerges from your Knowledge. Here you feel that you must do certain things. It is not a matter of personal preference. It is not even driven by fear. "I just must do this!" You are able to do these tasks with such strength and conviction, such single-mindedness. You will not be a pure and immaculate person, but you must do this one thing. Then you become able to do things in the world very effectively, without fear. You will have concern, and your personal side, what's left of it, will have its usual kinds of anxieties, but there is something more important now.

Fear is escaped because there is something more important! If the house were on fire, who would be sitting around worrying about when they will find a relationship? Something now is more important. There is purpose now, for a little while, to preserve life in a dangerous situation. Fear is escaped because there is something more important than fear that takes you out of it.

You do not need dire circumstances if the source of your Wisdom is being attended to. It will grow slowly, and it will bring about gradual change in your life because for the vast majority of people it must be very slow. Some people want it to move very fast and so they do extreme and difficult spiritual practices, the hardest they can find—the "path of fire," they call it. But those who follow the slow, methodical way go faster.

One of the most important qualities is stillness. In developing stillness, you are able to see things you could not have seen otherwise regarding yourself and subsequently the world. You are increasingly able to look at situations, individuals and even objects and see what is actually there, not what you are interpreting to be there. All students of Knowledge must develop some degree of stillness so that they can start to see things. This also develops their desire for peace because peace is very still. Peace is not simply the absence of conflict in the world. Peace is stillness. As long as stillness is greatly feared, there will be war because the struggle for stimulation will produce conflict.

When you are cultivating Knowledge, you are always facing fear and choosing either to go with Knowledge or not to go with Knowledge. When you go with Knowledge, something happens that is wonderful. But when you do not go with Knowledge—well, you find out that going with Knowledge would have been a better idea.

In developing stillness, you also develop patience because Knowledge does not reveal itself upon demand. If you feel you must make a decision and Knowledge is silent, well, maybe you do not need to make a decision. Maybe you cannot make a decision. Maybe any decision you make will have no true potency. So, patience naturally must arise. With patience come tolerance, faith and trust—all very fundamental things. When you are still, the Presence is with you, your Teachers are with you, and the power of your Spiritual Family begins to emanate through you. When you are still, you become more a mirror or a window than a wall.

You must recognize at this point that I am talking about you, not about your husband or wife or friend or client. *You* are the subject. So, the idea is not, "How can I make this other person have these qualities?" or "What can I do for this person?" It is *you*.

Another aspect of escaping from fear I would like to mention is that you must begin to think about your life beyond the world. I can say that I am without fear because my foundation is not in the world. That does not mean that I do not take my role in the world seriously. I am not free from the world totally. I have to work here. There are better places to work! But I am fed by my life beyond. I am a rich person. I have relationship. The world cannot hurt me. So, you must have a foundation beyond the world.

Because of their early religious training, some people cannot say the word God. So, whatever word you need to use to give yourself permission to think about your life beyond the world, please use it because your role in the world is dependent upon where you have come from. People look to the world saying, "Give me meaning. Give me purpose. Give me direction. I have come looking for the truth of my life." But the world cannot do that. That is like a doctor walking into the patient's room saying, "Who am I, please? Tell me!" The world needs the truth you have within yourself. The world cannot give it to you. But once you give it, the world will bear witness to Knowledge because Knowledge is everywhere. A mind without fear can see this. A mind with fear can only see its own thoughts and interpretations. It is not free to see or to know. It is out of relationship with life. Your life must be beyond this world for you to experience this because you are here such a short time. It is very important, then, to think about your life beyond the world.

It is very important to associate with individuals who have devoted themselves to Knowledge. Knowledge is good. You cannot find it and misuse it. As soon as you claim it for yourself, you lose it because it works through you. If you can become still and open, you will begin to shine like a beacon. You will feel moved to be with certain people and to do certain things. Your life will be very simple. That is why we say you must take time to become still, or you will be as frantic as the world and as unhappy. Increasingly, your happiness and your relationship with others will come from Knowledge.

Therefore, you *can* escape from fear. And you will see your fear, oh yes! It will be standing in your way and saying, "You cannot enter here." Fear can be identified because it has no depth. It is very superficial, though it can be very strong in its inducements. It does not have substance. In this, it is very different from Knowledge. Knowledge is quiet but has tremendous Presence. It is extremely intelligent, but it does not think all the time. It is a different state of mind. The world is kept going because there is a sufficient number of men and women of Knowledge in the world, and Knowledge moves other people who do not know anything about it.

*Everything
becomes clear
when
your mind
is
still.*

Twenty-six

STILLNESS

DEVELOPING STILLNESS IS VERY ESSENTIAL to the cultivation of Knowledge and to the resolution of personal difficulties. I have not talked about stillness a great deal because many people are not yet practitioners in the reclamation and development of Knowledge. Stillness is relevant because it will give you an emphasis to use in developing your own abilities and in recognizing the requirements that are necessary for you to utilize your greater powers of mind.

People are very anxious to have very big answers to very big questions. They seek resolution to long-term problems, but when it comes time to talk about practice, well, that is a different matter. Many of the things that are your true goals in life require much development to achieve because you cannot be satisfied with explanations or philosophy or answers alone. Answers are not enough. You must cultivate the real abilities that are essential for successful living here. There is no way around it. There are many shortcuts that are promised, but the methodology is secondary to your will in the matter and to your desire for truth and resolution, which in time will be greater than all other things.

So, why is stillness of mind essential? Its rewards are quite apparent if you think about it. A still mind is a focused mind. It is a mind that is using all of its resources. It is concentrated upon one thing. It is without the vexation of little distractions. You are able to concentrate your greater strength of mind on one area, and this gives you much more profound insight than you would normally have. Because your mind is quiet, you are not trying to give the situation answers or explanations, so you are able to witness things as they truly exist. Simple enough, but very profound.

With stillness, you can exercise the great powers of your mind; you can have a greater ability for observation and discernment, and you are able to see the necessary way that you must follow. In stillness things become obvious that would never be apparent to a mind that was in distress or in conflict. This power of concentration will give you tremendous ability in the world, but that is the lesser of its rewards. Its greater reward is that you begin to discern and to experience your own Knowledge, which is the True Mind that you have brought from beyond this world to contribute here.

Not all of you wish for the complete reclamation or discovery of Knowledge. Many of you just want to have a problem solved. Here the lesser rewards of developing stillness of mind will give you what you need as well. But I don't want to talk simply about the incredible resolution and sense of purpose, meaning and direction this state of mind will yield to you. I would also like to talk about what happens along the way.

You are where you are. You cannot be somewhere else in your development. You may dream or think or wish that you could be in a much higher state of mind with greater abilities to contribute, with greater powers over mundane things and so forth. Yet, the most valuable thing is the means for getting there. Getting to a place of stillness is even more important than the result, for in achieving this you begin to have the fundamental qualities of concentration, discernment, patience, perseverance, faith, compassion and forgiveness—all things which are very essential.

Now, when you are concerned about a problem and are in conflict regarding it, the last thing you want is to become still. You are very eager for answers. "I need the answers right now! I am desperate!" And you go through all the possible answers that you have ever considered or heard about. Maybe the problem is emotional. Maybe it is physical. Maybe it is medical. Maybe it is philosophical. Maybe it is spiritual. And so you go all through the inventory of answers and possibilities because you are afraid. How can you afford stillness of mind? It does not seem to yield any result.

Very few of the problems you consider require immediate action. So, the first step is to withdraw from the situation. Do not try to answer the question. The first step is recognizing that you must take a more comprehensive approach rather than simply trying to resolve the situation by putting an answer on top of it. This separates you from the problem and establishes that you are greater than the problem itself because you are establishing the means for its resolution.

Next, you must take inventory of your preferences regarding the matter. "What are my preferences regarding this situation?" To the degree to which you have strong preferences, it will be more difficult for you to experience Knowledge or know what to do. You will think you know what to do. You will think you have the answer or possible answers, but you have not found the real answer because the greater mind deep within you is not yet able to speak to your conscious mind.

So, withdraw from the problem and then begin to review your preferences or anxieties about it. Preferences and anxieties are very similar. They both distract you from focusing upon that place within yourself where the answer can emerge.

Then, you must see if you really want resolution. "Do I really want resolution?" It requires a great degree of honesty to come to a genuine answer here. If you are not sure, it is better to say no. If you say yes, then in order for this to be genuine, you must be willing to follow any course of resolution, even if it leads away from the preferred outcome that you seek.

You see, problems are not hard to solve. The problem is that people do not want their problems solved. What people seek is a resolution which will give them their preferred outcome and relieve them of the discomfort which they are feeling. Then there is plotting and scheming. Here outcomes are considered to be more important than the truth until the truth becomes more important than the outcomes.

When you finally reach stillness of mind, you don't care about any of this. You are past negotiation. To approach stillness—this deep state of alert observation in the face of difficulty or dilemma—means that you are at least willing to become quiet and observant rather than struggle for resolution or to achieve something.

Developing stillness is one of the essential qualities in healing, in spiritual evolvement and in practical problem solving. Yet it seems so impractical, and this makes you confront your own personal conflicts. This is good, for it makes you confront these things in order to achieve stillness, not to resolve things. If you are attempting to have a still mind and you are still trying to resolve something or get something, you will not be successful.

Another by-product of developing stillness is that you develop trust— a very deep trust in your true nature, a very deep trust in God and a very deep trust that there are forces working on your behalf. This means that you do not trust your thoughts or feelings alone. You are trusting something greater within you and beyond you. This is an inherent trust.

People say, "Oh, I have a terrible problem. You must help me," and I say, "Well, the first step is stillness." "Stillness? What about the answer?" And I say, "Stillness is the answer."

Most people's problems are hypothetical anyway. There is the problem and there is the interpretation of the problem, which can be quite different from the problem itself. People say, "I want to have a relationship in my life now," which may not be the problem. So, why should I try to resolve something that is not the problem? The problem is not that they do not have a relationship, but that they need to develop something else that is more important! That is very often the case, but people do not see that as the avenue that they must follow. They are lonely, so they want a mate. But, I say "stillness."

Now, some people must not attempt stillness because the problem facing them is quite immediate and they must take action. But overall, to realize what Knowledge is, to experience its power and efficacy in the world, you must develop some degree of stillness. To achieve this, you must persevere and have patience because you do not get instant results. You must fortify your faith that this is genuine and within your reach.

I have often said, "Do not be satisfied with answers. It is really the experience that matters." I bestow experience. Experience requires involvement, participation and trust. Anyone can play with answers, like a hot potato! I have given many answers as well, and they are like seeds. They can be planted in the mind and grow over time. But it is still your preparation and experience that are most important.

People often ask, "How can I be in contact with my own Inner Teachers?" I say "stillness." They are still; you are not. That is why you cannot perceive them. Here you are rushing about with your mind grinding

Impulsivity   vs.

thoughts down into powder, always trying to sort things out or see a new way around things, always trying to get the better angle, and your Teacher is standing there. In stillness, you will feel the presence of your whole Spiritual Family. They are calm. You are not.

So, unless immediate action is required, calmness is often the best first step. It cannot be a complacent or a passive calmness. It is calmness with a very great intent. It is an intention for resolution without attempting to resolve the situation yourself.

In all ages, in all societies, even in all worlds, stillness is one of the primary challenges. Even if you live a very busy life and have lots of work and commitments, it is still relevant. Only a few minutes a day in stillness is necessary. It is not appropriate to say, "Well, I do not have time. I cannot fit it in." If you cannot fit it in, then you should eliminate some things because your life is out of balance and out of proportion with your true needs.

I will share with you a perception of humanity in this day and age, if I may. People in your society have a great deal of information available. You are concerned with many things and are very intelligent, but you are not very strong—either physically, mentally or emotionally. Part of the reason for this is that your mind is concerned with so many things that are unrelated. The fewer things you focus on, the more powerful your concentration will be and the greater the results you will achieve, if a result can be achieved. Therefore, to achieve any kind of stillness or depth within yourself, there must be greater simplicity in your life. *true, but what to let go of?*

One of our main themes is the cultivation of Knowledge. This is a profound state of knowing, which can be applied to immediate and practical problems as well as to a greater emphasis in life. Knowledge is not something that you can simply dabble with if you have any hope for success because it is more important than this. Since its rewards are so great, it requires a greater investment on your part. That is why it is very important to settle down into a form of practice sooner or later. You have read enough books. There are enough issues to concern yourself with. You have seen all these techniques. Now it is time to practice.

It is very important in practice not to try to get results. Most forms of spiritual practice—which is training your mind and applying your abilities—involve simple observation without judgment. This is practicing stillness. Here you begin to set aside the agenda that is wrapping you all up. For students of Knowledge, we have different kinds of practice. We have practice for when you cannot settle the mind down. We have practice for when you can settle it down a little. And we have practice for when it settles down all by itself. There is practice for the dabbling student. There is practice for the semi-serious student. Then there is practice for the serious student. By semi-serious, I am not being critical. It is just that you want some Knowledge, but not all Knowledge. And if you are a dabbler, you just sort of want to see what it is all about and get your feet a little wet. If you want all Knowledge, well, you just jump in! So, we have three overall categories. You don't give similar practices to people in different categories.

When your mind is very noisy, you practice counting or breathing or listening to your pulse. If your mind is a little unsettled and there is a possibility you may settle down, then we practice with sound. If your mind is settled down, well, you are practicing already. Then we guide your mind to the presence of the Teachers directly. The Teachers are like a reflection from Heaven. They fill your mind full of light. You cannot enter Heaven and still be in the world, but you can experience yourself as an intermediary. Overall, that is the final goal. When Heaven, your Home, has been partially established here, then you will be able to serve in a higher capacity. That does not mean the world looks any better. It simply means that you are carrying your Home within you.

Our practices are mind-proof. No matter how clever your mind is, the practices are more clever. Why? Because they make conflict unnecessary. If I say, "Look at the floor for thirty minutes," who can do that? If I say, "Say this word for thirty minutes," how many people can do that? I can say, "Say your name for thirty minutes," how many people can do that? "But my relationship? What can I do about it?" I say, "Say your name for thirty minutes. Nothing else." How many people can do that? Not many. To be able to do that means that you have the power of concentration and other qualities as well that are most beneficial to you and to others.

I am going to really drive the point home. "I am having so much trouble with my practice!" Stillness. "I can't." I say you don't want it. You are still trying to settle things yourself. Observation and tremendous alertness are all you need for most problem solving. To be alert, you cannot be thinking of something else. Nor can you be satisfied with thoughts or emotions. You are looking for a deeper feeling of resolution. Anyone who has achieved even a small incremental state of stillness of mind is such an asset to other people. You give them your calmness. Most people, you know, simply need a little reassurance that it will be okay and that they have the ability to take effective action.

No matter what you are facing in life, no matter what you have or do not have, develop stillness of mind. You will not know what the result will be, but even at the outset you will feel a tremendous relief and relaxation if you are successful. If you have difficulty, you will begin to realize what is standing in your way in everything.

A mind that is unfocused cannot perceive correctly, cannot recognize resolution and cannot act effectively. That is why we often recommend for students of Knowledge to simplify their lives so that they can draw on greater resources of energy and concentration and have time to experience some peace. Now, people want many things that they do not need at all. Isn't that true? And sometimes things people never think of are absolutely the essential thing!

I can teach stillness because I am still. Particularly when I am not in the fish tank with you, when I am Home, I am still. I am not rushing about, solving the problems of the universe! You have your own little life to try to manage. I have so much more to manage. But I don't have a busy schedule with a secretary because I have learned in life, as you are learning now, how to distinguish between action and contemplation. There is a time to act. And there is a time to not act but to be alert, like a hunter who must wait oh so long for the right moment to act. This ability to stalk your prey, whether it be an animal on the hunt or Knowledge within yourself, is something that has been lost in your society to a great extent. People are so over-stimulated that they have no sense of proportion.

Everything becomes clear when your mind is still. Make a problem list, practice stillness and things will come to you. You don't need to try to work it out or create a better angle. If a problem requires a resolution, an answer will come through you. It will come through you in stillness or it will come to you when you aren't thinking about it. That is why it is good when people play musical instruments, do sports or something like that where they are not trying to fix anything. Or if they are trying to fix something here, it is often something so totally unrelated to their dilemmas that there is a possibility that the mind may have an opening and the resolution will simply slip through, like someone escaping from prison. Answer got through! Messenger got through the enemy lines!

Stillness is related to escaping fear. Why is this? Because you cannot be still if you are afraid. So, you must get tired of being afraid or give up on it to some degree to relax enough to be still. Here you must affirm either consciously or unconsciously that you have faith in a Greater Power and that your Home is not this world. When you know, truly, that your Home is beyond this world, then you can begin to relax in the world. Then the world's consequences are not so dire. This does not give rise to passivity. It calls upon a greater responsibility, which indicates that you have come here for a purpose. You have come here to contribute something. This requires development and preparation, focus and true priorities. It calls upon a greater and much more substantial emphasis in life, which is hardly passive. The luxury of being able to relax and to be truly alert, which is not being asleep or dozed off, is that you are settling into a Greater Reality which you yourself possess.

We have a very noisy world here, yes? Lots of noise. Why is there noise? Because people are addicted to stimulation. They are afraid of stillness and must have noise constantly going. They must have an outer environment that correlates to their inner state, which is continually turbulent. Turbulence is very stressful and causes all manner of pain and disease. Therefore, for those of you who realize that you are seeking peace more than stimulation, stillness is the way.

There are some very fundamental premises for approaching stillness. The first premise is that you possess Knowledge and that you have thoughts. These are the two aspects of mind within you. There is your personal side, which contains all of your beliefs, assumptions, demands, requirements, feelings, fears and wishes and so forth. Then there is your Knowledge, which you have brought with you from beyond, and which is still, concentrated and cannot be defiled. It is hidden within you until you have developed enough for it to emerge.

Another premise is that you need great assistance to truly develop yourself, assistance both within the world and from beyond. A third premise is that you have come here from your Home to contribute something and that you are not doing this for yourself alone. The next premise is that there is God somewhere and that God is always seen as watching. The next premise is that you must become very honest, so much more honest than you thought. Instead of knowing what you want, you must want what you know. That is the honesty I speak of.

So, given all of these premises, you can begin to develop stillness. To do this you must enter a formal preparation at some point. A person who can prepare will achieve the true results. That is being intelligent. To think about things and not prepare is not intelligent. If you cannot prepare, it is then better to go out in the world, be a totally worldly person, enjoy the fruits of this world and accept its pains and tribulations.

If you are really interested in cultivating your Knowledge and in deepening your experience of God and your sense of purpose, then be very active in your pursuit. Do not hold back and say, "I don't know. I must think about it some more." Take action. Then your life will be moving, and you will not be standing by the side of the road thinking and pondering and wondering. Sometimes it is better to go down some road actively than not to move at all. Many people wish to pursue relationships that have no purpose or promise. They cannot be dissuaded, so we say, "Go! Do it all the way!" And then they do it. They come back and say, "You told me to do it!" Boom! "But you told me to do this. It did not work. Why?" I say I had no other choice. There was only one answer to your question. "I must have what I want to have. I must, I must." Now, if a person is a little bit more open, then we say, "Practice stillness. Cultivate Knowledge." If a person is even more open, we say, "Oh, better not go that way. Nothing there. There is something over here, however."

If you cultivate stillness, you will cultivate many other things that go along with it. If you allow your Knowledge and your true reality to gradually arise within your mind and your outer life, then you will take the most expedient way to true achievement. That is why we place such a great emphasis on preparation. I could be more dramatic, you know! I could talk about popular, metaphysical subjects and get you very stimulated. But I will tell you something. Most metaphysical information is not worth very much. It is more playthings, more things for the mind to chew on, more things to do before you truly prepare.

How many people can be truly intimate with another? Not many. But many people have a great deal of information on the study of relationships—"The Dynamics of Relationships and Communication." Oh, they can talk about it all day long, but how many people can be truly intimate? Many people talk about spiritual things, but how many people can be quiet while their mind settles down? Do you see the difference? Your time is precious in the world. It is such a precious opportunity to be here. When you truly prepare, you have cast your fate a little bit, yes? That is good! It is good to move in a true direction. If you are making a mistake, you will know soon enough.

So, to practice stillness, let all things come to a rest except the keenness of your mind. Here your mind is all looking and no thinking. Your ears are all listening. Your body is all feeling. Of all practices, stillness is the greatest and the most useless. I say that because to your personal mind, it will be the most useless and to your True Mind, it will be the most useful. The mind that is still can permeate anything in physical life.

The life of Knowledge is such a greater life. I cannot compare it to your life here favorably because it possesses such great, great joy. It is still. That is why we practice the state of mind that replicates your true state of mind. Then the bridge between your personal state and your greater state becomes so small that you slip over it easily. The gap has been narrowed and now the transition occurs.

*Why is there
disappointment
in life?
Because
there is so much here
that
is not important.*

Twenty-seven

DISAPPOINTMENT

W E FIND DISAPPOINTMENT to be a very great opportunity. Because it is a natural fact of life that you will encounter disappointment, it must then be seen as an advantage, not always something you can appreciate at the outset, but an advantage nonetheless. There is very great effort by many people to avoid disappointment at all costs, but we want to encourage you not to avoid disappointment. Bring it on! Let it happen! There are lessons you must learn in life, and disappointment will illustrate many of them. We do not encourage people to repeat their mistakes, of course, but certain lessons are waiting for you. Taking advantage of them means that they can unburden you so that you may walk lightly through this world. The burden of avoiding disappointment is a far greater burden.

We are not in control of things that happen to you, but we provide an opportunity for you to view things that happen to you in such a way that you may be able to find an open door there. There is always a door open for you. The reason this cannot be apprehended is because you are trying to do something else with your life. When you are committed to getting what you want in life, then you see only those things that are relevant to your pursuit. These pursuits exist in each person, whether they are acknowledged or not. Often there are a great many pursuits that are unknown to you, and these must be revealed. Then you begin to understand your behavior and to understand why your consciousness is so selective. Here it becomes apparent that there are certain things that you have been missing, perhaps for a long time, though the evidence of them is quite apparent. Often people say when they discover that they know something, "Well, I have known this for a long time. I just have not thought about it."

This occurs because you are trying to do something else and only see what is relevant to your pursuits. Many of your pursuits are unnecessary for your happiness and for your true calling in life. Because it is very difficult to give up a pursuit that is cherished and is still seen as a positive factor, disappointment then begins to have real meaning. This is what reduces you down to your essential Self. You are at the surface of life no longer.

When you are experiencing disappointment, the first key is acceptance. Do not fight it. There always is a relief in this. The second key point is alertness, becoming alert to what is happening. The third key point is leaving the explanation open. The fourth key point is mourning for the loss and the last key point is committing yourself to action. So, let us talk about each of these.

When disappointment is evident, things are not turning out as you had planned. It is not going to happen that way, and it may not happen at all. Accepting this enables you to step back from the experience and become truly observant of your environment, the situation at hand and your own response. This empowers you immediately because it gives you the freedom and the strength to become a witness. This enables you to become alert. One of the most profound and important aspects in all of your education, regardless of what you do in life, is alertness. It seems so commonplace that no one thinks of it when they talk about personal development, spiritual training, and so forth. People talk about awareness, but awareness is not the same as alertness.

When you are alert, you are watching things around you. When you are aware, you are rarely aware of things around you. You are aware of yourself thinking of things around you. When you are alert, you are looking with very little thinking involved. If you were trying to listen to a conversation in the next house down the street, you would have to listen very carefully, yes? You couldn't be thinking, "How am I doing right now? Here I am listening to the conversation in the next house. Why am I here anyway? What's going on with me? I feel this way and my body hurts."

That is the difference between alertness and awareness. Awareness is very important, but alertness is more important. The person of Knowledge is extremely alert, which makes life very exciting.

When you become aware of yourself and your mind too much, it bogs you down and leads to a very unfortunate kind of self-preoccupation. It is giving too much attention to something that is inherently confused. Besides, you have to be outside of your mind to do anything with it. Otherwise, you are running about trying to plug up the holes and keep it all moving along, like a car that is always in disrepair. It is like always working on your car and never going anywhere!

Life conspires to make you alert because until you are alert, you only see those things that are relevant to your interests and pursuits and nothing else. Therefore, your frame of reference is far too limited to comprehend the meaning of your life and to experience and enjoy the Mystery of your life. Disappointment is tremendously valuable in making you alert by shaking you out of a fixed mental reference and framework.

Once you become accepting and are alert, then you can begin to witness what is happening. The next important point is to leave the explanation open. For those of you who have taken courses and read books, it is very tempting to give an explanation immediately. "I know why this is happening. It is for this reason. This must be about this. That must be about that." When you do this, you cease to be alert. You now become complacent again with your explanations. Leaving the situation unexplained enables you and requires you to be alert. Now you must watch. Life has your attention.

Before we go further, let us explain why people become disappointed. As I said, we do not control matters. It is you who are conspiring to bring yourself into the open. It is you who are choosing things that do not work in order to shift your emphasis. Why else would you be committed to things that have so little promise if it were not to bring you to a place of true recognition? Many of your pursuits are very much in alignment with your real purpose, which is yet to be discovered. But many of them are not. Conflict and friction will bring about the necessary recognition.

So, we have acceptance and alertness. We have the necessity of refraining from giving an explanation. This is frightening sometimes because if the explanation is not immediately available, then people go into anxiety and feel out of control in the situation. But it is this vulnerability that makes true alertness have meaning and potency.

Then comes mourning. It is very good to mourn for a loss, but not for too long—intensely for a short period of time. Mourning is embarrassing and belittling to your idea of yourself, but it enables you to take the next step. Remember, if you are alert, you can know what is happening. You now can follow each step. You just do not have an explanation yet. Then you reach a position to be ready for action, for each disappointment opens a new door—perhaps something you had never thought of or perhaps something you had thought of at the very beginning of your life and now it is there awaiting you, as a new opportunity.

Mourning is especially evident in relationships because there is so much disappointment here, yes? Where there is ambition there is disappointment. We don't want to discourage your ambition. We wish for it, instead, to lead to its conclusion. Many people want to know the purpose of their lives, the meaning of their experiences and the meaning of the events occurring around them, but you cannot know these things from the surface of your mind. You must be taken deeper.

It is a very interesting phenomenon that in human thought, hell is associated with the unconscious and with the depths of the world where there are fires and demons. It is analogous to your inner life. That is why those individuals and powers in the world that have been fearful of humanity's true Knowledge have attempted to persuade people to stay on the surface of their minds. We are encouraging you to go deeply into your True Mind where things can be known. This is what we mean by Knowledge. Your successes and failures will bring you here, if you are alert, attentive and open-minded.

When we say that you bring yourself to disappointment and that you choose the things that bring you to this experience, we must ask you, "Who is this *you* who is conspiring to do this?" It must not be the you that is thinking and planning your life. You will not let yourself stray from your true discovery. There will always be pressure here. You will never be content until you find your purpose in life. Accept this. You cannot be content with less. You have come here for your purpose to be discovered when you reach maturity. If your purpose is neglected, avoided or discounted, you will live with a stress that no one can alleviate. This is not cruel. It is, in fact, the very essence of life that makes this possible. As you become a witness to your life, you will see this Greater Force which is like an undercurrent. You will feel it. But you will not understand it, and your philosophy will not be able to explain it.

True spiritual training is very disappointing. Why? Because you find that your philosophy, your idealism and your hopes must be left at the entrance to the temple. Only those who argue philosophy remain outside on the steps. In the sanctuary this has no meaning.

This is a teaching in The Way of Knowledge in the tradition of the Greater Community. Our aim is great. We do not guarantee anything short of the discovery of your purpose, which is purely an experience that you will discover. Your purpose is to discover Knowledge, to follow Knowledge and to allow Knowledge to express itself through you. That is everyone's purpose. This statement indicates that there are three stages: there is discovery, there is following and there is expression. When you truly want to learn about the Mystery of your life and when you see that the Mystery of your life is the source of all of your true happiness and contentment, you will find that there will be disappointment. It will not be as great as the immediate relief and joy you will feel, but there will be disappointment, and with disappointment there will come relief.

Let us spend a few moments talking about peace, peace of mind. It is very hard to pursue peace. You are at peace when you are not at war. Therefore, peace is a quiet state. It is not a state born of getting all of your requests fulfilled. That may produce momentary excitement and happiness, but these are very soon lost, for the yearning of your True Self has not been answered. The happiness that goes with the discovery of your purpose is so far greater than any disappointment that it literally absorbs the disappointment in moments. It is a moment of grief leading to a moment of laughter. It is as if you finally set down this great burden you have been carrying. Now, in peace, there is acceptance, there is alertness, there is openness of mind and there is no need for explanation. However, we must treat peace as a result and not a goal. If it is held as a goal, then you will attempt to act peacefully, behave peacefully and mask your conflict. That prolongs the conflict and makes it more difficult. Peace is a result.

Peace in the world is something very few people have ever attained. It is something so inexplicable. Therefore, let us then think of it in terms of satisfaction because satisfaction is something you can acquire in a state of action or movement. You are in physical life, in a world of movement where everything is moving and colliding and mixing. And yet you have a purpose in being here and a calling in life to carry out a specific role.

When people are profoundly disappointed, then they turn inward. They slow down and God catches up! This is true elsewhere in the universe as well. Your predicaments here are shared by other societies in the Greater Community beyond your world. It is no different there. Very few individuals have acquired Knowledge or discovered Knowledge. So, having the best approach requires that you be open to disappointment and even welcome it. If it must be, and if it will lead to greater happiness in your life, greater certainty and a greater sense of purpose, meaning and direction, then welcome it. Then you will have the opportunity to truly see what is going on. Then our Presence will begin to make sense to you. We have only one goal. You have many. When your goal is our goal, you will feel as intimate with us as you would with your own child, as close as your brother or sister.

To armor yourself against disappointment is to cast yourself in chains. Now your preparation requires more time and is more difficult to bring about. This means that there is more suffering. Therefore, to end suffering in the world, we teach the reclamation of Knowledge. A more daring and adventuresome pursuit you cannot imagine. This makes climbing great mountains like boy's play! A more thorough involvement with your True Self and all of your important abilities you cannot find. You must honor yourself to even begin to consider it. You cannot be a pathetic person and think it is a worthy pursuit for you. There must be something in you that is truly valuable that is worth this kind of investment of your time.

There is great assistance available to help you alleviate suffering. Here it is very important to realize that suffering is not the same as disappointment. To have something you want not turn out for you is not suffering; it is disappointment. Suffering is when you long for something that cannot be or when you long for something that you do not really want. That is suffering. What attends that kind of suffering is hope and disappointment. Hope recommits you to your suffering and disappointment offers escape from it.

We have said on a number of occasions that the great spiritual leadership in the time to come will be primarily given to women, for this is the Age of the Women. Part of the restructuring of society is for this purpose, and it is happening naturally. Therefore, many women will become true leaders. The disappointment for these women is that they cannot take men with them. These women I speak of who have a true calling to be spiritual leaders, rarely will they be able to take a man with them. That is part of their maturity. It is going unchaperoned into a greater life. Women want to find a man first and then go to God because they do not want to go to God without a chaperone. They want to have a man to make sure they will not be lonely. But how can you be lonely in God? God is like having all men at once! To lament not having a man when your heart is going for God represents confusion. Therefore, these women must be disappointed. No man? Go for God. Mourn for no man. Go for God. Don't go for belief in God; don't become a philosopher. Let God and your Spiritual Family fill your life. Then things will begin to happen. If you yearn for a man and a man is not there, you are wasting your life. You might as well yearn for something that is there. Not every woman will be with a man, not in the normal sense. And yet women will still need men very much because they will need to be nourished as women.

In many other societies in the Greater Community that have attained Wisdom to any degree, their greater leadership are all females. Males run society and females provide the Knowledge. For races very similar to yours, this is usually the case. Because your world and societies now are preparing for emergence into the Greater Community and because you are preparing to unify your race, this issue of the role of women is quite relevant now. It is not merely a potentiality. It is actually happening.

Certain women who have a great spiritual calling in life must approach their calling without requiring a man to go along with them. In other words, they must take complete responsibility for their calling. If they can respond to this, they will be so nurtured by life. With women on the rise, men feel quite helpless and confused. Women outperform men in many, many ways. But women have weaknesses as well. Women for centuries have carried the flame of spirituality in the world. Now they must carry the responsibility. This is very different. Here they will be able to have compassion for men, for they will see why men's errors and successes came about.

This is also the era of the Spiritual Family. That is why there is so much of this kind of spiritual communication going on. That is why the women will respond. Family is their domain, yes? That is why we use this terminology. Very exceptional men will respond, too. Most men are concerned with the day-to-day function of physical things, and that is a big challenge in and of itself. Men have plenty to do. I am making this point because women carry their disappointment about men like a great yoke, while in reality it is a means for their freedom.

You cannot take a man with you. If a man cannot go, you will have to go alone. I give no guarantees from then on. You go alone because you must. In this way, you honor your nature and you honor the truth within yourself. If a man comes, that is wonderful. If a man does not come, that is wonderful, too! Anyone who goes to God, goes alone. They go based only on the power of Knowledge within them. Nobody knows what going to God looks like. Many people wish to look like they are going to God when they are just creating a new social strata, just pretending.

As long as women are willing to respond truthfully within themselves and not require that men go with them or wait for them, then they can proceed. You do not choose Knowledge because it guarantees that you will have all the things you think you must have. You choose Knowledge because you *must* choose Knowledge. You come into the world because you *must* do that. That is Knowledge. You must not let your small self dictate your decisions here.

It is very disappointing when something real happens. It is very disappointing when a true spiritual force emerges in life. You cannot be in relationship until you learn disappointment because until you do, you are living with your thoughts about someone rather than your relationship with them. To know your true Inner Teachers, you must go beyond your thoughts about them and enter true intimacy. That is profound.

When you are disappointed, let the emotions come forth. Be a witness to them. You are greater than any emotional state. Your Teachers stand by while you go through everything. Most of it is quite boring to them, but they are waiting for the opportunity, and they are providing you with the quality of love and the orientation that you will never find in the world.

It is very interesting to us, though understandable, that even *Steps to Knowledge* students still debate whether their Teachers are real. It is very hard to be in a relationship with someone who spends so much time wondering whether you are real. You can't even begin the relationship. "Are they real? Are they good? Do I have to give up anything to be with them?" Sometimes people get past all that and see that this relationship is as natural, normal and integral as anything they experience in life—in some ways, more so, for the Teachers have no form. Here, you can experience relationship in its truest context—pure affinity, pure transfer of mind.

At the surface of the mind, everything is deliberated. At the depth of the mind, everything is known. When things are known, you are in a position to witness the world and to have Knowledge of the world. Here, you have already been disappointed sufficiently so that you do not want anything from the world. Now you can begin to know things about the world. You are then in a position to contribute because you can give everything in the direction it is meant to be given. And if it does not work out the way you want, well, that is okay.

We are not worried for the world. But we wish to eliminate suffering. That is what we work on. We are rarely successful in the moment. Yet, we are certain because the truth lives with us. You must find yourself while you are in physical life. We are a very good demonstration that you have life beyond the physical, that life is continuous and that you do have purpose for coming into this world.

Everything that happens that is genuine is disappointing to someone. Everything that is truthful that happens is disappointing to someone. Someone tells the truth; others are disappointed. You are disappointed. But everyone is relieved. Even when there is true loss and disappointment, a door is opened, for in this state of loss you can see something that is rarely seen otherwise.

People often ask, "I have a loved one who has died. Can I communicate with them?" I say, "Yes. Be still and they are there. Call for them and they are there—in your permanent state, which is where Knowledge lives."

If you are not afraid of disappointment, even in your current state of mind, you will be able to embrace life. Here you have already set down half of your burden. If you are very willful and are demanding that your life be a certain way and yet are open to whatever may happen, you are partially liberated already. Therefore, if you seek that which is true, prepare yourself for a little disappointment. And remember always that your disappointment will be momentary and slight compared to the relief and happiness that you will find.

We want to speak about one other thing and that is emptiness. What is emptiness? Emptiness is being calm when you want to be stimulated. It is a moment when nothing is going on. It is the one thing that people at your level of development will do anything to avoid. Look at your world and see how noisy it is, how much stimulation! The more affluent you are, the more forms of stimulation are available to you, all to avoid this moment.

Disappointment brings to you the experience of emptiness. In this state, you experience how afraid you are of everything. That is what makes it hard. But if you keep going, all that fear dissipates, and you begin to enjoy emptiness. It is like a luxury. Those of you who are students of Knowledge are beginning to find stillness to be a luxury, as it truly is. A more gracious luxury you cannot imagine. Disappointment brings you there. For a moment, you don't know what to do about anything. If you do not panic with this, you will see that you can just simply be available in that moment, and it becomes a very special moment. When tragic things happen, it gives rise to very great moments in people's lives. Great moments are great opportunities. If everything were going the way you wanted it or demanded it to be going, well, great moments would be hard to find.

There is a very great purpose in life, for all of you and for me. It is very great! So, in The Greater Community Way of Knowledge, we teach people to gain access to this experience of purpose and to gain access to this state of mind. Ideas about teachers and schools and learning—well, many of these ideas have to be disappointed. They are assumptions only and are not born of true experience but are temporary expedients to bring you forward and to give you ideas.

You have a calling in life that will emanate out of your purpose once you have developed sufficiently. Yes, you are made specifically to do something. Until you find this thing, you will always be trying to change your nature, change yourself, rearrange your priorities and make yourself look better. That is why, when you find your calling, it is a profound experience of self-acceptance, which is love. You are custom-made for something you have not yet found.

You see, I will tell you a very interesting thing. In this day and age when there is so much luxury in your society, it is harder for people to choose Knowledge. It takes longer to be disappointed. There are always new thrills, always new things to lose yourself in—so many distractions. In earlier times, physical life was not so glamorous. Your advantage is that you can read my words in this book. I can speak to you and you can listen without serious consequences, without being hurt. Yet, your life is so much more stimulated. The experience of Knowledge is entirely different. It is ninety percent stillness and ten percent action, instead of the other way around.

That is why we teach The Way of Knowledge. I don't want to add things on to people. I want to subtract things. I want to be like a good shower that washes away all the dirt! What happens in The Way of Knowledge is that we engage people in what is absolutely essential for them, and we do not put much emphasis on anything else. By "essential" I mean the things that are essential in your outer life. What is absolutely essential that you must do? That is what we concentrate on. That produces vitality, harmony and a uniform life. It produces power because you are becoming more focused—and power is the result of focus. Power is not good or evil. Power is concentration, and to be concentrated you must simplify your life. So, the preparation requires a certain amount of reduction. This is so simple, yet people never think of it.

What should you reduce? What is essential? What is not essential? What is taking up your time and energy? If you spend twenty minutes a day concentrating on developing Knowledge in your preparation, it would be remarkable what you would be able to produce. But practicing twenty minutes a day is a major accomplishment for many people. You see, this illustrates the problem. The solution here becomes very obvious when the problem is really comprehended.

Your purpose here in life is to find out what is important. That is one way of saying it. When you know what is important, then you know where to devote yourself. Until you get there, devote yourself to whatever is most important now, be open and alert and allow for disappointment. Then you can embrace your life. "Here I am! I am open! But I prefer things to be like this." That is okay. You can have preferences. Be open, though. "I hope this relationship works out, but if it doesn't, please free me." Why is there disappointment in life? Because there is so much here that is not important.

You already
have
power.
The object here
is not
power.
The object
is
Wisdom.

Twenty-eight

USING POWER FOR GOOD

OW WE WILL TALK ABOUT USING POWER for good. We say "using" power, which is very different from "having" power, and we say that power can be used for good. So, in order that everyone understands what we mean by power, let me give you a definition which is relevant to my discourse: Power is the ability to transfer energy from one domain to another.

This is a very specific definition which itself requires much consideration. It is relevant to your individual needs because your main emphasis is to integrate your life. Being integrated means that all of your resources are brought to bear and made available and that you are brought out of conflict into inner harmony within yourself. Then you will be in a position to recognize this energy and transfer it consciously. Many people want power and the ability to have influence without this integration. We, as Teachers, could never provide this, for it would not only be hazardous to the individual but detrimental to the world as well.

So, let me give the definition once again: Power is the ability to transfer energy from one domain to another. In other words, it is the ability to bring something forth that you have realized within yourself and to make it actual in life. It is the ability to transfer something from your spiritual life into your life in the world. To do this, you must become a bridge; you must have access to both these realms without attempting to master either of them. If you attempt to master the physical realm, you will not be able to have a real association with your spiritual life. If you try to master your spiritual life, then you will not be able to have access to your physical or intellectual life because in this world you have to live with your mind and your body and with the minds and bodies of others.

Having access to these realms is essential for your happiness here and for successful accomplishment, which will yield satisfaction to you. My definition of power, then, is somewhat mysterious because it requires a deep self-examination. If you cannot undertake this examination, you will think it odd and will go no further. Yet, we wish to stimulate your thinking and to give you a different perspective regarding your individual needs and opportunities.

As I have said, your primary need at this point is for integration. Yet, if you attempt to appease all aspects of yourself, your inner conflict will continue and grow worse. If you attempt to make all parts of yourself feel comfortable and included, you will experience profound conflict. Yet, there is a greater resource within you that can integrate you naturally. The reason you cannot integrate yourself is because you are not in full awareness of all of your aspects, and you do not see their relevant association with each other. You are too involved with certain of your aspects and not involved with others at all, and at any one moment you are representing some aspect of yourself without regard to the others. If you were beyond all of these aspects, you could possibly integrate yourself, but we cannot expect that of anyone here.

You need true assistance to help you do this. You need Teachers because they can activate that part of you which integrates you naturally. This process is something in which you participate very directly, but you will not be in charge of it. We must make this very clear. People sometimes think, "Well, if I am to become powerful and resourceful within myself, then I must learn to rely completely upon my ability to do so." Or people sometimes think, "I must rely completely on spiritual powers or the Teachers." But in actuality, you must learn to rely on both. A true Teacher will call upon you to use your inner resources very specifically and will create a context where it is necessary to do so.

Therefore, you need guidance, but you also need to become powerful within yourself. This you must learn to do through participation. You cannot do this intellectually. The more aware you become of yourself, the more you will realize that some aspect of you is in a state of confusion at all times or even suffering. Here you may try to be comfortable at all moments by caring for that aspect or allowing it to express itself. That is a step towards health, but you are not yet integrated. You are still disassociated. When you are disassociated, you will vacillate between unhappiness or despair and a temporary feeling of power and direction. You are not yet stable.

Because we are speaking of a greater experience of satisfaction, harmony and ability than most people would strive for, it is perhaps beyond the range of your individual goals to achieve such a state. Yet, in order to use power for good, you must achieve this state. There must be something greater moving in you that you can accept, translate and contribute where it is meant to be given. You are like a channel for power now, not attempting to control or dominate the process but an active participant. To do this, you must be a person of tremendous concentration, ability and openness of mind—a person capable of a direct experience of life.

Power itself can be measured in terms of an individual's ability to concentrate—attention and concentration. If you can accept this idea, then it becomes apparent that there are minds more powerful than yours. Even in physical life this is true. This is not a very popular idea because everyone wants to be equal at all times—with the same abilities, the same potential, the same resources, the same level of development, and so forth. But in reality this is not the case. There are minds more powerful than yours. And because power is not the same as Wisdom, there are more powerful minds that are working against Knowledge and there are more powerful minds that are working for Knowledge. It is very important to understand this. This requires discernment and Wisdom within yourself. Wisdom comes from Knowledge, but power is a resource in life that is available to anyone. Therefore, you can use power for destructive purposes. If you are dedicated, determined and concentrated, you can translate energy from one form to another. That is why our discourse is on using power for good.

How do you know if power is good? Because you have the ability to make this distinction within yourself. That is Knowledge. Knowledge comes from beyond this world. You have an inborn power of discernment within yourself that we wish to cultivate here. Yet, there are also raw powers that can be used and are used. There is physical power. There is mental power. There is spiritual power. That is why when you are concentrated only on using power, it is a very dangerous situation. Your mental institutions are full of people who have attempted to use power without the necessary development and have found themselves involved in something they could neither understand nor control. The love and the grace that you have brought with you are born of your Knowledge. Knowledge will naturally utilize the power that is available here in life for good.

There are minds more powerful than yours. A mind that is more powerful than yours can influence you, even dominate you. That is one of the reasons you are so afraid of relationship and of losing your ground to another. And if you have advanced to a certain extent, you realize you have a certain propensity for following a mind that is more powerful. This is not bad. It is natural. You should follow a mind more powerful than yours, but you must learn to avoid those which are detrimental to you. This is Wisdom, not morality. It is simply learning to negotiate your environment and your relationships successfully.

One of the reasons that the Wise remain hidden in life is because they do not want to influence people. Their presence itself is a tremendous influence. Therefore, I want to emphasize this one point, though it may be uncomfortable, that it is possible for you to be dominated. It is possible for you to dominate others. You cannot help but influence others. Even if you hid yourself away with no contact with the outside world, your mind would still exert an influence upon others. The greater your concentration, the more influence others would feel. Therefore, you have a responsibility in life to cultivate yourself, to accept assistance and to make use of this opportunity to learn how to use power because you are already influential. When you are not preoccupied with your own mind and your own circumstances, you begin to see the influence that people have on one another.

Here it becomes very advantageous to have Inner Teachers. Though you may very seldom experience them, it is very comforting to know there is someone watching over you that can intervene on your behalf if it becomes absolutely necessary. The reason your Teachers do not spend a great deal of time with you in general is because their influence is too great. If you read about spiritual teachers living in physical life, you will recognize that, except in extremely rare cases, they seldom gave their full attention to anyone individually and then only for very brief periods of time. Why is this? It is because their influence is too great. They must be responsible for this influence and use it wisely for good. This is a universal fact. The temptation for power—for the domination of others, for personal gain—becomes very severe here. If individuals have not been properly prepared, their concern for their own survival, a very powerful force in and of itself, can sway them dangerously.

Wisdom must accompany power or it is better that you not have power—better for you and better for others. If you are in confusion regarding your direction, meaning and purpose in life, then you are not concentrated and, therefore, your influence will be minimal. A mind that is concentrated and absolutely determined is tremendously powerful because most people are still very much in a state of confusion.

There is no independence in life. Everyone is influencing everyone. But within you there is an independence that saves you for what is good and protects you from what is ill, and that is your Knowledge. This is a relief, for with Knowledge you have the ability to sense what is going on. With Knowledge, in a personal relationship of great intimacy, you will influence each other for good. And your purpose with each other will be far greater than what you individually could accomplish because now you have the right influence.

We are adamant that students of Knowledge become very conscious of their influences. What is influencing you? Often this question is seen as a limitation of your personal freedom, but it is more a form of protection for you because as your mind begins to open, you become much more vulnerable. Here you are more easily persuaded, and until your powers of discernment have grown strong, you can be influenced in all kinds of directions. You are less shielded now. You are more open. Therefore, it is important that you become more discerning and more attentive.

I want you to think about whether you are a good influence on people. It is very comforting to think "I am a good influence." But this requires greater discrimination and observation. In every person, there are good and bad influences. No one is a totally good influence. No one is a totally bad influence. Some of you already have some degree of power. What are you doing with the power that you have? People want more power, but they don't know what they are doing with what they have. Do you want everything in your life to be accentuated? Do you want fear to be accentuated—more fear, more excitement, more everything? If not, then do not seek for more power. Instead, seek for more clarity with the power that you have now. You already have power. The object here is not power. The object is Wisdom. You will not be happy with more power. You will simply have everything that you are now experiencing become more accentuated. That is why we are not encouraging people to have power. We are encouraging people to have Wisdom. Then power becomes a source of satisfaction and not a source of frustration or conflict.

I'll tell you a secret. There are people who are suffering because they have more power than they can handle. They have not even accepted the power that they have now. I cannot in good faith give them more. The next time you are afraid, do you wish to be three times as afraid? If I add power, I accentuate everything in your experience. That means you are three times as happy, but your happiness is not stable. Therefore, when you fall from happiness, you will fall into a deeper pit.

The issue is not more power. It is more Wisdom. There is already lots of power around, but who can wield it? Who can use it for good? There are people with great vision in life who are killing thousands of people! It is justifiable, is it not, to that person? Those who start wars always think that they are doing it for a good reason. Wars are not started by nations. Wars are started by individuals. In all cases, the devastating wars that you have seen in your world were generated, maintained and carried out by the will of very few people. In other words, a few people used many other people to carry out their intent. People can be used if they are afraid, if they are vulnerable, if they are weak, if they are underfed and if they are disadvantaged.

There is power everywhere. Knowledge will guide you to use it in the proper proportion for the right course of action. Without this guidance, you may try to seize upon it for other reasons. That is why we place such a great emphasis on the development of your abilities. People often cannot see this because they are only thinking of their personal motives and goals. They do not see their value to others. That is why I am speaking in a larger context.

When you are not preoccupied with yourself, you begin to see yourself as a participant in a larger arena. This is where your Knowledge is meaningful. You were not sent into this world to figure out who you are. You were sent here to utilize an ability that is inherent within you and that will require that you realize your true nature, even as you prepare to realize it. You have all come prepared to do something very good for life. That produces satisfaction. When you are doing something very good for life and are not harming yourself, it is very satisfying and produces the greatest happiness. Then you can be at ease. You are not at war with yourself. You have compassion for life's difficulties, and you can enjoy its pleasures.

We have power. That is why you do not experience us very much. Even power for good can be too strong an influence if it is prolonged. You as a recipient must have the capacity for this influence. It may take years for you, if you are inclined and if it is necessary, to have true intimacy with your Teacher. Like any very important relationship, it changes your experience of yourself, and it changes your experience of what your individuality really is.

We have cautioned people about their intimate relationships with one another because of the level of influence involved. If an individual has a very strong addiction or disability, he or she will naturally promote that in others. Everyone has minor disabilities. That is okay. You cannot do anything about that. Your internal experience will determine if you are to be involved with someone. You do not need to judge or analyze the person. Knowledge will guide you towards those influences that are best for you. It is very easy to be enraptured or in love with someone who is not good for you and in the name of love to commit yourself to that situation. That is harmful. People are naturally fascinated with other individuals who are very different from themselves. That is a normal fascination. In all your years of having intimate relationships with others, you can learn Wisdom—where to give yourself, where not to give yourself, and how relationships begin, survive and end. It is about Wisdom! Relationships are very easy to start but very hard to finish.

Using power for good is important because it is the source of your satisfaction. Yet, the greater the resource of good that you can contribute, the more competent you must be. This elevates and develops you on an individual level. This is your education, truly. If you are not committed to only doing good, then your gifts can be misconstrued, misused or misappropriated. The evidence of this is very great, and it leads to tremendous disappointment.

I have emphasized that there are minds that are more powerful than yours. For this reason, you must learn to shield yourself when that is appropriate and open yourself when that is appropriate. This is a voluntary act. If you are completely open, well, you will find life to be very harsh. As you have skin and bone to protect your internal organs, you must have a shelter for yourself mentally. It need not be a prison house. It must be a dwelling you can enter and leave at will. Then you can use your emotions at will. They will not use you. You use your shelter at will. It will not conceal you like a prison. You can use your abilities. They are not functioning in spite of you or only latent within you. It is because we wish great happiness for you that we speak of these things.

You see, there is never really a shutting down or opening up. There is just transferring your attention. If you are opening up internally, it looks like you are shutting down externally. If you open up externally, sometimes it looks like you are shutting down internally. Your attention must be placed somewhere; it cannot be everywhere. It is how you shift the balance here. You are only as aware as you are at any given moment, and during each moment you can shift the balance of your focus. Therefore, you must then see what is influencing you now and begin to determine what is healthy and what is not, or you will feel increasingly aggravated being in the world. You see, this is very confusing for the person who is ambitious because in developing real power, you become more sensitive. With real power, it looks like you are less capable of being in the world. You look less powerful. You look weak! And you think that because you can't handle everything, you are not a strong person.

Therefore, take stock of your influences. Begin to determine which influences are good and which are not. You already know this, but there are many things from which you cannot yet disengage. You are too fascinated with too many things. You see, with power comes responsibility— the ability to respond. There is Wisdom and there is responsibility. The greater your Wisdom and responsibility, the greater the power you can access and the more you can transfer energy from one domain to another. So, then, let us cultivate Wisdom and responsibility. This means that you must do in life what it is necessary for you to do. That is recognizing what needs to be done and having the strength to do it. Then everything will proceed. You must find people to help you do this. You cannot do it alone.

Do you know how Knowledge becomes strong within you? The ability to know—do you know how it becomes strong? You follow it, in spite of everything else, when that is necessary. Something will come up and you will need to follow it.

The more
you experience
that your life is
in service
to something greater,
the less afraid
you will be.

Twenty-nine

FAITH & FEAR

NOW I WILL TALK ABOUT FAITH AND FEAR, which is of particular relevance since many of you are on the verge of taking great steps forward. Whenever a true change comes upon you, it is a very important opportunity. In fact, it is an opportunity that is long anticipated by those who watch you from beyond. People are very fortified against true change because it affects them deeply. It is not merely that they have a new set of circumstances or are engaged in new activities and disengaged from old activities. Something very deep inside is being touched.

It takes unusual circumstances to bring about genuine change within an individual. When people attempt to keep their circumstances stable or the same, it is more difficult. So, the more you try to control your environment, the more difficult it is for you to find yourself. Life wishes to move you forward. That is why you came here.

Therefore, it is important to manage your personal affairs but to leave a great door open for something new to happen. As I have said, the important change will affect you very deeply. It will change your experience of yourself. It is rare that you will remember that particular moment when your experience of yourself changed, but that change is the really important thing. You know, people go to many places in the world, have many new experiences, new relationships and so forth, but nothing has touched them deeply. They go to great lengths to have a new experience of themselves, but nothing yet has touched them deeply.

Yet, when that happens, it is a very important time to understand the meaning of faith.

Now, in an ordinary sense, you have faith that life is good and that there is a God out there somewhere—not too close at hand but out there somewhere. God is certainly there if you need a God, yes? But not so much a God that there is any interference with your plans. Sort of a convenient God. Like a life insurance policy. In case things get beyond your control, maybe there is someone that can help you.

So, the usual idea of faith is that if you have faith, everything goes well, yes? But that is only in the ordinary sense. I will speak of faith in a deeper sense, a real sense. This is important because if you have faith in God, or in a Greater Power, or in life or whatever you wish to call it, and everything is going along fine, well, that is good; you have faith. But if things do not go so well, maybe your faith is shaken a little bit. It is more difficult to have faith now, and it takes more effort to shore up your faith once again. But when you are touched very deeply within yourself, which will occur at some point, then it requires a whole new kind of faith, and I'd like to explain this a little so that you can understand.

What is the most cherished thing a person has in the world? What is the thing that people will defend against all adversities, the very source of their survival instinct? What is this? Is it the preservation of the physical body? In an ordinary sense, you would say yes. That is a fundamental motive for self-protection. But there is something greater than this. It is something that you will rarely ever think of. It is something so fundamental that it is not even part of awareness.

The thing that people are most afraid of is that their idea of themselves will be changed—the *idea* of themselves. It is quite apparent that people will commit suicide physically to maintain an idea of themselves. People are very protective of their idea of themselves because that is their identity in the world. So, when real change is occurring, the idea of self is affected.

Now, this idea of self goes far beyond your wish to minimize or eliminate the negative aspects of yourself and enhance the positive aspects. That is still at the surface. Yet, when your fundamental idea of self is being affected, your life truly changes. That is real change. That is important change. That is what people are longing for most deeply and are most fortified against. All of your habits and compulsions maintain your idea of self. I use this expression "idea of self" to give you an understanding that what you are truly afraid of is changing something very fragile—your idea of yourself.

When you are experiencing true change, true development and true progress, well, the idea of self undergoes tremendous change. And while it is changing, you go through periods when you don't know who you are or what you are doing—you seem out of control. These are the most important times. This is when something very important happens. That is when a new direction is recognized and new abilities are discovered. You see, that is what all this development and personal growth is for—to bring you to this. And when you are really going through this change, you begin to understand something very important about other people and about yourself. Making progress means that you are going into the unknown, and the unknown is really a state where you are not so sure who you are.

It all sounds very simple. Yet, why is there so much fear? There is so much fear! If you begin to become aware of yourself, you realize you are in a state of fear most of the time—a kind of low grade fear and occasionally a high grade fear like panic. This is unnecessary.

What you really want is to discover Knowledge because that holds the promise for your life, and that is beyond your idea of self. You must go past the idea of self to find this, to really find it. It is far greater than simply having some intuitive experiences. It leads you to the reality of the Greater Self within you.

Here you must have faith that there is something within you that is worthwhile. And you must also have faith that you have assistance within the world amongst people and assistance from beyond the world as well. This must be your foundation. You cannot proceed into the unknown without guidance and assistance. It is not an individual pursuit. You see, the idea of self is how you remain a separate identity in a universe that represents a unified identity. In other words, this is how you maintain your idea of yourself individually. So, when two people come together in relationship, there is much negotiation over "How much of my individuality will I give up?" and there is a great deal of effort to express and establish each person's individuality.

Why are people afraid of embarrassment or disapproval? It is all to protect the idea of self. When you are alone, all you have is your idea of self. You do not yet have your True Self. Following Knowledge returns you directly to your True Self. Here you must go through periods where your idea of self is lost and you are not so sure who you are. Here faith is necessary. This is a far greater faith, more important than simply hoping that there is something good out there to make sure that you don't lose your money or have a bad time.

When you begin to discover the power of Knowledge within yourself, you will also see where all fear comes from. You will see this within yourself because it is always standing in your way telling you to go back, to go back to the known, to go back to the familiar, to stay where you are, to not do anything, to not move forward. "Hold back, protect what you have, don't risk it!" Now, I am not advocating that people go out and risk what they have just for the sake of doing it. That is ridiculous. What I am saying is that when true change in life is upon you, it is essential that you be able to respond to it. It does not come every day. Yet, there are junctures in your life where true change becomes not only possible but necessary. These are the great opportunities.

You are not the source of this change. That is very important to understand. It is the result of your own deeper will and the Greater Will of all life working together. In other words, it is the result of the truth. There is no individual truth and no one can have a total understanding of the truth—only a partial and perhaps momentary understanding. There is something greater that is bringing about this change within you. You are responding. And if you can respond, then others will respond to you. You will spark something in others as well. That is why when any individual begins to truly experience Knowledge and to follow each step towards Knowledge, others will begin to be motivated in the same way. Here you begin to teach as a natural part of your life.

So, what do you have faith in? That is important. You cannot have total faith in an idea of self if you have looked at yourself honestly because you are not consistent in your thinking or behavior. What is worthy of trust must be consistent. It must be strong. It must be good. It must always be there.

There are only two things in life that qualify for this—two things. One is Knowledge, which is the part of you that is part of God. The other is God, or all the Knowledge in the universe, if you want to say it like that. Some people do not like the word God; it brings back memories of childhood or something, but we talk about God anyway.

So, there are only two things worthy of your faith. Having faith in your Knowledge restores your own value to yourself. If you can follow it, it will demonstrate its reality to you. It can only do that if you follow it. Having faith in God restores your relationship with life and with the universe. So, you have part of God within you that you must reclaim and you have relationship with life that you must reclaim. Here you begin to build a foundation for true happiness. Here your life makes sense and you realize why you are the way you are. You have been specially made for something that you have not discovered yet. Until you realize this to be true, you are always trying to be like other people and are angry about it, and those people you are trying to be like will always have great influence over you, which will cause much conflict. You will never be at ease around people whom you emulate. This all produces conflict. This makes relationships very unstable.

You don't discover Knowledge all at once. It comes to you in increments. Each part must be accepted. Why? Because it changes your idea of self slowly. People often have big experiences. These experiences produce only a little tiny change in idea of self, and people think that they have gone through some kind of metamorphosis. Only a little change in self seems so big to them. They begin to experience things a little differently perhaps, but it is only the beginning of change because who you are is not your idea of self. Who you are is only using your idea of self, but you must go past the idea of self to see this and to know this to be true.

Why am I here with you? Because you have come into the world to reclaim yourself in the world. This is not the path of personal fulfillment. You do not meet all of your criteria for being a wonderful, perfect, magnificent person. It is more of an undoing than a doing. It is more about letting go than taking on. When you begin to experience yourself more directly, then you will be in a position to take on real responsibility in life. So, here I am talking about the idea of self, but it is only a temporary expedient because to experience me you must know me in a very deep place in yourself, or I am merely a phenomenon that you either like or do not like, agree with or do not agree with. It does not matter. It is all at the surface only. Deep within you, where real experience emerges, there is true relationship. That is also the case between yourself and others. You may have been together for many years, intimately, and not have touched each other yet—really touched, really experienced relationship very deeply, beyond understanding the relationship, beyond behavior and shared interests.

You see, what I am talking about is where all of the goodies are! Everything else is just stimulation, something to keep you occupied momentarily to ward off insecurity. That is not bad. It is simply not very important. Within each person, there is the expression of their true Knowledge. It is to bring this forth in the midst of all other ideas, influences and tendencies that is the purpose of our being here together.

You can only have faith in Knowledge and in God. Knowledge is God in you. God is Knowledge in the universe. Why fear? Because you are afraid you won't know who you are. You know, people jump off a bridge and say, "I am doing this to tell you all who I am! To make you remember my idea of myself." If an idea of self becomes too damaged or destroyed and you do not have Knowledge, you can go crazy and try to kill yourself because your idea of self is too small to fit you. That is why when people begin to open to greater experience, they must have true support and assistance because at times they will not know who they are as they eclipse their idea of self to find the True Self. That is why we have always discouraged people from attempting to do this on their own. You cannot do this on your own. This takes you beyond yourself. This brings you into true relationship with other people.

When I say have faith in God, I mean have faith in Knowledge in others because that is the most real demonstration of God in the world. Someone is doing something beyond their own personal interest. That is greatness in the world.

But people become afraid. "What will I have to give up?" It is not about giving anything up. It is about finding something. You can keep what you have now if you are truly interested in it. That is fine. If you are not interested, that is fine. It is all fine. But you must love and trust your True Self to know that you will not lead yourself into deprivation.

The man and woman of Knowledge do not need much from the world, unless they have a very big role to play, and then they need things temporarily. It is all used to express something greater. Being a musician? It is to express something greater. Being an athlete? It is to express something greater. Being a leader amongst people? It is to express something greater. It is this experience that you wish to have. That is what gives everything meaning.

One of the difficult things that the student of Knowledge must learn to do accurately is to be able to discern fear, to know when he or she is afraid and say, "Oh, I am afraid!" When you say that, half of your burden is gone in the moment. People are afraid and think it is something else, it is someone else or that something is going on. But they are only afraid. When you are afraid, you are without Knowledge. If you are acting crazy, you cannot respond. If you are closed, no one can reach you. I am not speaking here of the fear that you experience when you are obviously very frightened of something. I am talking about your normal state of mind. I say this only to give you an indication that there is something far greater waiting for you.

You see, I'll tell you a great secret, from beyond the world. God does not care if you are a "nice person." That is not important. God does not care if you look good. Not important. There is only being real. If you are real and it is important to look good, well, you will look good! It is not a problem. It is simply an expedient in order to communicate with others.

There are only two things in life—I make everything simple. I could write a book with only two sentences. "There are only two things in life. There is Knowledge and there is looking good." It is true. Looking good! Why look good? To protect an idea of self. If you think I am kidding, then go outside one day dressed completely inappropriately for who you think you are and see how you feel. You will be afraid. Go out dressed like people you do not like. You will be afraid. You do not really need to do this, but some of you are very adventurous and want to try out everything, yes? Lifetimes are spent trying out all the things the world has to offer, and in this day and age the world has so much more to offer. A very exciting place, yes? Then you realize that everything the world has to offer is all the same, and only your desire for Knowledge remains.

You can go out to your car, open the door and experience Knowledge. The most ordinary action. This may be much greater than going to the Pyramids around the world. You know why? Because the Pyramids do not mean anything. The only thing in the Pyramids that means anything is the Knowledge that was experienced when they were built. Other than that, they are just more "stuff" in an interesting shape. The same is true with all places considered holy or sacred. Their only value is the Knowledge that has been experienced there. So, you go to those places and the Knowledge that was experienced remains there, for any place where Knowledge has been experienced is a holy place. You can experience Knowledge in a bathtub. Then it becomes as holy a sanctuary as the great cathedral! People often have an experience of Knowledge in the most ordinary circumstances because for a moment they are not trying to be anything. So they are themselves. They fall back into themselves. Wonderful moments! But then they must return to protecting an idea of self.

There are two kinds of fear. I would like to make a distinction here. There is the fear that constitutes fear of survival of self, which constitutes about ninety-nine percent of the fear you will ever experience. Then there is another kind of fear, which is not really fear at all. It is more like cautious observation, like climbing a mountain. Not fear, but cautious observation. You are very attentive now. You are cautious. That is good. To be truly cautious, you must be alert and observant. To be observant and alert is a profound state. It is very rare. It is so easy for the alert person to be successful in life because there are so few alert people. Alert means you are not preoccupied with yourself. You are observing things around you objectively without attempting to define things or judge things. If you were crossing ice cold water in a fast river, you would not be judging the river, you would simply be watching it to know where to put your feet. This is a very alert state. Caution is like that. Some people may think this is being fearful, but it is not.

The rest of fear will become increasingly unnecessary and recognized as just an aggravation of mind as you begin to trust Knowledge within yourself and beyond. This is a relevant subject, particularly if you are facing real change in life. Knowledge is the foundation. It will make your passage far easier, and you will be able to gain true value from change. Otherwise, it is not important that you go from this place to another place or that your circumstances change. It is all forgotten anyway. The only thing you take from this world is the Knowledge that you have discovered here and the relationships that you have truly established. They are permanent. That is what is truly meaningful. Therefore, the fewer distinctions you have, the more clearly you can see. But they must be very important distinctions, and they will require much openness of mind.

Now I wish to talk about service a little bit. The more you experience your life is in service to something greater, the less afraid you will be. It is not sacrifice to something greater. That is wrong thinking. It is service to something greater. When you serve, you cannot lose. But when you try to acquire things for yourself, there is always a great risk of failure and loss. You may lose that which you have here already, and you may not succeed in what you are attempting to acquire. This does not mean that you should not acquire things, but I am speaking of a different state of mind. When you are in service to something, you are acknowledging an inherent relationship already and are in position to receive from that relationship. Achieving a state of total service is a profound state of giving and receiving. There is very little fear here. You will still have an idea of self, but it will not be in contradiction to your true nature. Everyone here has an individual nature to use while you are visiting here in the world, and you have a true nature, which is permanent. Your permanent nature is not important to discuss. It is simply there when you run out of other things to do. But your individual nature is very important because this is where the foundation for self-love must be established.

I'll tell you something very interesting and worth thinking about. People are afraid to be still, and they are afraid to act with great determination. These two experiences are very complementary. When you learn stillness, you learn to act with great determination, and you also learn to wait for what stimulates great determination. So, when you are confused and in doubt, become still. You can't be still asking questions, "Where is the answer? I am being still. Where is the answer? I am being still. I have been still for five minutes!" You see, your questioning mind is not where the answer is.

God in life you cannot follow. Knowledge in yourself and in others you can follow. Therefore, be with those who exemplify what I am talking about. If you want to know something important to do in life, be with someone who is doing something important. Don't be with people who are as confused as you are. You will amplify each other's confusion, and there will be endless discussion about how it all should be or could be. Instead, find someone who is doing something important and spend time with that person. This is not complex.

There are two things in which Knowledge expresses itself in this world. There is stillness and there is determined action. That is where people experience Knowledge. Some people need to become still to know something. Other people need to do something to know something. But you all need to be still a little bit. That is the first step.

*Direct experience
means that you are
experiencing
a reality
that is beyond
your interpretation.*

Thirty

PERCEPTION

IN THE GREATER COMMUNITY WAY OF KNOWLEDGE, answers are not always easy to find. Things are not always immediately accessible. This is because you must go deeper. You must penetrate things that are simple and obvious to find what is really at the heart of your life and what accounts for the mystery of your life. In The Way of Knowledge, we take people through many stages of development. There are other Teachers who are disseminating information at various levels to help people on their way, but our role is a little bit different. We actually present a curriculum for training in Knowledge according to the ancient schools in the Greater Community.

Now I will speak about perception, reality and Knowledge. First of all, I would like to say a few things about Knowledge so that you will know what I am talking about. At the very surface of Knowledge is the experience of profound intuition, the experience of profound insight and knowing. That is at the surface of Knowledge. Beyond the surface is the total experience of life in this world and beyond this world for you to have while you are still here. That is what reassociates you with life beyond and enables you to fully be a contributor while you are in the world. In all practical aspects, this is complete fulfillment while you are here.

We do not speak of enlightenment because enlightenment is entirely relative to various stages of development. When you reach a state of enlightenment, you will find you are a beginner in the next stage. So, when people talk about total enlightenment, they are talking about reaching the climax of the stage that they are in. There are great turning points within physical life that very few people achieve—these are generally regarded to be enlightenment.

Because a great deal of public teaching is going on now, public teaching from sources that are beyond the world—or beyond your range of perception, let us say—it is important to note that those instructors who are most popular are disseminating information to the largest numbers of people. Disseminating information is a very different role from being an initiator. It is a different function to fulfill. Disseminating information alone requires a great deal of verbal skill and a facility in working with people individually and collectively. This in itself is a complete role. Beyond this, there are instructors who actually carry on the initiation process but rarely take a public stance. They have very few students because there are very few who are actually prepared to take the journey in its advanced stages. Those Teachers that disseminate information prepare those who eventually will begin the actual reclamation of Knowledge. They prepare the way.

Therefore, much of what is said by the Teachers who are disseminating information is only preparatory. In other words, it is to orient you in a correct direction. What is given are not statements of ultimate truth. It is merely a beginning, like preparing the soil for planting great seeds. When you are preparing the soil, you realize that that is the stage you are in, and you do not confuse it with later stages of development. So, disseminating information is preparing the mental soil, preparing minds to receive Knowledge.

When we speak of perception, we speak of your interpretation of the reality that you can experience. Let me say that again. When we speak of perception, we are speaking of your interpretation of the reality that you can experience. What you experience is interpretive. It is very rare that people have a direct experience of anything! Direct experience means that you are experiencing a reality that is beyond your interpretation. A very rare and great experience this is. It could be the common denominator of your experience, but in fact it is quite rare and phenomenal because 99.9% of your experience is interpretation of the reality that you can experience. When I say "the reality that you can experience," I mean that you can only experience a little bit of reality because of your limited capacity and range of perception. So, it is not merely the interpretation of reality at large; it is interpretation of the reality that you can experience.

That is why people live in their minds and not in life. This is the source of all of your difficulties. You are more engaged with your ideas than you are with life. Being engaged with life means that you are directly involved and are having a direct experience. Now, obviously, you can sit and be totally involved with your own mind and be totally uninvolved with everything around you, unaware of forces that are influencing you—forces that are helpful for you and forces that are not helpful for you. This is a profound disadvantage! This is why people are having problems.

There is not a problem with reality, but there is a great problem with interpretation and self-absorption. At the very beginning of true learning, then, each person must become aware of their self-absorption—how much they are involved with their own mind and how little they are involved in life. Often it can seem very upsetting or disappointing and even insulting when you find out that you are actually experiencing very little of life and thinking a great deal. Because we value true experience, that is what we wish to orient you towards.

There are many Teachers who are disseminating information and there are a few Teachers, such as myself, who are initiating students. It is a different role. It is not necessarily better; it is just a different role. It means that my responsibility is to prepare a handful of individuals for Knowledge. In the process of doing this, I will, of course, disseminate a great deal of information, but disseminating information is a very small part of my role.

The problem, then, is that people are involved with their thoughts and not with life. This creates a very great gulf in your experience. So, when people say, "You create your own reality," what does this mean? It is only meaningful in the realm of your own thoughts. It assumes, if you think about it, that there is no reality beyond your own thoughts. In the beginning—the very beginning—people are told, "You create your own reality. You must change your thoughts to have a different reality." Isn't that what you have read? Yet, this is only a first step. This requires that you look at your thoughts to see how fully involved with them you really are. There is reality beyond your thoughts. In fact, beyond your thoughts is the only reality because your thoughts can only interpret. There is a reality within you that actually creates, but it is entirely beyond your mind. If your mind is open and has become balanced and whole, then the reality that creates can create through you. That is the greatest experience of satisfaction and fulfillment in the world.

In contrast to this creative reality, your personal problems are very small, just requiring certain adjustments here and there. Like maneuvering a car down the street, it requires that you steer a little here and push a button there and make adjustments along the way. Even with the great responsibility of driving a car down the street and all the terrible things that could happen to you, you don't think about it much, do you? You just do it! You learn how and you do it! So it is that Knowledge is so much greater than personal problems that personal problems become easier to solve. In fact, all personal problems are very easy to solve. The problem is that people want the problem and not the solution. The frustrating thing about teaching is always the ambivalence about learning. That is why the initiation process takes a long time. It is not an easy path. It is not a difficult path, either.

Therefore, when you say, "I create my reality," what you are saying is that you are creating an interpretation of what you can experience. If you can only experience this much of life, and it is all your interpretation, then you see your range of perception is very limited. But your Knowledge, which you carry within yourself, is capable of opening up your perception completely. Without so much incessant thinking, wondering, asking, pondering, manipulating, planning and scheming, and so forth, the greater part of your mind, your Knowledge, can begin to show you things.

It is not difficult to have direct experience. You simply must not be doing anything else. Having direct experience means you are not doing anything else. So, then, true preparation requires that you learn to be still, to become observant, to disassociate yourself to a certain degree from your own judgment of things, to become open to the presence of intimacy and love, to accept true relationship, and to begin to accept at least the idea that there is something greater than your own thoughts. Not a bad deal!

The fact is you only create interpretations of reality. A better interpretation may be more pleasant temporarily, but you are still disassociated from yourself and life. It is this disassociation that must be bridged. Life is happening all around you, an incredible panorama. But you cannot experience it. Your Teachers are with you, helping you in amazing ways, but you do not know that they are there. There are genuine relationships waiting for you in life, waiting for you to be ready and desirous of them, but you must have the capability and the desire.

There is a reality that creates beyond the interpretation that you create. You do not need to create reality. It is created for you. You can enjoy its creation. Therefore, it is very important to become a happy recipient of reality. Then you will see that you have brought something from beyond the world to give to the world. It is not good to come to the world and say, "Give me reality, world! Give me what I had from beyond! Give me intrinsic relationships! Give me peace of mind! Give me equanimity! Give me meaning! Give me purpose! Give me direction!" The world cannot do any of these things. These are things that you bring to the world. It is like being a parent and asking the child to take care of you! You are the parent. The world is a where you have come to contribute. It cannot give much because it is only a child. In this you find your responsibility. You begin to accept your true worth and the resources that you have brought with you.

Why is the world such a difficult place for human beings? Because they have come from beyond. It is not so difficult for plants and animals, but it is difficult for people because they come from beyond. They have come from a much more pure reality. This makes it very difficult, then, to adjust to being here. You do not need to change the world. But you do need to find out who you are, why you have come and what you have brought with you. You are only here for a brief time, after all. Before you know it, you are back Home, like nothing changed! It is always the same there.

What people are seeking for in life is purpose, meaning and direction. They have brought these with them. The world is waiting to receive them, but people are looking for them in the world. Do you see the complication here? It is like the parent saying, "Take care of me, baby! Be my daddy and mommy."

Becoming a true contributor in life, guided by your own Knowledge and unfettered by your own interpretation of reality, is the greatest achievement possible and one that will make you a great resource for everyone you come in contact with and for people whom you will never see. Your mind, being open, will provide an opening for other minds. This is entirely natural and is actually more an unlearning than a learning process. All the books, all the lectures, all the ideas and all the processes— you must leave them all at the temple gate, the outer gate, to enter in. You simply enter and your Teachers are there to take you in. They have successfully completed the development of Knowledge in physical life. Therefore, they are prepared to enable you to do so as well. That is the great promise.

Not all the seeds that are thrown onto the ground from the tree will hatch, but some will. You will always find that the most direct way does not attract great crowds because people find the requirement is too great. "I just wanted some information. I don't want to have to do anything!" Ideas are simple. They require very little of you. They also give very little to you. But relationships require a great deal and provide a great deal. Having a meaningful marriage and raising children require a great deal and provide a great deal.

The emphasis here is Knowledge. It is not your personal Knowledge because there is no personal Knowledge. In Knowledge there is only individual expression. There is no individual reality. Drawing from a Greater Reality means that you have passed beyond your own interpretations sufficiently that you can now have a direct experience of life. You can see in a new way, hear in a new way, speak in a new way and experience life in a new way.

Therefore, when you hear others talking about "creating their own reality," see this only as a sign pointing in the right direction. What this means for you is that you must take responsibility for the content of your mind. What are you thinking at this moment? What you are thinking is relevant to what you are experiencing. This is accurate. But beyond this is reality, and that is the great gift. Achieving this, then, is more a settling down than a building up. It is the result of becoming still and observant so that you can penetrate your own interpretation. A still mind is a mind that is collecting its own power. It can direct its full resources in any direction, and that is the definition of power in the world.

Concentration is power. A more concentrated mind will have a great effect on less concentrated minds. If that mind is concentrated on evil or destruction, it will still have a great effect on less concentrated minds. That is why we have said in recent discourses that great wars are perpetrated only by individuals who are dedicated to those wars. Their influence on less concentrated minds is quite apparent.

Yet, a mind that is concentrated on good is even more powerful. That is why the Wise are hidden and do not make a show of themselves. They do not want to have too great an impact. They don't want to attract too much attention from the wrong people. They save themselves for certain individuals whom they realize are actually prepared for their gifts.

You see, I am painting a bigger picture here. Do not be satisfied with ideas or little truths. Knowledge is still within you. It is sleeping like a giant. Until it becomes manifest in your life, your life is still interpretive. You are not in direct relationship with life yet. Life is relationship. That's all life really is. If you are feeling lonely, you are not experiencing this relationship. The only thing that you can experience apart from life is your own ideas, yes? After all, life is everything. It is very hard not to experience it. To do that you must create your own internal reality that is interpretive, and you must be in relationship with it.

The Teacher of Knowledge brings you out of relationship with ideas and into relationship with life. That is the process. Each step of the way renders great rewards. It leaves you freer and more lighthearted. In Knowledge, everything is very simple. In fact, your life is so simple that you can devote yourself to other lives, helping and caring for others because your life is so simple. You are free, then, to participate beyond your own self. This is the great happiness, and this enables you to be in meaningful relationships.

Knowledge waits for the moment and then gives the remedy.

Thirty-one

HEALING

HEALING IS A SUBJECT I do not often address because of how people approach it. There are many, many ideas— even philosophies—about healing. Beyond the purely mechanical repair of the physical body, there is a great deal of speculation on the cause and nature of illness and the reparation of illness. Remedies vary depending on how far you want to go. Because any dysfunction, mental or physical, is part of your total life here, it cannot be isolated and separated out. If you wish to address a chronic problem, you must address your entire life. But because addressing your entire life is a far greater quest than most people are willing or desiring to undertake, they merely wish to address the symptoms of the discomfort and erase them as quickly and as easily as possible.

Our job is to talk about the larger picture and to deal with healing in a very complete framework. I have not wanted to speak of healing very often because people bring all of their aches and pains to me and say, "How about this one? And how do I take care of that one? And this one and that one?" as if I am dispensing remedies like a pharmacist. So I say, "The most important thing is to discover your Knowledge." Well, often people want only a remedy, which they can take home and try out. Of course it has very limited success. It may ease discomfort if they follow the directions. But very few people will take the real remedy because then they must deal with their whole lives. So, let me give you a few ideas so that we can explore this subject together.

First of all, the physical body has no magical powers. It is an instru-ment, a vehicle. People are confused about this because they confuse the levels. They confuse Spirit with the body. They want to make Spirit and the body alike, having the same properties, but Spirit and the body do not have the same properties. This does not mean that they are disassociated. It simply means that you cannot expect the same qualities from both, or you will diminish the whole experience of your spiritual life and try to elevate your physical life to an immortal state.

The physical body is a vehicle. Your personal mind is a vehicle, too. This is very important to understand because when you see that you have a vehicle, it leads you to ask the question, "What is this vehicle for?" A vehicle is to take you someplace to do something. It is not merely a mask that you wear. A vehicle is to take you someplace for a purpose.

To come into physical life you must have a body and a personal mind. You have a body so that people can experience your presence, and you have a personal mind so that you can communicate to people through the body. They are both vehicles. They are not meant to be perfected. They are both subject to wear and tear, breakdowns and problems. They can be maintained very well if you care for them, but they are not infallible because they are vehicles.

It is when you try to make a vehicle the object of your attention completely that you lose perspective on what it is for. If the body becomes the total emphasis, then you will require more of it than it can produce, and you will make its symptoms and its problems extremely complex when, in most cases, they are very simple. Because the personal mind and the body are very closely related, they have tremendous influence upon one another. Obviously, your physical body affects your emotional states, yes? If you have an ache or a pain, if you feel bad, it is very hard to think of anything else. Likewise, your emotional states have a direct impact upon your body because they both work together as vehicles.

Knowledge is not a vehicle. It is your True Self in the world. It is your True Mind. It is not an individual, though it seeks an individual expression. It fulfills the mind and the body by expressing itself through them. Here your body is fully used and is something to be appreciated, not maligned. Your personal mind is something that is employed and finds its own self-love here.

So, what is illness then? Why do things break down? As I have said, bodies break down and personal minds break down too because they are vehicles. But they can be maintained at a very high level of functioning. It is not complex to do this. You simply must have the desire, and they must be seen as vehicles. That is very important. Without this understanding, you will make them the object of your life, trying to keep the body and the personal mind comfortable. Then, beyond having nice chairs to sit in and pleasant food to eat, you will try to keep the personal mind always calm, satisfied and happily stimulated. But that is not the purpose of life, for when you leave this life, you leave behind these vehicles. If you identify too much with your vehicles, you will think that that is all you are. Here you are afraid to go beyond, and your life is fearful because your vehicles can be taken away from you. They are easily threatened.

Now, if you think that your vehicle is your self, you will hate the vehicle because it will seem to trap you and you will feel imprisoned, bound and limited by it. If your vehicle is all that you experience, then your whole life will be about taking care of the vehicle or about taking care of other people's vehicles in an attempt to be happy and to keep everyone happy. But your deepest need has not been met, and you have not found your foundation yet. Even faith in God is not enough of a foundation. You must experience God because religion is experience. You only need faith when you are not having the experience that *is* the experience. Then your faith will confirm that the experience was real. That is what faith is for—to carry you to the next real experience. It is something you take into the shadows with you when you return to blindness—that is faith.

So, our remedy is very great, but it is also very complete. It is very comprehensive. It enables you to have compassion for the world. Healing must happen in life, but it is not the kind of healing that people often think of. People think of healing as everyone being happy and everyone having equal opportunities, yes? They think of healing as a state where there are no physical problems, where emotional states are stable and where people are not having friction. It sounds a little ridiculous when I talk like this, but really when you examine your model for life, it can resemble this very closely—a life where everyone is supposed to be comfortable. But comfort is not why people have come here. Obviously, there is very little comfort in the world, yes? For such intelligent beings there are more comfortable worlds, but not this one! There is something else happening here, but very few people know about it. The ones who do know about it often feel tremendously isolated because their experience of life is very different.

So, you have mental and physical problems, aches and pains, things that break down. If you do not feed the body right and take care of it, and if you do not take care of the personal side and give it some personal pleasures, they break down and have problems. But hey can be attended to without a great deal of investment if you realize these things are the vehicles for something greater. There are people lying on their death bed, with their body ninety percent gone, who are dispensing more God into life than the person running up and down the street in full health.

God does not ask that your vehicles be perfect because they are temporary expediencies. God does not ask you to look beautiful. That is not why you came here. It is much nicer on the other side! That is why so many people want to leave when they give up hope here. But this is where you yearn to be, so you are here and you are here for a purpose— each of you. Deep within you, like a secret cargo, you are carrying your purpose in life, but you cannot figure it out in your mind. It is not an idea or an explanation. It is a profound experience that rearranges your life, giving it direction and restoring self-love to you. It comes from within you and it restores your relationship with the universe because its source is the universe. It protects you from making false assumptions about yourself, and it reunites you with life.

Sickness in the mind is always the result of isolation and self-absorption because you are out of relationship. That produces sickness in the mind. Sickness in the body is because the mind hates the body and hurts it. But there is also sickness in the body because it gets old and wears out. Not everyone is going to die in their sleep. Not everyone is going to live life without a day of sickness. So this is not expected.

What is important is that you find your Knowledge through experience. It is very powerful. It is not subtle. It is so powerful, in fact, and so present that most people are afraid to take even little baby steps towards it for fear it will take everything away from them.

God is so close to you that you cannot even turn around. God is so big and so magnificent that if you had only one leg and one arm and God, you would do well. So, when I speak of healing, I am not merely speaking of repairing the vehicles. There is already a great deal of information about that. If the problem is purely mechanical, go to a doctor and fix it. If it deals with your mind, which is often the case, or has a mental equivalent, well, you need to go work with someone a little bit to get back into relationship, restore your self-expression and gain some perspective on your life. But it is very important, in all of this, that you give your attention to what is beyond your personal self. It is not self-neglect to do that. Your personal self needs some things beyond food, shelter and clothing. It needs some things just like your physical body needs some things— but their needs are not your life.

My Presence here is important in this regard because I represent your life beyond the world, if you can accept my reality. If you come into relationship with me, the memory returns. Yet, I am not the object of your devotion. I am merely a reminder that your life in this world is part of something far greater and that God is not merely a romantic ideal or a great big person up there. God is organizing everything to return to union, but God is doing it in God's own way. It is good that this is the case because people's idea of union ends up being very oppressive when applied to society.

When you begin to discover Knowledge and experience its thinking and its quietness and learn how it takes action, then you will see that there is a very different approach to healing things in the world. One of the most important aspects of healing things in the world, beyond yourself, is leaving things alone. Ninety percent of the time you leave things alone, like someone cultivating a garden. Ninety percent of the time you leave things alone. Ten percent of the time you carry out a very specific action that makes everything else possible. By leaving things alone, I am not saying you neglect things because the good gardener never neglects the garden, but he or she understands that there is a greater process that actually produces and brings about the results in a predictable manner.

This is a new way of helping people. Often when people help others, they want the other person to look good so that they themselves can feel okay. It is very upsetting having someone around in misery, crying and making a big fuss! You can't have a good time with someone like that, and if you don't help them, well, you feel terrible about yourself. But Knowledge is different. Knowledge waits for the moment and then gives the remedy. The rest of the time it seems to be asleep, like God. It seems to be doing nothing about the situation, like God. The reason people don't experience God is that God is not moving very fast because when God moves, everything moves. Then civilization changes. Yet, God is active every moment.

Knowledge seems to be quiet ninety percent of the time. So, as you go about your basic worldly responsibilities, you can be quiet ninety percent of the time. If Knowledge is not indicating for you to do something, do not do anything. Just carry out the obvious duties in your life. Then, if you are taking care of sick people, just take care of sick people. Do the normal things and once in a while Knowledge will move you to do something, so do that. If Knowledge is quiet ninety percent of the time, well, then, you can be quiet too. People can barely be quiet one percent of the time, so you can see that being quiet ninety percent of the time is a very peaceful state. And yet it is an extremely alert and powerful state. The person of Knowledge has great impact on other people because he or she is living a different life and always has a reservoir of energy.

The person of Knowledge can act very deliberately. This action has tremendous impact. Whether you are working in a hospital and dressing wounds or working in a factory, there is a moment of action when your Knowledge can change another person's life. It is not you that changes the other person's life. It is that your Knowledge has activated Knowledge in another, and someone has turned a very important corner within himself or herself. That is healing. That is really it! Beyond repairing the vehicles and keeping them functioning, that is really it.

Something must touch you very deeply and must ignite life within you to such an extent that you start to burn with it inside. But the ignition is only the beginning. There is also the preparation, and now your preparation becomes very conscious. It becomes mysterious too because, you see, the preparation for Knowledge is not the same as the preparation that people prescribe for themselves. Even your prescriptions for enlightenment or getting better may not be similar to the process that you are really in. Your real preparation is more about clearing things away than adding things on.

If you want to know the purpose of your life, you will know it, but it will not be an explanation. It will be more like a great door has been thrown open and you must go through. Then things will really start to move in your life. Once you see the power of this movement, you will have no doubt that it is effective, and you will see why you were not ready for it before.

So, my prescriptions for taking care of the body and the mind are very simple. They are not complicated. People make the problem complicated because they are not sure if they want the solution. So, they have all of this technology for getting better, and it gets them in deeper and deeper with their problem. For example, governments like to study problems which they are not prepared to resolve. Is that not true? So, the commissions come together and they write thousand-page reports. They hire experts, and everyone knows what to do about it, of course, but no one wants to pay the price.

The person of Knowledge is only looking for Knowledge. If you get too involved in studying your personality, there will be a great deal of motion but not much movement, like splashing around in the water but not really getting to the other shore. You think things are happening because you are making such a splash, stirring yourself up. Going from a hot shower into the cold ocean, back and forth, back and forth, is very stimulating to the body, but not much is really happening.

Knowledge is very close at hand, but you cannot grasp it. Yet, it is available when you begin to ask what you *know* about things. Here you must distinguish what you know from what you want and what you think. Then there are all the things you *think* you know or *want* to know. If you can get past all of this, you will get right down to the very core of yourself. Knowing anything, even knowing something very simple that is right in front of you, will take you to the very core of life where everything is simple. God is simple. But ideas about God are very complex. All these levels, and angles and shapes and forms. Sometimes people have to create all that just to get to God. But in the end, it's like coming home to Mama.

To take care of your body, feed it properly. Find out if there are some foods aggravating you or not. Be sure to exercise, and practice some form of meditation or time of quiet. For ninety-nine percent of the people, this is adequate. If you have special physical problems, you must attend to them. That is okay because bodies are vehicles and sometimes they don't come out of the assembly line absolutely perfect.

When you are no longer in the world and you are thinking about your life here, you will not be concerned with vehicles. You will be thinking of how far you got in the world. Did you deliver your cargo or not? Did you come Home with the packages unopened? I want you to have a good life because it enables you to deliver your cargo. But if your body or your mind are always in a state of aggravation, you cannot do that. You will be broken down by the side of the road, and you can't go anywhere. When you are not trying to get everything in life, well, things get much simpler, and you can begin to see which way to go. After all, there are people who have nothing and are happy. There are people who own a great deal and are happy. There are people who have nothing who are miserable, and the same is true for people who own a great deal.

In The Way of Knowledge, you realize that everything is for a purpose, and you understand that purpose does not come from your intellect but from a very deep place within you. You do not understand it very fully because Knowledge always transcends understanding. That is what makes you able to do something really important in life. If you came here to do something important and you are not doing it, you will not feel good. You will become sick and bogged down in yourself.

So, for the personal side you need healthy self-expression and relationships; you need tenderness and intimacy; you need times of quiet and you need to be in the process of allowing your Knowledge to emerge. It is the same with children. Sometimes you realize that when they are upset about something ridiculous, you need to give them something else to do.

"Here, do this!" Then they forget about themselves, they go do it and their tears dry up. "Here, do something else."

If you had nothing important to do in life, this world would indeed be a tragic place. But you have all come here for a purpose. If you can accept that, you will start to look beyond your vehicles. Looking beyond your vehicles means you must learn to become quiet and observant and refrain from your own self-judgment. It means you must have Mystery in your life. Mystery is the source of everything important—the Mystery of your life. You may think you have everything figured out and under control, but leave the door of Mystery open. When you learn to trust Mystery and see that it is not going to deprive you, then your life will become a tremendous discovery from moment to moment.

Knowledge is very different from personal ambition. With Knowledge, healing others is something that simply happens naturally, and you don't even know what is happening. If you are pregnant with Knowledge, you will activate Knowledge in others, and hopefully you will know not to interfere with the process. Hopefully you will know it is not you who is doing it, though you are playing a significant role.

Therefore, I am presenting you with a very big remedy. This remedy requires a real investment of yourself in a very special way. If you take a physical ailment, erase it and go back to the way your life was, it will recur. If you are not at ease with yourself, you will certainly feel it physically, and eventually you will do something to yourself to bring yourself to a halt. Crash your car! Fall off a roof! Then you are lying there in the hospital, everything is catching up with you, and you are starting to become a visionary. Believe me, lives can be changed dramatically for people who do that, but that is a very radical way of finding things out.

So, I am giving you the big remedy. Some of you will use it and won't know why you are using it; it's just the thing to do because Knowledge is moving you. When Knowledge is moving you, there is incredible Mystery in your life, and there is wonder. Wonder is not something you can make yourself have. You either have it or you don't. If I say, "Go out in life and have wonder," you can't add that on to yourself—"Today I will try to have wonder!" You either have wonder or you don't. If you don't have wonder, don't have it. Look at everything and go, "Yuck!

It's all boring stuff! Junk! It's all junk!" You can be a grouch and go around sneering at people. When people are being nice and they don't feel good, the first thing is to get them to feel worse. Then they can come closer to being happy. At least one step closer.

If you have one leg and one arm and one eye and one ear and you look ridiculous, you can still be one of the most powerful people in history. Why? Because something is happening in your life, and it does not just happen in *your* life. It happens to everyone who comes in contact with you. You are not just an individual now trying to fulfill yourself. You are something bigger. You are your entire Spiritual Family. Your life is like the tip of the pen that touches the paper, but what is feeding your life is actually the vessel that holds the reservoir of ink. That is when you feel that you are the place where Heaven and Earth touch together. You don't have to have that experience often, but if you have had it once, it will be enough.

To keep your physical vehicle and personal side of your mind content while you do more important things, it is very good to have a simple life. If you want to have some quiet in life, it will require some simplification. Simplifying your life is very important because then you begin to ask the question, "What is essential in my life?" That is an important question because Knowledge deals with the essential things. What is essential in your life? Here you will begin to see how much is not essential and how it is taking a great deal of your life. This leads you to realize, "I have only this much energy." Do not think that you do not. You only have so much. It is nice to entertain yourself by thinking that you have unlimited energy and you can be superman or superwoman, but you only have so much. It is a limited amount. So, what are you doing with it?

If everyone had no money and I gave everyone ten dollars and said, "That is all you've got. Go out and do something in life," what would happen? Life is like that. You have a few years, you have your waking and sleeping time and you have a tremendous opportunity. Realizing this, you begin to care for yourself and to appropriate your energy more consciously. Your encounters with people become more important and less mindless. Things become more important, but you are more lighthearted about it.

When you are with Knowledge, you will move beyond error. On a personal level, you will still be sort of ridiculous, but it is more a source of fun now. And your body will still be a little ridiculous, but it is not a problem. It is not you. Can you be happy if your car has a dent or mud on it? Can you be happy if your bumper is falling off? Can you drive up to a fancy hotel with your bumper dragging on the ground? Do not look at crippled people and feel pain. If they have Knowledge, there is no problem. They are being fed by life itself. They are bigger than the world.

It is very
important
to see
what
achievement
really is
&
what it
requires.

Thirty-two

ACHIEVEMENT

I WOULD LIKE TO SPEAK ABOUT achievement and relationship. Sometimes people are uncomfortable with the things
I say. To a certain degree, this cannot be helped because not
everyone likes everything. Sometimes I put a little pebble in your shoe, so
to speak, because it is good to think about things. Often when you are
engaged in discussing very important matters, it is very easy to maintain
self-comforting ideas and to rely upon them to answer all the controversies that may arise. To penetrate the real truth within your life, however,
sometimes you must let these controversies rage a little and see what happens. Sometimes you must think very carefully about your own assumptions and be able to distinguish your assumptions from those things you
really know to be true. In other words, you must distinguish between
belief and direct experience.

Life is very intelligent. It is always conspiring to move you into a
larger sphere of experience. A part of each person always wants to stay in a
smaller sphere of experience, which is actually not experience at all. It is
merely a realm of self-assuring ideas. Therefore, sometimes it is necessary
to sort of break things up a little, to bring in some new ideas or say some
things that are challenging. This is healthy. Here there must be trust that if
something that is held very deeply is challenged, there is something else
within you that is really sound, true and stable. You are all trying to get to
that because that is where all meaning and true direction come from.

When you experience life, it is always interpretive. In other words, what you see is interpretive. What you hear is interpretive. What you feel from within yourself is interpretive. However, the Source of Knowledge within you is not interpretive and the more that you can set aside interpretation, the greater your direct experience of life will be. This will give you a vision of life that is quite profound and extremely useful. You will be able to perceive situations around you with greater clarity of mind. You will be able to see what is there rather than what you want to be there because your preferences are exerting less influence upon you. This makes your vision clearer and your presence more powerful.

There are many popular spiritual ideas that are very deeply cherished, and people often think that these are not ideas but absolute truths themselves. But they are really ideas. Anything your mind settles on is an idea. What is most important is where true ideas come from. That is why we have often said, "Do not be content with ideas alone." Whether they be comforting or not, find out where they come from. That is the great opportunity.

You have all come here to achieve something. It is a possibility. There are no guarantees that you will do it in this life because that is up to you. You have all come to do something specific. By achieving that, you will be able to end separation within yourself and therefore be able to complete your work at this level. However, this thing you have come to do is not so obvious. Do not say, "I know what it is already. It is to do this!" That may be a very comforting idea, but not terribly helpful. If you sense that you have something in life that you must achieve, it is important that there is someone in your life who loves you enough to challenge you when that is necessary, to comfort you when that is necessary and to reassure you when that is necessary.

An achievement has two aspects: the first is realization, the second is accomplishment. You cannot separate them. They must happen together. Some people want the realization without the responsibility of the accomplishment. Many people want to experience accomplishment and just bypass the realization. "Just tell me what it is. I'll go do it tomorrow. Or maybe I'll do it tonight, if it is important. Just tell me what it is. Tell me what to do!" So, in my discourses I have given some very lofty goals to achieve. They are not so easy, but they are worthwhile. I want everyone here to aim very high in life, perhaps higher than you think you can go. That is good.

The realization is very important because it gives you the power of accomplishment. It also resolves many other issues that can be very substantial in themselves. The accomplishment is very important because here you leave your mark upon the world. Then you achieve a satisfaction that very few people will ever achieve. You have completed something that is absolutely fundamental to your being here. There is satisfaction even in. approaching the accomplishment and in all the various stages of the accomplishment. Here you do not need to question your reality. You do not need to continually ask the same question, "What am I doing? What am I doing? What am I doing?" You are able to give yourself increasingly to a primary focus in life, and that in itself ends conflict.

There is something else very important about achievement. You must be extremely concentrated, not only concentrated in terms of your perspective, but concentrated in terms of your life force. You must have tremendous vitality to go in the direction that you must go. You will find this quality apparent in all individuals who are achieving something important in any area—a tremendous concentration of energy and focus.

When you learn to concentrate, you find out it is not so easy to do if you are not used to it. At first, it can seem very self-limiting to concentrate like this, but as you proceed, it begins to generate spiritual power in your life and to harmonize your outer affairs. In fact, this concentration requires that other things be resolved. This begins to generate a tremendous build-up of power that is quite essential for your achievement.

To achieve anything in this life, you must exert tremendous energy to do it, and yet the achievement that we are speaking of is not only an achievement based upon your own ability, but the achievement of carrying a Greater Power in your life that far exceeds anything that you individually can do alone. But the Greater Power cannot do this without your development as a vehicle and your development as a partner. This is very exciting!

Very few will actually be the seed people for the accomplishment. They will require a community of people to help them do whatever it is given them to do, and everyone who can help them will be uplifted in doing that.

When you are concentrated, you will have power. Whether it be for good or for ill, you will have power. Those who are committed to destruction can be very concentrated. That is why they are so influential. If the general population is not concentrated, either individually or collectively, it can be easily manipulated. This is sad but true.

Therefore, if you wish to make a contribution in life, it is very important to increase your concentration on your power and development. This means pulling yourself in and focusing your emphasis on only one or two areas. This magnifies your presence and power and brings about resolution to your conflicts. When you are truly engaged in achievement, you are concentrating on what is essential. What is essential is gaining your attention and involvement. This concentrates your life, and with concentration comes the resolution of conflict. More and more of yourself is aiming in one direction, and there is less and less division internally.

The Greater Community Way of Knowledge is for people who know they must carry on in achieving what they came here to achieve. Beyond their personal preferences or desire for comfort, there is something now that is driving them forward, and they must proceed. The Way of Knowledge is for these people.

We wish to give a very honest and clear picture of what true preparation is and what it requires. Then people can become more honest about the issue of achievement. Now, in normal conversation people talk about the great things that they want to achieve or intend to achieve or will achieve someday or should achieve, and so forth. The word "commitment" is used very lightly here, and the word "dedication" is used very lightly. These things deserve reverence. Indeed they do. When you have a taste of what it really means to be committed and devoted, to be inner-directed and to give yourself completely to something, then you will see the difference and how important it is.

Somehow you must find your place in life and you must find a way to gain access to that part of you that has come here to achieve something. It is not true that you are here merely to make up for past mistakes. It is not true that you are here merely to resolve personal dilemmas. That is not true! That is a very limited viewpoint. It does not hold respect for your origin, your Source or your true Community beyond this world.

Often we have spoken of Spiritual Family, and we would like to say a few words about this because many people who have heard this are not yet certain what I mean. In life thus far, you have had a physical family, a family of the world that has made it possible for you to be born, to be raised and to be educated in the ways of the world. Likewise, you have a Spiritual Family that is waiting to prepare you, to activate your spiritual life and your Knowledge while you are here in the world. All sparks of achievement come from beyond the world. The achievement may have a very physical manifestation. It may have a very mundane application, but the inspiration for it has come from beyond the world—all achievements for good, that is.

Therefore, you have a physical family, a worldly family, that has raised you from birth and that has educated you to prepare you to be in life. Maybe they did not do such a good job, but that is beside the point. Then you have a Spiritual Family into which you are born in a new world. Here you develop and you become educated so that you can become a spiritual presence in life.

Now, when you first begin to realize this process, it is very important to know that you will be like a child in this new realm. Like all little children, you will want everything but will actually have the capacity for very little. Here it takes time to understand how your wants are relative and dependent upon your capacity. Even though a little child wants to have everything interesting for themselves, they must learn what things are and what things are for good and what things are not for good. They must develop a capacity for having things and for being responsible.

The same is true with your spiritual development. At the beginning you want it all. "I want it all!" But you cannot really receive very much yet because your capacity is quite limited and your education has not been brought about. So, you must be raised within your Spiritual Family and educated as well so that you can assume the responsibilities.

Therefore, we wish to talk about achievement in terms of your Spiritual Family and your Ancient Heritage, which you are privileged to bring into this world from beyond. We applaud all achievement for good in life. Yet our role is to cultivate a greater level of achievement. To prepare for this requires a great deal, yet whatever it requires is small compared to what it gives. It is an achievement that at the outset looks very intangible. You do not quite know what you are doing. It is not like building a better car or a business. That all seems very predictable. In these cases, many of the steps seem to be laid out in front of you. You merely need to follow them and be intelligent and committed to what you are doing.

In the reclamation of your true Spiritual Heritage, however, the process of achievement is much more mysterious. The steps are not so evident at the beginning. You enter because something inside of you is moving you to do that. To trust this requires that you relinquish self-hatred and self-doubt and begin to honor the Spiritual Presence that is emerging inside of you. You are taken through various stages of initiation. Then, anything you do will have a lasting impact on the world, not only because of what you may do physically, but because of the state of mind that you are in. Achieving this state of mind, in essence, *is* the greatest achievement, but it requires the greatest preparation as well. We don't expect this achievement of all people. In fact, we only aim at a few people, but everyone who is closely aligned with these individuals will be raised as well. So, our job is to initiate these individuals, and for everyone else we offer important ideas.

In order to do something important in life, your life must become simplified, directed and more concentrated. If I say to someone, "Go become a surgeon," well, becoming a surgeon requires a great deal. It is not something you can do in your spare time. That is achievement.

Therefore, with all the talk of achievement and people's expectations of others for achievement and the expectations of the human race for achievement, it is very important to see what achievement really is and what it requires. That is why I want to talk now about relationships.

There is something very important to see when you look at people who are involved in great achievements. Often they are not very well-rounded people. They are very advanced in one area and not so advanced in other areas. In terms of purely worldly achievement, this is always the case. But in terms of achievement at a higher level, this *cannot* be the case. Purely worldly achievement requires using relationships to bring about an intended result, but achievement at a higher level has an entirely different emphasis on relationship. Here relationship *is* the result. What you achieve, you achieve *in* relationship. If you happen to build a building, or bridge or hospital, that is secondary. In fact, people who are achieving this mysterious thing I am talking about rarely do anything! They don't leave lasting things. They leave lasting relationships. Did Jesus Christ build anything? Did he carve his initials anywhere? Buddha, what did he do that is tangible? What is their achievement? They made it possible for many people to achieve. They ignited relationships at a very high level.

Of course, people do very stupid things too, but that must be expected. You cannot judge a teaching based upon what people do with it, and anyone who is giving the teaching must know this. They must know that it will be horribly disfigured by subsequent practitioners. This is a very important thing to think about.

So, a person who is involved in worldly achievement will use relationships to meet his or her aim. But for a higher level of achievement, relationships *are* the aim and those who achieve this level of relationship will leave the greatest imprint, the most lasting effect. They will produce a movement that will stay in motion for a very long time.

All of this is very relevant to what you want to do with your life. Do you want to squander your life seeking little things which do not satisfy you, or do you want to concentrate on something very important? Many people seem to be happy with little things. That is okay. But these people usually don't read books such as these. People respond to my words because they have a deeper hunger that has manifested itself, at least to some degree. Many people are merely curious. "I want to see what this is," and then they laugh about it later. That is okay. People laugh all the time about the truth. I don't mind. Then other people respond because something is stirring in their lives, and they must do something about it. They must give it recognition and validation, and that is good.

If you want to achieve something tangible, then all you have to do is dedicate all your time and energy to doing that and use all of your talents and the talents of other people to help you, and you will make a strong impression in life. There are other factors involved in this, but generally that is it. It is not that difficult! But to achieve a greater achievement in the realm of relationship, well, that is something else. Here you cannot have part of you being an idiot and another little part of you being brilliant and be a brilliant idiot who can only do one thing very well and be handicapped in everything else.

Our emphasis, then, is on this greater achievement. Any step in this direction makes you more powerful, more generous, wiser and more efficacious in life. Here you must be concentrated, but your focus is much more mysterious. Your poor mind won't have much to hold onto because your Spirit will be moving things. That is good. It is a different kind of training, a different preparation for a different goal. Here you will achieve something that affects the Mystery of life, where all meaning comes from. In tangible matters you are focusing on something physical that needs to happen. That is very commendable, and I do not want to belittle it. But these two levels of achievement are in different realms.

To see where you are aiming yourself, you must become aware of your own nature. If you think that your life was to achieve something and it hasn't happened so far, well, it's a good chance that that is not your goal. People say, "Well, I would be so magnificent if only I had no barriers!" I cannot tell you what a ridiculous thing it is to think like that. This is not helpful. What this says is that your barriers have all the power, and who you are is something meek, only a potentiality. It belittles what is real and gives great weight and authority to what is not real. This is not helpful! You will always end up condemning yourself and justifying error, so please don't think like that.

There are always barriers. You will always have limitations in this life. You will have psychological limitations and physical limitations. This ceases to be such a problem when you are involved in something greater, however. That is why, in the most practical sense, true healing deals with being involved in something greater. When you have nothing greater to be involved in, you fall back on your wants and your fears. That is the prison house because what you want in that little realm is hardly enough to satisfy you. And so there is a constant war within yourself to achieve little things which you do not really want anyway. True resolution comes when you are assuming something greater that pulls you out of this morass and allows you to concentrate, which you must do.

I have often given the example of the house on fire because if the house were on fire, everyone would jump into high gear. Who cares if you wanted a soul mate? House on fire! My God! Who cares if you wanted more pay for your job? House on fire! Who cares if you wanted a body that never aches? House on fire! Everyone goes into gear. Do you wonder why people let situations become intolerable? That is a very marked tendency in human beings, both individually and collectively. People wait until the situation is dire because then everyone *must* go into action. But you cannot thrive upon catastrophe alone. Emergency is not enough to give you a sense of real purpose in life. Desperation is not a good foundation to live upon.

You are remarkably free to consider what you really want to achieve in life. I am giving you a perspective on the Greater Community of Worlds in order to illustrate your remarkable freedom and how much we encourage you to take advantage of it. Most of the universe on the physical level is enslaved in contrast to your life, which is relatively free and casual. Often, teaching greater things works better with people who are enslaved because they take it more seriously, but it takes longer for them to move into a position where they can actually do something with it.

You are very free. So what do you want to do? You can have little things, but they are not very satisfying. You live in a spiritual and a mental world as well as a physical one. To be fully responsible means that you are accountable in all three realms. Here you do not neglect the physical because you are only interested in spiritual matters. Likewise, you do not neglect the mental because you are only interested in physical things. Achievement, at the level that I am pointing to, requires accountability in all three realms. Achievement on a purely physical level, a manifest level, requires accountability only in the physical and the mental realms, though in the mental realm it may not require a great deal. If you are clever, rational and patient, you can do a great deal because there is not much competition.

Sometimes, people think that I am too hard on everyone, but I am not. I am too easy on everyone. The reason I seem too hard is that I know who you are. So, I offer great things. If I did not think you were great, I would offer little things. If I thought people were sort of stupid, I would offer things for stupid people. But because people are great, I offer things that are great. You must do something great to know you are great because this is a world where things are done. When things are done, they are demonstrated and that is the level of teaching here. When things are demonstrated, that is achievement!

We teach about relationship. Anytime people come together based upon the deeper impulse of Knowledge, something remarkable happens. But because this does not happen very often, it seems to be too rare to rely upon. It requires that you re-evaluate relationships and what attracts people to each other. Here demonstration is very important. People come together for many reasons. Much of this is for unlearning things. It is for disillusionment. This is not easy, and though we wish to save people these pains, we can only do so much. When you become tired of little things that are temporary and that do not last, there is a good chance in a very sober moment you will say, "Oh, my God, this is my life! What am I doing with my life?" And then you will perhaps stumble across something that has been waiting for you all along. Disappointment always opens a door, and it can be a remarkably rewarding experience if you can take advantage of it.

Sometimes people only want temporary comfort in relationship. Sometimes people want an extended holiday. Sometimes people want something really lasting. It is very important to look and see what you want in this regard because relationships that are based upon Knowledge will be lasting. Their effects will be with you forever, even beyond this life. That is how permanent these relationships are. The discernment that you need to develop will give you a real sense of their contrast to everything else.

Your purpose in life is waiting to be discovered once you have reached a state of maturity. One of the qualities of maturity is that you begin to value things that last. You want to invest in things that have promise not only for the present but for the future as well. You look for things that are more substantial, and you look for different qualities in people. In relationships, you look for compatibility now, not beauty, excitement, romance or infatuation. You look for compatibility, honesty, productivity, and so forth. These are different criteria. Unfortunately, these things are not highly valued in this world. Here in your world, romance is the ultimate expression of union—self abandonment in a profound love state where you forget all problems, past, present and future, in order to have a glorious moment with another person. For this moment, you will sacrifice a great deal and will expend your resources to a great extent.

When you reach maturity, you are not going for things that are momentary. You want things that last. You want to build something. You are thinking not only of immediate satisfaction. You are thinking of future providership. You are thinking of yourself in terms of making a contribution, not only for the present time but in times to come. Here your life becomes much bigger. You are living in a bigger world. You are seeing yourself participating in a larger time frame. This represents maturity. Out of this state comes a desire for achievement that is markedly different from your former state.

At times we have been very hard on adolescent mentality, which is quite rampant here. It would be fun to have this mentality, if it were not so tragic. It is actually very silly, and it is unfortunate that so many resources are being spent for it when it provides so little.

As I have said, your worldly family initiates you into the world, but your Spiritual Family initiates you into the Mystery. You were born from the Mystery. You will die into the Mystery. Mystery is where you have come from. Everything that is lasting comes from the Mystery. Everything that is transitory comes from the manifestation.

There are two things that last in this world: There are tangible, physical manifestations and there is relationship. Of the two, relationship is far more lasting because it continues long after your death. After all, buildings fall down and society changes, but what you have begun continues to move.

When you begin to experience your Spiritual Family, you enter a whole new realm of relationship. There are many illusions that go along with the idea of spirituality, of course, and many things are hoped for. But when you begin your education with your Spiritual Family—those individuals both within and beyond the world who are working on your spiritual development directly—it will require that illusions be seen as such and be discerned from those things that are really true.

There is kind of a romance about spirituality, too, and it is all right because it is predictable. Without direct experience, what can you have but assumptions? So, the sooner you can have the direct experience the better because assumptions become cherished, particularly if they have become the foundation of your identity. Then, even if they are not true, you will not want to admit it for fear that your life will be wasted. If an idea lasts too long and if an identity is built upon it, it will be very hard to relinquish that idea. That is why ideas need to stay in motion and not become solid. Your true identity is beyond all ideas. Ideas can either help or hinder you in your progress. They are temporary expedients.

Now, the question of relationship is not really that complex. Everyone wants everything right away, but things that are important do not come immediately. They must come at the right time, and you must prepare for them. There are not many people who are prepared for successful marriage. That's why there is so much divorce. It's not hard to get married—not really—if you really want it. Just talk someone into loving you, find out what they want, try to be that, and for a period of time they will be convinced. Perhaps.

Therefore, there is a great deal of experimentation in relationships. This is necessary to a point, but again we are aiming for something substantial and lasting. When you begin to realize your true powers of discernment, it will become increasingly difficult to make mistakes in relationships. Ultimately, it will become very hard to make any mistake. At the beginning you have this resource to fall back on. We call it Knowledge and this is what we teach.

To reach a greater achievement, the whole question of relationship must be re-examined. If you want something lasting, it requires different criteria. It may seem great to fall in love, but it often does not lead anywhere, and it carries with it a very great price. Likewise, it may seem fun to have a party and make love and all that, but it all carries a price. As you get a little older, you begin to realize the price—what it has cost you to invest yourself so greatly in little things. Therefore, if you feel you have reached a place where you want something truly substantial and lasting, it will require a different set of criteria for relationships. This requires patience.

There are only two things in life: There is relationship and there is ideas. As you abandon ideas, you become more available for relationship. So, don't look for new ideas because you will have to abandon those too.

When I say relationship, people always think of romance because at this level that is what most relationship seems to be. Romance is a very small part of life. Romance is simply enjoyment between people who are united. When did it become the sole object of life where people will spend all their money and all their time preparing themselves for this little romantic dance, which at best offers only a few glorious moments? It is very intoxicating, but not much real love comes out of it.

When I say relationship, people think, "Oh, boy meets girl. How wonderful!" I am not talking about that. I am talking about relationship in a bigger way, where you are really united with someone beyond your personal interests. As you let yourself follow what is being given to you, it will make you ever more reliant upon and ever more sensitive to the presence of your Spiritual Family. After all, to become truly united with someone, you must rely on them. This is hard to achieve in a society that places such a premium on individual self-reliance, where you try to be powerful and try not to need anyone. A true island! A fortress!

This is not the way to undo pathetic needs. Great relationships are established because individuals can rely upon each other. This is not simply because they have seen each other and have felt a deep affinity. Affinity is not yet relationship. Emotional attraction is not yet relationship. It is only potential for relationship.

When people do something in life together, it establishes relationship. When they carry weight together and when they rely upon each other, it establishes relationship. That is why we are interested in people doing things together, not simply being mesmerized by their recognition of one another. Recognition is important, but it is not the substance and foundation of relationship. You can experience great recognition with individuals that you will not be able to do anything with. You may experience a tremendous feeling of affinity with another, but in life you can do very little together. How often have people married because of an experience of affinity, only to find out that in real life they could do very little together? How often this has occurred.

You cannot carry on substantial physical achievement and spiritual achievement simultaneously because they both require too much time. It is possible that someone who has achieved something that is very substantial in the physical world will have a real spiritual emergence. But you cannot succeed in the two realms simultaneously, though many people are currently trying. They are trying very hard to be magnificent in all aspects and do you know what? They don't make much progress in any aspect. You see, you can't trick the way things are and find a new way to slip through a loophole in life. Look back in history. You are not smarter than people used to be.

If you really want to find out the Mystery of your life, if that is the direction you choose, then that will draw all of your primary energy. If you wish to be involved in manifest life, then that will draw all of your energy. People who want it all don't go very far because you must make choices along the way. You must let go of that to have this or this to have that. Why is this true? Because your Spiritual Family is extremely powerful and the attraction to your Spiritual Family is stronger than the world itself. Your attempt to maintain a precarious balance cannot last in the face of real forces. Likewise, the world is a real force and will captivate you completely, leaving little time or energy for other things.

Do not think that your barriers can keep you from Knowledge. But your desire for Knowledge must be greater than your barriers. If desire is weak, barriers are great. If desire is strong, barriers are few. Therefore, we don't look at barriers with a magnifying glass. We rekindle the desire for truth and Knowledge because these things give meaning everywhere and provide all good things in this world.

*To realize
your strength,
you must exercise
your authority.*

Thirty-three

PROVOKING CHANGE

NOW I WILL BE TALKING ABOUT CHANGE—provoking change. Obviously change is something that is happening all around you, but I want to focus on the kind of change that you yourself must instigate. There is much change that is happening to you that is beyond your control, not only in your environment and your world but within you as well. Something is happening. You are always in motion in the physical world.

Yet, there is also change that you yourself must be the source of and for which you must take responsibility. If you want to progress and to achieve important things in life and if you want to grow and to develop, you must take responsibility for conducting yourself according to the true requirements of life as you recognize them. This also means taking responsibility for instigating change with other people. In other words, at times you'll need to change the situation.

Most people are very passive when it comes to change. They will only change on their own accord if moved by desperation. That is a very destructive way to approach life. To instigate change when it is necessary means that you must trust yourself. You must trust what you know in the situation and yet be open to making a mistake because, you see, there are some mistakes you must make. So, why try to do everything right when there are mistakes that you must make? They are unavoidable. Many mistakes are avoidable because they only repeat the former mistakes that you needed to make. So, do not think all mistakes are for a good purpose. You get one chance to make a dumb mistake. That is for a good purpose. After that, you can repeat it many times, but the repetitions are not necessary.

We want to encourage you to take the initiative. When there is conflict, it means that something must move, something must progress. People want to be comfortable, and they associate comfort with living in a static situation. Comfort is associated with a state of no change. But when you are not growing, your life is shrinking. The walls are closing in upon you. Here we must qualify our remarks because many people change things that do not need to be changed. And likewise, they do not change the things that need to be changed. So, what should be changed and what should not be changed?

There are two arenas for change: There is the change you *want* to make and there is the change you *must* make. The "must do" category is the most important, for the things you must do, whether you want to do them or not, are very necessary. Human life and development are very much dependent upon this necessity. That is what keeps things moving forward. It is based upon purpose. All of you have come into the world carrying the seed of God within you, and in this seed is your purpose.

Now, obviously people do not want to think that they have no purpose, so they invent various purposes for themselves. Eventually, their real purpose will have the possibility of emerging and when it begins to emerge, they will realize that they have a responsibility to accept change that is necessary and to instigate change that is necessary. They will also realize that they have a responsibility to maintain themselves in good health, to become aware of their strengths and weaknesses and their favorable and unfavorable tendencies, and so forth. The emergence of purpose will require change in their thinking, behavior and perception and in their relationships with others as well.

Often people become very lazy here because they are waiting for something to change them. Then if it goes wrong, they have someone else to blame. "Hey, I was just there and it changed. Don't blame me!" But to take full responsibility means that you are cooperating with life in bringing about the necessary adjustments as you proceed.

Because of the routines of life, people often forget that they are actually trying to go somewhere. You're not just settling down, you're going somewhere. You're doing something. Part of this is in your conscious mind and part of it is in your deeper mind because, you see, you're operating in the world both as an individual and as part of a greater collective called the human race. Therefore, you are unconsciously pressing things forward in order for the race to progress. As more people become conscious of this, the evolution advances at a more rapid rate. This is certainly happening. Because this is a collective movement, people must now keep pace with it. This requires that you accept change in your circumstances and instigate change where it is necessary.

As I have said, there is change that emanates from your wishes and fears, and then there is change that is a necessity. There are two kinds of necessary change: There is necessary change when you are forced to do something or when you face catastrophe. Then there is necessary change when you *know* you must do something. Here circumstances are not forcing you into action. Instead, you are motivated by your own Knowledge here, a deep and profound intuition.

It is this state of Knowledge that we wish to cultivate in all students of Knowledge to enable them to see the direction of the race with vision and to be able to be very strong participants in the evolution of the world. To be able to function in this capacity, they must escape most of their personal dilemmas. They must be able to trade little problems for big problems. Since these people are destined to become important contributors in life, they are often very unhappy early in life because they get bogged down in personality conflicts, which they are usually unable to resolve. They have not moved into the proper position in life yet, and so their energy, focus and vitality become oriented to little things, and it is very hard for them.

So, we want to remind you that you are living in a very dynamic situation. You have come into the world at a very exciting time. Oh, my God, the change that you will see in your lifetime! Your ancestors could not dream of such things. To keep pace with this change and not merely be dragged along, kicking and complaining, to be able to actively participate in this and make a positive contribution, you will need to base your sense of security on something far more tangible than money or political stability and so forth. You must have a greater foundation within yourself.

Your life is attempting to move into true position. All personal growth is only for this purpose and not simply for self-indulgence. In fact, personal growth is really not even for you personally. All of this self-exploration and development of skills—they are not for you. Why would you need to do all that? You'd be happier sitting on the beach drinking beer! Have you thought of that? "Oh, let's all go to the beach and forget it all!" Many people do that, you know, but not you because you must advance forward. There is nothing for you to hold onto.

Your world is changing faster than you can even imagine. In your lifetime, you will see change that you would have a hard time accepting as possible at this present time. I am not speaking of calamities or catastrophes but merely the progress of human beings. Things are advancing very fast. It is not correct to say that you are responsible for it. You are, indeed, responsible for a part of it. But it was set in motion by your predecessors. Everyone now and in the past is responsible. What you are doing in life now is setting the stage for your offspring in future generations.

Not all change is good. Not all change is healthy. But as a whole, your race must become united, not in spirit because that is far too advanced for the human race yet. But you will be politically and economically fused together out of necessity. If you can see this happening, you will understand the trends now, and you will see that you will need to have a new relationship with change. You will see change not as something that has to be forced upon you and that you accept as a last resort but as something you can wholeheartedly promote. Things are going to change with or without your help, but if you help, you can generate a positive result.

There are certain things that are destined for the human race because they are evolutionary, but how things turn out—for better or for worse—is dependent upon your contribution. People think, "Well, I can do so little individually," but if they do not contribute, things will be worse! Things are as good as they are today because someone gave something of value before. Your prosperity, whatever you may have, is the result of what other people have accomplished. The car you drive, the conveniences of your home—people made contributions and sacrifices so you could have these things. You are walking on the ground that other people have laid out for you. They had to change to do this. Like the trees that grow from the soil of their own ancestors, you are now growing in the soil of your own ancestors, too. This is a wonderful thing to think about because it stimulates gratitude. It lifts you out of your personal preference about your life—what you want, what you are afraid of and your personal interests in the matter—and you see that you are a part of something bigger that is moving and changing and advancing.

People rarely change their behavior or thinking for themselves alone. They change because it is necessary for them to do something important in life for other people. When you are thinking of yourself alone, the difficulty in self-purification does not seem quite worth the effort. It is very hard to give your development the energy that it requires. But if it is for something greater, then people give more than they would for themselves alone, if their giving is true. If people are only giving to themselves, they give themselves aggravation.

Your first challenge regarding change will be with yourself. That is the most important. It will begin with yourself and in your primary relationships: your partner, your loved ones, your family and so forth. If you feel a spiritual emergence arising within you that you must respond to, you will have to change your relationship with your family. You cannot undergo this change and not have relationships around you adjust themselves to it. You must do it and not wait for someone else to do it for you.

If you wish to have true authority in your life, the authority that God has given you to exercise, then you must claim that which is yours to claim and not claim what is beyond your capacity. It is not your authority to determine the fate of the human race. It is not your authority to determine the fate of another person. But it is your authority to orient your life to Knowledge to the best of your ability.

Why improve your health? You do it for everyone. Why resolve a financial difficulty? You do it for everyone. Perhaps it meets a personal need and that is the most pressing thing, but you do it for everyone. Why give up bad habits? So the burden on humanity will be less. Why meet a challenging situation in marriage? So that people will be happier as a result. Therefore, you see, instigating change and service to humanity are very related.

There is a great deal of confusion in the world about the "authority problem." Who has the authority? Where does the authority reside? Where does it come from? Some people are very passive, thinking God is going to do everything for them like a servant, like a handmaiden. Some people insist that no one can do anything for them and that they are going to do it all and not let anyone else have decision-making capabilities within their own sphere. Some people will not let the government be the government. Other people will not take any authority, thinking that the government will do everything for them.

What is your arena of authority and what is not? I can only give you a greater perspective on this. You must find out for yourself where your authority can be established and where it cannot be established. You are responsible for your behavior and for your thinking. You are responsible for the demonstration that your life makes, but you are not responsible for who you are. You are not responsible for the destiny of the world, though in some respects you share this responsibility because it gives you direction. It is quite enough for human beings to manage themselves in their primary relationships with honesty, tolerance and determination. Very few people have done that.

Sooner or later you will do what you must do, either in this life or in the life to come. Situations keep presenting themselves to give you this opportunity. What gives you the strength and the power to make decisions is God and your Spiritual Family, who are devoted to your spiritual emergence. But still, the power of decision must be utilized by you. It is very hard to understand the idea that the world is moving in the direction that it must and you are moving there, too—willingly or unwillingly. Your contribution is to give what is good to that movement and destiny. You cannot control the overall outcome, but you can give what is good to it.

Often, when people come to this Teaching, they find out that their situation in life is not very complex. It is just that they are not sure if they want to take responsibility for what must happen. One of our first jobs is to unburden people by simplifying their dilemma. What makes a dilemma complex is when people want resolution and harmony, but they are unwilling to do what is necessary to achieve them. They create a great deal of speculation about themselves and their involvement and other people's involvement and who's at fault and so forth. It is as if you drop a glass of milk on the floor, and it breaks, and you stand there wondering how it could have happened and why it always happens to you and if you should be the one to clean it up. After awhile, the glass of milk on the floor is the least of your problems. Now you are entertaining your self-doubt, conflict and judgment, and it becomes a big issue beyond what happened initially.

Then, someone as wise as I am comes along and says, "Hey, you should clean that up. Then you can go on and do something else." And you say, "Oh, my God! You are so wise. What a magnificent teacher! All I have to do is clean it up and I can go do something else?" And I say, "Yes."

I am concerned with what is essential and not with what is non-essential. When you are dealing with what is essential, all of your actions have great impact. To do this, however, you must trust something deeper inside of yourself which you have learned to discover. We call this Knowledge, the power of Spirit expressing itself in your life. It is not an alien spirit. It is not from somewhere else. It is the truth about you. You are an expression of God. Do not think that you are God. That leads to some very grievous mistakes in perception and understanding. But you are very important to God.

Everyone here has things they know they must do. There are things you must change. Procrastination here is simply a form of self-neglect. To realize your strength, you must exercise your authority. You have great strength that is latent within you, but you must use it in the face of things that intimidate you to understand that it is there. Then you will understand that most complaining—not all but most—is because the people involved are neglecting what is essential and are procrastinating. When you are entertaining things that do not need to be changed and they are competing for your attention with things that do need to be changed, it all becomes very complex. This leads you to become passive because, after all, you cannot change it all, right? So, you sink back into reverie about it.

The man or woman of Knowledge who has cultivated Knowledge is not concerned with what is non-essential. Everything in life is very pronounced. It is very active. Even in meditation, things are very active. These people live in a vibrant world, not a world of dull pain and weak hopes. That is why if you wish to make advancements, you must cultivate your capabilities—your powers of discernment, honest communication, discrimination, humility, authority and above all, an abiding willingness to be wrong. You will be wrong! That is because the only way that you can find out and learn discernment is to make some of the mistakes that are waiting for you to make. If being wrong is associated with failure, if it is seen as an expression of your weakness or lack of worth, well, you will not be in a position to learn or to progress. You will simply use your life to keep yourself from attacking yourself. Here you are strangling yourself and cannot go anywhere. That is when the broken glass of milk is on the floor, and you are thinking about what kind of person you are. You don't know enough about yourself to condemn yourself. It is not your authority to determine your worth. When you start thinking like this, you are in error from beginning to end.

Most mistakes that people make are made because they are not looking. They are not present in the situation. They don't know how they got on the railroad tracks, and now the train is coming. The only reason you can't look or be present in a situation is because you are consumed with your own thoughts. Why does the man or woman of Knowledge who drops the milk and makes the mess clean it up just like that? Why? Because they have something important to do in life. They don't have time to try to contemplate their value.

When you are doing what you need to be doing in life, you will feel your self-worth. You may not admit it, but you will feel it. If you are not doing what you need to do in life, you will not feel good about yourself, not because you are a bad person but simply because you are not meeting a need. You have an internal as well as an external need to progress. Indeed, your internal need is even stronger than your external need. When your external need is as great as your internal need, then life is matching you. Do not resist this. When you resist this, you are not present to the situation. Making a wise decision then becomes very hard.

Some change is very hard to make. It brings forth emotional pain and takes great courage because you must override all other arguments and tendencies to do what must be done. You do not need to create change and exercise your authority as some sort of spiritual practice. There is always enough content in your life for real application. Sometimes when you identify the change that must happen and separate that from all the things that you think you should have or do, your whole life becomes clear. Boom! Then if you can accept what you must do, everything begins to make sense.

Now I want to talk a little about leadership. Everyone here must become a leader of his or her life, but one thing important about a leader is that a leader is a follower. You are not the source of leadership. You can only express it as it emerges in your own life. Either the Creator is guiding you in your leadership or something else is guiding you—anger, desire for power, grief or vengeance. They provide leadership too. All leaders must serve something. Be it God or be it their own ideas or ambition, they are serving something. They are not the source of their own leadership. When you realize this, it will make it possible for bad tendencies to be corrected and for you to gain the moderation you need to lead wisely. It will give you perspective and humility in difficult situations so that you do not overstep your authority.

God wants to lift you up, but for this to happen, you must be prepared. It is not something that happens like the wave of a hand and you are lifted up. People are raised the way a house is constructed. It does not simply appear. Why is this? Because people must exercise their authority and learn their true relationship with life. God can exercise authority, but if you do not exercise yours in conjunction with God's, then you will not advance. That is why when you are passive about God's Presence in your life and think that God will do everything for you and you can go merrily along, you do not understand your relationship with God. You are here to be raised up so that you can be able to serve the world. When you are raised up, what is raised up is the power of Knowledge within you. It is not a form of self-aggrandizement. Here you do not become inflated with yourself and start telling lies about yourself.

Fortunately, being human is always subject to error and comedy, yes? It is very hard to become too significant about yourself on this level. You have a personality, you have a body and you have Knowledge. Obviously, you cannot become too significant about having a body. It is full of flaws and is always growing old, my God! If the body is your emphasis, you will suffer greatly for it. Likewise, the personality, like the body, can be trained to serve a higher purpose, but in and of itself it is hardly worth the devotion of your life. That is why so many people are complacent about self-development. They think it is either for the body or for their self-image. It is not worth the effort! But when you serve something greater, then it is worth it because this is an act of profound love for the world and the regeneration of your self-respect.

People who read my words are often disappointed because I do not talk about metaphysical things. I do not talk about crystals and pyramids and all that sort of stuff. That is because I talk about important things. Occasionally, these things are useful tools for wise practitioners, but in the hands of the ignorant they become sources of superstition. Why become concerned about crystals if your life is calling for your action and decision making? Why indulge in things that in the hands of the powerful can have real meaning but are not necessarily germane to your immediate needs?

People progress because they *must*. It is rarely because of curiosity. Do you not live in a world of great necessity? Is it not a perfect environment for advancement? Sometimes people read my words and they say, "Oh, my God! This teacher is overbearing. I thought we were going to talk about spiritual things, and now he is telling me I must do this and that I must face that. Oh, my God, I'm getting out of here!" So, they go back to their metaphysical books and they read about things that are far away from them.

I want to talk about things that are very present now. Everyone has his or her own laboratory in life, yes? You are either sitting here not knowing why you are here or you are actively working on things that are important. Not only are they important, they are necessary. It is this necessity that is so important. It is necessary either because your outer life says it is or because your own Knowledge says it is. Either way, it calls for you to respond. If this is called for, do it! You won't know what's going to happen.

It is very hard to be reasonable about change or use logic regarding change. Change is often illogical, particularly regarding your relationships. Sometimes things don't work anymore and you must leave them. Nobody has to be blamed for this.

You have been given the greatest gift that God could ever give you, even greater than God's Presence in your life. You have been given

Knowledge to guide you—a perfect guiding, functioning reality within yourself. The less you have preference or insistence from your personal mind, the more you will be able to experience Knowledge and have it express itself through you. That is the greatest privilege and satisfaction. It has nothing to do with the human problems of identity, conflicts of interest and all that sort of thing.

I'll tell you something very interesting. It is very good to equate happiness with simplicity. Why is this? Because when something is simple, it does not fall apart very easily. It is more integrated. To be simple, however, does not mean that you do not have depth. It just means that you are uniform. When human beings become uniform, their power increases. Their range of perception and understanding increases. The effect of their life on life around them increases because power is concentration. The more concentrated you are as a human being, the greater the power you will have. For good or for ill, this is the case, but when your power is concentrated on what is good, you will exemplify that good. Then you will not be afraid of change because you will be able to trust yourself.

It does not do any good if you trust God and think that you are a rat! "I am a rat. God is wonderful. I am a rat." What can God do for you? God cannot raise you up now. You do not glorify God's Creation by being a terrible, lowly thing. But some people are in error and think that they can become God. They are either nothing or they are everything! Neither of these is correct. You are part of something. You have a role to fulfill at a certain level of reality. Do not make this level or this role absolute. It is not absolute. It is relative to where you are in time and space.

It is very exciting when someone is doing something that is absolutely necessary. It is not very exciting when people are doing something merely out of frustration or boredom, nervousness or compulsion. If you can see your life as part of a Greater Life here in the world and your contribution as part of the movement of your race, then will you have a perspective that will allow you to contribute and to initiate change without so much personal tribulation.

You are only as safe as your race, yes? People think of personal safety only in terms of their personal lives. You are only as safe as your race. Of course, that is part of the context in which you live. Why are you able to eat food at dinner time? Because someone provided it for you. Everyone is taking care of everyone, making a few mistakes along the way, but that is really what is happening. Likewise, if you want to do something for the race, you also must take care of your immediate requirements and development. You cannot escape into serving the race if your life is a mess! The race is then no better than your life. If your life is a mess, then the race is a mess.

People are unhappy because they do not see that they are a part of something. They do not feel their responsibilities. They only feel responsibilities that are not their responsibilities. People think that the advancement of the race is making everything look nice—everything pretty, no frowns on the faces, no bad appearances, spruce everything up! But, really, advancement has to do with the quality of relationship between people and their sense of identity together.

You must make the change and *then* you find the open door. Otherwise, it is all playing it safe, you see. If no one is ever at risk, nothing is ever opened. People want to know and then do. But it is not like that. You do and then know! Regarding substantial change in personal life, you do and then know.

When you serve something greater, you are greater. When you serve something less, you are less. You are what you serve. And service involves change: accepting change, directing change and provoking change.

*Your education
is
not for you.
It is
for the world.*

Thirty-four

RELIGION AS EDUCATION

I AM GOING TO TREAT THE SUBJECT of religion with a particular emphasis—as an arena of education rather than as a system of belief or a set of ideas or hopeful expectations. As education, religion requires the introduction of new ideas and their application to real life situations and the adoption of certain practices for personal development.

In education you maintain goals for your own development and for their possible use in the future. Yet, when people think of religion, they often don't think of education. They think of adopting, defending or struggling with belief. We don't wish to treat religion in this manner. Simply said, religion is practice. It is what you use to develop and to improve yourself and, from this, the world around you.

Therefore, let us leave conjecture and arguments behind and look at what can be done for you and what you can do for others. Our Teaching is religious in nature because it deals with applying a greater truth to the world. What is a greater truth? A greater truth is something people do not make up for themselves for their personal reassurance, comfort or for any other reason. It is something that is inherent within people. They either choose to acknowledge it or not, to use it or not.

People experience and interpret truth differently, but the truth is beyond interpretation. What people think of as their experience of the truth is their interpretation of the truth. The truth always beckons you to go beyond your ideals and your philosophy. As a great attraction that is beyond your own grasp, it keeps engaging you to move forward. Therefore, when people say, "I know the truth here," and they argue with others, they are arguing over interpretations and approaches. That is because the same truth appears to be different things at different stages of development. It has different value and application in these different stages. When someone at one stage argues with someone at another stage, they may not understand one another because their experiences are determined by their stages of development as well as their own personal preferences, fears and psychological make-up.

Why is the truth important for people to know? Because it is the source of purpose, meaning and direction in life. Purpose, meaning and direction are what all human pursuit is for. Even in the worst error or the most foolish behavior, someone is trying to experience purpose, meaning and direction. Beyond fundamental survival, this *is* the human quest—to know why you are here, what you serve, where you must go and what you must do. Purpose, meaning and direction. This is what religion is for.

I am going to talk about religion in terms of practice and not in terms of theological ideas or God. It does not matter if you think God is real or not. That just determines your form of education and what terminology must be selected for you to proceed. You are all religious people because you are involved in education. School is not out. It is moving forward. When you cease to learn, your mind begins to shrink. It is like a muscle in your body. It must be exercised and employed and given new challenges. That is why the goal of life is not to achieve complete understanding. The goal of life here is to be educated and to share your education with others. Here you have come very far and are at the beginning all at once because the truth is still beyond you. What does this yield to you? It yields purpose, meaning and direction—something the world itself cannot provide. This is the source of your inspiration, enthusiasm and experience of life.

So, first of all: God is real. Everywhere, real! But so what? What good does that do you today and tomorrow? The important contribution of religion is the development of the human mind and the advancement of the human spirit. Growth involves friction, confrontation, success, failure—everything. When people lose enthusiasm and vigor for life, it means their ability to learn in this environment has diminished or is complete. If it is complete, then it is time for them to leave. If they can do so in a conscious manner, it means that they can leave with very little regret, and that is good.

Most people are not in this position. They have lost vigor because they do not see their life as education. They do not see religion as practice. Solving dilemmas, within yourself and externally as well, is not the issue. Problems are healthy for you but can only be valued if you are involved in your development. Development means you are assuming a preparation that you did not invent for yourself. If you invent a preparation for yourself, you will merely entertain yourself with your past learning. That is not advancement. It takes great trust to engage in a curriculum you did not create for yourself. People say, "I do not want to learn this. It affronts my ideas. I do not believe in this, so I do not wish to study it or investigate it." That is not progressing.

We could talk about gratitude, but to do that we would need to talk about education, for it is the only thing you can be truly grateful for. Everything you see around you, people have worked to create to give you an opportunity, but the opportunity is not for comfort alone. It is for advancement. Everything you see, be it agreeable or disagreeable, is for advancement. But if you do not see advancement as your fundamental aim, then you will judge things merely on whether they please you or not or whether they provide comfort or not.

In The Greater Community Way of Knowledge we teach the reclamation of Knowledge, the greatest and most fundamental use of the mind. As Knowledge becomes developed in the individual, it provides a sound demonstration of the mind's true capabilities and of the assistance that is necessary both from certain individuals in the world and from forces beyond the world. This solves the question about God but not in an ultimate sense. It just means that you can experience a Greater Presence that you cannot account for and which you must in time acknowledge as a necessary part of your advancement.

Therefore, I have said education is for advancement and religion is for education. Now, let me make another important point so that you can understand what this means. Your advancement is not for you. This must

advancement
↑
Education
↑
Religion

be understood. Your advancement is not for you. Your advancement is your contribution because from it will come all the actions, words and demonstrations that are necessary. The advancing student of Knowledge will use both the greatest inspiration as well as the most foolish act for his or her advancement.

Now, people do not usually enter preparation with the idea of serving anything but their own personal interests. They want more pleasure and less pain. At least, that is the avowed goal. Genuine education seems to be confusing here because it provides challenge and asks you to apply yourself in the situations where you are needed the most, yet which may also be the greatest areas of avoidance. Here you may feel more pain. "I thought this education was to escape pain, to become a happy person, to finally answer the most important questions."

When I say that your education is not for you, it is very important that this be a tacit understanding. This requires asking the question, "What is my education for? If it is not for me, who is it for? Am I merely to be sacrificed for another will, even if it is greater than my own?" In truth, your education is for you and not for you both because you need to discern a Greater Reality in life, give yourself to it and participate with it through all the stages of your development. That is your greatest opportunity. Therefore, we aim to take people to the greatest pleasure, not to little pleasures to merely ameliorate their sense of loneliness but to great pleasure where loneliness is never thought of.

When you leave this world, you will return to your Spiritual Family, and this will all become so obvious to you. Your memory will then return to you, and there will be no question. But while you are here, this memory seems buried. It does not seem relevant to the world you see.

People who are not beset by personal tragedy are in a position to contribute a great deal to the world. Their contribution is their reward and produces satisfaction, purpose, meaning and direction not only for them but for everyone who can perceive them. What did the great teachers in this world do? Is there anything tangible left behind but their recorded words? Yet, their impact is greater than standing armies and natural disasters. You are still feeling the reverberation of their contribution. That is how great their contribution was. That is how great their satisfaction was.

You were created to give because you are an extension of God. You may not like the idea of God, but that is all right because you are a religious person. You may substitute your own words for mine if you find them too difficult.

Therefore, your education is not for you. It is for the world. The greatest satisfaction a human being can experience is being a vehicle for something greater that loves the world. All individuals who have contributed greatly to the world in any capacity, in any arena—by thought, word, action or deed—always felt a Greater Power behind them. Your greatness is to give greatness which you yourself have not created for personal aims. People become engaged in the study of Knowledge and they often say, "I don't know why I am studying this." As they advance, they realize that their desire for personal power, personal control, management of their lives and personal protection from pain or adversity is perhaps not being fully satisfied, but that something else is happening in its place that seems far more substantial, sound and reliable.

People want us to make their lives easy, and we want to make their lives genuine, so sometimes there is a misunderstanding here. When your life is genuine and you are doing something you believe to be truly important, then you will have a foundation for confidence and self-worth. Then you will realize that your ability to communicate with others and the need to maintain a healthy body and mind are simply necessary. When people do not do what they know they must do for their well-being, it is because they do not yet value their own life. You cannot simply create value by telling yourself you are worth it. Value comes because your life is for something greater, perhaps beyond definition, but for something greater nonetheless.

When people read our words, they are often very eager to have information about their future. That is all they want. "How will all this work out? Will I win?" Sometimes they are disappointed because we offer education. What is the value of an answer if it cannot be fully embodied? You already possess enough answers to enlighten a thousand people, but you do not have the desire or capacity yet to fully embody them.

When we talk of education, we have to talk of practice because practice is what people do. It is the practical expression of their devotion and adherence to their pursuit. People say, "I want to know my purpose," and I say, "Do this. When you do this, you will find out." Now, practice takes a long time. It is not quick and easy, and its rewards come in their own way. People do many foolish things with practice, but you cannot judge a teaching by the behavior of its students. How can the students' behavior be exemplary if they are being honest?

The greater the teaching, the worse the abuse will be because fewer will be able to use it and progress. The more simple, basic and short-lived the education, the more people can exemplify it, but over time it will not meet their overall need. The education that I am speaking of is not for everyone because not everyone is ready for it. In fact, everyone does not need to be ready for it, only certain individuals. If you are not satisfied with the normal range of things, this may qualify you. If you are looking for something greater, this may indicate that you require a greater education, which means a greater responsibility.

When people speak of religion and argue about which one is the best or truest or has God's blessing to the greatest degree, we must always ask, "What do you do for practice? What are you doing that is advancing yourself and enabling you to be exemplary to others?" That is the only question we need to ask about religion. God is not interested in religion, only in advancement. That is all that matters. If you think of it like this, it will make sense to you. You can leave all sectarian controversies behind for those who cannot practice. It is like learning anything, is it not? To learn a musical instrument or a physical talent, you must practice. It is like that. But practice must be specific and have guidance from someone who is competent. It also has a mysterious aspect which engages aspects of you which are beyond your understanding. It is appropriate that education have a mysterious aspect that cannot be logically approached.

This season you celebrate Jesus. Jesus is still having an impact because his education has a resonating effect throughout the world. It is actually a call to education. When he said, "Come follow me," which is the essence of his Teaching, he was saying, "Engage in the form of education in which I am engaged." But Christianity as a religion usually does not teach education. It teaches the necessity of belief and the fundamentals of moral behavior. Rarely does it actually engage people in fundamental education, particularly beyond the realm of simple personal behavior. Christianity's past errors are manifest, but that is not a reason to discount it as a real form of education.

Why are you being educated? You do not really know. Then why do it? Because you must. Understanding the purpose of your education is based completely on your advancement. Let us give this idea for you to consider. People who are not satisfied with the normal range of things ask very great questions that other people may find foolish or unnecessary, such as "What is the meaning of my life? Is there life beyond death of the body? What is the purpose of my life, if it has a purpose at all?" These things can only be known in hindsight. At the end of your life, you'll look back and see what has transpired. Then you will have a much more substantial view of your life's purpose than someone who is looking into the future and trying to speculate.

What is important about purpose is that it is something you wake up with in the morning and go to bed with at night. It is not a definition that you attempt to live by. It is a living experience in your life—perhaps fleeting, not every moment, but consistent enough that it provides consistency for your life. Here you realize that the truth does not fluctuate. You do.

Therefore, we tell people, "Follow Knowledge once you can learn to identify it within yourself." Very simple, but not easy to do. Here you will have more power than answers. It is a very vital form of education in all the ways that it manifests itself to you. Regarding great questions about life, these things are seen in hindsight and rarely understood in the moment. You may ask, "What am I doing now? Why am I doing this?" Look back. Without regret or disappointment, your past illustrates your preparation for education.

In a previous discourse, we spoke of education as having three levels. The first is education for physical survival, which is development of the body. The second is education of the personality for social survival, which is the development of personal behavior and forms of communication. Ninety-nine percent of the education that you can recognize has been for these two purposes. So, I wish to congratulate you for having succeeded! Your body has survived and you are able, to some degree, to function in society. Very good!

The third arena of education is the development of Knowledge. This is a whole new category of education. People often think that education in this category is completely mysterious and cannot be described, that it is all by chance. Some people think that this means that they can be passive and hope that some day God will do something for them—hopefully tomorrow, not today, and that if they sit back, God will give them some great avenue to travel. But in actuality, education in the realm of Knowledge, though it is mysterious and has a mysterious destiny, is as fundamental in its daily application as learning to tie your shoes or read books. It requires that you develop stillness, mental concentration, discernment in relationship, sensitivity to communication, patience, perseverance, self-application, trust, and tolerance—fundamental things that are actually part of your learning in the other two categories.

In terms of practice, the experience of Knowledge is not so mysterious and can be quantified and applied. Therefore, do not confuse the Mystery with the application. I am speaking of the practice. It is very simple: Do this and this once a day or once a week or whatever. Nothing mysterious. What is mysterious is that you do not understand how it works. But you do not need to understand how it works, unless you have experienced it sufficiently and are preparing to teach it to others. When you are learning to tie your shoes, it does not matter to you how the educational process works. It simply matters that you accomplish the task. Then, if necessary, you can study the methodology of learning this so you can teach it to another.

The Teaching in The Greater Community Way of Knowledge is in the third arena of education, but the third arena of education completes the first two. This means that as you begin to study Knowledge and experience it as an active living force in your life, it provides information, direction and discernment for you. In other words, it provides inner guidance. Here you realize that you will have to further develop your physical vehicle. You will also have to further develop your personality—who you think you are.

Knowledge will take you beyond these two arenas, but it will require their sound development as well. You cannot escape worldly problems and have any hope of true advancement in the realm of Knowledge. It will always bring you back to exactly where you need to be. Those who engage with it with a desire to avoid the irresolutions that have plagued them thus far will find little relief here, for there is little relief without the completion of past and present problems. This enables you to go into new territory because the past has been completed. Education is always for advancement. Advancement is always to take you beyond where you are today. This is religion.

Do not look to the world and say, "Give me purpose, meaning and direction." It is you who must give these to the world because the world is asking this of you. The world is asking you, "Give me purpose, meaning and direction." There is a great gulf between these two approaches. You are not the source of truth, but you are possibly a vehicle for its full expression, which will elevate you so far beyond your current self-evaluation that it will almost look like you are Godlike. You will be Godlike, but God is much greater. If you are truly a vehicle for the Creator, the Creator will express itself through you. Here you will be required to both acknowledge your advancement and to maintain a very healthy form of humility because you will always feel small compared to the greatness that is at hand. Though you may seem greater than you were in the past, something will always be overshadowing you, and from this you will derive your inspiration and your unique individual contribution to life.

Everyone has personal needs. Everyone has greater possibilities. When you truly entertain a greater possibility, your personal needs will be satisfied. If you entertain only your personal needs, nothing will be satisfied— not even your personal needs.

There are two arenas of learning that exist in people: They either learn through ideas or through feeling. They will learn predominantly in one avenue. Therefore, the preparation must be unique and have specific applications to different types of people with different orientations. Anyone who is advanced as a teacher will have learned this and will be flexible enough to administer it. Yet, because the education is not only for you but for the whole world, it has a uniformity that does not always conform itself to the personal preferences and idiosyncrasies of the individuals involved, and that is good as well.

The first thing that is important to learn and which seems so simple that people do not even think of it, is how to learn. People think they already know how to learn. You remember—study for a test and pass the exam. Yet, if you are learning something that is very important which you will be using for the rest of your life, you will want to learn it in a whole different manner.

Therefore, one of our first challenges in education is for people to learn how to be students. It is required for a student to have an open mind and to assume the responsibility of practice. This requires a very honest evaluation of your current skills. In other words, you must find out what your real starting point is, not the starting point that you wish for or hope for. Many people try to live as if they were living the life they want and not the life they have. Very few people are genuinely aware of their strengths and weaknesses at any given moment, so these things must be discovered to a great degree. That is part of the education.

It is absolutely necessary to teach the education once you have progressed in it. The first thing the teacher must learn is how to discern genuine interest and ability in students. The second thing the teacher must learn is how to be flexible in the teaching in order to reach people. The third thing the teacher must learn is how to be uniform in the teaching so that all people can be aimed in the proper direction.

Yet, the first goal of education is learning how to be a student. Then the advancement can happen more quickly. Here you must learn each step. Each step is very clear. What you don't understand is why it works or where it came from, but it is clear because it is practical and you can, in time, see its direct relevance to your situation.

Because you are religious people, you have come here for education. Education is to satisfy your deeper need for purpose, meaning and direction. Everyone must begin by learning to be a student, which means having an open mind, not claiming things that are not present and not denying things that are present. Students must accept the responsibility of training in a curriculum that they did not create for themselves. In this way, they are able to go where they could never take themselves.

Our preparation in The Greater Community Way of Knowledge begins with the development of Knowledge, which develops your ability to have profound insight in your current situations, beyond your personal preferences or fears. The preparation also develops your ability to act upon these insights in an effective manner. This is the education that we are here to represent, though it has been presented in other forms throughout human history, and indeed throughout the history of all races. Your advantage here is that the preparation is presented without the burden of human superstition, so it does not have the residue of the past to make access to it more difficult.

Superstition is the belief in something that is not there. If you think of your religious customs, consider how difficult it is to get to the real education. What is the real education? What is the practice? Superstition is when people attempt to use religion to gain power over one another, to ameliorate their own sense of guilt or blame or to satisfy their personal goals. The real preparation seems to be very difficult, so people wish to have ideas only and will accept whatever is most gratifying.

One of the first tasks in teaching is to bring people back to what they don't know. Then they can know something directly. People often say, "I thought I was going to know more as a result of studying The Way of Knowledge and now I know less!" I say that is very good. At least now they have an opportunity to know something that is worth knowing because they are becoming unfettered with trying to know things that have no value.

Superstition is the result of making conclusions without understanding. It permeates all of human thought. When people first encounter religion, that is often what they encounter—superstition. So, we have given you a new approach to religion by asking, "What is its practice?" and not "Is this truth?" Truth is beyond religion. Religion is an approach to truth. The approach is practice. Therefore, ask, "What is the practice?"

When you try to believe things that are beyond your experience, you run into problems. It is better simply to practice something that is useful and learn to become a student and a practitioner. I ask you, "Do you want to find out what you really know within yourself?" That is the starting point of preparation in The Way of Knowledge. Approaching Knowledge is like climbing a great mountain. On the way up the mountain, you find beautiful places to rest and to find comfort. You lie down and sleep for a few thousand years. "This is it! It is more beautiful than I ever thought!

High Places on Hind's Feet

Hanna

More wondrous! I can see! Now I can see the valleys below. I have true perspective. It is so beautiful here. I shall reside here." But the student must press on.

At some point you will ask, "What is it all for? Why am I doing this? Why not just find a nice place to live, get married and have a simple life? Call it a day! Why not do that? So simple. Other people are doing it. They are happy, somewhat. Why do I need more?" But you must take the next step. The preparation is mysterious because you do not know where it comes from or how it works, but it is not intangible in what it asks of you. I say, "Practice." Keep practicing. You may say, "But there are so many other things to do." I say, "Keep practicing." It will take you there. The practice is sufficient to take you there. Go with that. The way is not difficult. It seems confusing because people want other things.

The preparation in The Greater Community Way of Knowledge is very simple to do and very hard to understand because understanding is not necessary. Understanding comes naturally when you are progressing. Forget about understanding. Do the practice. Involve yourself in education. Like learning a musical instrument, one day you are able to play. But until then, you are working on it. Who knows when that day will be when you can sit down and play the piece?

I should like to make a point about practice. If you are to engage in a practice, you should give it a minimum of one year. If you begin and you find it is a practice that is good for you and you are making progress, give it at least a year. If you quit too soon, you will not find out. People are often getting new practices. They get tired of this one, and they go on to that one. Then they become tired of that one, and they go on to the next one. They never get very far. A practice is like a relationship; it is something you give yourself to. The practice does not wave a magic wand over your head and say, "Now you are wonderful!" You have a relationship with practice. Sometimes practice is boring. Particularly after the initial excitement wears down, it can become monotonous. That is when the real work begins. If it is the right practice for you, it will take you very far because you will have a greater relationship with it. Practice is like marriage. Do you throw a marriage away because things are becoming dull or difficult? It ceased to be a thrilling love affair, and now it is all work! Do you then

I kept on and this is even harder! Learning. Now I must just much both.

say, "This marriage is over. I will find a new marriage"? No, this is something that requires devotion and persistence. *BA + K*

The practices that we give are very simple to do. They require very little time but must be done consistently, regardless of what you think of them. They will work, regardless of whether you like them or not, if you keep doing them. These practices prepare the mind so that the mind can become a vehicle for a Greater Reality. Preparation can seem monotonous. But people do not prepare; they stimulate themselves. Anything that is important or that was made required skill and training. Someone did not wake up one day and build a piano. They prepared to do it.

Do you want to have the experience of Knowledge? Do you want to see God in everything? Then you must prepare. Then you will feel grateful to God. "Thank you for giving me this." Then you will know God is there because God has given you something to work on. This is not mysterious. Every day you get up and you do your practice. This is not mysterious. You just do it!

One of the most simple practices is to sit quietly and repeat the word "Rahn." Repeat that. "Rahn." That practice is enough to elevate your mind to a phenomenal level, but to get to that phenomenal level, you will go through all your attitudes, feelings and beliefs about the practice. One day it will thrill you. The next day it will bore you. The practice will take you through everything that you are already going through. If you do it consistently, it will provide consistency for you. It will empower your mind over time. Not everyone can do that practice. Some people are so mentally active, they cannot sit still for anything, so they have to do something. Other people are more contemplative and more introverted. That practice is easier for them. Anything you do that consistently engages your mind with something greater will yield a result you could not produce for yourself. *building a habit takes 28 days of doing it*

Why do people get involved in religion? Because they are looking for a result they realize they cannot produce for themselves. God becomes real when you need God. When you realize you need God everyday and not just when things are bad, well, then you begin to acknowledge a greater relationship. If you want to see God in everything, then you must see everything as it really is and feel God while you are seeing everything as it really is. Otherwise, you will attempt to turn everything into a beautiful experience and become ridiculously dishonest about your life. If you look at a table and feel God, it's still a table. There is nothing magical about the table, but you can feel something greater while you are experiencing this. It has nothing to do with the table. God is like an invisible substance that permeates everything. It does not make things look better. That is why when you are experiencing God like this, which is called "practicing the Presence," you are not disavowing physical reality, you are simply experiencing something else while you are watching it.

We teach practices such as this to help people develop this sensitivity while they are engaged with physical life. But do you know what the greatest practice of all is and the hardest to do? It is to follow what you know you must do, regardless. To do that you need to have a powerful mind. You need a strong body. You need to establish confidence within yourself and to learn about the possible mistakes that you can make. This all requires training and preparation.

Saying the word "Rahn" is very good if you have an active mind. "Rahn" gives you something to think about. When you practice using a mantra like this, it brings up everything that your mind is already engaged in. You keep coming back to the practice—back, back, back—because the practice is more important than your thoughts or feelings or attitudes. Here your practice is like your God for awhile. It is the closest part of God to you, your practice. That is why we speak of religion in terms of practice. After all, God is the end. We are talking about the means. The means are what is important in religion, not the end. You will only know God when you get there, but you must do something to get there.

The personal mind
cannot
achieve peace.
It can only
achieve service.

Thirty-five

ACHIEVING PEACE

PEACE IS THE FULL ENJOYMENT of your natural mind and the complete utilization of your opportunity to be in the world. At the very core of this experience is stillness. From this stillness emanates a potency of action that is rarely to be matched in the world. So, at the very core of peace it is absolutely still. At its outer perimeter, it is very powerful action.

Therefore, those who are engaged in this kind of experience are very still on the inside and yet can function very competently in the world. As a matter of fact, they can function at a far greater level of efficacy than the average person because their mind is concentrated.

To concentrate your mind, to focus your mind to this degree, you must be still because stillness is what focuses you and concentrates you. This naturally emanates into the world and exerts influence in all aspects of human endeavor. Your world has been saved many times because of the cumulative effect of this. The few minds that are engaged in this kind of concentration have been able to protect the world from aggressive forces and from internal conflict. The calling for this concentration will certainly increase as time goes on.

Do not think of achieving peace in political or economic terms in the world. That is the wrong appropriation at this point because you are working internally now. Peace in the world is difficult to achieve because the world is not a place of peace. It is a place of activity, growth, friction, competition, disappointment and accomplishment—not exactly a quiet and still place. If you do not have peace at the center of you guiding your actions, and very few people do, then you will become engaged in the world of movement, living at the surface of yourself. Asking the world to be at peace is asking for people to be in a different state of mind than they are currently in. This is not easy to achieve! All of the people in the world do not need to achieve this equanimity; only a very few do, but those very few must achieve it. For them it is vital, and their achievement will resonate with others and keep the potency of this alive.

Therefore, let me make a very important point that we must spend some time with: To achieve the goal that I have indicated here you must have a different kind of mind than the kind of mind you are used to. You already have this different kind of mind. It is the mind that you have brought with you from your Ancient Home. The mind that you think with now is the mind that you have created since you have been here. We call this the "personal mind" or "personal side." It is not bad. You need to have a personal mind to function in the world. Otherwise, no one would understand you and you would not understand anyone. The personal mind is not your natural mind. The personal mind is meant to serve a Greater Mind, of which you are a part. It is cruel to demand that the personal mind achieve peace, power and harmony. That is like requiring your body not to feel pain. The personal mind was born in conflict and resides in conflict and will achieve peace only in service to a Greater Mind.

The Greater Mind is not a personal mind. It is a mind of which you are a part. You may be familiar with this idea, but I must make this emphasis because this is the critical one: You cannot achieve peace with the personal mind alone. This does not mean that you have to get rid of the personal mind, but that the personal mind cannot be the center of you because the personal mind cannot achieve peace. It can only achieve service. Do not be alarmed when I say this because you must realize that the personal mind is not who you are. It has simply been constructed and developed since childhood—even since birth—as a vehicle to enable you to function in the world as an individual human being. You did not originate as a human being, but to become competent in the world, you have had to create this mind. Actually, you did not really create it. You simply used the components that were available to you to put it together. People who do not effectively put together their personal mind do not function too well in society.

So, you all have personal minds. Congratulations! But it is not the personal mind that will achieve peace within yourself or within the world. Let me say it another way: The personal mind cannot be still. If stillness is at the very core of peace and generates peace, then it cannot emanate from the personal mind. Many people today are punishing their personal mind, driving it into servitude, trying to make it godlike, to elevate it, to give it lofty principles and ideals and to torture it into submission. They do this with very limited success. The personal mind can be elevated and will be elevated in The Way of Knowledge, but it cannot achieve a godlike state. Do not make a god of the personal mind. It is a temporary vehicle. It is meant to allow you to contribute in the world.

Until the Greater Mind of Knowledge has been rediscovered, the personal mind will dominate you, and you will be in service to it until it can find its true form of service. Your body was also made to serve a Greater Mind. Without a Greater Mind, what can the body do? Your only hope is to keep it comfortable until you die. And when you leave the world and go back to your Spiritual Family, you say, "Let me see. I don't think I got it done. When can I go back?" And they say, "Well, you have to wait in line!" Everyone who goes back to the other side unfulfilled is so eager to return. When you go back to your Spiritual Family beyond the world, it is so obvious what must be done here. The memory returns to you completely. From that vantage point, it is very clear what you must do. But when you return to the world, you are in the world's vantage point, and it is not very clear.

The purpose of this Teaching is to give you the vantage point that you had when you were not here, which will make everything very clear! When you are not here, you are not thinking with your personal mind. You are thinking with your Natural Mind. So there must be a way to regain the Natural Mind while you are here. You cannot contribute to the world that well when you are not here. You have to do it while you are here. You can root from the sidelines, yelling "Yay, Peace! Yay, Peace!" like we do, but when you get into the game, well, then you have a more direct engagement. So, we are relying upon you, and for this you will need to rely upon us. If you cannot gain access to your Natural Mind, you must learn to engage with someone who can. That is very simple to understand. If you wish to learn even a mundane skill, you must go to work with someone who has the skill, yes? That is very obvious, though you know, many people do not do it.

Now, let us talk a little of the Natural Mind. Very different it is from the personal mind. Your first experience of it will be emptiness. It will seem spooky, like entering a great temple where very little is said but a great deal is understood. Your first experience, if you are not used to this, is, "Gee, it's spooky in here!" Everything is very quiet; there is not a lot of noise or running around. That stillness can be very threatening at first because it is so powerful. So, the first experience of peace is emptiness because in a state of peace so much that you are used to seems to be missing. That can make it seem a little uncomfortable, even a little scary at first. But if you proceed in your preparation, you will discover that emptiness is not "nothing." It is something. It is simply so still.

When people approach peace, at first they often feel the weight of their own conflicts. If you were to enter a very quiet place and were to stay there, what is the first thing you would experience but your own stress and tension? The contrast between your current state and the environment in which you have placed yourself would be so great that it would illustrate to you your own strain. So, you may not want to go to that place because you feel more pain at first. But then, if you return, you will find that there is a sweetness there, a comfort there and a reassurance there you cannot find anywhere else.

The world will continue to be the world. Do not try to make the world like your Ancient Home. This is not a good idea. It will never be like that. It will always be a crazy place, okay? However, the world can be an environment where people rediscover themselves—a much happier place than it is now. But it will not be a place of absolute stillness and quiet. After all, people initially came to the world for excitement. But excitement is not exciting for very long. But that is another story.

So, you must rediscover your Natural Mind, which we call Knowledge. Knowledge thinks its own thoughts. But because it is very quiet, whenever it thinks, its thoughts are very potent. Whenever it moves you to act, your actions are very strong. When it is not thinking or moving you to act, it is very quiet. The more you experience this, the more you realize that Knowledge is both yourself and something greater than yourself. The more you establish relationship with Knowledge, the more you realize that you are now free to become quiet. You realize that when you think with Knowledge, your thoughts are powerful, and when you act with Knowledge, your actions are directed and strong.

To approach the reality of Knowledge, your personal mind will need to be reorganized. Perhaps certain things will have to be given up and other things acquired. Your body will change because it is now becoming a vehicle for a Greater Force, which is why we advocate physical fitness for students of Knowledge—not just to look better or to live a little longer, but to actually carry this Presence.

When you are still internally, your stillness is your contribution to the world. A still mind has a much greater impact upon the world than any other form of achievement. This is mysterious but true nonetheless. But please remember my words: You cannot have a still personal mind. That is like trying to make the blood stop flowing in your veins. The personal mind will continue to be very chatty, okay? The difference over time is that you are with it less and less.

Now, why is it so difficult for people to achieve peace? Well, it is a difficult thing. Theoretically, achieving peace would be easy if you wanted it and nothing else. But who is in this position? If you wanted it and nothing else, it would come to you so easily. In fact, you would be there. But who wants this and nothing else?

Knowledge will guide you, simplify your life, give you the freedom to be quiet and give you escape from your personal mind. Who wants to be with a chatterbox all the time? Who wants to be governed by little thoughts all the time? My goodness! That is like being stuck watching re-runs on television twenty-four hours a day!

The more you experience Knowledge, the less you will be concerned about loss and survival because you will have confidence that you will be guided by what you need to do. This will not lead to passivity at all but to a very heightened engagement and a very great sense of responsibility, a responsibility that is not motivated by fear. You will care for your body because it is a valuable instrument. You will care for your mind for the same reason. You will care for your affairs because they are important. You will value relationships because they are essential. This is not a passive state. It is not sitting around in dreamland all day long. Why? Because Knowledge will propel you into action in the world. You did not come here to lie on the beach. You lie on the beach when you go Home. Well, there actually isn't a beach, but you can lie there anyway. We could create a beach if someone wanted one!

So, how do you do all these things that I am talking about? People often want answers to their problems. "I am reading this because I need to find out what the hell is going on with me and how I'm going to fix this situation. I have been to several teachers and conferences and have read several books, and I have all these ideas and different recipes."

The answer to any problem is following a means to its resolution. Answers are nothing; they only generate more questioning. For instance, imagine that you were lost in the middle of the jungle and you were trying to figure out where you were and someone finally figured it out. "We are here, in the middle of the jungle in this particular country." And everyone goes, "Oh, I am so relieved! At least we know where we are." But you are still five hundred miles from the nearest outpost. So, you walk a mile and you say, "Where are we now?" And somebody figures it out. "We're in the middle of the jungle in this particular country." And everyone goes, "Oh, I am so relieved! At least we know where we are." Now you are four hundred and ninety-nine miles from your destination.

Therefore, there must be a means of achieving your objective, but you cannot figure this out with your personal mind. If the personal mind accounts for five percent of your mind, then what about the other ninety-five percent? Is it dead weight? Is it a bag of rocks? Is it empty computer disks? No. What this means is that only five percent of the preparation is for five percent of the mind. Ninety-five percent of the preparation is for the other ninety-five percent of the mind, which means that you are probably only aware of five percent of the preparation. That is why students of Knowledge often feel that they do not quite know what is going on. But they do feel more certain because their personal mind, which they are most engaged with, is being more greatly influenced by the Natural Mind that is influencing them, of which they are as yet not fully aware.

Let me say this in another way. Your personal mind, where you live, is being increasingly influenced by something very great which you do not understand. This may concern you as to who is really in charge of your life, but the fact of the matter is that your life now has greater purpose, meaning and direction than it did before. So, most of the real work is happening on another level anyway, beyond your control. All you can do is participate or not, and to participate will require a great deal of will. Therefore, you must have self-determination, which eliminates any hope of being passive in the situation. That is the funny thing. Achieving peace is the most active engagement. It is finding the way out of the jungle.

You may ask yourself, "Am I ready for this? Maybe I should get married first, have children, become successful in business or achieve great status in art or achieve all of my goals. Then maybe when I am an old person, when I have had my fill of all these things, then I can turn my mind to such pursuits." But what if I said that you will be called into the development of Knowledge and into your spiritual life when you are in the middle of the ladder, that when you reach halfway up the ladder, your spiritual life will begin. Then you find out at some later time that the ladder—remember, we are going for the halfway point—extends infinitely in both directions. Therefore, wherever you are is the halfway point. So when you are an old person, satisfied or sick of the world, you reach the halfway point. Some people reach the halfway point when they are on their deathbed, but they cannot do much then. Therefore, the halfway point is right now. There is no, "Well, these other things must be done first." The halfway point is whenever you begin.

The way out of the jungle is to follow a preparation. It cannot be a preparation that you have invented for yourself because the preparation you invent will only keep you where you are. Something greater in you must call it into being; something greater in you must engage you with it. You will need assistance from others as you proceed, both within the world and beyond it. Your spiritual advancement is a matter of worldly involvement and involvement from beyond the world.

You have Knowledge within you, waiting to be discovered. You have no hope for certainty outside of this, for everything that seems certain is contingent upon very weak forces. Your government is fragile, your economy is fragile, your body is fragile, your thought system is fragile, and your relationships are fragile. All these things are fragile without Knowledge. Knowledge is from beyond the world, but it is in you, and you are here. So, what is from beyond the world is here! That is what I am saying.

Let me outline, then, some of the things that must be cultivated. First, you must learn to develop stillness internally. This will allow you to gain access to your Natural Mind. You must begin to communicate honestly about your circumstances so that they can be arranged appropriately and so that many problems can be resolved in order to give you the freedom to penetrate deeper, both into yourself and into life. Your comprehension of your environment is directly proportional to your comprehension of your inner life. Therefore, as you become closer to your Natural Mind and more engaged with it, your engagement with your life in the world will be more meaningful, more penetrating and more genuine.

You must have a different foundation for establishing relationships. Some of this can be learned simply through experience, but your powers of discernment must be developed. Knowledge will do this for you naturally if you are able to become aware of it, to follow its indications and to learn to distinguish them from other impulses that may be ruling you. Knowledge frees you from all other impulses. That is what it means to become free. Having no one to tell you what to do is a very limited and unsatisfying freedom. Most people want to be told what to do and feel helpless and resentful when they are not.

The purpose of freedom, then, is to find your own freedom and to express it in the world. Then lack of infringement really means something. If you go out into the world where people are having fun and you listen to them beyond their personal minds, you will hear, "Give me something important to do! Tell me what to do!" This is a very, very loud call in the world. Lying on the beach, they are saying, "Give me something to do! I am dying here in this body. I am feeling dead. Give me something." If you listened beyond the personal mind, you would hear these things, which are very much in contrast to people's behavior and declarations. This will give you an entirely different experience of people, and a very compassionate one as well. You don't need to have theories about this. You simply need to listen and respond. That is another thing you must learn—how to listen to people. There are many, many things to learn and each avenue has various steps. In learning and living The Way of Knowledge, everyone becomes engaged with all of their complications, and all of their complications come undone.

Let me give another example regarding freedom. People often equate freedom with the ability to have choice, yes? "I am free to go this way or that way and that represents my freedom. Actually, I can go in a hundred different ways. That represents my freedom. This coming weekend I can go to a hundred places. Therefore, I am more free than the person who can only go to two places." However, the person who is really free can only go to one place. They cannot go to the other ninety-nine. They are free to go to the one place they really need to go to, so the burden of constant decision without certainty is not weighing upon them. How can you be happy if you must constantly decide everything? There is no happiness here. But there is another way.

Of course, not every moment will you have to be doing something where there is only one choice, so the rest of the time you can flop around. But when it's time to make an important decision, there is only one thing to do. As you can see, freedom requires a different understanding, as does everything now. This is very clear to your Natural Mind. Your Natural Mind will consider relationships differently—freedom, self expression, success, everything differently. It is a different perception altogether.

Commitment and devotion are natural in relationships of Knowledge. That is what relationship is! Finding the right person to be with? It is not difficult. Being with that person is a little more challenging because you have your personal minds to contend with and all of the business of life, but the relationship is intact. In order for you to do something of value in the world, your life must be simple and cannot be drained away with personal disasters and conflicts. You must be free to contribute. Then your vital energy is free to come forth from you. You are fully functioning. You are able, then, to become involved in greater things. This confirms your experience of your origin, of the Greater Power that is with you to help you and of the value of your relationships.

All you need to do in life is comprehend the next step and do it completely. Simple! Unfortunately, people want to do all the steps right now or do steps that are far down the way. If you will only do this step, then it will take you to the next step, and that is how you will progress. If there is no dysfunction in learning, you will be able to simply learn within this progression, and you will follow a straight path to your destination. The steps involve giving up what is non-essential and realizing what is essential. When you are doing what is essential, you feel essential. When you are doing what is non-essential, you feel non-essential because you always identify with what you are doing. This is normal. Even Knowledge is identified with what it is doing.

I want you to know here that I am giving you only part of the picture. Your understanding must always be incomplete. As soon as it is complete, you have stopped learning. Do not try to be comfortable with a complete cosmology where nothing new can come in. "My theories now cover every gap." The man or woman of Knowledge does not know what the hell is going on! Jesus did not know what the hell was going on! He did not know what was going to happen next. This probably concerned his personal side very much, at least at first. You do not need to know what is going to happen next; you simply need to know what you are doing now. That is freedom. Let God control the universe! Life is much better with God, if you are friends with God.

There are only two places to be in the world. (Because I want to make everything simple, I say there are only two!) However, before I make this statement, I must say that the simpler the truth, the more difficult it is to grasp. Truths that are very complex are very easy to think about because they don't require much attention. Truths that are very simple require a great deal of penetration. They require a greater engagement to comprehend them.

There are two places to be in life: You are either with your thoughts or you are with Knowledge. How is that? If you are not with Knowledge, you must be with your thoughts because there is nowhere else to be.

Being with the personal mind is very tiring. It's like listening to a two-year old all day long, or maybe a four-year old, if it's sophisticated! So, after awhile you want some relief, particularly if you have learned to become self-observant, which is a sign of maturity. You want some relief from the constant friction of the personal mind. That is a good sign. It means you are considering that there is a more important place to reside.

People are not that different from one another, but their evaluations of things vary greatly. When you are looking from the personal mind, personal minds appear to be very distinct. That is why it is sometimes difficult to let go of your personal mind because you think you are giving up your individuality. However, your real uniqueness is your expression in this life. That is a very joyful individuality because it does not separate you from anything.

So, all your beliefs have to be re-evaluated, which happens naturally when you achieve a relationship with the Greater Mind. Knowledge does not care about ninety percent of the things that concern people. At first, this seems like an affront. "Well, the things that are important to me apparently aren't important to Knowledge!" This seems very insulting, but after awhile you realize, "If Knowledge is quiet now, I guess I can be quiet too. If Knowledge is happy, maybe I can be happy. If Knowledge isn't doing anything right now, maybe I don't need to be doing anything right now." This leads to true relaxation. By the way, the value of true relaxation is to prepare for valuable action. So, it is always preparatory to doing something important. Most people view relaxation as a form of recovery, not as a form of preparation.

I said that often the first experience of peace is emptiness. Then I said that emptiness is not nothing. It is something. It is Presence. So, you go from feeling empty to feeling very full. If you stand outside of emptiness, it seems empty because it is so still and so great, like looking at the stars and thinking of the space between them. If you could, imagine that the space between two stars is actually full of life and that the stars themselves are the dead objects in comparison with what exists between them. Using this analogy, you could then understand that the space that is within you is incredibly vibrant and intelligent, but from the outside it appears to be empty because it is so still and so large.

To approach stillness, you must become still. The greatest things in the world are still, but they are rarely experienced because everyone is racing around going 100 mph. If life is going 5 mph and you are going 100 mph, then you are not going to experience what is happening. You are only going to experience your own acceleration and will not at all feel a part of what is around you.

You know, it has been our experience that whenever a truth is given, an antidote must be given with it, so people will not think that that truth is the whole picture and then fill in all the gaps. All serious errors begin as a truth that is considered to be complete. Therefore, the purpose of truth is to lead you further, not to end your search. That is why when you discover something of great importance, it gives you a whole new array of questions to ask.

To prepare for stillness obviously involves a readjustment of your outer life and the development of your mind to concentrate your mind. Here you learn to get used to stillness, and then you can penetrate it and receive its rewards. Everything that is valuable comes from stillness. The center of stillness is absolutely still. There is no movement there, but all movement comes from it. It is like that.

Where did the physical universe come from? It came from stillness. Where is the physical universe going? It is returning to stillness. Stillness is not dead. It is simply life without movement. You don't need to worry about that here because you have come here for movement, so it is very hard to comprehend life without movement. It is a state of incredible rapture. To prepare for stillness, you must practice a certain kind of meditation, you must have a teacher, you must have a method and you must have a community. These are what are necessary.

FURTHER STUDY

THERE IS A WAY TO STUDY AND PRACTICE what has been presented in this book. Study of The Greater Community Way of Knowledge is presented in the three texts, *Steps to Knowledge* and *Wisdom from the Greater Community: Volumes I & II*, which comprise the first level of study in the *Steps to Knowledge* Program. Offered in a self-study format, the Program provides the perspective, the insight and the method of preparation necessary to begin learning and applying Greater Community Knowledge and Wisdom.

Steps to Knowledge, the Greater Community Book of Practices, is the map that takes you to the discovery of Knowledge, the Knowing Mind, which is the source of your greater purpose in the world and your true relationships in life. It contains 365 daily "steps," each offering a special teaching and a practice in The Way of Knowledge. By exercising the two natural functions of the mind, stillness and focused inquiry, *Steps to Knowledge* mysteriously opens the mind to revelation, where purpose, meaning and direction become apparent.

The two volumes of *Wisdom from the Greater Community* present the perspective and insight of The Way of Knowledge in its application to the fundamental aspects of daily life. In chapters ranging from "Marriage" and "Freedom" to "Intelligence" and "Greater Community Realities," *Wisdom from the Greater Community: Volumes I & II* create an environment for coming to terms with what you really know about your life and the world around you.

The Sacred Books of the New Knowledge Library are published by The Society for The Greater Community Way of Knowledge. To order copies of *Steps to Knowledge* and *Wisdom from the Greater Community: Volumes I & II* or to learn more about The Society's other publications, educational programs and contemplative services, please contact: The Society for The Greater Community Way of Knowledge, P.O. Box 1724, Boulder, CO 80306-1724, (303) 938-8401.

ABOUT THE AUTHOR

*M*ARSHALL VIAN SUMMERS IS THE FOUNDER of The Society for The Greater Community Way of Knowledge and is the primary representative of Greater Community Spirituality in the world today. He is the author of *Steps to Knowledge, Wisdom from the Greater Community: Volumes I & II* and the other books of the New Knowledge Library. He lives in seclusion in the Rocky Mountains where he continues to receive the sacred books of the Greater Community Way. Several times a year he travels to introduce the Teaching to new audiences and to spread the message that the world is emerging into the Greater Community and for this humanity must prepare.

Wisdom from the Greater Community, Volume I, was received in a state of Revelation. It is a gift from the Creator to prepare humanity for its life in the new millennium.

ABOUT THE SOCIETY

THE SOCIETY FOR THE GREATER COMMUNITY WAY OF KNOWLEDGE has a great mission in the world. Our world is emerging into the Greater Community of Worlds and humanity must prepare. The Greater Community Way of Knowledge is the preparation. The mission of The Society is to present this message worldwide and to teach The Way of Knowledge through its publications, educational programs and contemplative services. The Society provides the materials, the instruction and the environment necessary for learning and living the greater Knowledge and Wisdom that this teaching and tradition represent.

THE SOCIETY WAS FOUNDED IN 1992 as a religious non-profit organization. It publishes the books of the New Knowledge Library, offers the Greater Community Services and provides special educational programs on Knowledge and Greater Community Spirituality by its founder Marshall Vian Summers. The Society is supported and maintained by people who are committed to learning and living The Way of Knowledge and who recognize that they have a greater purpose in life to fulfill.

AS A RELIGIOUS NON-PROFIT ORGANIZATION, The Society is supported primarily through volunteer activity, tithes and contributions. The Books of Knowledge are finding their way around the world through the power of relationships, where people are sharing the discovery of The Way of Knowledge with others. You can make a difference by reaching those who need Knowledge and Wisdom now and who feel the need to prepare. Share these books with them.

YOUR FINANCIAL CONTRIBUTIONS will make possible the ongoing publication of all the Sacred Books of Knowledge, many of which are currently awaiting funds for publication. In addition, your support enables The Society to offer the programs and services which make learning and living The Greater Community Way of Knowledge possible.

strength:
  think in metaphors
  determination
  committment
  cultivate a higher mind
  desire for spirituality
  seaching
  articulate communication

Announcing
STEPS TO KNOWLEDGE

STEPS TO KNOWLEDGE represents the essence of spirituality as it is taught, practiced and shared in the Greater Community of Worlds.

STEPS TO KNOWLEDGE is a gift from the Creator to enable humanity to establish a foundation for peace and cooperation within the human family and to spiritually prepare for its destined encounter with intelligent life from the Greater Community.

STEPS TO KNOWLEDGE provides the lessons and practices that are essential for learning and living The Greater Community Way of Knowledge. In its 365 practices or "steps" it presents the road map to Knowledge, the Knowing Mind, and lays the foundation for learning and applying Greater Community Knowledge and Wisdom.

STEPS TO KNOWLEDGE is for those who have the need to know and who feel the need to prepare.

"These words are a calling. This message is a calling. These ideas are a calling. The world is emerging into the Greater Community. You must prepare. The preparation is here. It is time to begin."

From the Introduction to STEPS TO KNOWLEDGE

Wisdom
from
The Greater Community:
Volume I

Wisdom I is the first Greater Community Book of Teachings. It serves as the introduction to the Program and along with *Wisdom II* presents the immense scope and application of The Greater Community Way of Knowledge.

Wisdom
from
The Greater Community:
Volume II

Wisdom II presents a more advanced study in The Way of Knowledge. It expands many of the ideas that are presented in *Steps to Knowledge* and in *Wisdom I* and introduces the reader to the larger arena of intelligent life called the Greater Community.

THE STEPS TO KNOWLEDGE PROGRAM

Steps to Knowledge and *Wisdom from the Greater Community: Volumes I & II* may be ordered individually or as a set:

QTY.   (PLEASE PRINT)

_____ **STEPS TO KNOWLEDGE PROGRAM:** *Steps to Knowledge* and
         Wisdom from the Greater Community: Volumes I & II @ $70 each   _____

_____ **STEPS TO KNOWLEDGE** @ $25 each   _____

_____ **WISDOM FROM THE GREATER COMMUNITY: VOLUME I** @ $25 each   _____

_____ **WISDOM FROM THE GREATER COMMUNITY: VOLUME II** @ $25 each   _____

         SHIPPING AND HANDLING: $7 for the program; $5 for one book;
         $6 for two books. $7 for three books. Add $1 for each additional book.   _____

         Colorado residents please add 4.1% sales tax.   _____

         Boulder residents please add an additional 3.11% sales tax.   _____

         TOTAL: _____

NAME: _____

ADDRESS: _____

CITY/STATE/ZIP:_____

PHONE (optional): _____

Referred by:_____

Please send this order form along with a check or money order payable to:
The Society for The Greater Community Way of Knowledge
P.O. Box 1724, Boulder, Colorado 80306-1724 • (303) 938-8401

THE STEPS TO KNOWLEDGE PROGRAM

Steps to Knowledge and *Wisdom from the Greater Community: Volumes I & II* may be ordered individually or as a set:

QTY.   (PLEASE PRINT)

_____ **STEPS TO KNOWLEDGE PROGRAM:** *Steps to Knowledge* and
         Wisdom from the Greater Community: Volumes I & II @ $70 each   _____

_____ **STEPS TO KNOWLEDGE** @ $25 each   _____

_____ **WISDOM FROM THE GREATER COMMUNITY: VOLUME I** @ $25 each   _____

_____ **WISDOM FROM THE GREATER COMMUNITY: VOLUME II** @ $25 each   _____

         SHIPPING AND HANDLING: $7 for the program; $5 for one book;
         $6 for two books. $7 for three books. Add $1 for each additional book.   _____

         Colorado residents please add 4.1% sales tax.   _____

         Boulder residents please add an additional 3.11% sales tax.   _____

         TOTAL: _____

NAME: _____

ADDRESS: _____

CITY/STATE/ZIP:_____

PHONE (optional): _____

Referred by:_____

Please send this order form along with a check or money order payable to:
The Society for The Greater Community Way of Knowledge
P.O. Box 1724, Boulder, Colorado 80306-1724 • (303) 938-8401